Service Parts Planning with mySAP SCM™

Jörg Thomas Dickersbach

Service Parts Planning with mySAP SCM™

Processes, Structures, and Functions

With 370 Figures and 18 Tables

Springer

Dr. Jörg Thomas Dickersbach
Tullastraße 17
68161 Mannheim
Germany
dickersbach@gmx.de

ISBN:13 978-3-642-06911-6 e-ISBN:13 978-3-540-32652-6

Springer is part of Springer Science+Business Media

springer.com

Softcover reprint of the hardcover 1st edition 2007

Cover-design: Erich Kirchner, Heidelberg

Preface

Service parts planning in mySAP SCM™ 5.0 is part of the service parts management solution that was developed in a joint effort of SAP AG, Caterpillar Logistics Services, Inc. and Ford Motor Company and generally released in 2006. This solution addresses service parts specific functions, and is based on new functionality within SAP APO™ (plus some functions for monitoring in SAP ICH™ and business content in SAP Netweaver BI™). The main planning areas of service parts planning are forecasting, inventory planning, procurement and distribution – similar as 'normal' SAP APO™. Nevertheless the functionality is significantly different. Also the 'look and feel' of service parts planning is quite different. At the same time the effort for the creation of F1-help was significantly reduced. Because of these reasons we use screenshots in this book to a comparatively large extent.

The purpose of this book is to explain the functionality of service parts planning with mySAP SCM™ and the covered business processes. The target audience of this book is anyone who is considering or is already involved in the implementation of the SAP service parts management solution – whether as project manager, as project member or as consultant.

This book aims to provide the reader with knowledge on three levels business processes, application and configuration. Therefore the concept of this book is to provide first an overview about the processes for service parts planning, and then walk through each process. Starting with an overview of the business process we explain step by step the planning functions and the related configuration. The focus of this book lies on the key planning processes, and this book does not claim to describe all the functionalities for service parts planning.

A key input for this book were the explanations and corrections from Michael Wilking, Michael Schweitzer, Olaf Dudat, Thorsten Bender, Kai Müller, Michael Krenbauer and Yue Chen, and I would like to thank each of them very much. I would also like to thank Claus Bosch, Jens Drewer and Volker Krebs for their corrections and comments.

Jörg Thomas Dickersbach October 2006

Contents

1 Service Parts Planning Overview

1.1 Supply Chain Management for Service Parts

Supply chain management is the process of planning, implementing, and controlling the operations of the supply chain with the purpose to satisfy customer requirements as efficiently as possible. SCOR structures the supply chain management processes into plan, source, make, deliver and return (SCOR 2006). Another way to structure the processes is to differentiate between goods movements within the company and goods movements to the external customer resulting in a structure as demand planning, order fulfilment, distribution, production and procurement (Dickersbach 2005). These structures fit for most of the companies – at least we are not aware of any counter-example – even though the supply chain and the supply chain management might look very different from company to company – especially across different industries. From this point of view, the same approach fits for service parts as well. Nevertheless there are several specific features for service parts planning which have justified SAP AG in alliance with Caterpillar Logistics Services, Inc. and Ford Motor Company to build a completely new solution for service parts management. According to the nature of the development partners, the primary industry focus within the service parts management solution is engineering, construction and automotive.

• *High Number of Service Parts*
Supply chain management for service parts deals usually with a very high number of SKUs. This becomes plausible when comparing the number of finished products of an automotive or an engineering company with the number of service parts for their primary products. Differing from the production, the service parts have to be available at several warehouses in order to ensure a fast delivery. This leads to a multiplication of SKUs.
Another factor is that service parts have to be available for quite a long time after the production of the primary product has ended. There are legal

retention periods for service parts but many companies keep service parts available even longer. Mercedes-Benz e.g. guarantees an availability of 10 years after the production end date (Arnold et al. 2002).

- *Authorised Stocking List*

Service parts logistics combines a high number of service parts with a high number of warehouses. At the same time many of the service parts are slow movers. Therefore the decision whether to keep a service part on stock at the different warehouses is more significant than for normal logistics. These stocking decisions are combined in the authorised stocking list.

- *Sporadic Demand*

One of the most distinct characteristics for service parts is the high portion of products with sporadic demand. Most of the service parts are required if there is a failure in the primary product – due to wear, accident or other. These failures are hardly predictable, and there is a multitude of possibilities for failure. Therefore the failures which relate to a specific service part are usually comparatively seldom, which results in a sporadic demand. Naturally there are also fast movers among the service parts.

- *Availability and Safety Stock*

If a vital or an essential part of the primary product fails, an immediate substitution (and repair) is required. The costs associated with the downtime of the primary product might be very high – in the case of a bottleneck machine up to the production downtime a complete factory, in the case of an automotive this might lead to a significant loss of customer satisfaction. Therefore the availability of the service part on stock is of high importance in service parts management. Taking into consideration that there is a high portion of sporadic demand (which is difficult to predict) and that the service part has to be on stock in case of need, the importance of safety stock planning becomes obvious.

- *Preventive Maintenance*

Preventive maintenance based on the operating time or the mileage (which is essential e.g. for aerospace) is not the focus of this solution. Naturally some service parts are requested for preventive maintenance as well – e.g. gear belts for automotives – but in the current release of mySAP SCM™ 5.0 there is no link to derive the demand from the installed base.

• *Service Parts Production*
Most companies have a separation between their main business – the production of the primary goods – and their service parts business. Often the service parts are produced in the manufacturing plant like the components of the primary product, but sales and distribution of the service parts belongs in most cases to a separate organisation (Arnold et al. 2002). In line with this organisational structure, the service parts management solution focuses on the distribution and the availability of the service part at the warehouses with in the supply chain. All service parts are considered as externally procured – either via scheduling agreements or via contracts.

• *Repair / Remanufacturing*
Depending on the value of the service part, repairing is an alternative to new procurement. This is especially the case in the aerospace industry. A common concept is to have remanufactured parts – e.g. engines – in a stocking and repair cycle. The planned availability of the remanufactured service part depends on the number of 'old' parts and the repair capacity. Within the current release of service parts planning only very basic functionality is offered for this process.

• *Profitability*
Another reason that justifies a new solution especially for service parts is the high profitability of the service parts business.

1.2 Systems and Processes for Service Parts Planning

The purpose of service parts planning is to determine the required inventory levels at the distribution centres of the supply network in order to meet the target service levels and to plan the procurement of the service parts from external suppliers and their replenishment within the supply network. In-house production is not considered in this solution – if the company produces the service parts itself, the production has to be modelled like an external supplier. Service parts planning is however only one part of the service parts management solution. Besides service parts planning, the service parts management solution covers:

- sales, claims and returns, and entitlement management
- procurement execution including ASN creation and validation
- stock transfer execution
- warehouse management
- monitoring and reporting of the service parts supply chain

The functions for the service parts management processes were developed based on the system landscape containing mySAP ERP™ 2005, mySAP CRM™ 5.0 (Customer Relationship Management), SAP APO™ (Advanced Planner and Optimiser), SAP ICH™ (Inventory Collaboration Hub) and SAP EWM™ (Extended Warehouse Management) within SAP SCM™ 5.0 and SAP Netweaver™ including SAP XI™ (Exchange Infrastructure) and SAP BI™ (Business Information Warehouse). Though some of the functionality might work in a different system landscape as well, e.g. only SAP APO™ and mySAP ERP™, so far service parts management is only released for this system landscape.
Figure 2.1 provides the overview of the systems which are required for service parts management. Service parts planning – which is the focus of this book – is entirely within SAP APO™. Monitoring – e.g. the alert monitor – is done in SAP ICH™ based on common tables within mySAP SCM™. SAP BI™ offers reports for the measurement of the supply chain performance towards the customer, within the supply chain and from the supplier based also on the data within these common tables.

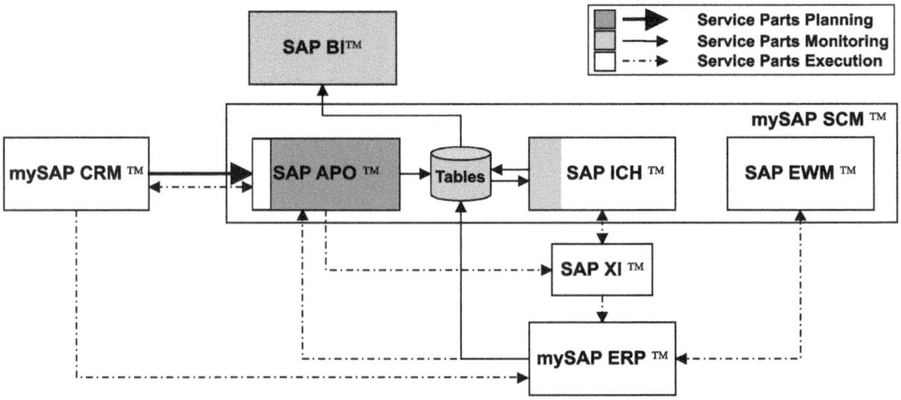

Fig. 1.1. System Landscape for Service Parts Planning

• *Service Parts Execution*
Sales order taking, claims and returns and entitlement management is based on mySAP CRM™. Other parts of the order fulfilment process are the ATP check in SAP APO™, the processing of the delivery in mySAP ERP™ and the goods issue in SAP EWM™. The order fulfilment processes include sales from stock and sales from a third party vendor to the customer as triangular business. Chapter 13 provides a brief overview of the sales from stock process.

Procurement execution starts with the releases for scheduling agreements or the purchase requisitions for contracts and involves SAP ICH™ (where the supplier creates ASNs), mySAP ERP™ for the validation of the ASN and SAP EWM™ for the goods receipt. The procurement execution is sketched in chapter 9.7 subsequently to the procurement approval and the release creation.
The execution of stock transfers is based on stock transfer orders that are created by service parts planning (in deployment or in inventory balancing). The stock transfer orders are sent from SAP APO™ to mySAP ERP™. Goods issue at the source location and goods receipt at the target location are performed in SAP EWM™. Chapter 10.8 gives a short description about the stock transfer execution.

• *Service Parts Planning within SAP APO™*
The focus of this book is the service parts planning processes which are entirely within SAP APO™. Though service parts planning covers similar processes as Demand Planning and Supply Network Planning in SAP APO™, it relies on completely new functions. Therefore there is no process interface with the 'normal' SAP APO™ functions, and mixing service parts planning with the SAP APO™ modules DP, SNP or PP/DS for the same location product is not intended and might lead to inconsistencies.
Service parts planning does however use the same master data objects for location, product, transportation lane and procurement relationship – though in most cases separate fields. All these master data object have been enhanced with new fields. The integration of service parts planning with mySAP ERP™ is done via CIF like for 'normal' SAP APO™. Compared to DP and SNP in SAP APO™, service parts planning offers some additional functions, is missing some functions – e.g. aggregated planning and macros in forecasting – and uses a different logic for similar functions.

• *Service Parts Planning Overview*
Service parts planning is concerned with the forecasting, inventory planning, procurement and distribution of the service parts to the customer facing locations in order to keep the target service levels. The processes for service parts planning are shown in figure 1.2 and range from the capturing of the demand to the planning of the procurement and the stock transfers.

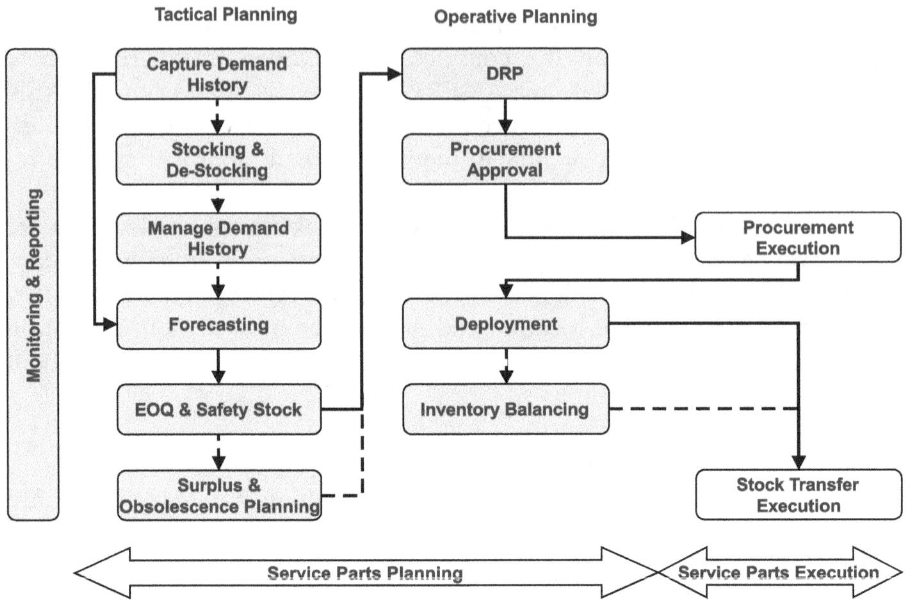

Fig. 1.2. Overview of Service Parts Planning Processes

The processes for tactical planning span the medium- to long-term range and are based on time buckets of months, fiscal year periods or even weeks. The processes starting from the capturing of historical demand to the stocking decision, the adjustment of the demand history, the forecasting and the determination of the EOQ (economic order quantity) and the safety stock levels (and optionally surplus and obsolescence planning) are considered as tactical. The results of the tactical planning are

- decision about stocking or de-stocking
- forecast based on the demand history
- safety stock and economic order quantity

for each location product and – optionally – the scrapping of surplus quantity. This information is used by the operational planning processes which are based on daily buckets. DRP (distribution requirements planning) determines the required procurement quantity depending on the stock and order situation in the network. The procurement proposals are checked in the procurement approval process and released. Sending the releases to the supplier, receiving ASNs from the supplier and posting goods receipt are parts of the procurement execution. Based on the received inventory the service parts are replenished to the warehouses in the deployment process. In case that lateral stock transfers between warehouses are required, inventory balancing is used. In both cases stock transfer orders are created and sent to mySAP ERP™ for execution. The result of service parts planning is that the stocked customer facing warehouses have sufficient inventory to fulfil the customer requirements. Each of these processes is described in the following chapters.

Chapter 12 explains how supersession – i.e. the replacement of one service part with one ore more other service parts – is applied for service parts planning.

Service parts planning is almost entirely based on forecast, and sales order fulfilment is not part of service parts planning. Nevertheless chapter 13 gives a brief overview of the order fulfilment process for sales from stock. Monitoring and reporting finally are sketched in chapter 14.

• *Scope and Limitations of this Book*

Not all functions of the service parts management solution are described in this book – even not all functions for service parts planning. The focus of this book lies on the planning functions, therefore monitoring and reporting is not explained in their due depth. Even within planning some topics as virtual locations for consolidated ordering and contract packagers are explained only very briefly. Planning with future BODs, remanufacturing and push deployment from the supplier are skipped altogether. The same applies to bordering processes like third-party order processing (TPOP) and kitting. For a complete picture of the service parts planning functionality please have a look into the SAP online documentation for service parts planning.

2 Master Data, Services and Basis Functions

2.1 Master Data

2.1.1 Bill of Distribution

One of the specifics of the service parts solution is that the supply chain network has a tree-like structure with one or more entry location – this is where the supplier delivers to – and for each entry location (optionally) one or more child locations. Looking from the demand side, there is a strict single sourcing. This fix and hierarchical distribution structure is modelled as a bill of distribution (BOD). The BOD is used throughout the whole service parts planning solution – from capture demand to inventory balancing.

• *Virtual Child Location*
Another characteristic of the BOD is that there is a functional separation between locations that deliver to the customer (also called customer facing locations) and locations that deliver to other locations (also called parent locations). If one location does both, a virtual child location is created for this location. All customer related data – e.g. forecast, safety stock, customer orders – are assigned to the virtual child location, and the location keeps only the transactional data for its role as a parent location. This implies that a stock transfer is modelled from the location to its own virtual child location in order to cover the customer related demand.

• *Example for a Bill of Distribution*
The modelling of the supply chain with the BOD is clarified with the example of a supply chain as shown in figure 2.1.

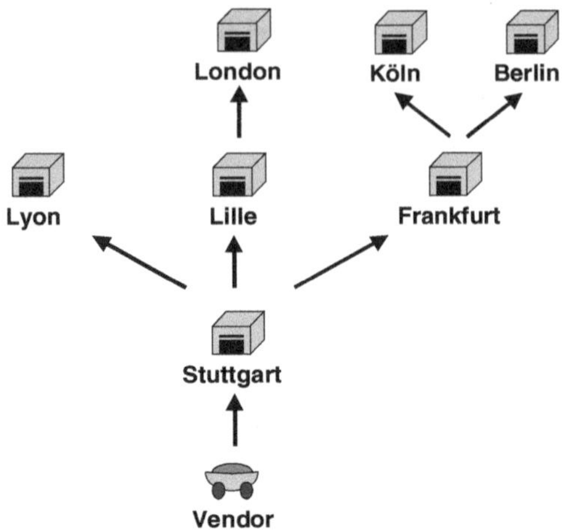

Fig. 2.1. Example for a Supply Chain

Each of the distribution centres – except Frankfurt – sell service parts to customers. Figure 2.2 shows the BOD to model this structure.

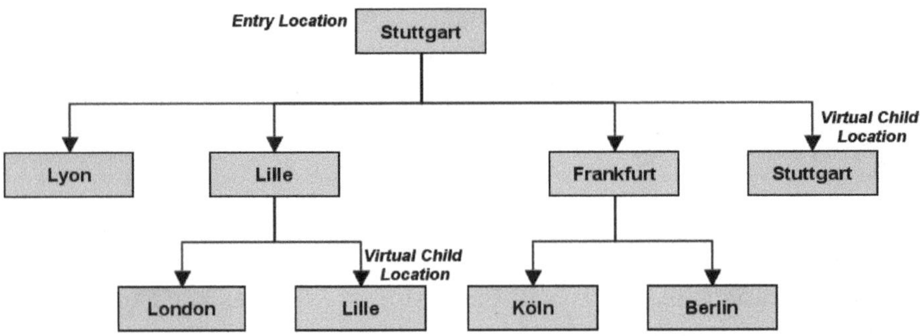

Fig. 2.2. Bill of Distribution for the Example

In this case Stuttgart is the entry location of the BOD, and all locations except Frankfurt are customer locations. The locations Stuttgart, Lille and Frankfurt are parent locations because they deliver to other locations within the network. Stuttgart and Lille have virtual child locations in order to separate their role as a parent and their role as a customer facing location. All locations except the entry location Stuttgart are child locations to their parent.

Restrictions in the modelling of the BOD are that the tree structure must be respected and that a location can only be used once within one BOD. It is however possible to have multiple entry locations within one BOD – e.g.

to model different supply networks in Europe and America. Figure 2.3 shows some alternatives for the modelling of a BOD.

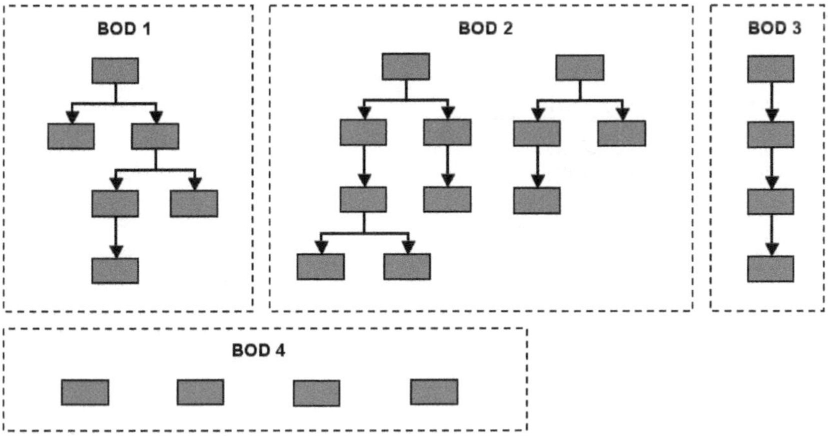

Fig. 2.3. BOD Modelling Alternatives

• *Hierarchy Structure*

The BOD is a kind of location hierarchy and is therefore based on the hierarchy structure. The hierarchy structure is defined with the customising path *APO → Master Data → Hierarchy → Define Hierarchy Structure*, figure 2.4.

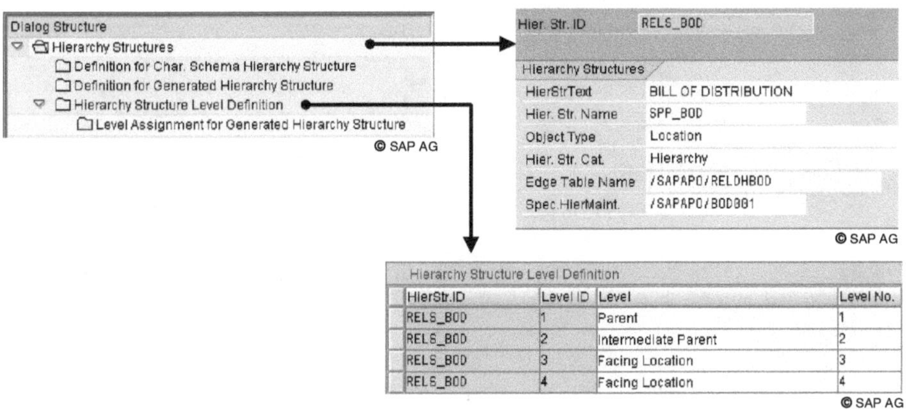

Fig. 2.4. Hierarchy Structure for the BOD

Note that the edge table name has to be /SAPAPO/RELDHBOD or else it is not possible to set the flag for virtual child locations. The hierarchy structure is linked to the transaction for creating the BOD by an entry in the customising setting as shown in figure 2.5 (customising path *APO → Master Data → Product → Maintain Product-Relevant Hierarchies and Hierarchy Structures*).

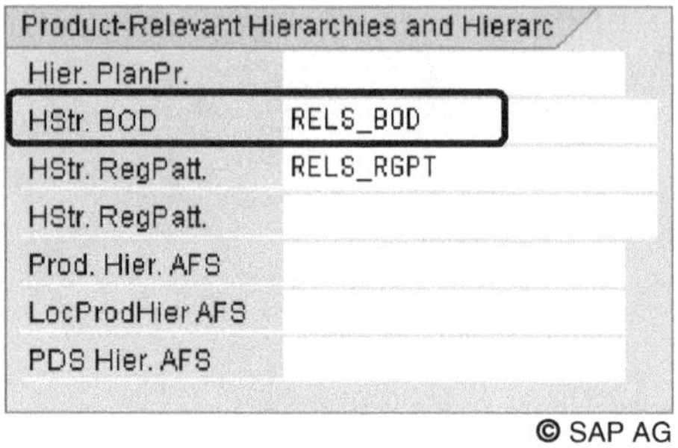

Fig. 2.5. Product-Relevant Hierarchy Structures

• *BOD Maintenance*
The BOD is maintained with the transaction /SAPAPO/BOD001. With this transaction the hierarchy structure is selected automatically, figure 2.6.

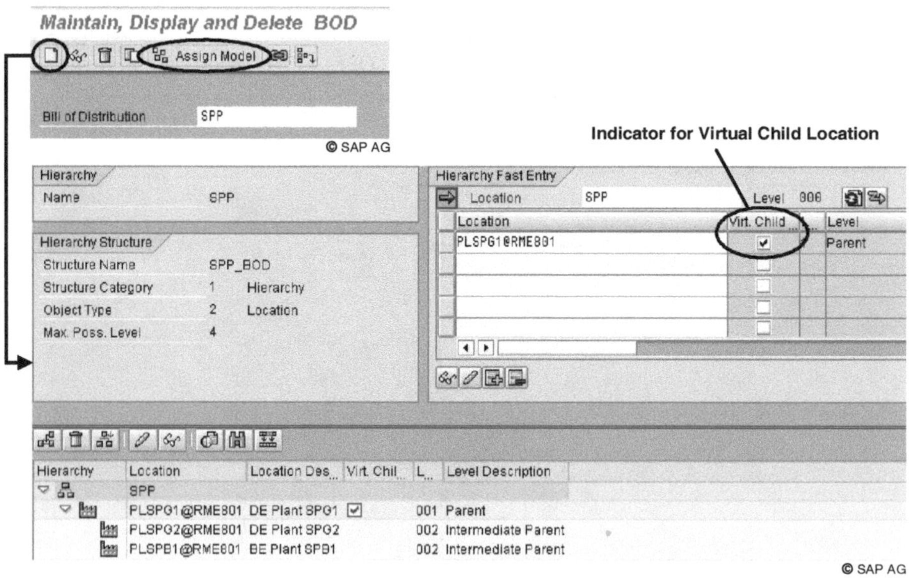

Fig. 2.6. BOD Maintenance

The tree structure of the locations is maintained in the bottom part of the screen. If a location has a virtual child location, the according indicator is set in the top right area. To display the location in this area, its parent has to be selected in the bottom area. When saving the BOD, it is checked whether transportation lanes exist. After saving, the BOD must be assigned to the active model 000 in the same transaction. There is no integration of the BOD from mySAP ERP™, but usually there are just a few BODs per company.

• *Product Assignment to the BOD*
The BOD is defined independent of the products. The assignment of the products to the BOD is performed with the transaction /SAPAPO/PROD2BOD_M as shown in figure 2.7. A product can be assigned to one BOD only.

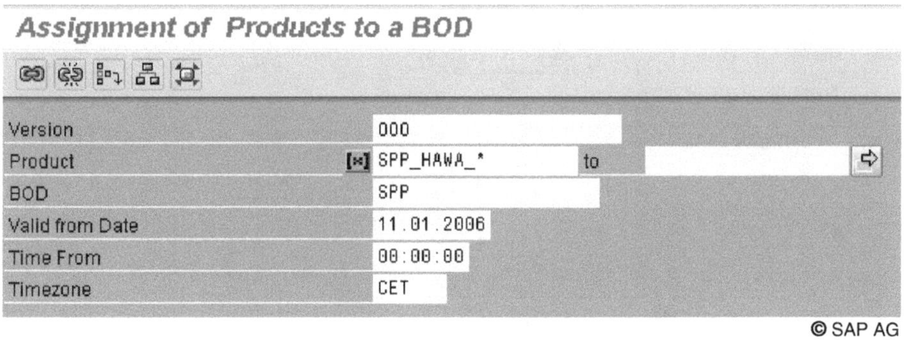

Fig. 2.7. Product Assignment to BOD

The validity date of the assignment must not be in the past. The assignment of products to BODs is displayed with the transaction /SAPAPO/PROD_DISP (products for BOD) or /SAPAPO/PROD2BODDISP (BOD for a product).

2.1.2 Virtual Location for Consolidated Ordering

Virtual locations for consolidated ordering (VLCO) are used to group locations which are geographically close and have only a small demand. This way the virtual consolidation location is considered like one location in DRP planning and all transactional data – stock, demand and fixed receipts – is aggregated to the preferred location. The preferred location is the location with the longest lead time and determines also the calendar, the deployment indicator and the rounding rules. As a consequence, netting is performed within the locations of the virtual consolidation location and only orders for the net demand are created.

The distribution to the real locations is done in deployment and inventory balancing. If a virtual consolidation location has registered a net demand, deployment delivers to the locations according to the demand of the individual locations. Using virtual consolidation locations has the benefit that netting is performed within these locations and that the data basis for planning is aggregated.

• *Regional Pattern*

Virtual locations for consolidated ordering are defined using a regional pattern. The prerequisite for defining the virtual locations for consolidated ordering is that all locations have the same parent. The regional pattern is a hierarchy structure like the BOD but has a different edge table (/SAPAPO/RELDHRGP), figure 2.8.

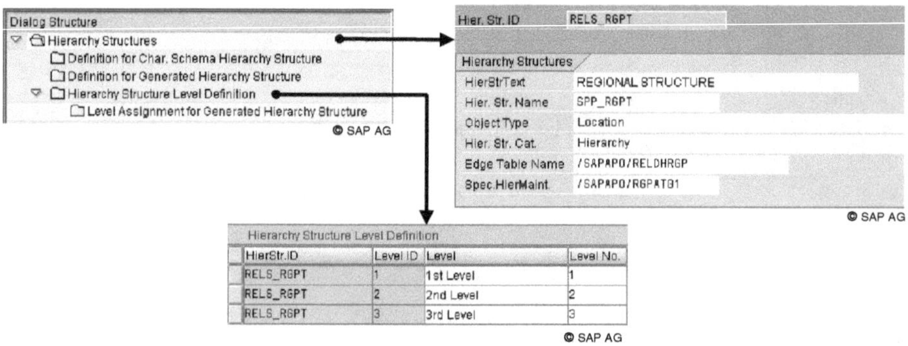

Fig. 2.8. Hierarchy Structure for Regional Pattern

The hierarchy structure is linked to the transaction for creating the regional pattern by an entry in the customising setting as shown in figure 2.9 (customising path *APO → Master Data → Product → Maintain Product-Relevant Hierarchies and Hierarchy Structures*).

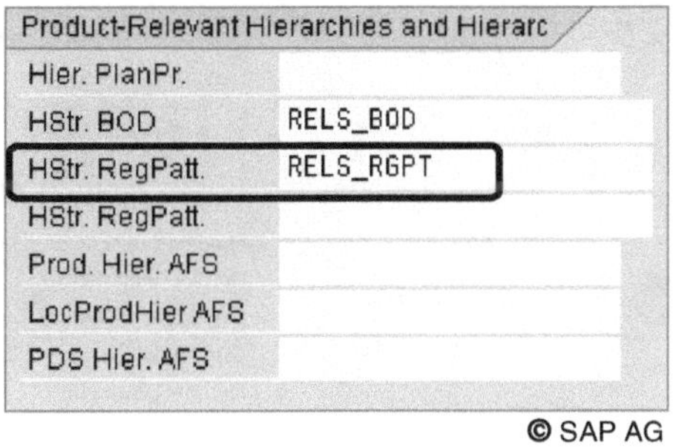

Fig. 2.9. Product-Relevant Hierarchy Structures

The regional pattern is created with the transaction /SAPAPO/RGPAT01. Figure 2.10 shows a regional pattern containing the locations PLSPG2@Q4L400 and PLSPB1@Q4L400.

Analogous to the BOD, the products are assigned to the regional pattern with the transaction /SAPAPO/PROD2RGP_M. The assignment is displayed with the transaction /SAPAPO/PROD2RGPDISP.

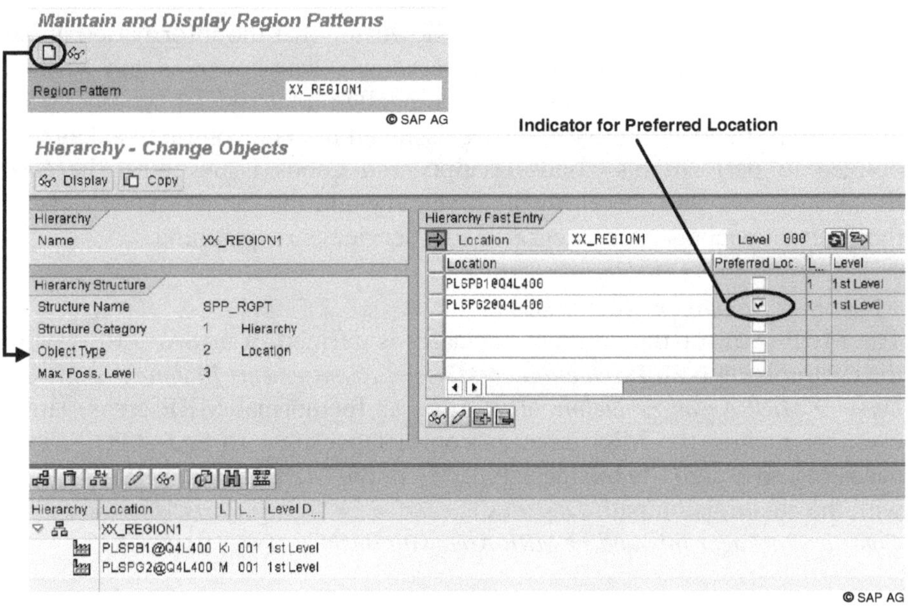

Fig. 2.10. Regional Pattern

Whether consolidated ordering is actually used for a service part is defined by the parameter 'consolidated ordering' in the 'SPP DRP'-view of the product master, figure 2.11.

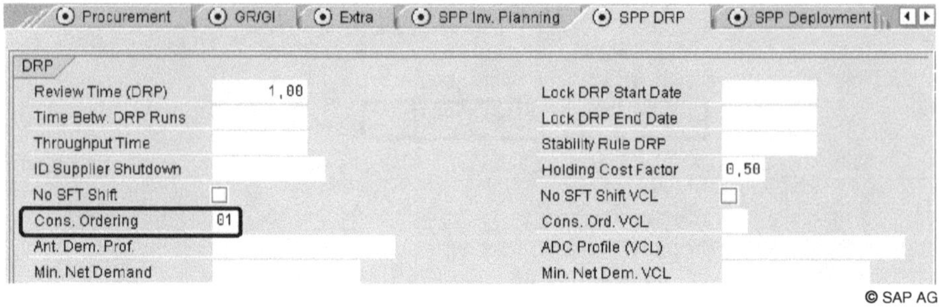

Fig. 2.11. Switch for Consolidated Ordering in the Product Master

2.1.3 Contract Packager

Contract packagers are subcontractors who perform packaging and re-packaging steps for the warehouses within the BOD. These packaging steps might be required for any location within the BOD. A contract packager is assigned to one location within BOD.

The subcontracting process has the downside that the information about the goods movements at the subcontractor's warehouse is not visible. Therefore the contract packagers are modelled as a special type of MRP area within the location that they are assigned to. The contract packager is obliged to perform his goods receipts and goods issues with the SAP EWM™ system, and therefore the inventory and the goods movements of the contract packager are integrated into service parts planning.

• *Contract Packager Master Data*

The MRP area for the contract packager is defined in mySAP ERP™ with the customising path *Production → Material Requirements Planning → Master Data → MRP Areas → Define MRP Areas* as for normal MRP areas. However, to transfer the MRP area as contract packager to SAP APO™, it is necessary to assign the business type '1' to the MRP area in mySAP ERP™ with the customising path *Logistics Execution → Service Parts Management → Contract Packager Inbound → MRP Area with Business Type*, figure 2.12.

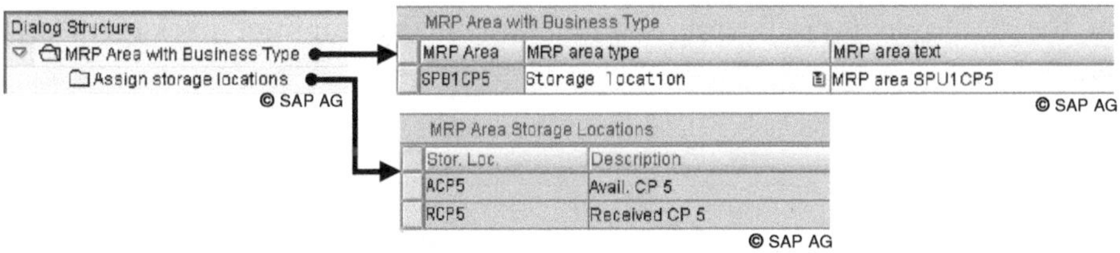

Fig. 2.12. Assign Business Type to MRP Area in mySAP ERP™

This way the MRP area is transferred to SAP APO™ as a contract packager with the location type '1007' and the business type '1', figure 2.13.

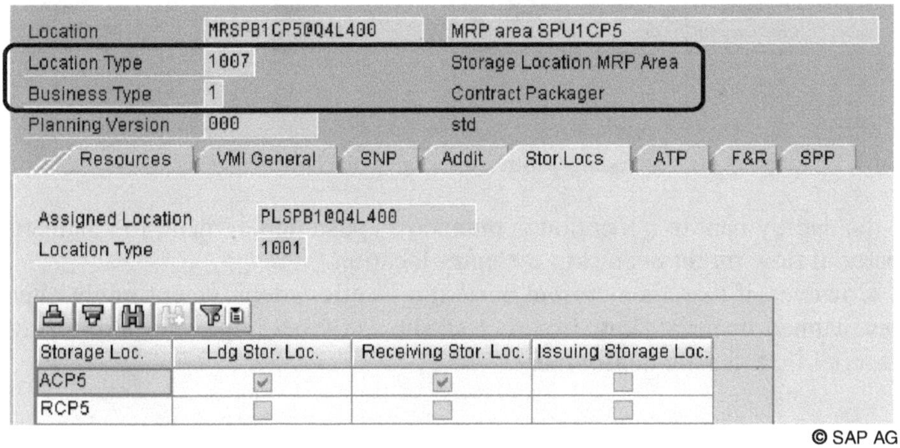

Fig. 2.13. Location for Contract Packager in SAP APO™

The contract packagers are not part of the BOD. If the contract packager is assigned to the entry location, the storage location for the contract packager has to be maintained in the scheduling agreement or the contract. For other locations info records are required.

• *Planning with Contract Packagers*

The material flow differs when contract packagers are used, because the service parts are first sent to the contract packagers before they are sent to the location that they are assigned to. The material flow depends on the deployment indicator which controls whether pull deployment or push deployment is assumed for planning (see chapter 10.2). The speciality of push deployment is that a goods receipt triggers the deployment run. Figure 2.14 shows the planned material flow – which DRP uses – depending on the deployment indicator and on how many contract packagers are used.

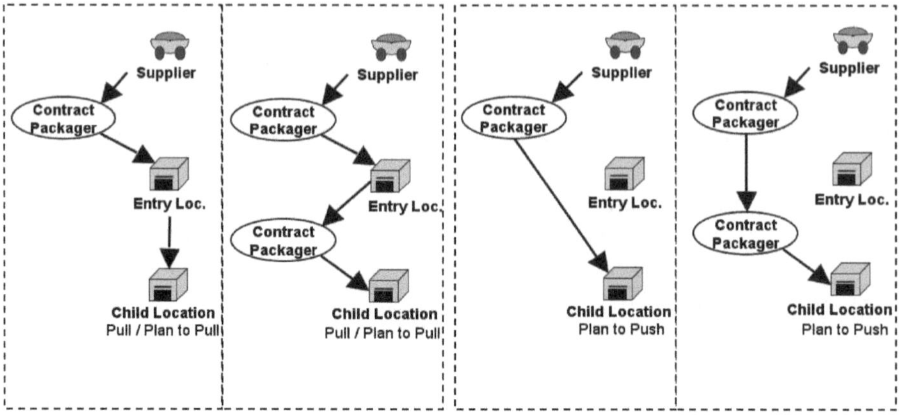

Fig. 2.14. Material Flow including Contract Packagers (for DRP)

If the deployment to a location is planned as push deployment, the planned material flow might even skip the entry location.

However, if there is a current need at a location, deployment might alter this planned material flow. Figure 2.15 shows two examples for a differing material flow during deployment.

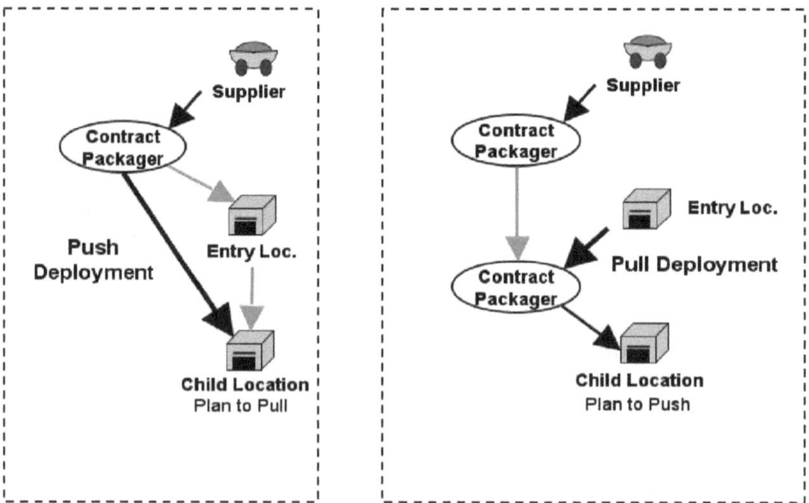

Fig. 2.15. Alternative Material Flow by Deployment

2.1.4 Product and Product Group

The product master has been enhanced for service parts management by approximately 150 new fields and the following product views:

- Properties of SPP
- Packaging data (used for SAP EWM™)
- Storage (used for SAP EWM™)
- SPP inventory planning
- SPP DRP
- SPP deployment
- SPP inventory balancing/surplus

The location master has been enhanced as well with an 'SPP' view. These views and fields are activated during the system installation with the report /SAPAPO/SWITCH_ON_SPP_MD_FLD.

• *Product Group*

The product group is used in service parts planning as a criterion e.g. for the stocking decision, for the exclusion from the stocking decision (see chapter 4), the phase-in forecast (see chapter 5.8), the product group procurement (see chapter 8.7.2) and for the determination of the deployment indicator (see chapter 6.4 and 10.2).

This product group is a new entity and has nothing to do with the product group used in mySAP ERP™. One or more product groups are defined for a product group type in customising. The customising path for the product group type is *APO → Master Data → Product → Product Group → Define Product Group Type*, figure 2.16.

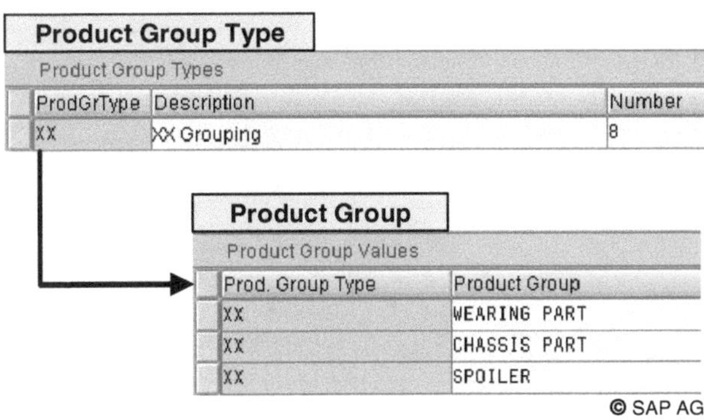

Fig. 2.16. Product Group and Product Group Type

The product group itself is defined with the customising path *APO → Master Data → Product → Product Group → Define Product Groups*. The product group and the product group type are assigned to the product master as shown in figure 2.17.

Fig. 2.17. Product Group Assignment in the Product Master

The restriction for the use of product groups is that only one product group is possible per product group type.

2.1.5 Location

The location master has been enhanced for service parts planning with the 'SPP'-view. This view contains the profiles for stocking and de-stocking that are used by the services for the stocking decision and the warehouse space savings profile for inventory balancing. Other entries are the threshold values for surplus planning and the target service level for monitoring.

In the 'calendar'-view of the location a new calendar is included – the planning calendar for service parts planning. This calendar can be used (if defined in customising) for the scaling of the demand history (see chapter 3.2) and for the scheduling of planned stock transfers (see chapter 8.3). Figure 2.18 shows the maintenance for the planning calendar for SPP in the location master.

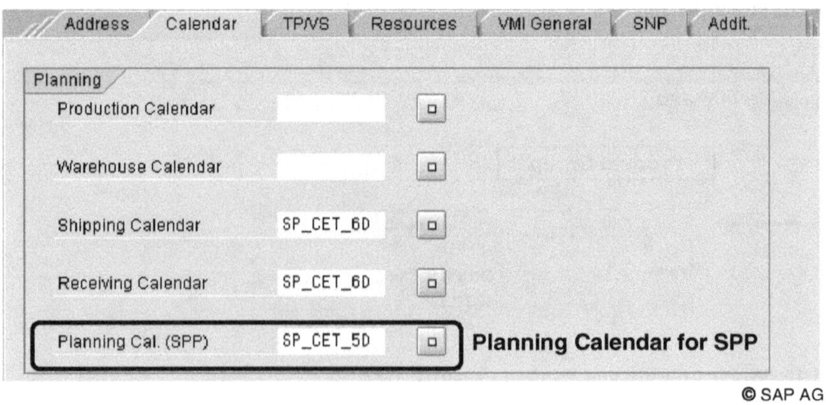

Fig. 2.18. Calendars in the Location Master

2.1.6 Rounding Profile

The rounding profile is based on the packaging specification and is used in inventory planning, DRP, deployment and in inventory planning. Since the packaging specification is used also for SAP EWM™ it contains more information than actually required for service parts planning. Figure 2.19 gives a simplified overview of the objects within the rounding profile – only those objects are mentioned that can not be avoided from a service parts planning perspective.

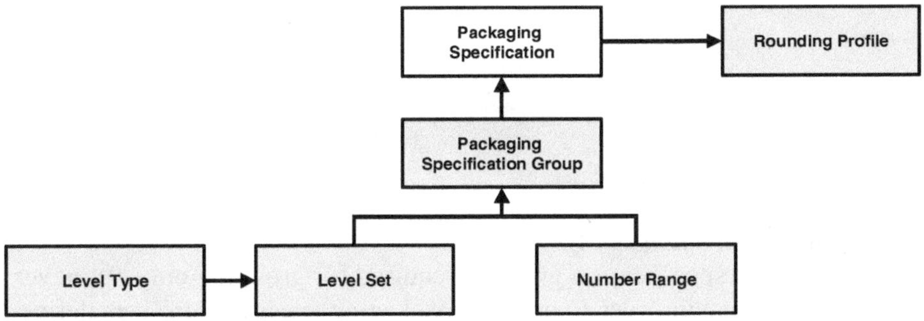

Fig. 2.19. Entities for the Rounding Profile

The rounding profile is assigned to the service profiles for EOQ and safety stock calculation, DRP, deployment and inventory balancing. Using the rounding profile is however optional.

• *Level Type and Level Set*

The packaging specification can have several levels – for example spark plugs are packed into a box, several boxes are packed into a carton and several cartons are packed to a pallet. The level type defines e.g. whether this level is relevant for kitting or rounding, and the level set defines which and how many level types are used for the packaging specification group.

Level type and level set are maintained with the customising path *EWM → Master Data → Packaging Specification → Maintain Structure of Packaging Specification → Define Level Type respectively → Define Level Set*, figure 2.20.

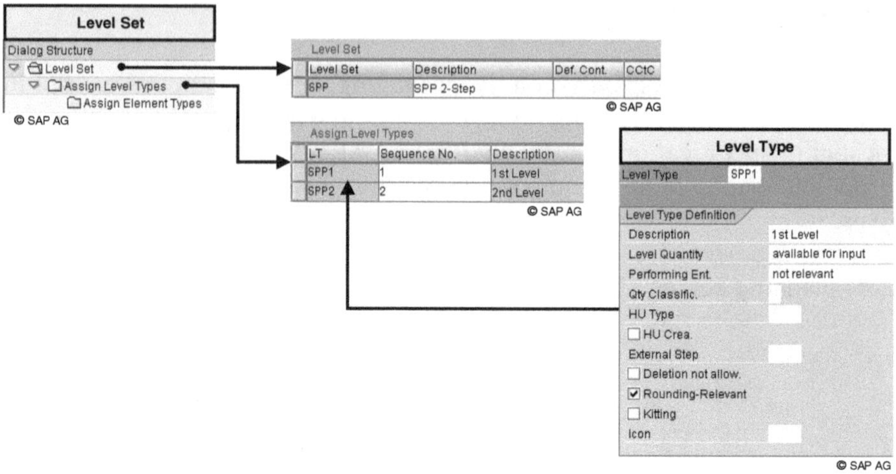

Fig. 2.20. Level Type and Level Set

• *Packaging Specification Group*

The packaging specification group is required for grouping only but nevertheless necessary in order to create a packaging specification. It is defined with the customising path *EWM → Master Data → Packaging Specification → Define Packaging Specification Group*, figure 2.21.

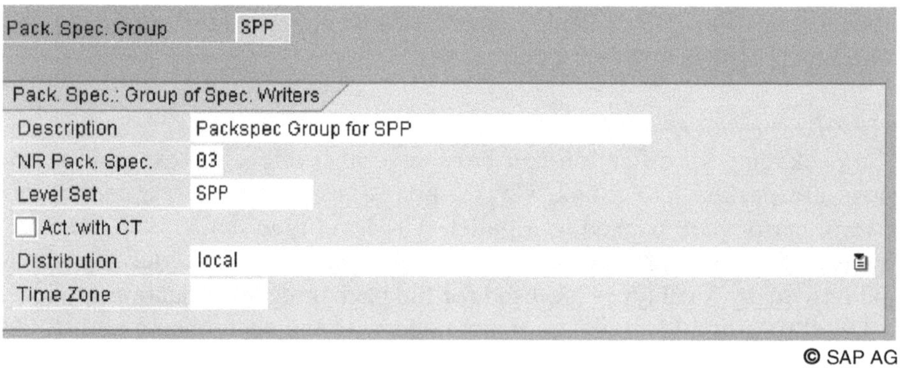

Fig. 2.21. Packaging Specification Group

• *Packaging Specification*

The packaging specification itself is a master data and maintained with the transaction /SCWM/PACKSPEC. Figure 2.22 shows the maintenance of the packaging specification SPP0002 which was assigned to the packaging specification group SPP.

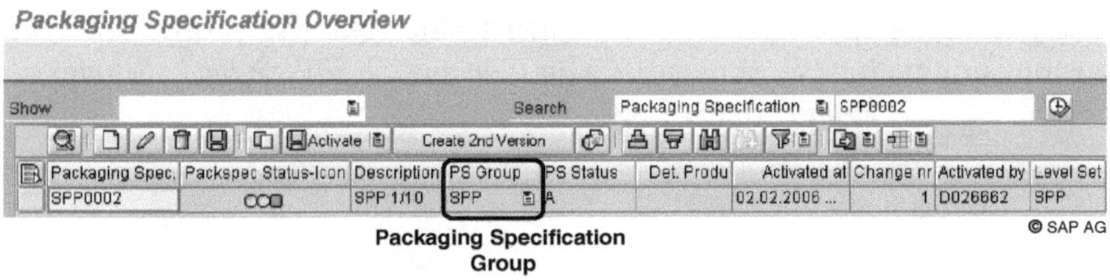

Fig. 2.22. Packaging Specification Overview

This packaging specification contains two levels (as defined in the level set), the first level rounds to full quantities only, the second level to 10 pieces. Figure 2.23 shows the packaging specification with the upper and lower rounding limits of 20 % and the target quantities of the rounding levels (1 piece for first level, 10 pieces for the second level).

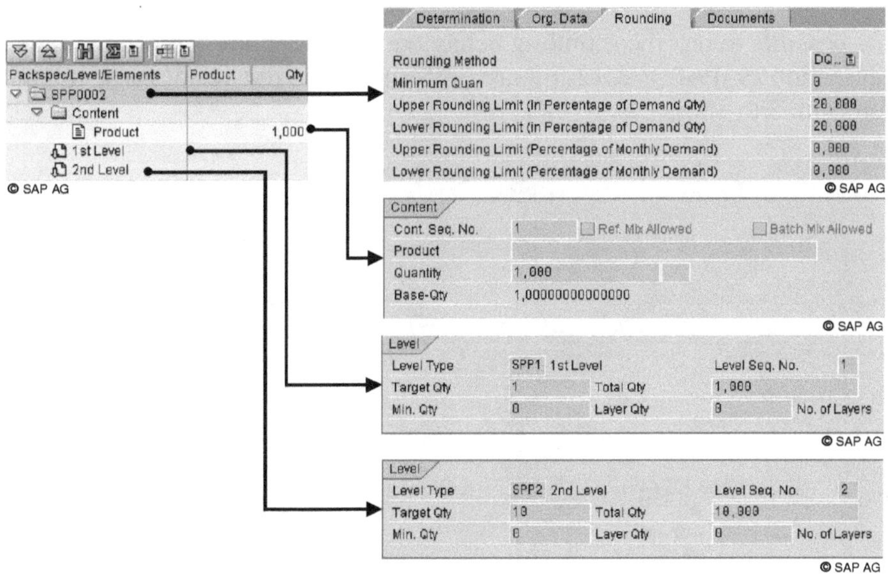

Fig. 2.23. Packaging Specification

The target quantity of each level defines how many units of the previous level are rounded. Therefore the target quantities of each level are multiplied – i.e. in case of a third level with a target quantity of 20 pieces the smallest quantity at the third level would be 200 pieces (and not 20 pieces).

• *Rounding Profile*

The packaging specification is assigned to the rounding profile with the customising path *APO → Supply Chain Planning → SPP → Basic Settings → Define Rounding Profile*, figure 2.24.

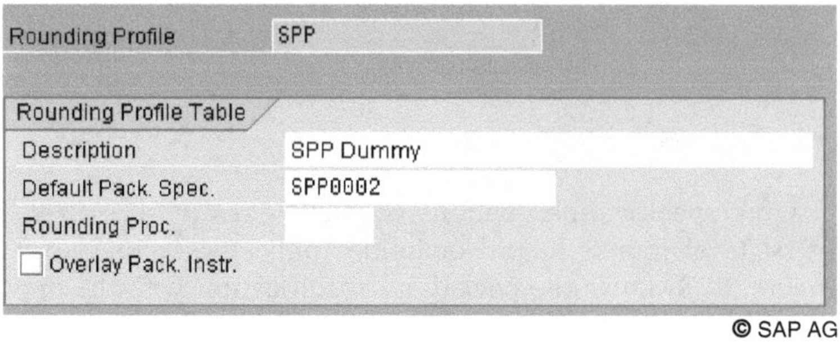

Fig. 2.24. Rounding Profile

It is possible to test the rounding behaviour of the rounding profile with the transaction /SAPAPO/AC12. Figure 2.25 shows the test result for a simulation from 8 to 15 pieces.

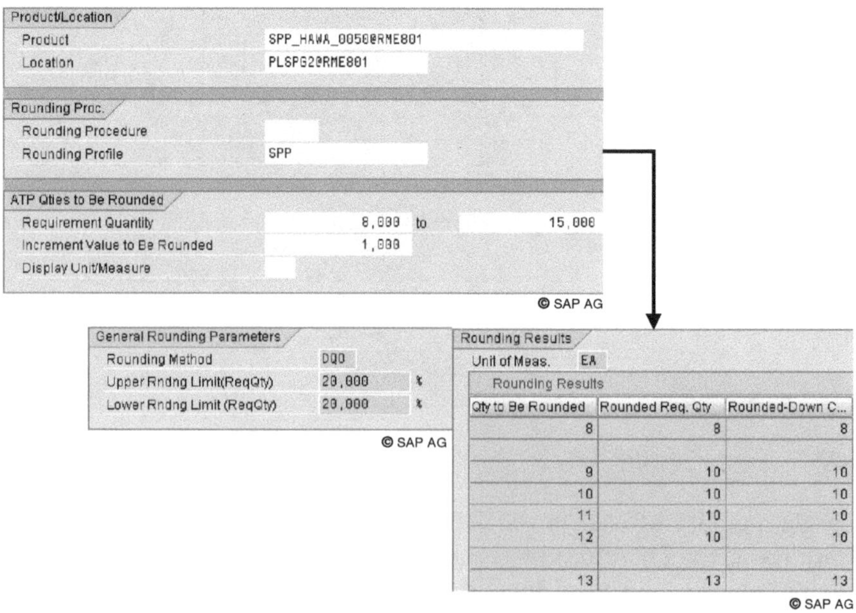

Fig. 2.25. Test of the Rounding Profile

Due to the upper and lower rounding limit of 20 percent quantities which are less then 20 percent from the rounding value are rounded up (in this case from 9 pieces to 10 pieces), and quantities which are not more than 20 percent above the rounding quantity are rounded down (in this case 11 pieces and 12 pieces to 10 pieces).

2.2 Planner

For service parts planning the planner (transaction /SAPAPO/PLANNER) has additional areas of responsibility as shown in figure 2.26.

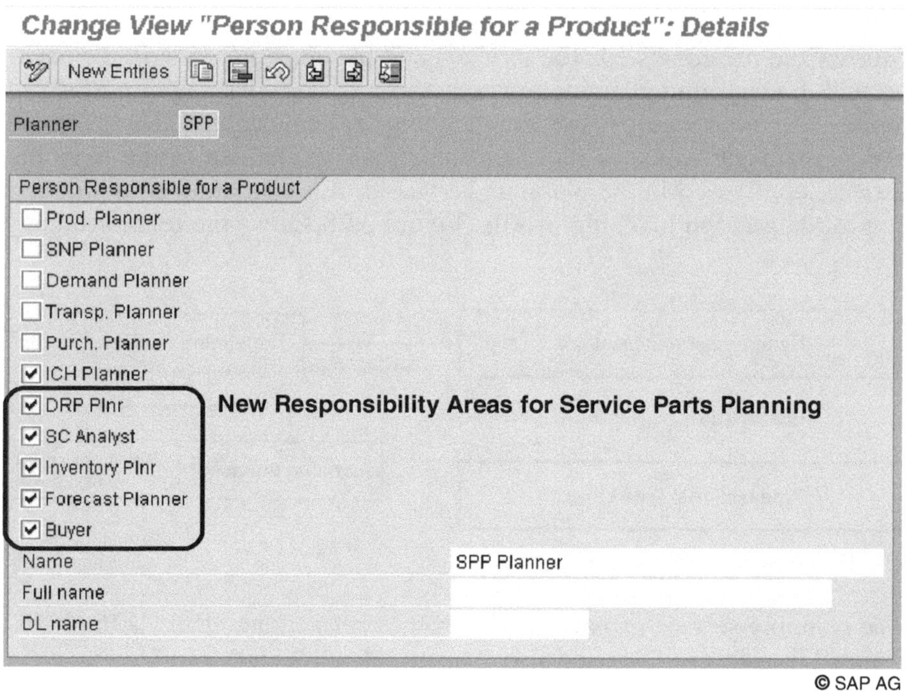

Fig. 2.26. Responsibility Areas for SPP Planners

These areas correspond with the assignment in the product master. In service parts planning the planner is not only used for selection but partially for authorisation as well. Therefore the user has to be assigned to a planner with the transaction /SAPAPO/USRPLAN, figure 2.27.

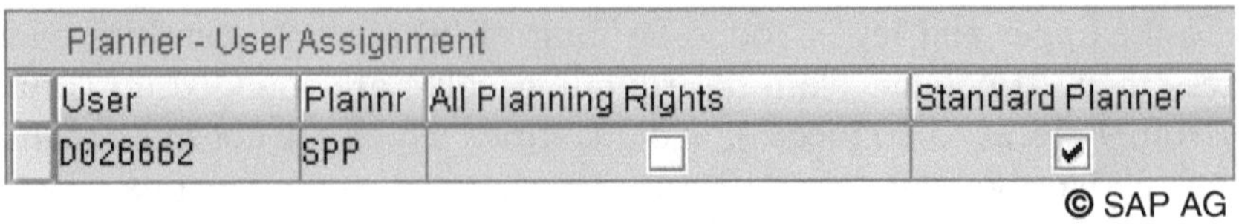

Fig. 2.27. Assignment of User to Planner

A user is only allowed to plan the products which have the same planner assigned.

2.3 Planning Service Manager

Most of the planning steps for service parts planning are done in the background. Background planning – whether as a background job or performed at the planner's request – uses the planning service manager. The planning service manager executes the algorithms that are defined in the planning service, configured in the planning service profile and bundled with other control data in the planning profile. Figure 2.28 shows the relationship of these objects.

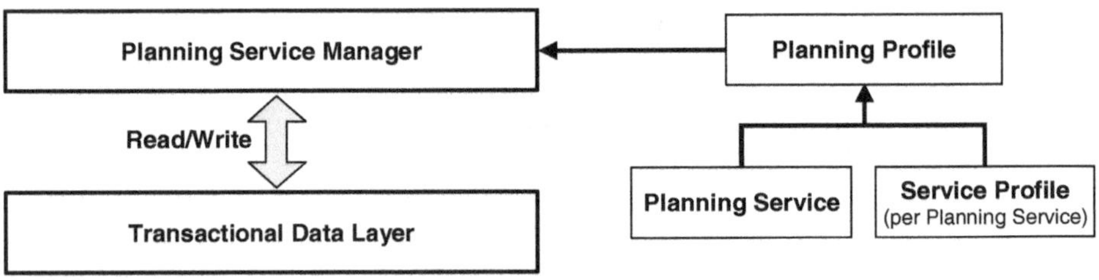

Fig. 2.28. Planning Service Manager

The planning service manager accesses the transactional data via the transactional data layer (TDL, see also chapter 2.4).

• *Planning Service*
The planning services contain the planning algorithms and are configured by the planning service profiles. Table 2.1 lists some of planning services which are described together with the corresponding planning service profile at the respective process chapters.

Table 2.1. Planning Services

Service Description	Service
Realignment (Stocking)	SPP_PDEM_STOCKING_RLG
Realignment (Supersession)	SPP_PDEM_SUPERSESSION_RLG
Forecast	SPP_FCS_SERVICE
Forecast Disaggregation	SPP_FCST_DISAGGREGATION
Forecast: Standard Deviation	SPP_FCS_SERVICE_MSE
Forecast Approval	SPP_FCST_RELEASE
Calculate Historical Forecast	SPP_RECALC_HISTFCST
Stocking Decision	SPP_INVP_STOCKING
De-Stocking Decision	SPP_INVP_DESTOCKING
EOQ and Safety Stock	SPP_EOQSFT_SERVICE
ABC Classification	SPP_INVP_ABCCLASS
DRP Planning	SPP_DRP
Anticipated Demand Coverage	SPP_PFR
Procurement Approval	SPP_DRP_APPROVAL
Deployment	SPP_DEPL
Inventory Balancing	SPP_INVENTORY_BALANCING
Supersession	SPP_SUPERSESSION
Surplus Planning	SPP_SOS_SURPLUS_DETERMINATION
Obsolescence	SPP_SOS_OBSOLESCENCE_CHECK
Shortage Analysis	SPP_SHORTAGE_MONITOR

• *Planning Profile*

All the information that the planning service manager requires is maintained in the planning profile. The planning profile contains one or more process blocks, and each process block contains one or more planning services with their planning service profiles.

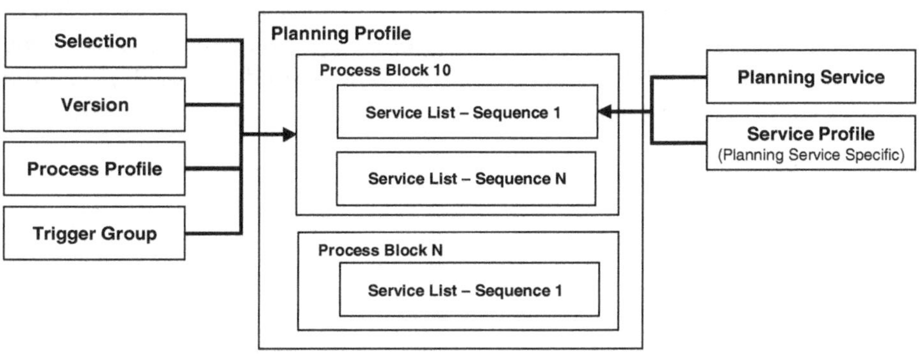

Fig. 2.29. Planning Profile Structure

The selection of the products, the planning version, the technical settings in the process profile and the trigger group are maintained per process block – this way it is possible to group services into one planning profile that require e.g. different process profiles. Figure 2.29 provides an overview about the entities which are required for planning with the planning service manager.

The planning profile is maintained with the transaction /SAPAPO/PE_CFG. Figure 2.30 shows an example of a planning profile for forecasting which contains one process block with four planning sequences.

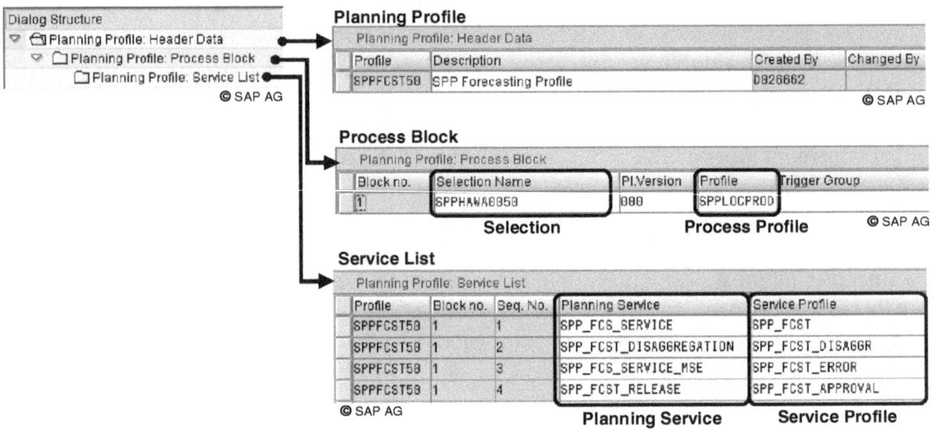

Fig. 2.30. Planning Profile

• *Selection Profile*

The selection profile defines the scope of the planning. There are different types of selection but for service parts planning either the selection type location product or the selection type product is used. Table 2.2 lists the services which require one or the other.

Table 2.2. Selection Types and Planning Services

Selection Type **Location Product**	Selection Type **Product**
Realignment (for Stocking)	Realignment (for Supersession)
Forecast (Forecasting, Disaggregation, Standard Deviation & Approval)	Surplus Planning
Calculate Historical FC	Obsolescence Check
Stocking & De-Stocking Decision	Shortage Analysis
EOQ and Safety Stock	
DRP Planning	
Anticipated Demand Coverage	
Procurement Approval	
Deployment & Inventory Balancing	
Supersession	

Figure 2.31 shows the selection profile of the type location product.

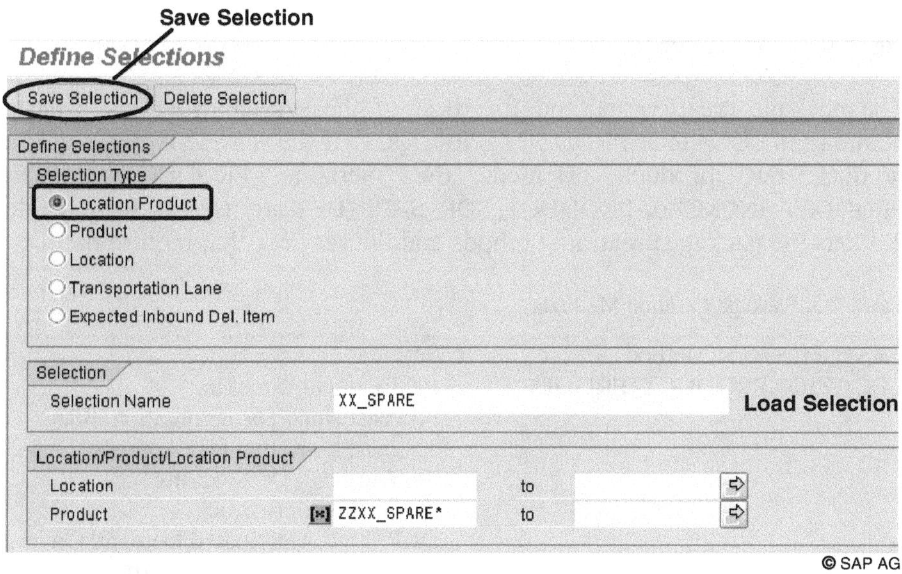

Fig. 2.31. Selection Profile

• *Process Profile*

The process profile contains the method of the package creation in the service and controls the detail of the logs. The process profile is maintained with the customising path *SCM Basis → Planning Service Manager → Define Process Profile* as shown in figure 2.32.

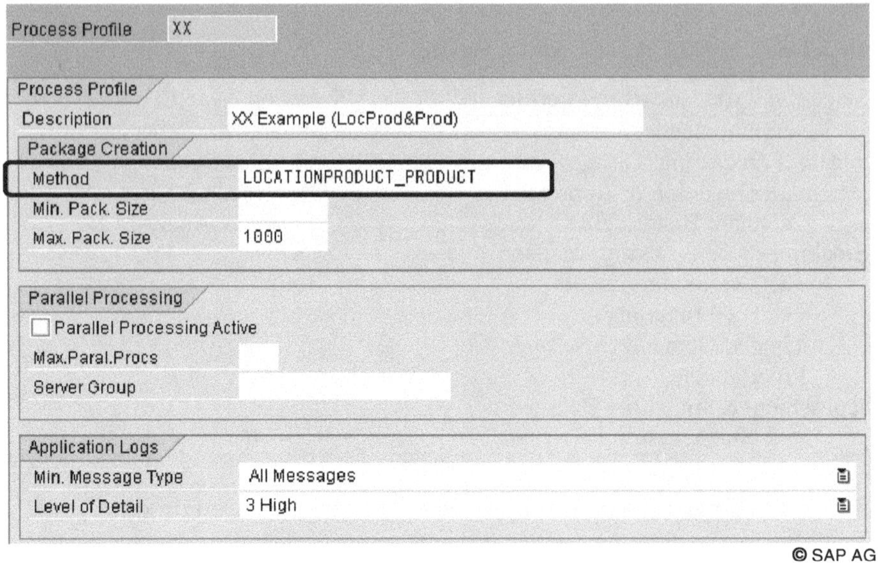

Fig. 2.32. Process Profile

The package creation method for most of the services in service parts planning is LOCATIONPRODUCT_PRODUCT. If the service is not location product but product oriented, the methods PRODUCT_SIMPLE, PRODUCT_INCMD or PRODUCT_SOR_SRPL_DET are used as well. Table 2.3 lists the package creation methods and the services that require them.

Table 2.3. Package Creation Methods

Package Creation Method	Service
LOCATIONPRODUCT_PRODUCT	Realignment (Stocking)
	Forecast (incl. Disaggregation, Standard Deviation and Approval)
	Stocking and De-Stocking
	EOQ and Safety Stock
	DRP (incl. Anticipated Demand Coverage and Procurement Approval)
	Deployment and Inventory Balancing
	Supersession
PRODUCT_SIMPLE	Obsolescence Planning
	Shortage Analysis
PRODUCT_INCMD	Realignment (Supersession)
PRODUCT_SOR_SRPL_DET	Surplus Planning
SPP_LOCPROD_FCSTRECALC	Recalculation of Historical Forecast
SIMPLE_GENERIC_METHOD	Version Copy

• *Planning with the Service Manager*

The planning service manager is called with the transaction /SAPAPO/PE_RUN and the reference to the planning profile. To run the planning service manager as a background job (transaction SM36) the report /SAPAPO/PE_EXEC is used.

• *Log*

The logs are displayed either with the transaction /SAPAPO/PE_LOG_DISP or with the transaction SLG1. In the latter case the object /SAPAPO/PE contains all logs that are created by the planning service manager (the object /SAPAPO/PDEM creates the logs for the data staging via SAP BI™ as used for the capturing of historical demand).

• *Trigger*

In order to reduce the volume for planning not all products within the selection are planned but only those who have planning relevant changes. The concept of net change planning is realised in service parts planning using triggers. Differing from planning file entries, many different types of triggers exist – depending on the action that caused their creation. Triggers are displayed, set and changed with the transaction /SAPAPO/TRIGGER, figure 2.33.

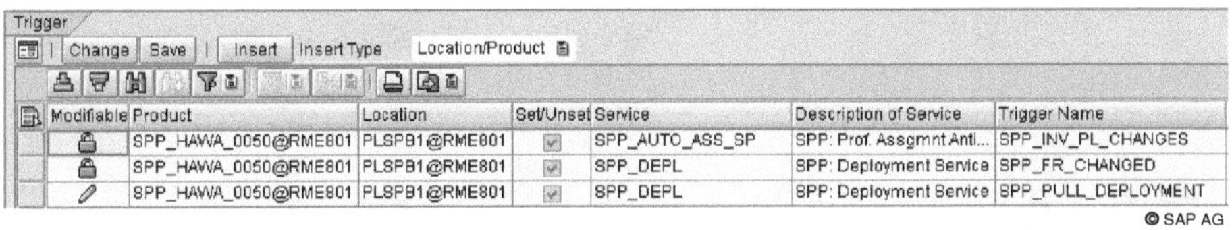

Fig. 2.33. Trigger

Table 2.4 lists the different types of triggers and the planning services that they affect. This follows the concept of publish and subscribe: the use of the triggers can be restricted by trigger profiles with the customising path *SCM Basis → Planning Service Manager → Data Management Layer → Triggers → Define Trigger Groups and Attributes.*

Table 2.4. Trigger Types and Services

Trigger	Service
SPP_ENTRY_POINT_VOID	SPP_DRP
SPP_EXPEDITE_FIRMHOR	SPP_INVENTORY_BALANCING
SPP_FACILITY_REDUCED	SPP_INVENTORY_BALANCING
SPP_FCST_CHANGE	SPP_EOQSFT_SERVICE, SPP_PFR
SPP_FCSTMODEL_CHANGE	SPP_FCSTHIST_CALC
SPP_FR_CHANGED	SPP_DRP, SPP_DEPL
SPP_INV_BALANCING	SPP_DRP
SPP_INV_PL_CHANGES	SPP_DRP
SPP_INV_PL_MD_CHANGE	SPP_EOQSFT_SERVICE
SPP_LEADTIME_CHANGED	SPP_EOQSFT_SERVICE, SPP_DRP
SPP_MANUAL_TRIGGER	SPP_INVP_STOCKING SPP_INVP_DESTOCKING SPP_EOQSFT_SERVICE, SPP_DRP
SPP_NEW_PRODUCT	SPP_PHASE_IN
SPP_NEW_REGION_ASSIG	SPP_INVP_STOCKING SPP_INVP_DESTOCKING
SPP_NON_ST_DEMAND	SPP_INVP_STOCKING
SPP_OVERDELIVERY	SPP_DRP
SPP_PHASE_IN_CALC	SPP_FCST_RELEASE
SPP_PICK_DENIAL	SPP_DEPL
SPP_PULL_DEPL_NOSUCC	SPP_DRP, SPP_INVENTORY_BALANCING
SPP_PULL_DEPLOYMENT	SPP_DEPL
SPP_REPL_INDI_CHANGE	SPP_PDEM_STOCKING_PDEM SPP_DEPL
SPP_RLD_DONE_BOD	SPP_INVP_STOCKING SPP_INVP_DESTOCKING SPP_FCS_SERVICE, SPP_PHASE_IN
SPP_RLG_DONE	SPP_FCS_SERVICE
SPP_SCHEDULE_CHANGED	SPP_DRP
SPP_STK_EXC_RULE_CHG	SPP_INVP_STOCKING SPP_INVP_DESTOCKING
SPP_STOCK_ADJUSTMENT	SPP_DRP, SPP_DEPL
SPP_SUPERSESSION	SPP_INVENTORY_BALANCING
SPP_SUPPLIER_CHANGED	SPP_EOQSFT_SERVICE, SPP_DRP
SPP_USEUPFLG_CHANGED	SPP_SOS_SURPLUS_DETERMINATION
SPP_WAREHOUSE_RESTR	SPP_DEPL

These triggers are activated with the transaction /SAPAPO/SPP_TG_ACT using the selection 'SPP*' for all service parts planning services.

2.4 Transactional Data Layer

With the transactional data layer (TDL) a new entity is introduced to control the source of the data storage for service parts planning. The general idea is the de-coupling of the business objects from the storage technique in order to gain more flexibility. The planning service manager accesses the transactional data layer using semantics Figure 2.34 shows how the planning service manager accesses the TDL as an abstract data storage for time series, orders or inventory. Within the TDL customising the real storage for the data is defined.

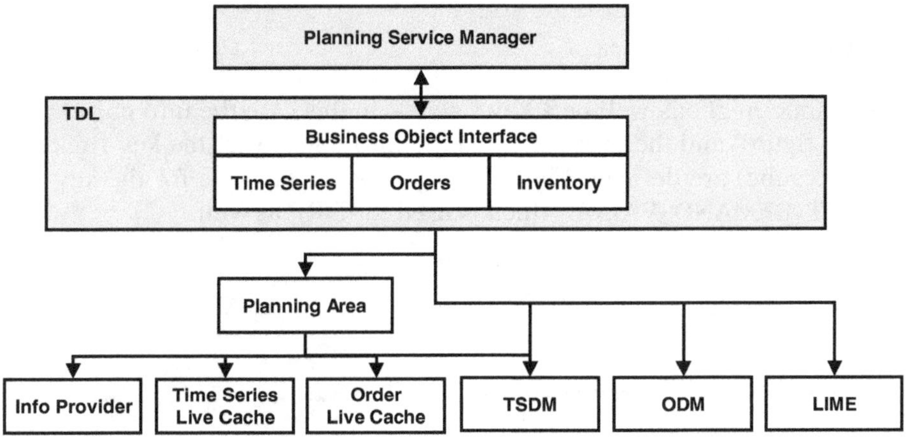

Fig. 2.34. Transactional Data Layer

• *Semantics*
The business objects are represented by semantics. The mapping between semantics and the storage technique is done either via a time series type, an info provider or a planning area. The info providers are only used for the reading of data. Figure 2.35 shows an example for the assignment of the semantic TS_DRP_RESULT (which is used for DRP) and the time series type DRP with the transaction /SCMB/TDL_SEMANTIC.

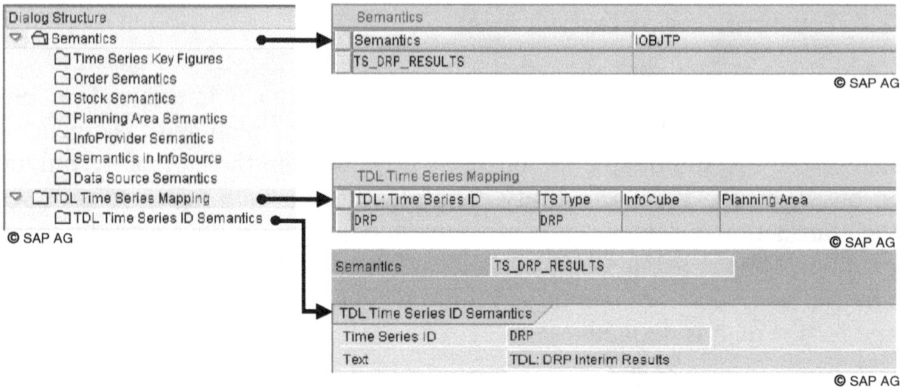

Fig. 2.35. Semantics Definition

A semantic might as well be a key figure – in this case the info object type is 'key figure' and the info cube and the info object (i.e. the key figure of the info cube) are defined. Figure 2.36 shows an example for the key figure NET_DEMAND_VALUE which is used for DRP as well.

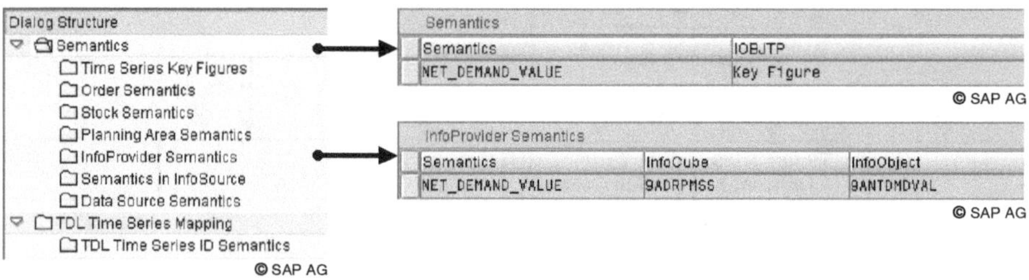

Fig. 2.36. Semantics Definition for Key Figures

This definition is done with the same transaction as above. Other object types are characteristic, time characteristic and unit.

• *Time Series Type*

The data storage is either defined via planning area, info provider or via a time series type (as in figure 2.35). The configuration of the time series types is done with the transaction /SCA/TSDMCFG, figure 2.37.

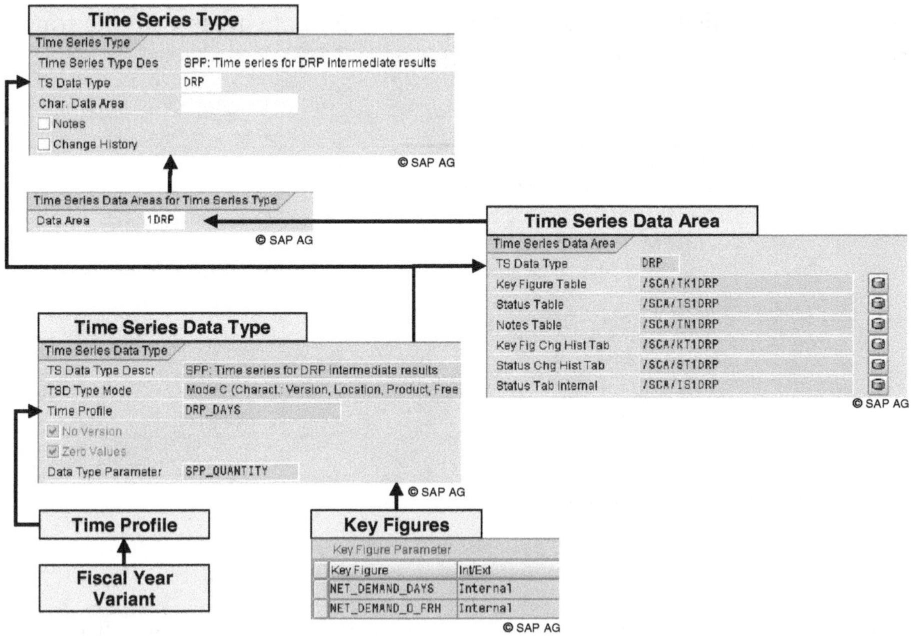

Fig. 2.37. Configuration of Time Series Types

The OSS note 913863 contains additional information about the TDL. A helpful transaction when dealing with the TDL is /SCMB/TDL_TOOLS because it contains the link to most of the customising steps and the transactional data management.

• *Definition of Number Ranges and Activation*

One prerequisite for working with the TDL is that the number ranges for the TDL orders are defined. This definition is done with the transaction /SCMB/TDL_ORDERGUIDS as shown in figure 2.38.

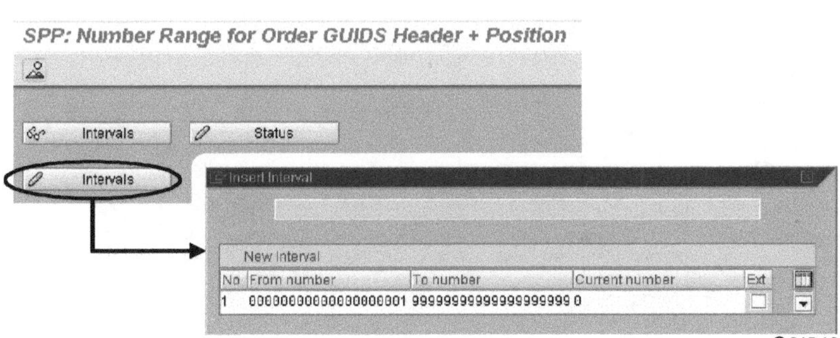

Fig. 2.38. Number Range for TDL Orders

Another prerequisite is the activation of the TDL data areas with the transaction /SCMB/TDL_TOOLS as shown in figure 2.39.

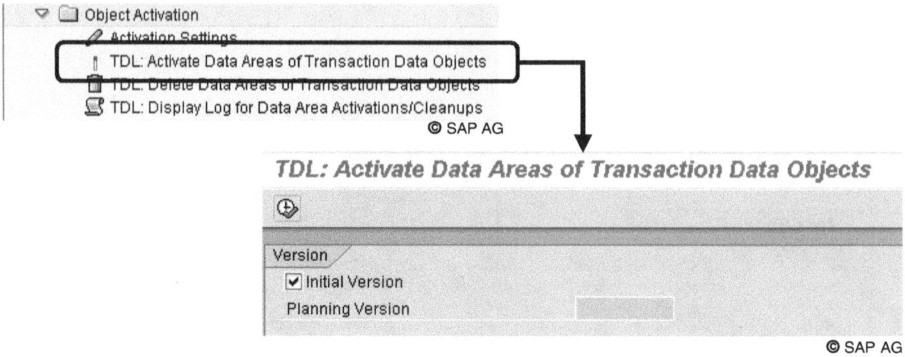

Fig. 2.39. TDL Data Area Activation

• *TDL Data Access*

The TDL contains (or links to) time series, orders and inventory. It is possible to access the TDL data via the semantics.

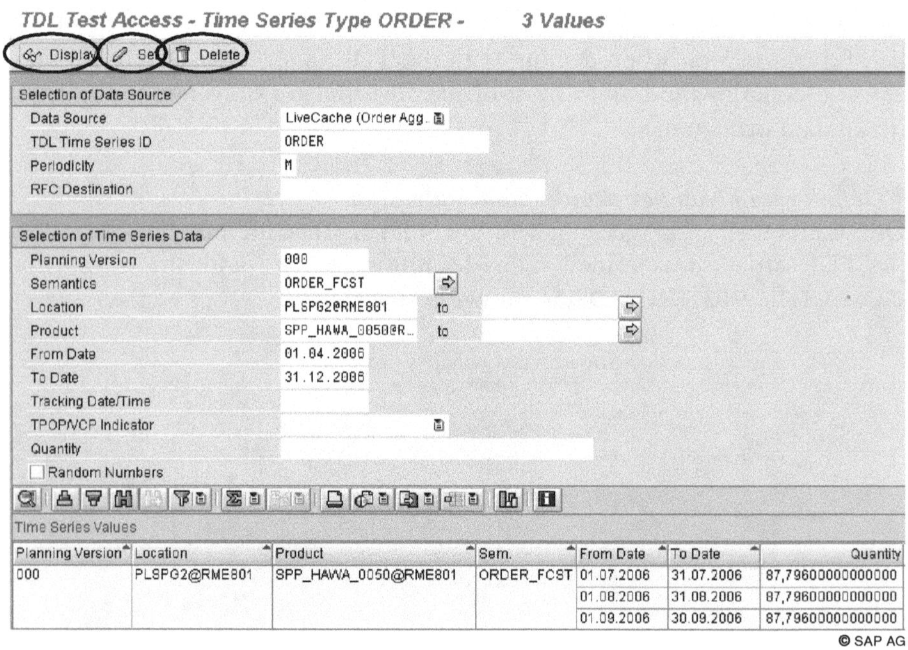

Fig. 2.40. Data Access to the TDL Time Series

For the data access the following transactions are used:

- transaction /SAPAPO/TDL_TS_TEST for time series
- transaction /SAPAPO/TDL_ORD_TEST for orders
- transaction /SAPAPO/TDL_INV_TEST for inventory

Figure 2.40 shows the access to the time series with the semantics ORDER_FCST.

2.5 Simulation

Simulation is part of service parts planning as it is in 'normal' SAP APO™. The transactional data is stored in versions. The active version – the version that communicates with mySAP ERP™ – is version '000'. It is however possible to copy the data from the active version to an inactive version and perform simulations. These simulations are analysed with the same tools as the operative data. It is however not possible to transfer the data from the inactive version to the active version because in the meantime the data basis might have changed. To transfer the information form the inactive simulation to the operative version, the planning steps have to be repeated in the active version.

In order to perform a simulation, first an inactive simulation version with a copy of the current operative data has to be created. The simulation version is created with the transaction /SAPAPO/SPPSIM as shown in figure 2.41. In order to avoid unnecessary data and to keep the performance high, it is possible to restrict the data – either by a selection profile or by products directly. Another option to restrict the data is by application, i.e. whether the data is required for a simulation of forecasting, stocking decision, EOQ and safety stock planning, DRP or pull deployment. The new simulation version is also displayed in the model and version maintenance with the transaction /SAPAPO/MVM.

Simulation versions should be created only with this transaction (and not with the version copy /SAPAPO/VERCOP) in order to ensure that all the data of the TDL is copied. For the copying of the TDL data however a version profile is required. This version profile is created with the customising path *APO → Supply Chain Planning → SPP → Basic Settings → Simulation → Define Version Profile* – figure 2.42 shows an example. Note that two process profiles are assigned to the version profile – one for copying and one for deleting the transactional data. These process profiles require a package creation method of the type SIMPLE_GENERIC_METHOD.

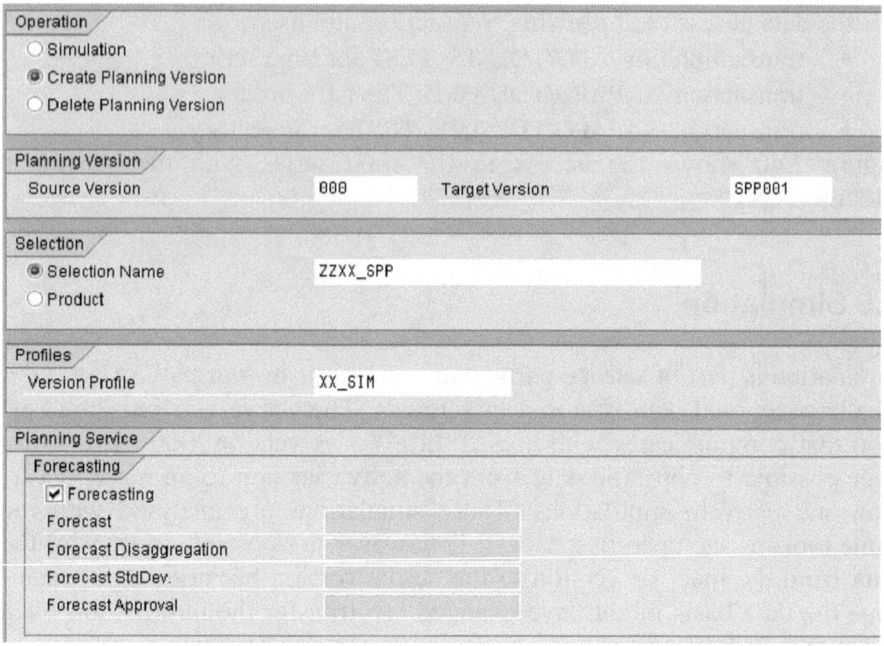

Fig. 2.41. Create Simulation Version

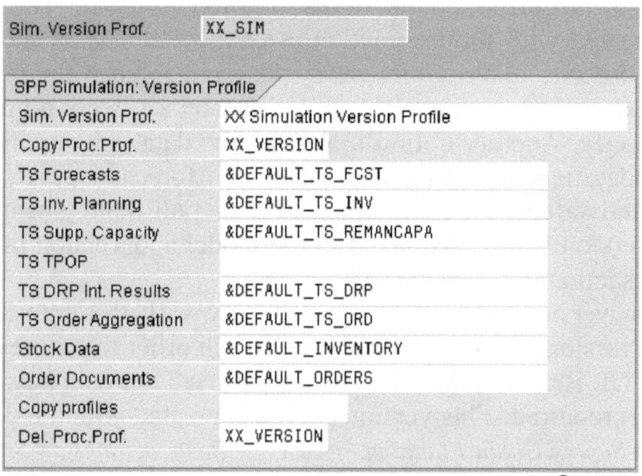

Fig. 2.42. Version Profile

In the second step planning is performed in the inactive simulation version. With the same transaction /SAPAPO/SPPSIM it is possible to execute planning with the service profiles without having to create new planning profiles for the simulation version. Figure 2.43 shows how to set up forecasting for the simulation version.

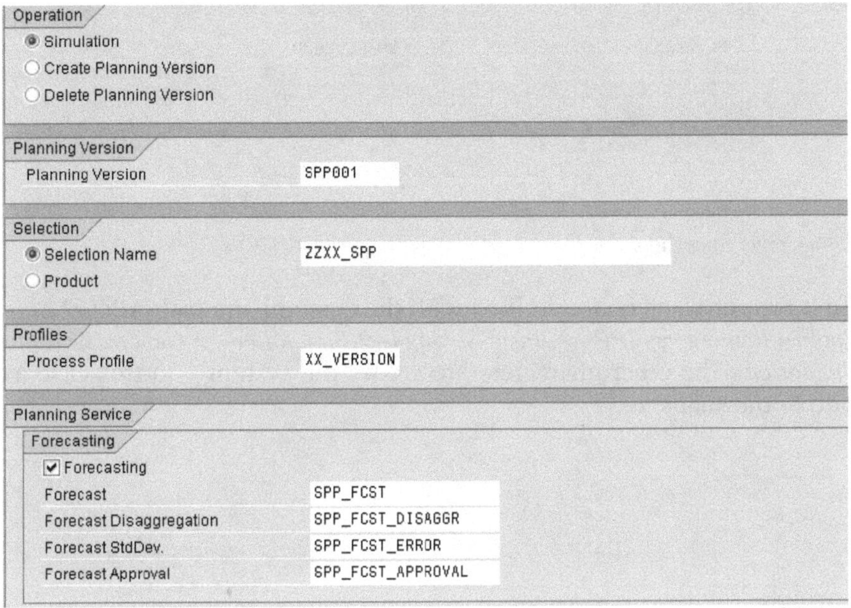

Fig. 2.43. Simulation

It is also possible to use the tools for interactive planning for the simulation version.

• *Snapshot*

The idea of the snapshot is to save a copy of the current planning situation into a simulation version in order to perform a simulation with this data at a later point in time. For example, the planning situation of the first of April is copied as a snap shot. Two months later, at the first of June, this snapshot is used and different planning steps are performed. The speciality of the snapshot is that the planning applications pretend that the point in time for the planning is the creation date of the snapshot. This way it is possible to analyse what the effect of a different planning decision would have been.

A snapshot is created with the transaction /SAPAPO/SNAPSHOT as shown in figure 2.44. The snapshot is not restricted by products or applications but contains the complete active version.

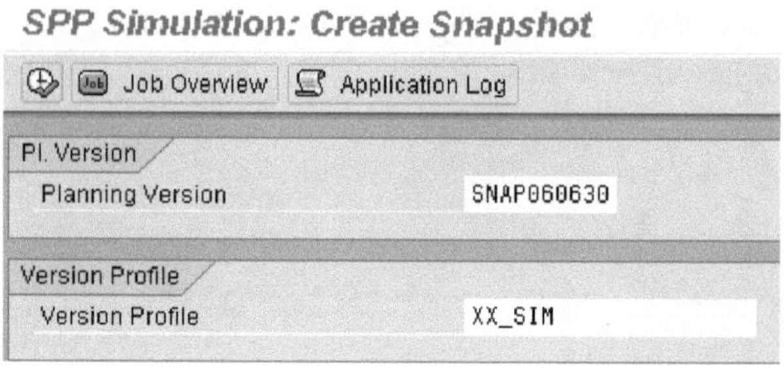

© SAP AG

Fig. 2.44. Create Snapshots

The first four characters are defined with the customising path *APO → Supply Chain Planning → SPP → Basic Settings → Simulation → General Settings for Simulation*. The other characters are set by the system – in this case as the date of the snapshot.

3 Capture and Manage Demand History

3.1 Process and Data Flow Overview

The demand history is the basis for forecasting and the stocking decision. Therefore the capturing of the demand history is the first step for service parts planning. The sales history is loaded from mySAP CRM™ (or for test purposes from a flat file) using the SAP BI™ data staging process. During the upload the data is processed in order to fit the specifics of service parts planning – e.g. an aggregation along the BOD is performed and other steps which are explained in chapter 3.2.2. The demand history is stored both on item level (in the ODS object 9ARAWDAT) and on aggregated level (in the info cube 9ADEMAND).

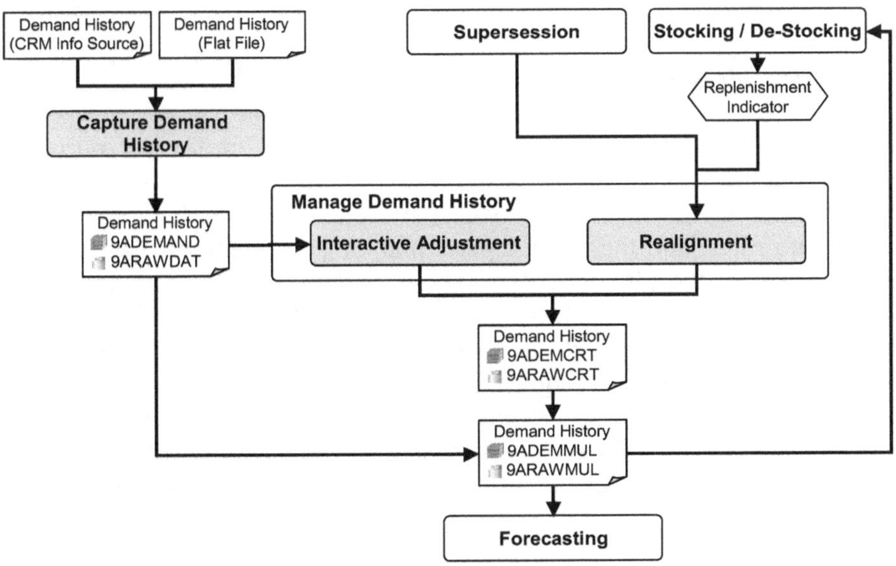

Fig. 3.1. Capture and Manage Demand Process Overview

For several reasons it might be required to adjust the demand history. Examples are realignments due to a change in the stocking decision (see chapter 4), supersession (see chapter 12) or to separate demand caused by promotions. In total 9 planning services trigger realignment, figure 3.1 shows only two examples. Another example for demand adjustment is removing demand that is caused by a unique and exceptional occurrence – e.g. the replacement of exhaust pipes due to a legal change. This increase in the demand is not representative and should therefore not be the basis for future forecasting.

Managing historical demand contains the realignment and the interactive demand adjustment and writes the changes to the ODS objects 9ARAWCRT for order items respectively 9ADEMCRT for aggregated demand history per period. The final demand history that is used by the applications forecasting, stocking and de-stocking is the sum of the captured demand history and the changed demand history. The technical realisation is done using the multi-cubes 9ARAWMUL for order items and 9ADEMMUL for aggregated demand history per period. Figure 3.1 shows the process overview of capture and manage demand history.

3.2 Capture Demand History

3.2.1 Data Flow Overview

The demand history is loaded from mySAP CRM™ (or for test purposes from a flat file) using the standard SAP BI™ data staging functionality. Nevertheless there are many service parts planning specific functions in the update rules, and the service parts planning application requires a defined format of the info providers. The SAP BI™ business content for the data upload from mySAP CRM™ and from a flat file is part of the service parts planning solution and has to be activated before loading data. The SAP BI™ content is also required for the data processing of the service parts planning applications because the transactional data layer accesses SAP BI™ objects as well (see chapter 2.4). Figure 3.2 shows the data staging structure and some of the SAP BI™ objects for the upload of the demand history.

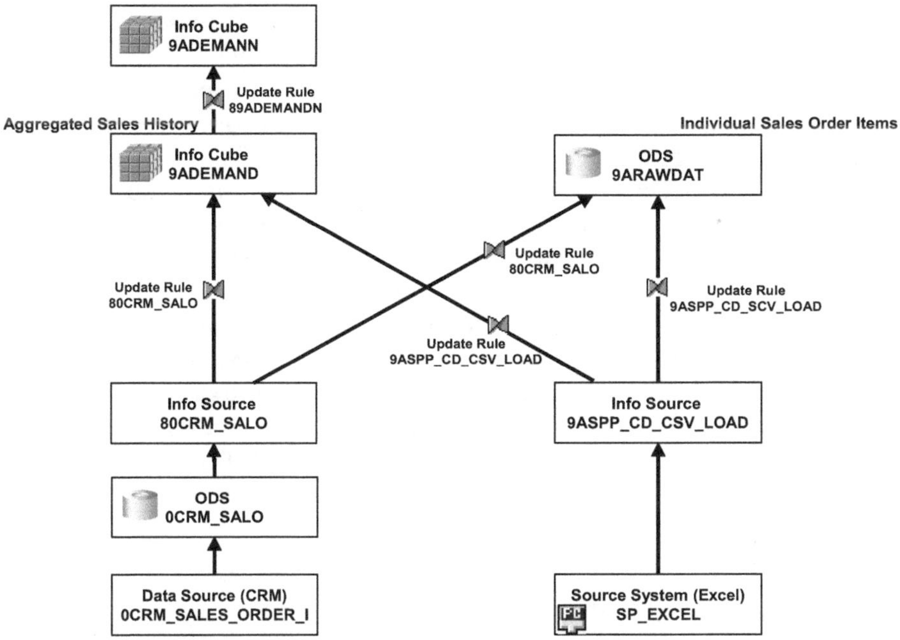

Fig. 3.2. Upload Structure for the Demand History

For the activation of the SAP BI™ business content the replication of data sources should be selected as '3.x datasource' (and not as 'datasource').

3.2.2 Processing of the Demand History

During the upload of the demand history the data is already processed for the service parts planning applications. Mainly the following processing steps are performed:

- demand category determination
- determination of future dated orders
- determination of the facing and the first stockholding location
- aggregation per period
- scaling of the demand history
- aggregation along the BOD

The reason and the details of these processing steps are explained in the following.

• *Determination of the Demand Category*

To each order item a demand category is assigned which determines whether the item is relevant for forecasting or not. The default demand category is NONE which is relevant for forecasting. The reason for demand categories is to treat certain customer orders differently.

Service parts planning is mainly a make-to-stock (respectively procure-to-stock) scenario which implies that individual customer orders are not considered in planning. There are however exceptions, e.g. if a big customer places an order of considerable quantity some time in advance. The demand category for customer orders is introduced to separate these kinds of customer orders. The demand categories (NONE, FDO_DEM, ADJ_DEM, PROMO_DEM, ...) are modelled with the info object 9ADEM_CAT as shown in figure 3.3 (transaction RSDMD). These demand categories are predefined and activated as business content (info source 9ADEM_CAT). It is not recommended to change these categories. Figure 3.3 shows that the demand category FDO_DEM for future dated orders is not relevant for forecasting. The info object for the forecast relevance is 9AFCSTABLE.

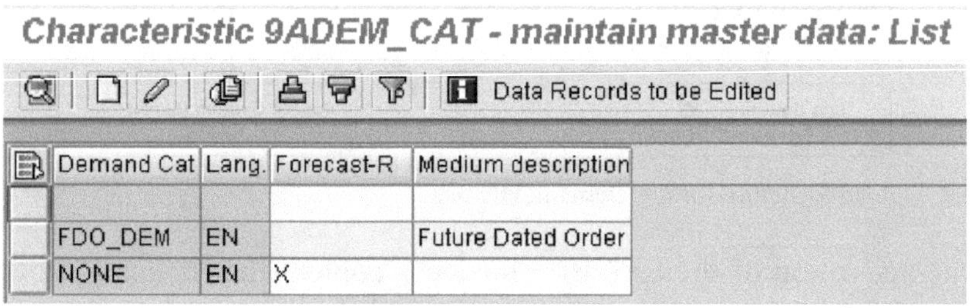
Characteristic 9ADEM_CAT - maintain master data: List

Data Records to be Edited

Demand Cat	Lang.	Forecast-R	Medium description
FDO_DEM	EN		Future Dated Order
NONE	EN	X	

Fig. 3.3. Master Data for Info Object 9ADEM_CAT

Though there exists also a table for the customising of the demand categories (transaction /SAPAPO/PDEMCUST) those settings have no impact.

• *Determination of Future Dated Orders*

Future dated orders are determined either based on the order type or based on the difference between the creation date and the requested date. If this time difference exceeds the defined horizon of the order item a demand is classified as future dated order (FDO) with the demand category FDO_DEM. This classification is done based on the customising settings defined with the path *APO → Supply Chain Planning → SPP → Basic Settings → Make Settings for Customer Demand* as shown in figure 3.4. In this example the requested date must be at least 90 days in the future at the time the order is created.

Fig. 3.4. Definition of Future Dated Orders

The implication of excluding future dated orders from forecast is that they will not contribute to the demand history. Therefore no forecasting is done for this kind of orders. To procure the requested service parts nevertheless for these orders, DRP considers the demand of the future dated orders additionally to the forecast.

• *Customer Facing and First Stockholding Location*
In the service parts planning solution the customer facing location and the first stockholding location are distinguished in order to keep the demand history consistent throughout changes of the stocking decision. The *customer facing location* is the first location which is checked. The customer facing location might however not be able to confirm the customer request– either because it was decided that the service part should not be stored at this location or because it has simply run out of stock. Since rules-based ATP is used for the SPM solution, other locations are checked and the sales order will probably be confirmed in one or more of these other locations. The locations which confirm the customer request are the *ship-from locations*. The *first stockholding location* however is the first location in the check sequence which is defined as stocked (i.e. the replenishment indicator is set to 'stocked') and therefore should be able to confirm the customer request – independent of which location actually confirms the request.

The demand history for service parts planning is based on the first stockholding location. If the customer facing location and the first stockholding location differ, it is checked during upload whether an ATP rule with a location substitution procedure for both locations exists.

• *Base Unit of Measure*
If the sales unit of measure differs from the base unit of measure, the demand quantity is adjusted to the base unit of measure.

• *Periodicity and Aggregation for Forecasting and Inventory Planning*
The relevant date of the customer order item is the requested date. During the data upload, the order items are aggregated into weekly, monthly and posting period respectively fiscal year period buckets. Both the order quantity (info object 9ADEM_QTY) and the number of order items (info object 9AORD_LINE) are aggregated. In the info cube 9ADEMAND the date of the demand element is not stored but only the week (info object 0CALWEEK), the month (info object 0CALMONTH) and the fiscal year period (info object 0FISCPER) with the fiscal year variant (info object 0FISCVARNT). All the three periodicities are calculated and stored – independent of which periodicity is used.

The definition of the periodicity for forecasting and inventory planning is done with the customising path *APO → Supply Chain Planning → SPP → Basic Settings → Determine Forecast Periodicity*, figure 3.5.

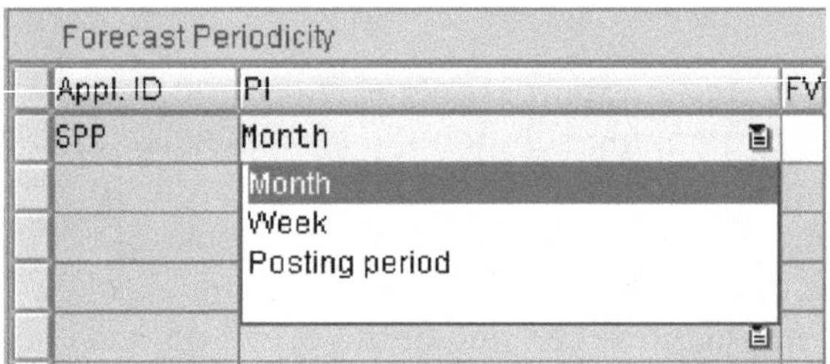

© SAP AG

Fig. 3.5. Periodicity for Forecasting

Forecasting and inventory planning is performed either in time periods of weeks, months or posting periods (using fiscal year variants).

• *Mandatory Fiscal Year Variant*
Though the fiscal year variant is only used in the case that the periodicity is set to 'periods', due to the data staging content it is required that a fiscal year variant is assigned in the general settings for the demand history with the customising path *APO → Supply Chain Planning → SPP → Forecasting → Make General Settings for Demand History* as shown in figure 3.6. As a default the fiscal year variant 'K3' is used.

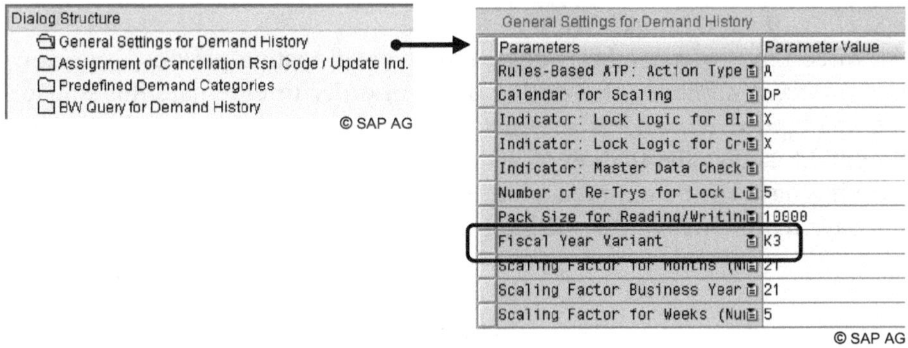

Fig. 3.6. Assignment of the Fiscal Year Variant

The fiscal year variant is created with the transaction OB29 in SAP APO™. If the same fiscal year variant should be used as in mySAP ERP™, it is possible to upload the fiscal year variant from mySAP ERP™ with the transaction RSA1 (or RSA1OLD) using the SAP BI™ functionality for the transfer of global settings, figure 3.7.

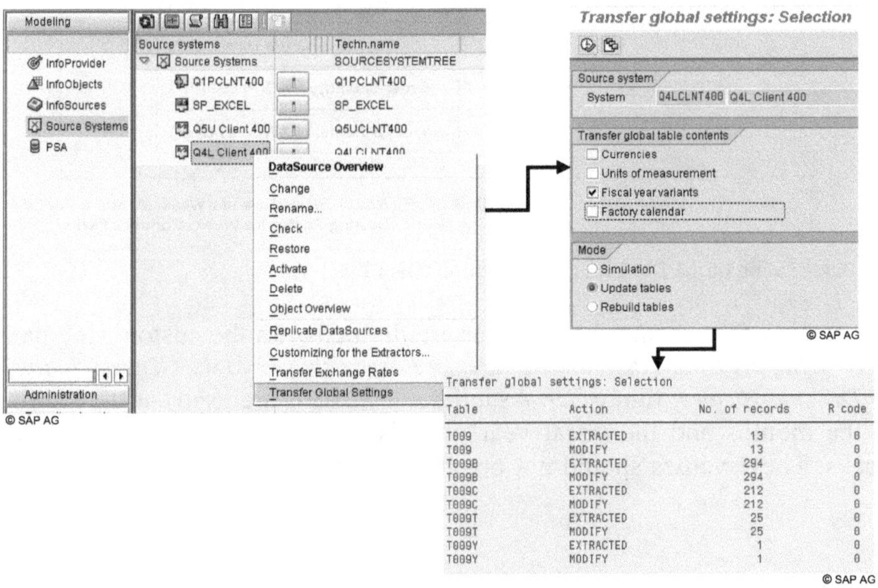

Fig. 3.7. Upload Fiscal Year Variants from mySAP ERP™

In this case the upload is triggered in SAP APO™ using the source system for mySAP ERP™.

• *Scaling of the Demand History*
All three kinds of periods - weeks, months and posting periods – can contain different numbers of working days. In order to eliminate this impact, the aggregated demand is scaled to a constant number of working days. Figure 3.8 shows the scaling of the demand with the ratio of the number of working days (as determined using the calendar) and the number of working days maintained in the scaling factor.

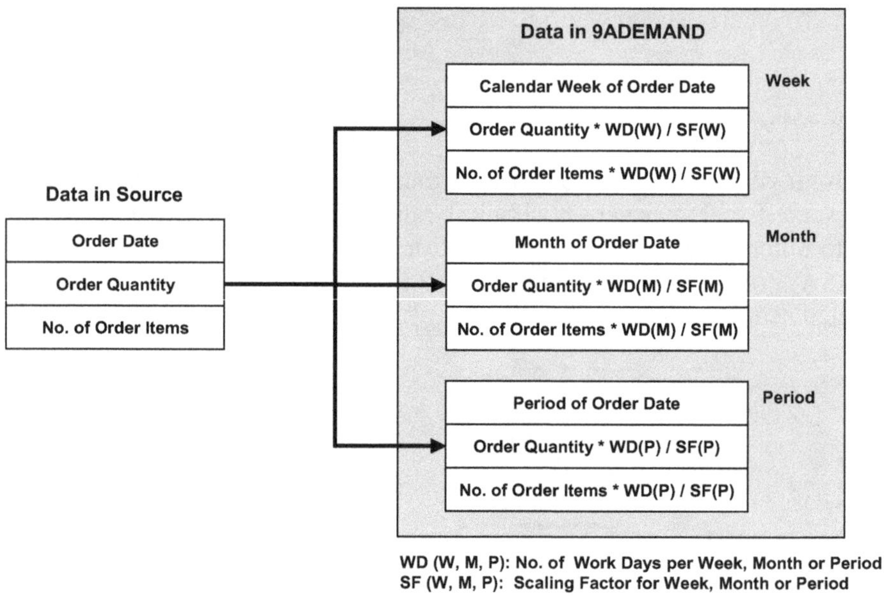

Fig. 3.8. Scaling of the Demand History During Data Load

The scaling factors and the calendar are defined with the customising path *APO → Supply Chain Planning → SPP → Forecasting → Make General Settings for Demand History*, figure 3.9. As a default 21 days are used for the scaling of the months and the fiscal year periods and 5 days for the scaling of weeks. These values should not be changed unless there are reasons to do so.

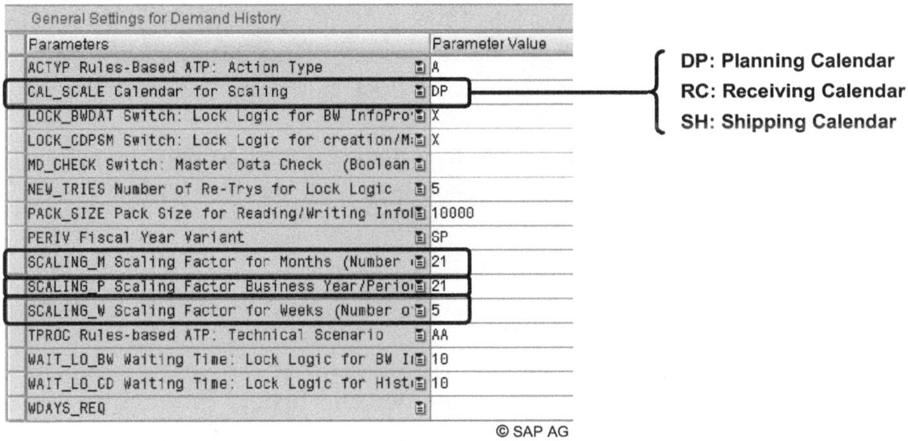

Fig. 3.9. Scaling Factor and Calendar for Demand Aggregation

Three alternatives exist for the calendar for scaling – the planning calendar, the receiving calendar or the shipping calendar. All the three calendars are maintained in the location master (see chapter 2.1.5).

• *Aggregation Along the Bill of Distribution*

For forecasting not only the demand at the customer facing location is used but also an aggregated demand along the bill of distribution (BOD). The purpose of this aggregation is to perform a forecast based on a bigger data base (see chapter 5). The result of this aggregation is that the customer order items and the order item quantities are stored both for the first stockholding location – where they actually belong to – and for the parent location, figure 3.10.

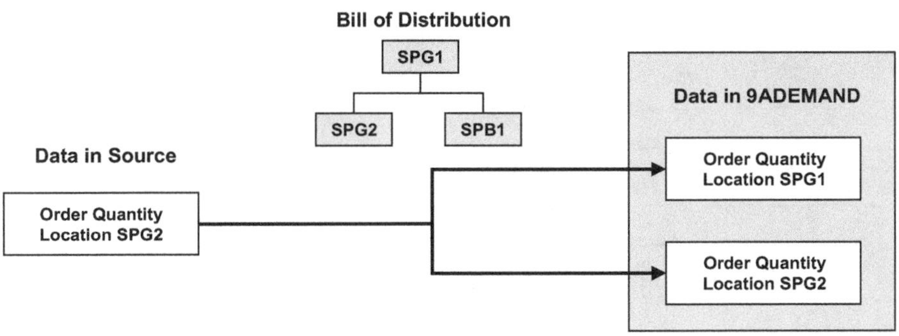

Fig. 3.10. Aggregation Along the BOD

As an example, if the location SPG2 has a customer demand of 10 pieces and SPB1 of 20 pieces, at the parent location SPG1 additionally 30 pieces are stored – though the parent location does not have any customer demand by definition.

The implication of this aggregation is that the service part must be assigned to a BOD before loading demand history. Therefore a missing BOD assignment causes an error.

3.3 Manage Demand History

The purpose of the management of the demand history is to adjust – i.e. change – the demand history either by realignment (due to a change in the stocking decision, supersession, in order to separate promotion demand or other) or by interactive adjustment. These changes are stored via SAP BI™ real time data staging in ODS objects (9ADEMCRT for the aggregated demand and 9ARAWCRT for the order items). The history for service parts planning is taken from a multi-cube which adds the original history and the changes to the final history. Figure 3.11 shows the data flow for the aggregated demand.

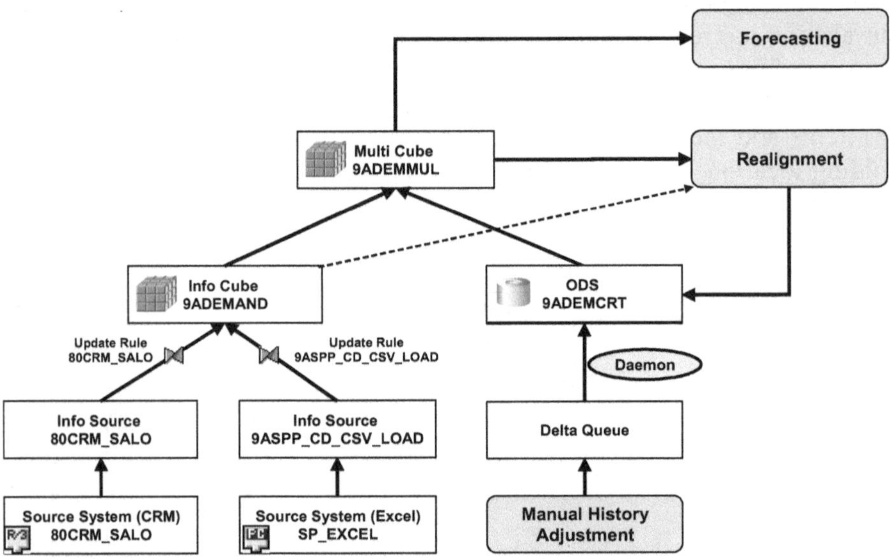

Fig. 3.11. Data Structure Overview for Manage Demand History

• *Interactive Adjustment of the Demand History*

The interactive adjustment of the aggregated demand history is performed per location product with the transaction /SAPAPO/SPPDMDH. Figure 3.12 shows the maintenance in the key figure 'demand: adjusted history'. The demand history – as uploaded into the info cube 9ADEMAND – is displayed as well but can not be changed. For both key figures – original and adjusted demand – the scaled values are also calculated and displayed.

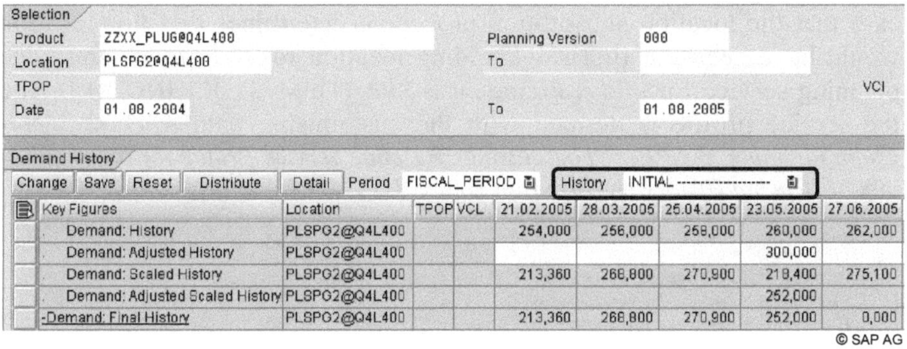

Fig. 3.12. Manual Adjustment of the Demand History

Another feature in this UI is to call directly SAP BI™ reports to analyse the history (with the drop-down menu 'history'). Also the definition of promotion demand is performed in this transaction by maintaining the value '1' in the key figure 'promotion' (not displayed in figure 3.12) for periods with promotions. In this case the realignment service for promotion determines the difference between the demand and the historical forecast and changes the demand category for this difference to the non-forecasting relevant category PROMO_DEM. This applies only if the demand is higher than the historical forecast.

Analogously it is possible to adjust the demand history for the order items with the transaction /SAPAPO/SPPDMRD.

• *Realignment*

Realignment is performed e.g. after a change in the stocking decision, after supersession or in order to separate the historical demand due to promotions. For realignment the information of the order item GUID, the product number, the order item type (e.g. TAN) and the customer is required, because a rule evaluation within rules-based ATP is performed in order to determine the customer facing location and the first stockholding location (an ATP check is not performed). This implies that the demand history on order item level is required for realignment.

• *Realignment after a Stocking Decision*

As an example for realignment the realignment after a stocking decision is explained (realignment after supersession is explained in chapter 12.3). If the replenishment indicator changes from stocked to non-stocked, the demand history of this location has to be transferred to the new first stockholding location. In the opposite case, if the replenishment indicator changes from non-stocked to stocked, the demand history of the old first stockholding location is transferred to the newly stocked location – in the case that the location substitution procedure determines that this location would have been the first stockholding location for the order items. The planning service for this realignment is SPP_PDEM_STOCKING_RLG, and the service profile is defined with the customising path *APO → Supply Chain Planning → SPP → Forecasting → Define Service Profile for Reorganisation of Demand History* as shown in figure 3.13.

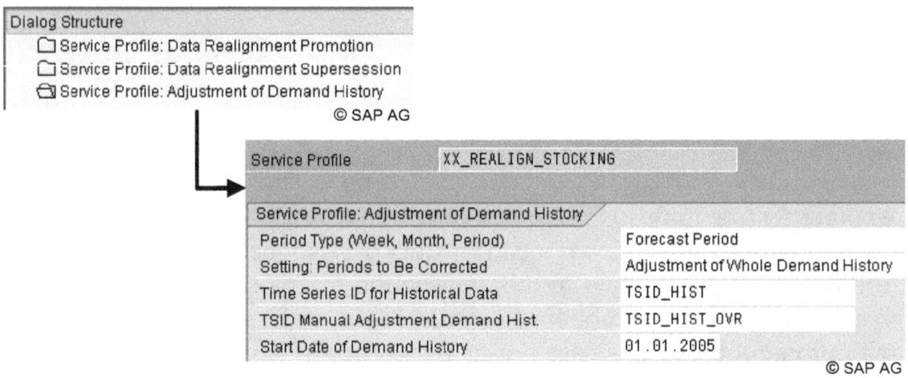

Fig. 3.13. Service Profile for Realignment Due to Stocking Decisions

4 Stocking Decision

4.1 Process Overview

One characteristic of service parts planning is the huge number of products and locations. In order to reduce inventory and warehouse costs not all products are kept in all locations. The decision whether a product is stored in a location depends on the demand and on the costs for the products. The decision is recorded in the authorised stocking list (ASL). The function of the ASL is modelled in SAP APO™ by the replenishment indicator, see next section. There is however no standard report to display the replenishment indicator for multiple products.

The decision to stock or de-stock a service part at a warehouse is based on the demand history of the product. Figure 4.1 shows this process.

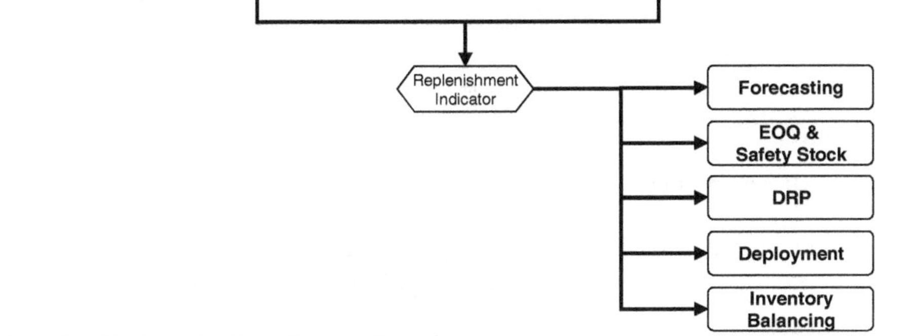

Fig. 4.1. Stocking Decision Process Overview

The thresholds for the stocking and the de-stocking decision depend on the cost of the service part and are based on the demand quantity, on the number of order items, the product group or a combination of these.

4.2 Replenishment Indicator

The replenishment indicator controls whether a service part should be stocked at a location or not. It is a prerequisite for most of the planning functions that the replenishment indicator allows stocking. If the replenishment indicator of a service part is set to 'not stocked' at a location,

- no forecasting is performed
- no EOQ and safety stock planning is performed
- DRP ignores forecasts and safety stocks.

The customising path for the replenishment indicator is *APO → Master Data → Product → Define Replenishment Indicator*. Though it is possible to create own values for the replenishment indicator, the stocking and de-stocking service consider only the standard ones. The replenishment indicator is assigned to the location product, figure 4.2.

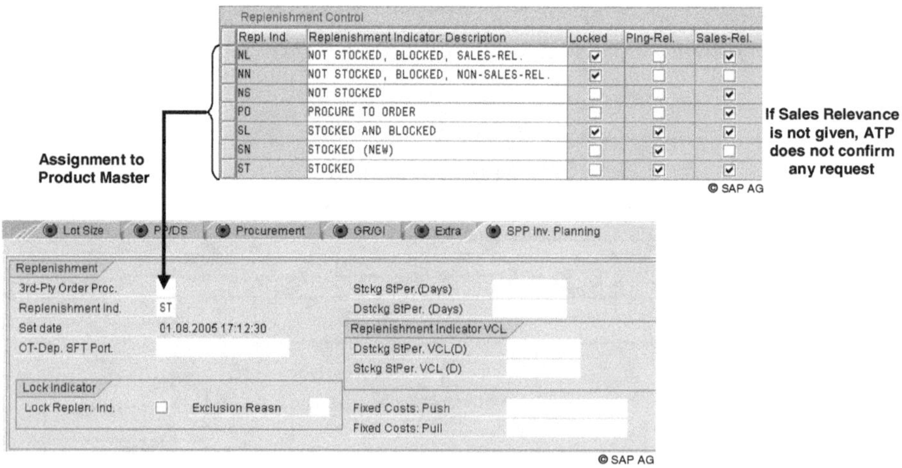

Fig. 4.2. Replenishment Indicator

The replenishment indicator is set by the stocking service and the de-stocking service. Figure 4.3 shows the cycle for the replenishment indicator.

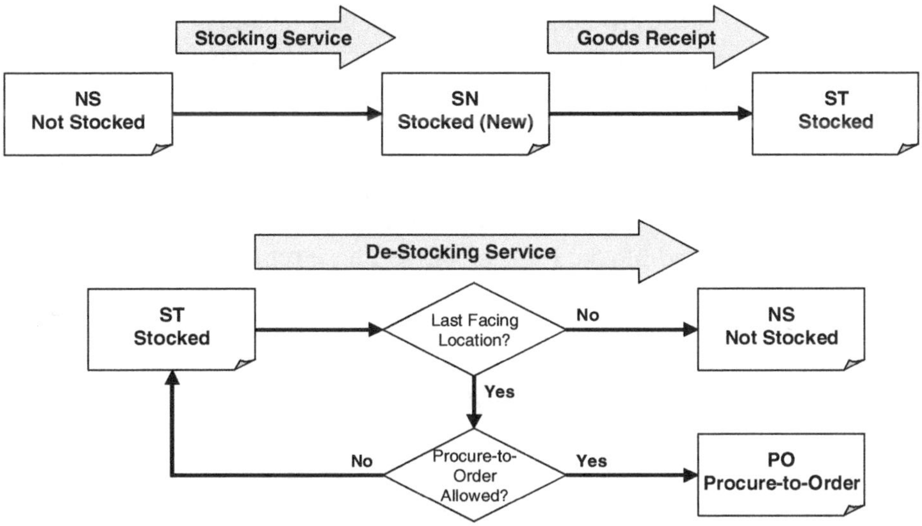

Fig. 4.3. Cycle for the Replenishment Indicator

If the stocking service decides to stock a previously not stocked service part, the replenishment indicator is set first to 'stocked (new)'. Only after goods receipt – i.e. when the service part is really stocked – the replenishment indicator is changed to 'stocked'. The threshold for the change of the replenishment indicator is defined with the customising path *APO → Supply Chain Planning → SPP → Inventory Planning → Define Limit Value for Replenishment Indicator*, figure 4.4.

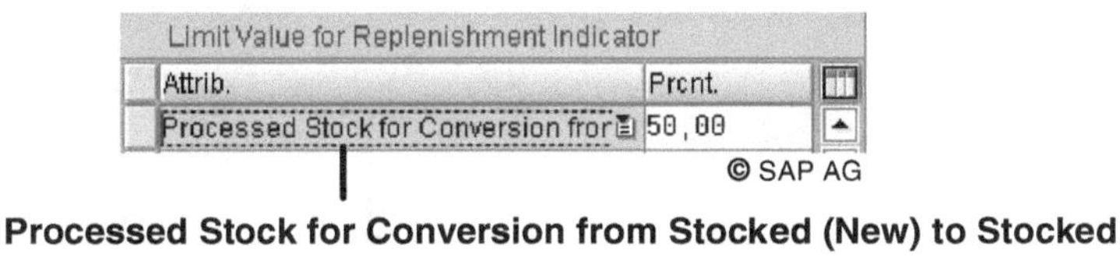

Fig. 4.4. Threshold for Change of the Replenishment Indicator

The percentage relates to the demand within the replenishment lead time – i.e. the demand which is due immediately. In this case, after a goods receipt of 50 % percent of the demand quantity, the replenishment indicator is set from 'stocked (new)' to 'stocked'.

In the other case, if the de-stocking service decides that a previously stocked location should not be stocked anymore, the replenishment indicator is set to 'not stocked' – unless it is the last facing location below the entry location. If the setting in the product master allows it, the replenishment indicator is set to 'procure-to-order'. The implications are that the safety stock is set to zero and the economic order quantity (EOQ) to one – if a customer places an order for this product, the order quantity is procured from the supplier and distributed along the BOD to the facing location.

It is possible to inhibit an automatic change of the replenishment indicator by using the replenishment indicators NL (not stocked, blocked, sales relevant) or NN (not stocked, blocked, non-sales relevant) for non-stocked and SL (stocked and blocked) for stocked. These replenishment indicators have to be set and changed interactively.

4.3 Rules and Decision Tables

Depending on the demand and the cost, the stocking and the de-stocking services change the replenishment indicator. The threshold for the decision depends on the demand quantity or the number of order items and the procurement cost. The axis and the thresholds are defined in the decision table, and one or more decision tables are combined to a profile. One profile for stocking and one profile for de-stocking is assigned to the location. Figure 4.5 shows the interdependencies of the objects for the decision tables.

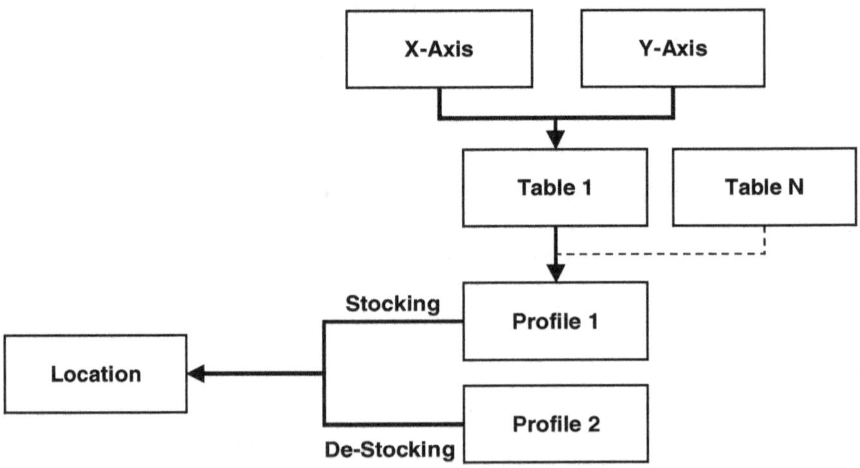

Fig. 4.5. Interdependencies of the Objects for the Decision Tables

• *Decision Tables*
The maintenance of the decision tables starts with the definition of their axis – both the dimension and the values. This is done with the customis-

ing path *APO → Supply Chain Planning → SPP→ Inventory Planning → Set Up Decision Tables for Stocking / De-Stocking* as shown figure 4.6.

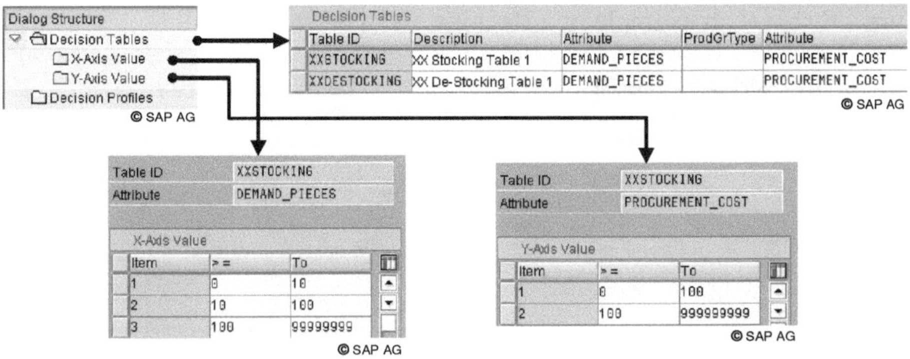

Fig. 4.6. Definition of the Decision Table

Possible dimensions for the axis are demand quantity (DEMAND_PIECES), number of demand items (DEMAND_ENTRIES), product group and procurement costs. Normally for the x-axis the demand quantity, the number of demand items or the product group is used. An example for the use of product groups is to model the ABC-indicator as product groups. If product groups are used as x-axis, only single values for the names of the product groups are maintained (the 'to'-field remains empty).The y-axis is usually the procurement costs which are defined in the 'procurement'-view of the product master.

In the next step it has to be defined for which combination of demand quantity and procurement cost respectively number of demand items and procurement cost a decision needs to be taken. This is done by setting a flag for the appropriate combination.

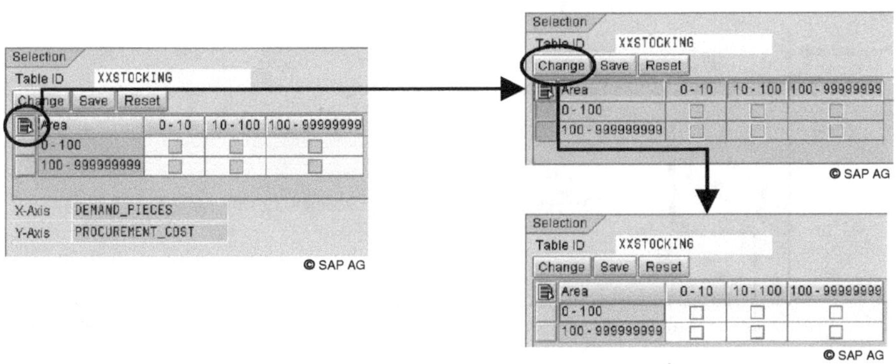

Fig. 4.7. Maintenance of the Decision Tables

Figure 4.7 shows the maintenance of the decision tables with the transaction /SAPAPO/SPPINVPDEC. By setting flags for the combinations it is defined where stocking respectively de-stocking should take place. Figure 4.8 shows an example of a stocking and a de-stocking table.

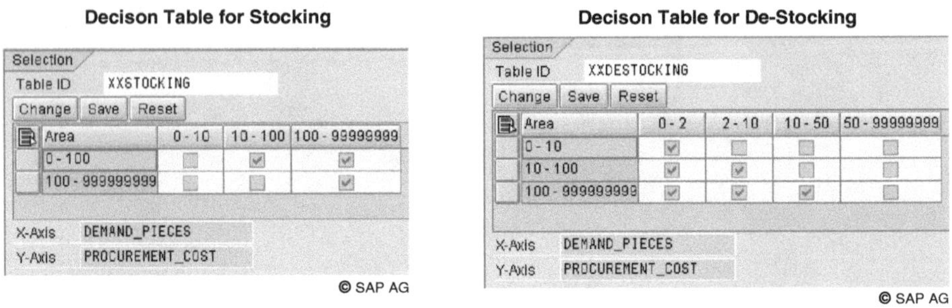

Fig. 4.8. Example for Decision Tables

In this case the product should be stocked at a location if the monthly demand is above 10 – unless the cost for the product is above 100, then the demand has to be above 100 to stock the location. In the other case a product with a value below 10 is only de-stocked if the demand drops below 2, if the value is between 10 and 100 the product is de-stocked if the demand is below 10, and if the value is above 100, a demand below 50 will lead to a de-stocking decision.

The decision for stocking and de-stocking is based on the demand history of the customer facing location (unless product groups are used as x-axis). The weighted demand history of the previous six months is used, where the most recent three months are weighted with 60 % and the earlier three periods with 40 %. Figure 4.9 visualises the rules as defined in the decision tables shown in figure 4.8.

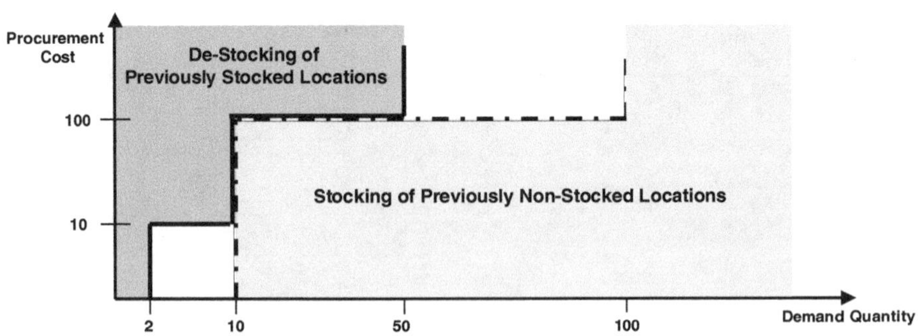

Fig. 4.9. Visualisation of the Example for Decision Tables

The areas for stocking and de-stocking do not have to cover the all combinations – e.g. in the case of a demand for 5 pieces and procurement costs below 10 no decision is taken and the replenishment indicator remains unchanged. The forecast for the service parts has no impact on the stocking and de-stocking decisions.

• *Decision Profiles and Rules*

The decision profiles are defined based on the decision tables with the customising path *APO → Supply Chain Planning → SPP → Inventory Planning → Set Up Decision Tables for Stocking / De-Stocking* – the same as for the definition of the decision tables. Figure 4.10 shows the maintenance of the decision profiles.

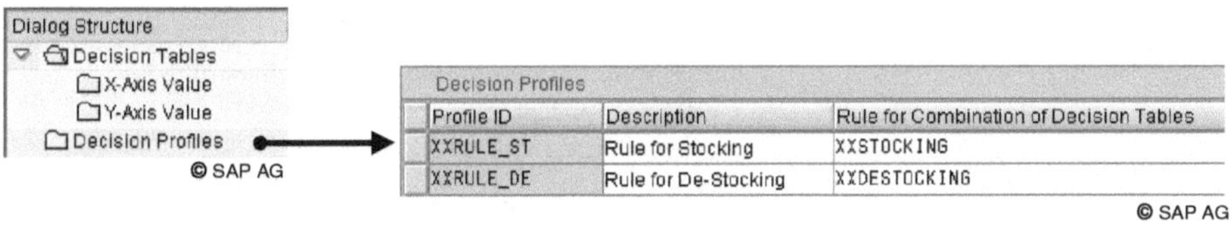

Fig. 4.10. Decision Profile Maintenance

The logic for the decisions might require the combination of decision tables – e.g. that both the demand quantity and the number of demand items have to be below their threshold to change the stocking. For combining the decision tables the BAdI /SAPAPO/PINV_STDEC has to be implemented.

The decision profiles are assigned to the location with the transaction /SAPAPO/LOC3 in the view 'SPP' as shown in figure 4.11.

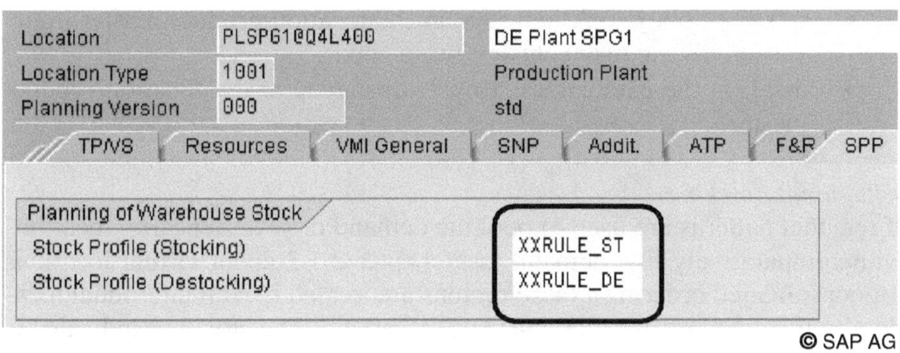

Fig. 4.11. Assignment of the Stocking and De-Stocking Rules to the Location

• *Exclusion Tables*

In some cases the stocking decision for a service part does not only depend on the demand and the cost but also on other criteria like legal regulations. Some hazardous goods for example might not be stored in certain countries. For this case it is possible to exclude product groups from the stocking or de-stocking service using exclusion tables. Figure 4.12 shows how to maintain them with the transaction /SAPAPO/PINV_EX_MAIN.

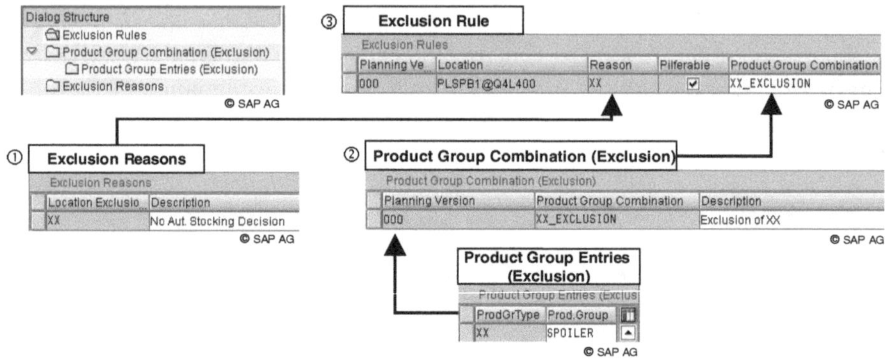

Fig. 4.12. Exclusion Table

The exclusion reason is used for descriptive purposes and defined with the customising path *APO → Supply Chain Planning → SPP→ Inventory Planning → Define Exclusion Reason for Location*. If a location product is excluded due to an exclusion reason, the de-stocking service

- sets the replenishment indicator to 'non-stocked, blocked',
- sets the policy lock indicator in the location product master in order to indicate the exclusion reason and
- displays the exclusion reason is displayed in the location product master.

• *Regional Stocking*

If regional patterns are used to pool the demand of several nearby locations with comparatively low demand (see chapter 2.1.2 about virtual locations for consolidated ordering), these regions are treated like an individual location by the stocking and the de-stocking service. The stocking indicator is set for the preferred location. The preferred location is either defined in the regional pattern or selected as the location with the highest demand.

• *Stability Periods*
To prevent an oscillation of the stocking decisions from stocked to non-stocked, it is possible define a stability period in the product master as shown in figure 4.13.

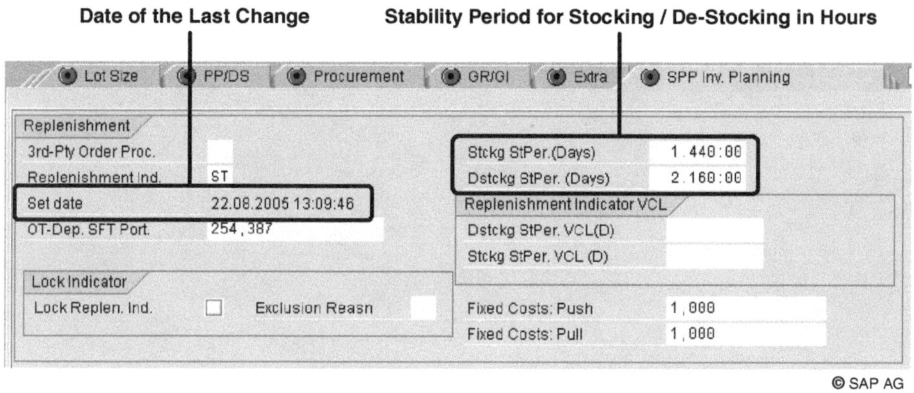

Fig. 4.13. Stability Periods for Stocking and De-Stocking Decisions

The last change of the replenishment indicator is recorded in the product master as the 'set date'. In this example the replenishment indicator of the location product will not change to non-stocked for 20 days (1440 hours) counting from the date of the last change (22.8.2005 13:09:46).

4.4 Stocking & De-Stocking Service

For stocking the planning service SPP_INVP_STOCKING exists, for de-stocking the service SPP_INVP_DESTOCKING. Since the parameters for stocking and de-stocking are maintained in the master data, the service profiles for these services are very lean – they contain only the key figure for the demand history (TSID_HIST), figure 4.14.

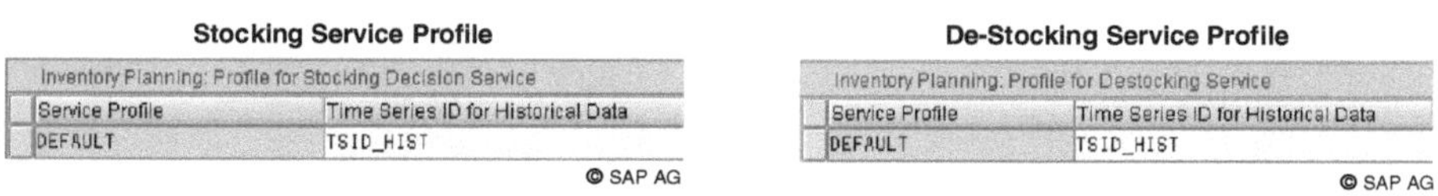

Fig. 4.14. Service Profiles for Stocking and De-Stocking

The service profiles are defined with the customising paths *APO → Supply Chain Planning → SPP → Inventory Planning → Define Service Profile for Sto-*

cking Decisions and *APO → Supply Chain Planning → SPP→ Inventory Planning → Define Service Profile for De-Stocking Decisions.*

5 Forecasting

5.1 Process Overview

Since service parts planning is mainly a make-to-stock respectively a procure-to-stock process, planning is almost entirely based on the forecast. The forecast drives the procurement and replenishment of service parts either directly or indirectly as an input for the safety stock determination. The basis for forecasting is the aggregated demand history (including re-alignment and interactive changes). Depending on the forecast strategy, not only the demand quantity but also the number of order items and the average demand quantity per order item might be used as an input (per forecast strategy only two out of the three).

The forecast is calculated by using a statistical forecast model. This forecast model and its parameters are defined in the forecast profile. Figure 5.1 shows an overview of the forecasting process.

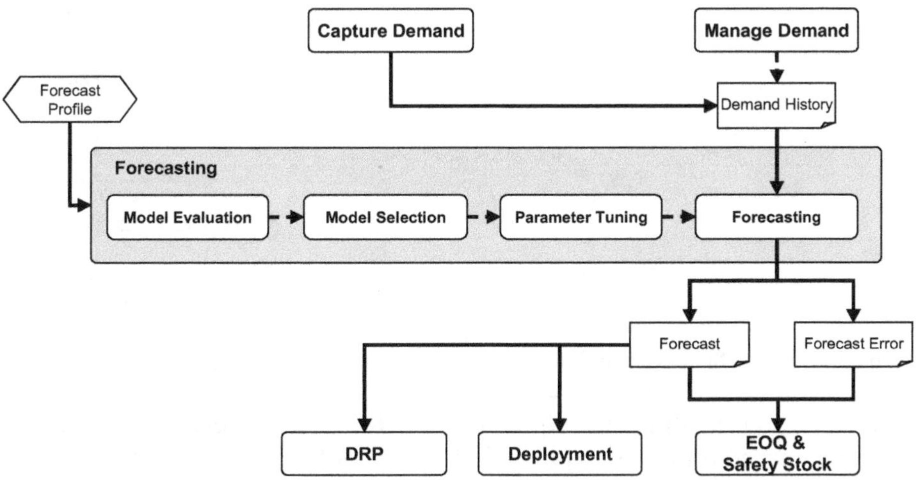

Fig. 5.1. Forecasting Process Overview

The forecast model and its parameters have a significant impact on the quality of the forecast. Since service parts planning deals usually with a huge quantity of service parts it is also important to offer functions to monitor and adjust the forecast model automatically. This is done in the process steps ‘model evaluation’, ‘model selection’ and ‘parameter tuning’. The forecast model and its parameters are stored in the forecast profile. If the performance of the forecast model (measured by Trigg’s tracking) exceeds the defined thresholds and the stability rules in the forecast profile allow to change the forecast strategy, an automatic model selection is performed and the forecast parameters are tuned. The new forecast strategy and the new parameters are saved in the forecast profile. With these parameters forecasting is performed. The combination of these four process steps – model evaluation, model selection, parameter tuning and forecasting – is called composite forecast. All planning steps are performed with the same planning service. Figure 5.2 shows the process steps within forecasting.

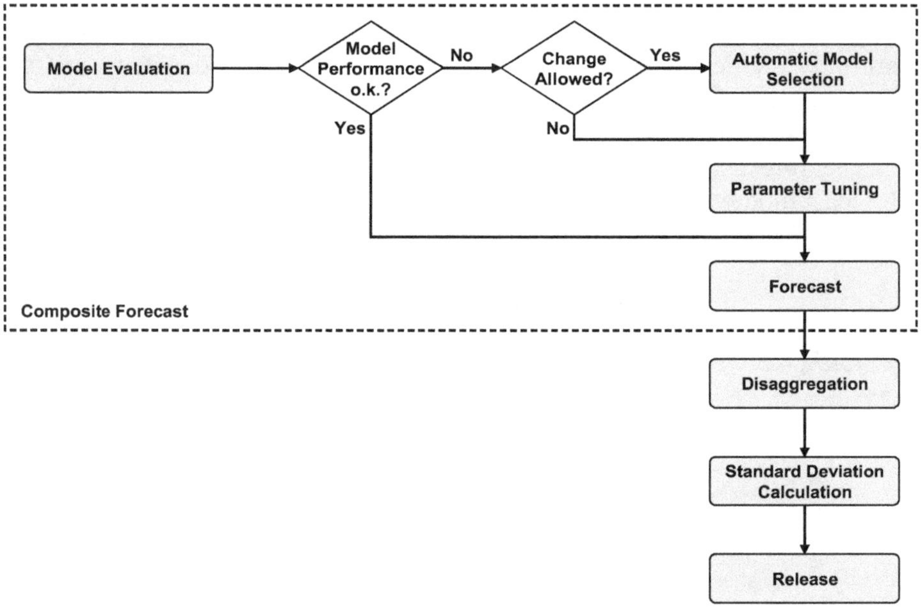

Fig. 5.2. Process Steps Within Forecasting

For the forecast strategies which contain forecast models with smoothing parameters additionally tripping is used in order to measure the whether the smoothing parameters are still appropriate. If this is not the case a new initialisation of the forecast model is performed.

The next process steps within forecasting are the disaggregation, the calculation of the standard deviation and the release of the forecast.

• *Aggregated and Disaggregated Forecast*
The forecast is calculated on two levels, on detailed level (at the child locations) and additionally on aggregated level (at the parent locations). In service parts planning the forecast on aggregated level relates to an aggregation along the BOD (and not to an aggregation along products – which is not possible in service parts planning). The reason for the aggregation along the BOD is that the forecast is less sporadic and that the forecast is usually the more accurate the bigger the data basis is. Therefore the forecast on aggregated level is usually more accurate than the forecast on detailed location product level. In the next step the forecast on aggregated level is disaggregated according to the detailed forecasts of the individual child locations. Figure 5.3 visualises this procedure.

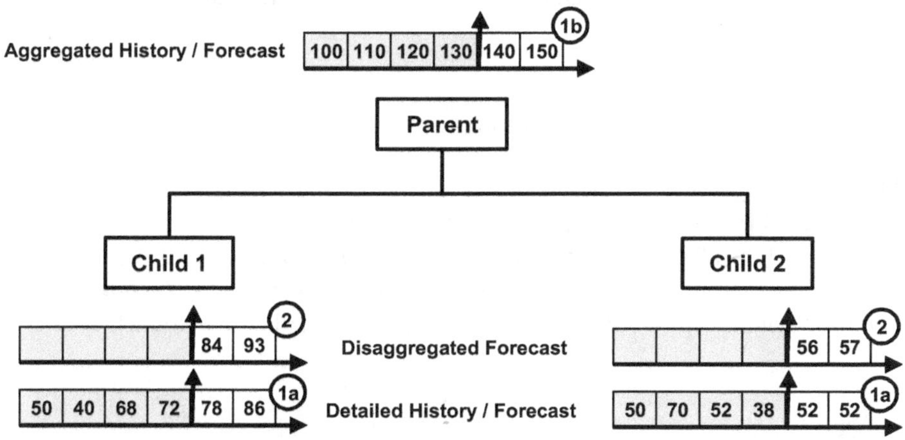

Fig. 5.3. Forecast on Detailed and Aggregated Level

The forecast is first performed on the detailed level for each location product based on the demand history (1a). Within the same forecasting service the forecast is also performed on aggregated level at the parent (1b). This is done based on the aggregated history along the BOD. In a second step the aggregated forecast is disaggregated according to the values of the detailed forecast (2).

• *Forecast Error and Release*
The forecast error is calculated as a standard deviation between the forecast and the demand history. Differing from Demand Planning in SAP

APO™, forecasting in service parts planning does not use the ex-post forecast but the forecast history.

The forecast is released automatically as long as the deviation of the new forecast to the previous forecast does not exceed the threshold defined in the forecast profile. Else an interactive forecast release is required. Order for the forecast are only created with the release, and only these are used by DRP.

The result of forecasting is the forecasted demand (demand quantity, number of order items and average demand per order item) and the forecast error – measured by the standard deviation. The forecast and the forecast error are inputs for EOQ and inventory planning in order to determine the safety stock (see chapter 6). The forecast is used directly for procurement and replenishment by DRP and deployment.

5.2 Planning Book, Forecast Profile and Forecast Service

5.2.1 Planning Book for Forecasting

The planning book for forecasting is called with the transaction /SAPAPO/SPPFCST. Accessing planning books in SPP differs from other SAP APO™ handling. The picture at the top of figure 5.4 shows the selection screen for planning books in SPP (not only for forecasting but also for inventory planning, DRP, procurement approval and deployment).

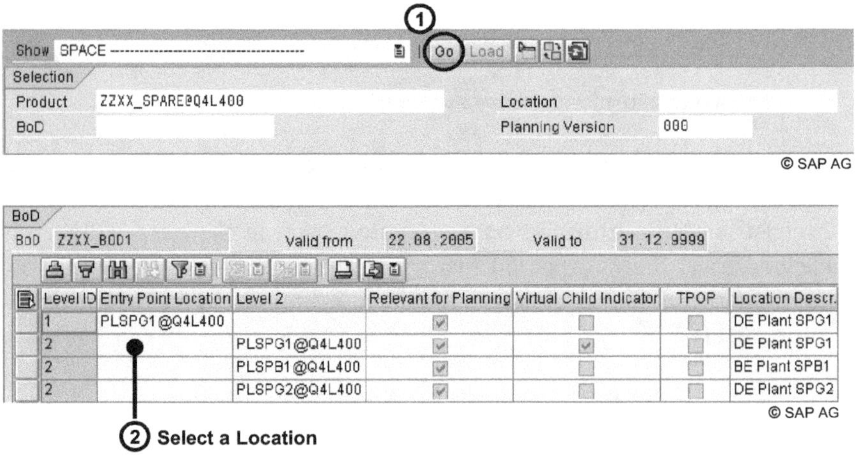

Fig. 5.4. Enter a Planning Book in Service Parts Planning

The product and the version are mandatory selection criteria, the location is optional. After entering the selection criteria, with the button 'go' the selected location products are displayed as shown in the picture at the bottom of figure 5.4. If no location is selected, all the locations of the BOD are displayed.

The transactional data for a product location is displayed by double click on the location – in figure 5.4 on the virtual child location of PLSPG1@Q4L400. The planning book itself is displayed as a third element within the screen below the selection and locations as shown in figure 5.5.

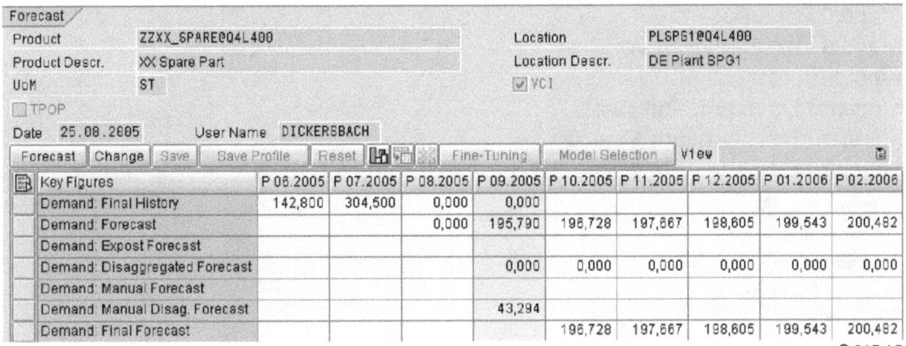

Key Figures	P 06.2005	P 07.2005	P 08.2005	P 09.2005	P 10.2005	P 11.2005	P 12.2005	P 01.2006	P 02.2006
Demand: Final History	142,800	304,500	0,000	0,000					
Demand: Forecast			0,000	195,790	196,728	197,667	198,605	199,543	200,482
Demand: Expost Forecast									
Demand: Disaggregated Forecast				0,000	0,000	0,000	0,000	0,000	0,000
Demand: Manual Forecast									
Demand: Manual Disag. Forecast				43,294					
Demand: Final Forecast					196,728	197,667	198,605	199,543	200,482

Fig. 5.5. Planning Book for Forecasting

In the header of the planning book the product, the location and the virtual child indicator are shown – this is helpful to make sure that the right location was selected. In this example posting periods are used – months or weeks would also be possible.

• *Key Figures*

The planning book contains a set of key figures for the demand history, the forecast, the standard deviation and others. For the demand history, the forecast and the standard deviation there are separate key figures for the demand quantity ('demand'), the number of order items ('item') and the average demand quantity per order item ('demand/item').

Because the forecast is calculated on detailed and on aggregated level, there are different key figures for the detailed forecast ('forecast') and the disaggregated forecast. At the entry location the key figure for the disaggregated forecast is empty.

In forecasting it is possible to overwrite the system proposal interactively in the key figure 'manual forecast'. A manual forecast at the child location is not aggregated along the BOD, but a manual forecast at a parent location is disaggregated to the children (key figure 'manual disaggregated forecast'). The final forecast finally contains the released forecast. Table 5.1 gives an overview about the available key figures.

Table 5.1. Key Figure in the Planning Book

Key Figure	Demand	Item	Demand per Item
Final History	X	X	X
Forecast	X	X	X
Ex-Post Forecast	X	X	X
Disaggregated Forecast	X	X	X
Manual Forecast	X	X	X
Manual Disaggregated Forecast	X	X	X
Final Forecast	X	X	X
Standard Deviation Forecast	X	X	X
Standard Dev. Disaggr. Forecast	X	X	X
Standard Deviation Final Forecast	X	X	X
MAD	X	X	X
Basic Value	X		
Trend	X		
Season Indices	X		
Tracking	X		
AMS Forecast	X		
AMS RMSE	X		

The ex-post forecast is only displayed when performing an interactive forecasting run. This key figure is not saved.

• *Planning Book Configuration*

Compared to Demand Planning in SAP APO™ there are less possibilities to configure the planning book (e.g. no macros are possible for service parts planning). The main tool to configure planning books in service parts planning is the use of the key figure view, which allows to de-select key figures and to change the sequence of key figures. Figure 5.6 shows the customising of the key figure view.

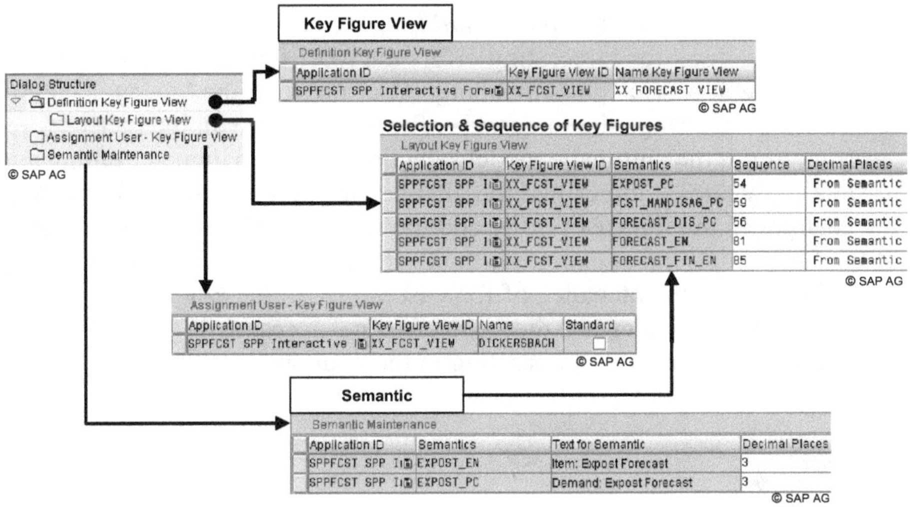

Fig. 5.6. Key Figure View

The customising path for the key figure view is *APO → Supply Chain Planning → SPP → Basic Settings → Settings for User Interfaces → Assign Key Figures*. Figure 5.7 shows how to switch between key figure views in the planning book.

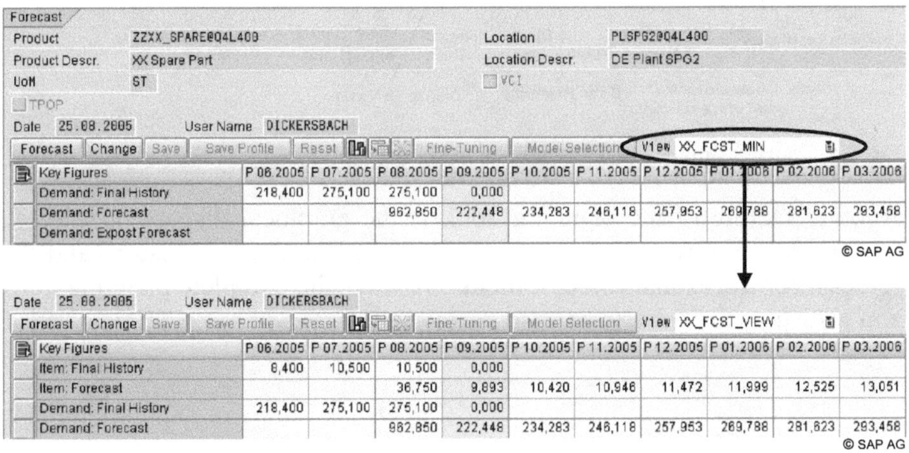

Fig. 5.7. Switching Between Key Figure Views

It is possible to use additional key figures with the BAdI /SAPAPO/SPPFCST_KF. However, first the key figure has to be created in the TDL with the transaction /SAPAPO/TDL_APO_SEM with a semantic (see chapter 2.4).

• *Interactive Forecasting in the Planning Book*
The planning book for forecasting offers the most functionality for interactive planning in service parts planning. After pressing the 'change'-button, it is possible to change the forecast profile and perform an interactive forecast run, to run the automatic model selection and the parameter tuning and to save the values – either just the changes in the forecast profile or both the changes in the forecast profile and the forecast. Alternatively the result of the forecasting run is undone with the 'reset'-button. Another possibility is the interactive maintenance of forecast values in the key figure 'manual forecast' – these values are then used as final forecast. Figure 5.8 shows the options for interactive forecasting in the planning book.

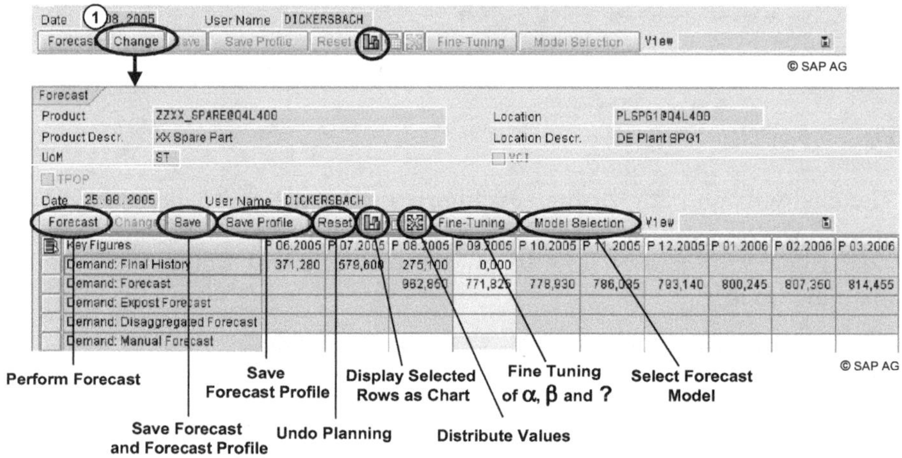

Fig. 5.8. Functions in the Forecasting Planning Book

Another feature of the planning book is the graphical display of selected key figures. Figure 5.9 shows the graphic for the demand history and the forecast for a seasonal forecast model. Always the complete planning horizon is displayed.

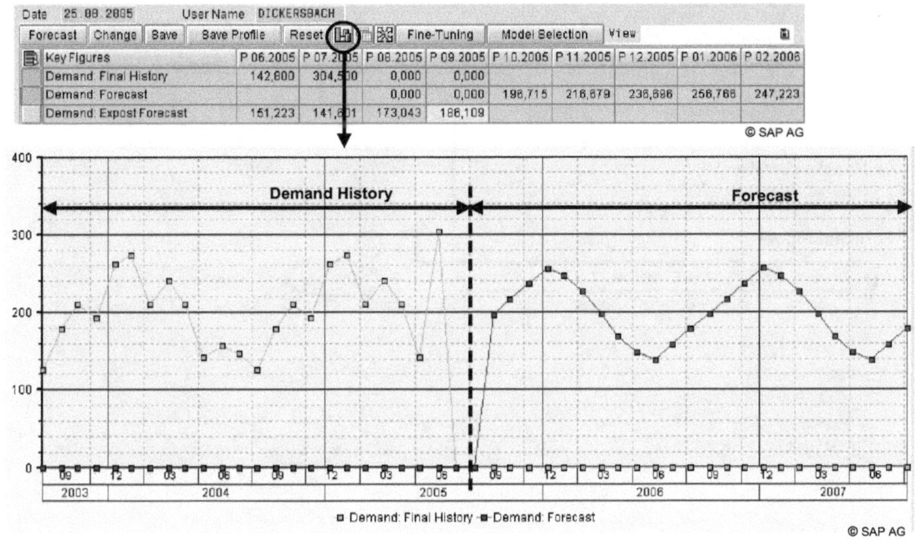

Fig. 5.9. Chart for the Key Figures 'Demand: Final History' and 'Demand: Forecast'

5.2.2 Forecast Profile

The forecast profile contains all parameters for the general proceeding of the forecast run, the forecast model, the forecast model parameters, the model evaluation, the model selection and the model initialisation. Some of the parameters can be maintained per product but most are maintained product location specifically. The forecast profile is maintained with the transaction /SAPAPO/SPPFCSTPRF, figure 5.10. The forecast profile is also changed in interactive forecasting or by the planning steps 'model selection' and 'parameter tuning'. For mass upload of forecast profiles from a flat file there is also a BAPI BAPISPP0007_TEST_PR7_CHANGE.

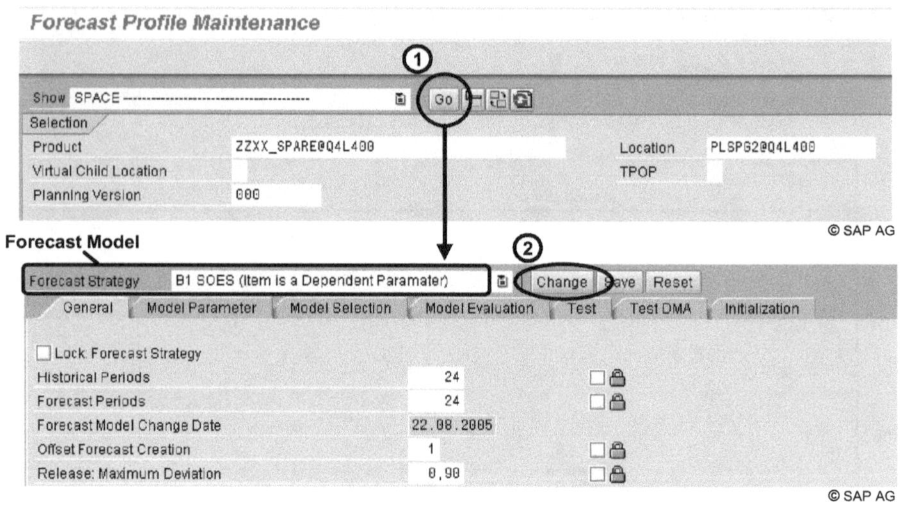

Fig. 5.10. Forecast Profile

Probably the most significant parameter is the forecast strategy. The other parameters of the forecast profile are grouped in views. Figure 5.11 shows the structure of the forecast profile.

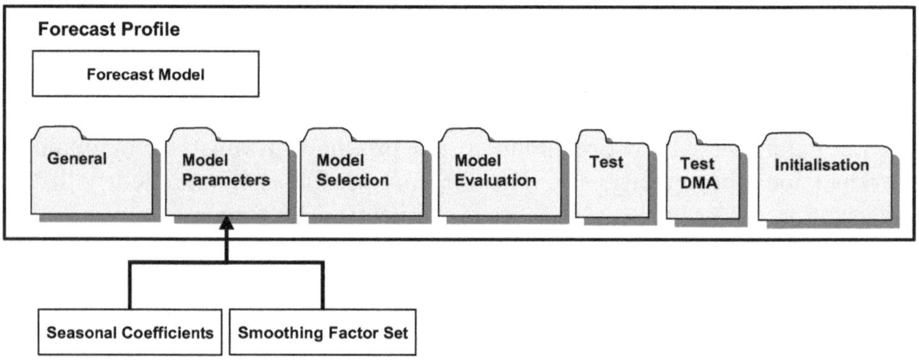

Fig. 5.11. Forecast Profile - Structure

Some of the forecast parameters are only displayed if they are applicable to the forecast strategy. The parameters for the forecast model and the initialisation are described in chapter 5.5, the parameters for the model selection in chapter 5.4 and the parameters for the model evaluation in chapter 5.3.

• *General Parameters*

The general parameters contain – among others – the definition of the number of periods for the demand history and the forecast (see also chapter 5.5.1), the threshold value for the forecast release (see chapter 5.7), the switch whether to use the forecast on the detailed level or the disaggregated forecast and whether outlier correction should be applied or not (see chapter 5.5.3). Figure 5.12 shows an extract of the general parameters of the forecast profile.

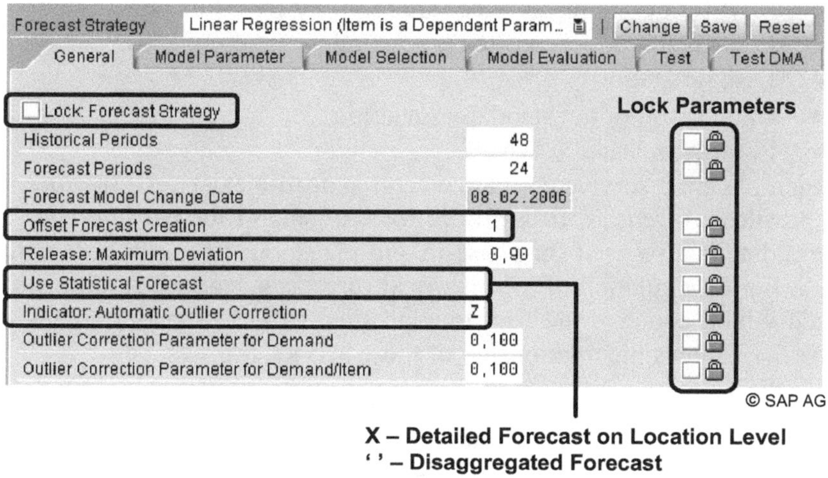

Fig. 5.12. General Parameters in the Forecast Profile (Extract)

Locking an entry in the forecast profile prevents a change of the parameter by inheritance. Automatic model selection or parameter tuning will change these parameters even if the lock is set.

The parameter 'offset forecast creation' is explained in chapter 5.3.1 about the historical forecast and the parameter 'indicator: automatic outlier correction' in chapter 5.5.4 about outlier correction.

• *Forecast on Detailed Level vs. Disaggregated Forecast*

Whether the forecast at the location product or the disaggregated forecast is used as final forecast depends on the setting 'use statistical forecast' in the forecast profile. This parameter is set at the parent location and refers to the child locations. The default setting is to use the disaggregated forecast since it usually provides better results.

• *Inheritance of the Forecast Profile*
The virtual child location uses the forecast profile of its parent – as long as no settings are maintained in the forecast profile on virtual child level.

5.2.3 Forecast Service

Forecasting requires – unlike other planning processes – more than one planning service and accordingly more than one service profile. As shown in figure 5.2, four planning services are required for a forecasting run:

- Forecasting or composite forecasting
- Disaggregation
- Calculation of the standard deviation
- Forecast release.

For each planning service a separate service profile exists. All the four service profiles reference a fifth profile for the general forecasting data. The general data is also used for phase-in and phase-out forecasting, see chapter 5.8. For a calculation of the historical forecast a separate service profile is used which contains the first four profiles from forecasting to release. Figure 5.13 shows the relationship of these service profiles.

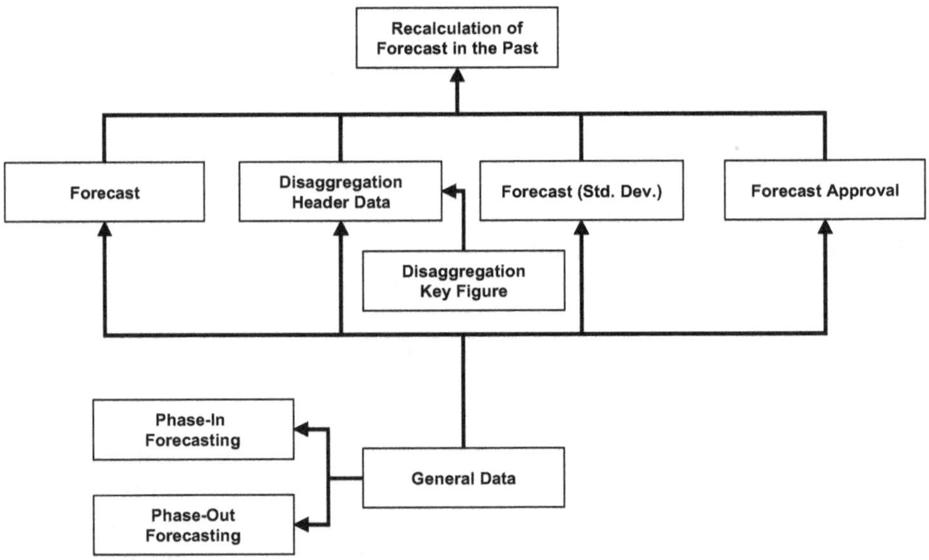

Fig. 5.13. Service Profiles for Forecasting

All these service profiles for forecasting are defined with the customising path *APO → Supply Chain Planning → SPP → Forecasting → Define Forecast*

Service Profile. Figure 5.14 shows the profile for the general forecasting data which contains the selection type, the number of periods for the demand history and the forecast, the threshold (in workdays) whether a forecast should be performed for the current month (see chapter 5.5.1) and the definition of the key figures for historical data and forecast.

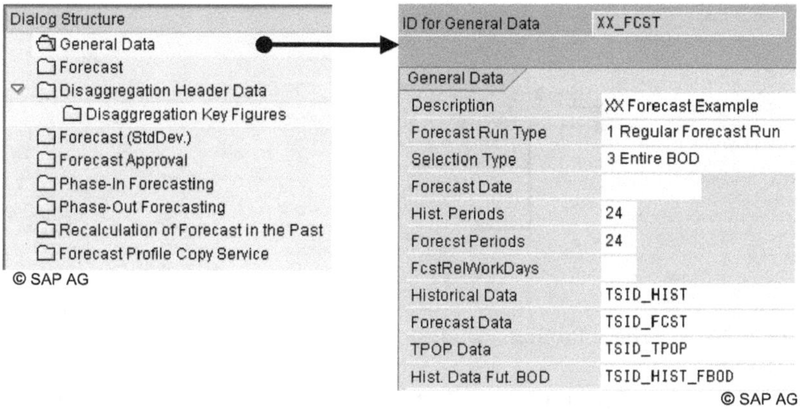

Fig. 5.14. Forecast Service Profiles – General Data

Only the selection type 'entire BOD' includes all locations of the BOD into the forecast run. The selection type 'selection' e.g. does not include virtual child locations.

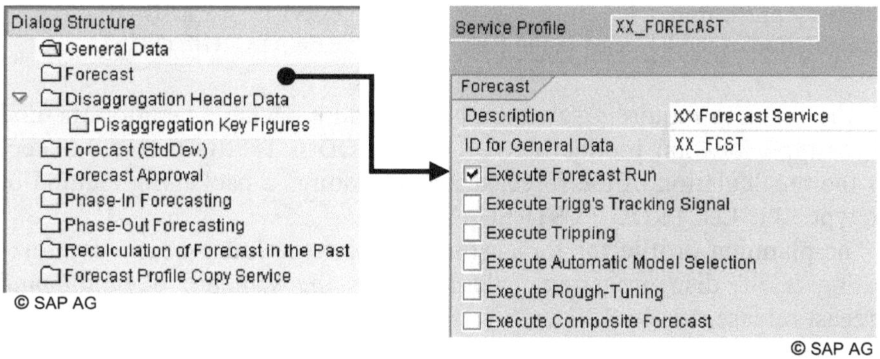

Fig. 5.15. Forecast Service Profile

Since most of the data is defined in the 'general data'-profile, the forecast service profile contains only the reference to the 'general data'-profile and whether composite forecasting should be executed or just a single function of composite forecasting. Composite forecasting would be the common choice, but for test purposes any other function can be selected as well, figure 5.15. It is only allowed to select one function.

The service profile for the disaggregation contains – besides the reference to the 'general data'-profile – the key figures for the disaggregation of the demand quantity (PC), the number of order items (EN) and the average demand per order item (PP), figure 5.16.

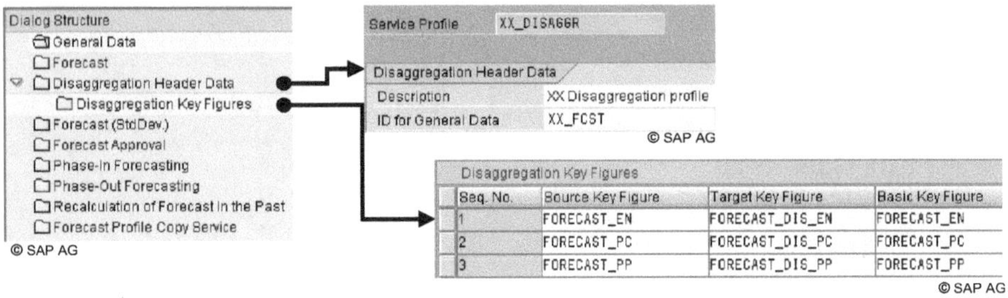

Fig. 5.16. Forecast Service Profiles – Disaggregation

The names of the planning services for forecasting are listed in table 5.2.

Table 5.2. Services for Forecasting

Service Profile	Service
Forecast	SPP_FCS_SERVICE
Disaggregation	SPP_FCST_DISAGGREGATION
Forecast (Standard Deviation)	SPP_FCS_SERVICE_MSE
Forecast Approval	SPP_FCST_RELEASE
Recalculation of the Forecast in the Past	SPP_RECALC_HISTFCST

All the services require a selection profile and a package creation method of the type location product (LOCATIONPRODUCT_PRODUCT) – except for the recalculation of the forecast which requires a packaging method of the type SPP_LOCPROD_FCSTRECALC.

The planning profile for forecasting contains the four services for forecasting itself, disaggregation, calculation of the standard deviation and forecast release, figure 5.17.

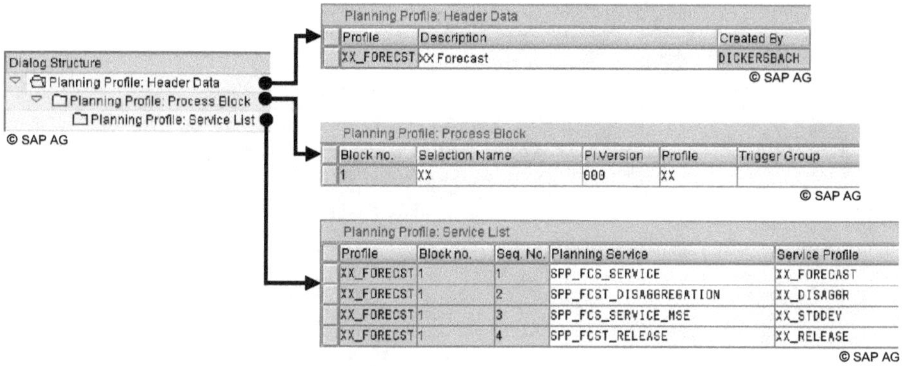

Fig. 5.17. Planning Profile for Forecasting

5.3 Model Evaluation

5.3.1 Historical Forecast

The model evaluation, the calculation of the standard deviation and the outlier correction are based on the historical forecast. The historical forecast is usually the forecast for the next period – but calculated at a point in time in the past. For each period the forecast is saved, and the forecast values of the respectively next periods compose the historical forecast. As figure 5.18 shows, this historical forecast is displayed with the transaction /SAPAPO/SPPFCSTTRACK. The forecast values which compose the historical forecast are highlighted.

The number of past periods that are displayed for the historical forecast depends on the forecast strategy and the required number of periods for the standard deviation (this parameter is set in the 'model parameter'-view of the forecast profile). If no historical forecast exists (or if the forecast model changes) the historical forecast is recalculated by performing a forecast run for each past period – pretending that the forecasting date is in the past.

Historical Forecasts

Forecast Strategy	Linear Regression (Item is a Dependent Parameter)
Number of Periods for Standard Deviation	12
Offset Forecast Creation	1

Chart

Key Figures	M 06.2005	M 07.2005	M 08.2005	M 09.2005	M 10.2005	M 11.2005	M 12.2005	M 01.2006	M 02.2006	M 03.2006	M 04.2006	M 05.2006
M 06.2005	176,134	179,486	182,838	186,190	189,541	192,893	196,245	199,597	202,949	206,301	209,653	213,005
M 07.2005		180,876	184,382	187,888	191,394	194,901	198,407	201,913	205,420	208,926	212,432	215,938
M 08.2005			183,081	186,443	189,804	193,166	196,528	199,890	203,251	206,613	209,975	213,337
M 09.2005				185,728	189,010	192,292	195,575	198,857	202,139	205,422	208,704	211,986
M 10.2005					190,372	193,806	197,239	200,673	204,107	207,540	210,974	214,408
M 11.2005						192,837	196,163	199,489	202,814	206,140	209,466	212,792
M 12.2005							197,539	201,017	204,496	207,975	211,453	214,932
M 01.2006								199,853	203,202	206,551	209,900	213,249
M 02.2006									96,487	87,979	79,471	70,962
M 03.2006										87,979	79,471	70,962
M 04.2006											79,471	70,962
M 05.2006												110,610
Historical Forecast	176,134	180,876	183,081	185,728	190,372	192,837	197,539	199,853	96,487	87,979	79,471	110,610

Fig. 5.18. Historical Forecast

In order to recalculate the historical forecast sufficient periods for the demand history are required. The recalculation of the historical forecast starts with the first period of the demand history which is not zero. Depending on the forecast model, a couple of demand periods are required for the initialisation of the forecast model. There should be at least sufficient demand history to recalculate the forecast history for the number of periods for the calculation of the standard deviation.

• *Offset for Forecast Creation*

Per default the forecast history is calculated using the forecast values for the respectively next period as figure 5.18 shows. For example, the historical forecast for June 2005 is the value that was calculated in June 2005. The idea is that the reliability of the forecast decreases the further it looks into the future. However, using the parameter 'offset forecast creation' in the 'general'-view of the forecast profile it is possible to compose the historical forecast e.g. by the respective forecast values for the third period into the future with an offset of '3'. In this case the historical forecast for June 2005 is a value that was calculated in April 2005. Figure 5.19 shows the difference in the historical forecast depending on the offset for forecast creation. As indicated by highlighting, the values for the historical forecast differ, and it becomes clear that the values are shifted to the right (within the same row) or upward (within the same column) by increasing the offset.

Number of Periods for Standard Deviation	12
Offset Forecast Creation	1

Chart

Key Figures	M 06.2005	M 07.2005	M 08.2005	M 09.2005	M 10.2005	M 11.2005	M 12.2005
M 06.2005	169,888	173,252	176,617	179,982	183,346	186,711	190,076
M 07.2005		173,852	177,305	180,758	184,211	187,664	191,117
M 08.2005			176,867	180,263	183,659	187,055	190,451
M 09.2005				179,883	183,222	186,561	189,899
M 10.2005					183,759	187,173	190,587
M 11.2005						186,775	190,132
M 12.2005							190,720

Number of Periods for Standard Deviation	12
Offset Forecast Creation	3

Chart

Key Figures	M 04.2005	M 05.2005	M 06.2005	M 07.2005	M 08.2005	M 09.2005	M 10.2005	M 11.2005	M 12.2005
M 04.2005	162,983	166,329	169,674	173,020	176,365	179,711	183,056	186,402	189,747
M 05.2005		166,870	170,292	173,713	177,135	180,557	183,978	187,400	190,821
M 06.2005			169,888	173,252	176,617	179,982	183,346	186,711	190,076
M 07.2005				173,852	177,305	180,758	184,211	187,664	191,117
M 08.2005					176,867	180,263	183,659	187,055	190,451
M 09.2005						179,883	183,222	186,561	189,899
M 10.2005							183,759	187,173	190,587
M 11.2005								186,775	190,132
M 12.2005									190,720

Fig. 5.19. Impact of the Offset for Forecast Creation in the Historical Forecast

• *Planning Service for the Recalculation of the Forecast History*

The recalculation of the forecast history is done with the planning service SPP_RECALC_HISTFCST. Figure 5.20 shows the service profile (customising path *APO → Supply Chain Planning → SPP → Forecasting → Define Forecast Service Profile*) which contains the four service profiles for forecasting, disaggregation, calculation of the standard deviation and forecast release.

Service Profile	SPP_FCST_RECALULATE
Recalculation of Forecast in the Past	
Description	SPP Forecast Recalculation in History
Service Profiles	
Forecast Service Profile	SPP_FCST
Disaggregation Service Profile	SPP_FCST_DISAGGR
Fcst Service Prof. (StdDev.)	SPP_FCST_ERROR
Fcst Approval Service Prof.	SPP_FCST_APPROVAL

Fig. 5.20. Service Profile for the Calculation of Historical Forecast

The relevant trigger for calculation of the historical forecast is SPP_FCSTMODEL_CHANGE, and the trigger profile is ignored.

5.3.2 Tracking

Tracking is the function to determine whether the forecast model is appropriate or not. The basic idea of tracking is to check whether the deviation of the forecasted values always tends towards one direction. If this is the case, it is likely that the forecast model is not appropriate and automatic model selection is triggered.

Tracking signals are set for a period, if the ratio of the smoothed average deviation (SAD) and the mean average deviation (MAD) exceeds a threshold value. The smoothed average deviation SAD (t) is calculated as described in formula 5.1:

$$\text{SAD}(t) = \alpha\,[\text{Demand}(t) - \text{Forecast}(t)] + (1-\alpha)\,\text{SAD}(t-1) \tag{5.1}$$

The mean average deviation is calculated similarly, only that the sign of the difference between demand and forecast is ignored, formula 5.2.

$$\text{MAD}(t) = \alpha\,[\,|\text{Demand}(t) - \text{Forecast}(t)|\,] + (1-\alpha)\,\text{MAD}(t-1) \tag{5.2}$$

If the deviations are in both directions – i.e. sometimes the real customer demand is higher and sometimes lower than the forecast – the SAD will be much smaller than the MAD. Therefore the ratio of SAD and MAD is a good measure whether this is actually the case.

Table 5.3. Example for Tracking

Period	1	2	3	4	5	6	7	8	9	10
Demand	95	102	98	104	102	105	103	102	100	98
Forecast	100	100	100	100	100	100	100	100	100	100
SAD	-0.2	0.24	-0.21	0.63	0.9	1.72	1.98	1.98	1.58	
MAD	1.8	1.84	1.87	2.3	2.24	2.79	2.83	2.66	2.13	2.1
|SAD/MAD|	0.11	0.13	0.11	0.27	0.4	0.62	0.7	0.74	0.74	0.41
Threshold	0.6	0.6	0.6	0.6	0.6	0.6	0.6	0.6	0.6	0.6
Tracking	0	0	0	0	0	1	2	3	4	4

To calculate the tracking signal, one period is required for initialisation – when the previous values of SAD and MAD are zero, the ratio of |SAD/MAD| is one. Table 5.3 shows an example for the calculation of |SAD/MAD| for a tracking smoothing factor α of 0.2.

The ratio of |SAD/MAD| rises as soon as the deviation of the actual demand tends toward one side – in this example above the forecast values – from period 5 to 8. As soon as the deviation changes its direction – in period 10 the actual demand is below the forecast – the ratio of |SAD/MAD| decreases. In this example the threshold for tracking is 0.6, and the tracking horizon is 10 periods. If the number of tracking signals within the tracking horizon – in this case 4 – exceeds a certain limit, a tracking exception is raised.

The values for the tracking smoothing factor, the tracking horizon, the tracking threshold and the number of tracking signals within the tracking horizon are defined in the forecast profile. Figure 5.21 shows these entries on the 'model evaluation'-view.

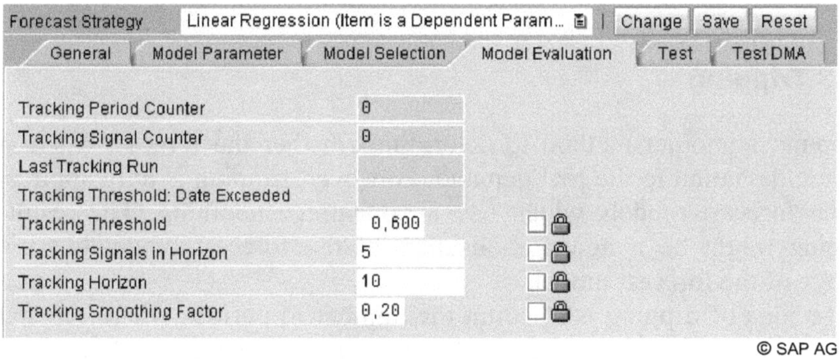

Fig. 5.21. Parameters for Tracking in the Forecast Profile

To perform tracking, the forecast planning service SPP_FCS_SERVICE is used. In the service profile (customising path *APO → Supply Chain Planning → SPP → Forecasting → Define Forecast Service Profile*) either tracking or composite forecast has to be selected, figure 5.22. Tracking is only performed for the demand quantities and not for the demand items.

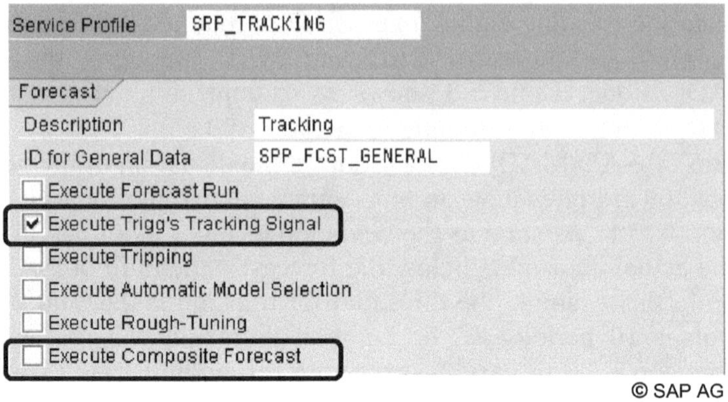

Fig. 5.22. Forecast Service Profile for Tracking

If the number of tracking signals within the defined horizon exceeds the threshold that is defined in the forecast profile, an automatic model selection is executed.

5.3.3 Tripping

Tripping is another method to determine whether the forecast has a systematic deviation to the real demand. However, tripping is only applicable to the forecast models which use exponential smoothing. The result of tripping might be a new initialisation of the forecast model but not a change of the forecast model.

The idea of tripping is to count the number of periods where the actual demand is outside the forecast plus its standard deviation. For tripping only the number of subsequent values outside the standard deviation (to one side) count. The tripping counter increases with each value that is outside the standard deviation (signs are used – i.e. the tripping counter increases by one with each value that is above the forecast plus the standard deviation and it decreases with each value that is below the forecast minus the standard deviation). If the next value is within the standard deviation, the tripping counter is reset to zero. If it is outside the standard deviation but to the other side, it is set to one (or minus one, depending whether it is above or below the borders). Figure 5.23 visualises the function of the tripping counter.

The tripping counter is also reset if the forecast model changes or the parameters change.

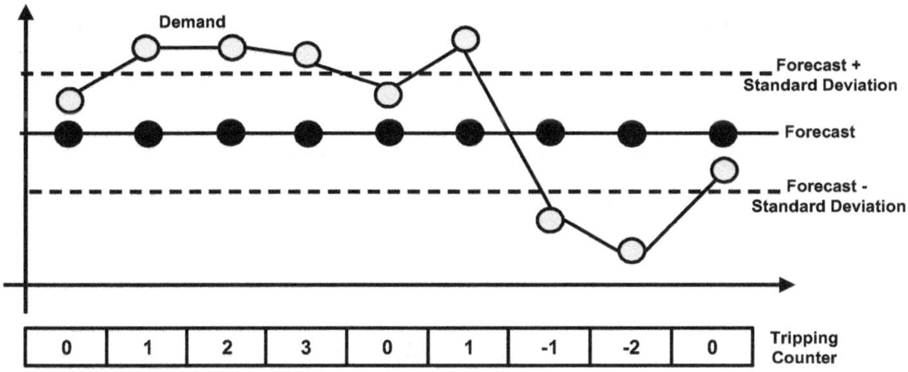

Fig. 5.23. Tripping

Tripping is performed independently for the demand quantities, the demand items and the average demand quantity per item. It is however only available for the forecast models first and second order exponential smoothing and the intermittent forecast model.

The parameters for tripping – the limits for the trip length for the lower and the upper demand – are defined independently for the demand quantity, the number of order items and the average demand per order item in the forecast profile. Figure 5.24 shows these settings.

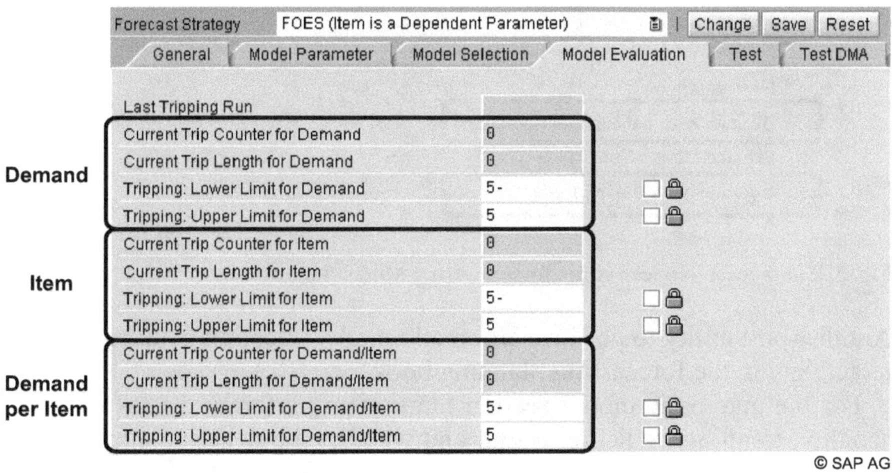

Fig. 5.24. Parameters for Tripping in the Forecast Profile

If the trip length exceeds the limits that are defined in the forecast profile, a new initialisation of the forecast model is performed – starting from the point in time where the trip length exceeded the limit. This implies that the history before this point in time does not influence the forecast results any more.

5.4 Model Selection and Parameter Tuning

5.4.1 Model Selection

Automatic model selection is either performed as a part of the composite forecast or if model selection is configured in the planning service profile for forecasting (see figure 5.25). As part of composite forecasting the automatic model selection is only performed if the model evaluation indicates a bad performance of the model. If the automatic model selection is chosen in the service profile, automatic model selection is performed anyway.

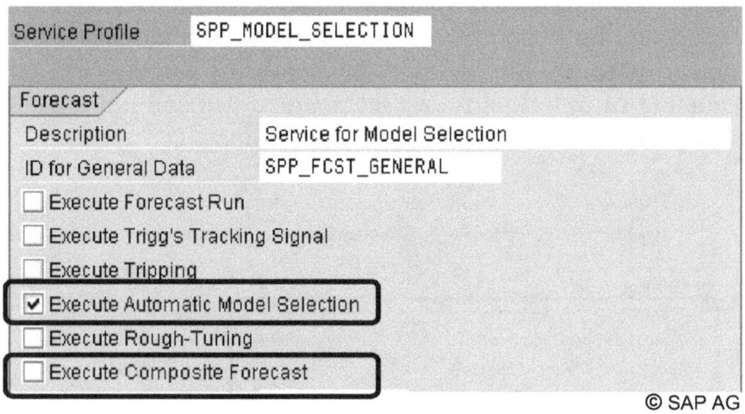

Fig. 5.25. Forecast Service Profile for Automatic Model Selection

Another possibility to perform automatic model selection is to trigger it interactively in the forecasting planning book.

For the automatic model section the system performs the tests for seasonality, trend, sporadic behaviour and whether the dynamic moving average model is relevant. The test sequence is defined with the customising path *APO → Supply Chain Planning → SPP → Forecasting → Configure Automatic Model Selection* as shown in figure 5.26. To each test one or more models are assigned. If the test is positive, one of the assigned models is chosen – the lower the weighting factor, the more likely the model is picked.

Table for Forecast Test Sequence

Test Sequence	Test Type	Forecast Strategy Sequ...	FS	Forecast Model Weighting
1	Seasonal test	1	F1	1
2	Trend Test	1	B1	1
2	Trend Test	2	D1	1
3	Sporadic Test	1	G1	100
3	Sporadic Test	2	H1	1
4	Other	1	A1	1
4	Other	2	B1	1
4	Other	3	C1	1
4	Other	4	G1	1

© SAP AG

Fig. 5.26. Customising for the Automatic Model Selection

In this example first a test for seasonality is performed and the seasonal trend model with fixed periods is selected if the test is positive. The test for trend will choose 2nd order exponential smoothing or linear regression. If this test is unsuccessful too, the system tests whether the demand history has a sporadic behaviour and chooses the intermittent model or dynamic moving average. Only then other forecast models might be chosen. The seasonal trend model is not considered by automatic model selection. If the seasonal trend model is to be used, it must be selected interactively in the forecast profile.

A change of the forecast strategy creates a trigger for the recalculation of the historical forecast with the new forecast strategy. The change date of the forecast strategy is recorded in the forecast profile.

To prevent a change of the forecast strategy it is possible to lock the forecast strategy in the forecast profile. To prevent frequent changes of the forecast strategy it is possible to use stability periods in the forecast profile. Figure 5.27 shows these settings.

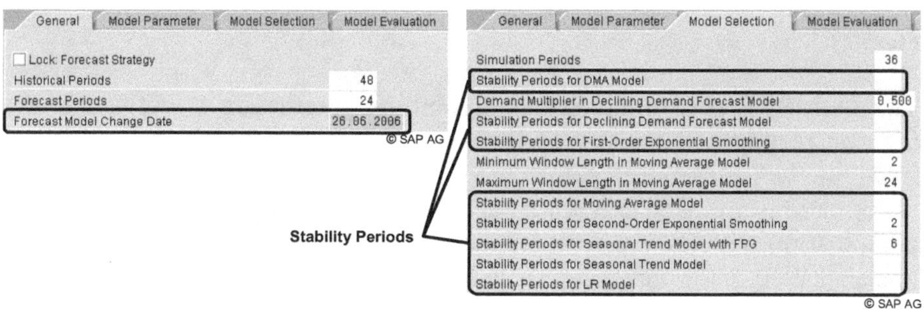

Fig. 5.27. Locking and Stability Periods for the Forecast Strategies

5.4.2 Parameter Tuning

Parameter tuning tests changes of the values for the alpha, beta and gamma factor in order to reduce the forecast error. This function is only applicable to the forecast models first order exponential smoothing (FOES), second order exponential smoothing (SOES) and the seasonal trend model.

Two different functions exist for parameter tuning – rough-tuning and fine-tuning.

• *Parameter Rough-Tuning*

Rough-tuning of the parameters is performed as a part of the composite forecasting (if the model performance was not satisfactory) or if it is defined as a separate forecast planning step in the service profile.

The prerequisite for the automatic parameter tuning is that a smoothing factor set is assigned to the 'model parameter'-view of the forecast profile (see figure 5.29). The smoothing factor set is defined with the customising path *APO → Supply Chain Planning → SPP → Forecasting → Define Smoothing Factor Set*, figure 5.28.

Smoothing Factors Set

Smoothing Factor...	Counter	Alpha	Beta	Gamma
SPP_SMOOTH	1	0,10	0,20	0,20
SPP_SMOOTH	2	0,10	0,20	0,30
SPP_SMOOTH	3	0,10	0,30	0,20
SPP_SMOOTH	4	0,10	0,30	0,30
SPP_SMOOTH	5	0,20	0,20	0,20
SPP_SMOOTH	6	0,20	0,20	0,30
SPP_SMOOTH	7	0,20	0,30	0,20
SPP_SMOOTH	8	0,20	0,30	0,30
SPP_SMOOTH	9	0,30	0,20	0,20
SPP_SMOOTH	10	0,30	0,20	0,30
SPP_SMOOTH	11	0,30	0,30	0,20
SPP_SMOOTH	12	0,30	0,30	0,30

Fig. 5.28. Smoothing Factor Set

The forecast is performed for the smoothing parameters as defined in the forecast profile and for any of the smoothing factor combinations as defined in the smoothing factor set. For performance reasons only these combinations are used and not a permutation of each parameter value. The combination with the smallest standard deviation is used, and the parameters are saved in the forecast profile.

• *Parameter Fine-Tuning*
Fine tuning is only performed if it is triggered interactively within the forecasting planning book – e.g. because rough-tuning was not satisfactory. Fine-tuning is based on a start value, an end value and an increment for each smoothing parameter (if applicable). These settings are maintained in the 'model parameter'-view of the forecast profile as shown in figure 5.29.

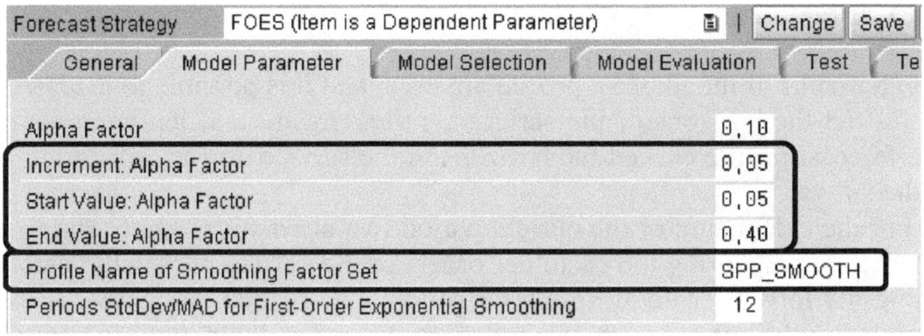

© SAP AG

Fig. 5.29. Settings for Parameter Tuning in the Forecast Profile

A permutation of all smoothing factor values is carried out. Therefore a big difference between start and end value and small increments might lead to performance issues.

5.5 Calculation of the Forecast

5.5.1 Forecast Horizons

Typically two horizons apply for forecasting: the number of periods for the demand history and the number of periods for the forecast calculation. These horizons are maintained in the 'general data'-profile of the service profile for forecasting and are restricted by the parameters in the 'general'-view of the forecast profile. Figure 5.30 shows these entries in the forecast profile and in the service profile for forecasting.

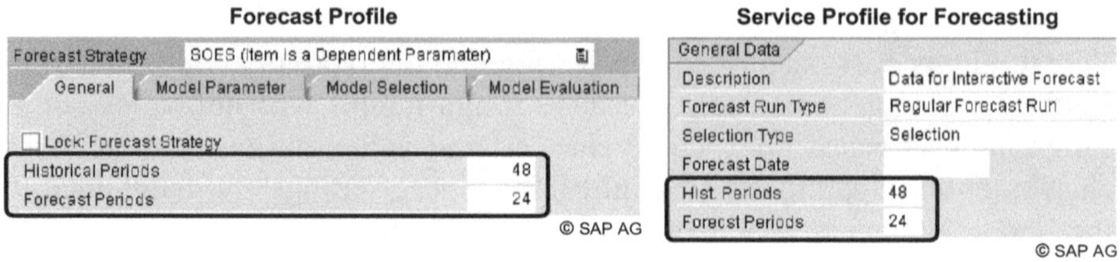

Fig. 5.30. Determination of the Forecast Horizons

The horizons of the forecast profile are used, and it is possible to extend or to restrict the horizons of the service profile. However, if the horizons in the forecast profile exceed the horizons in the service profile, a warning is issued.

For the calculation of the current period two alternatives exist. The first alternative is ignoring the customer orders of the current period and calculating the forecast without this information. The second alternative is extrapolating the current customer orders to the end of the period. In general the second alternative – to extrapolate the current customer orders – will provide the better results the later in the period it is used. The parameter 'forecast relevant workdays' in the 'general data'-profile controls that if the current workday is past this day the demand history of the current period is extrapolated. Figure 5.31 shows an example to visualise these alternatives.

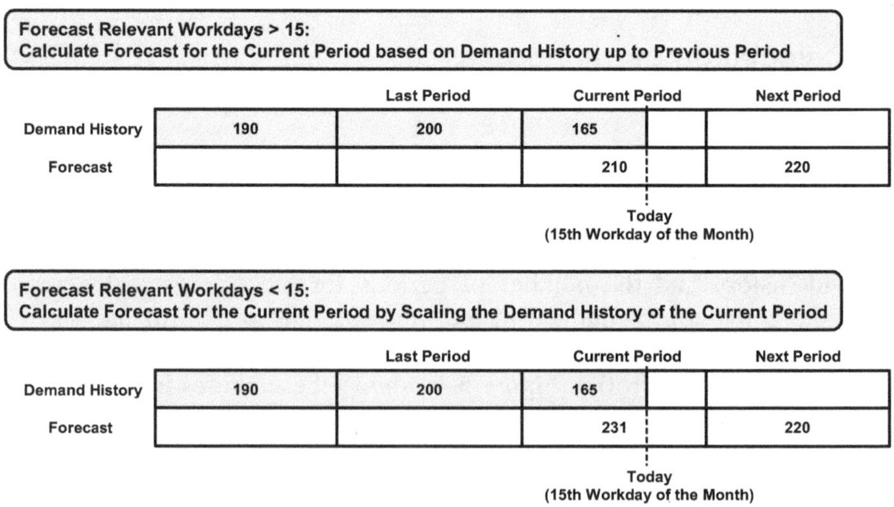

Fig. 5.31. Forecast Relevant Workdays and Forecast for the Current Period

The forecast is performed on the 15th workday of the month. If the parameter 'forecast relevant workdays' contains a value above 15, the information about the demand history of the current period is not taken into account. Assuming that the demand history contains a trend, an appropriate forecast model would calculate the forecast for the current and the next periods by extrapolating this trend – in this example the forecast for the current period would be 210 pieces.

If the parameter 'forecast relevant workdays' contains a value below 15, the forecast for the current period is not calculated by the forecast model but by extrapolating the demand history of the current month. In this example the demand history is 165 pieces – which relates to an average of 11 pieces per day and – assuming 21 workdays – to a forecast of 231 pieces. This value is also used as the demand history for the current period and is considered for forecasting.

5.5.2 Forecast Model Overview

Forecasting in service parts planning offers a couple of forecast models. All of these models are univariate forecast models – in the current release no causal relationship (e.g. to the installed base) is considered. Compared to Demand Planning in SAP APO™ some additional forecast models – especially for slow moving parts – exist (and some are missing, e.g. multiple linear regression). Depending on the forecast model an initialisation is required and outlier correction inherent, possible or not possible.

Table 5.4. Forecast Model Overview

Forecast Model	Name	Leading Parameter	Initialisation	Outlier Correction
1st Order Exp. Smoothing	A1	Demand	Yes	Yes
1st Order Exp. Smoothing	A2	Item	Yes	Yes
2nd Order Exp. Smoothing	B1	Demand	Yes	Yes
Moving Average	C1	Demand	No	Yes
Linear Regression	D1	Demand	No	Yes
Seasonal Trend Model	E1	Demand	Yes	No
Seasonal Trend Fixed Periods	F1	Demand	No	Yes
Intermittent	G1	Demand	Yes	Inherent
Dynamic Moving Average	H1	Item	No	Inherent
Declining Demand Forecast	I1	Demand	No	Inherent

The forecast is calculated for the demand quantity, the number of order items and the average demand per order item. Out of these three parameters only two are calculated independently, and the third is calculated by the other two. The leading parameter is either the demand quantity or the number of order items. The average demand per order item is calculated as a constant value using first order exponential smoothing (except for dynamic moving average), and the dependent parameter is calculated by the leading parameter and the average demand per order item. Table 5.4 provides an overview of the forecast models in service parts planning.

• *Initialisation*
If the forecast model uses a recursive algorithm – meaning the current value of a term depends on the previous value of the same or another term – some periods of demand history are required in order to provide these previous values for all terms. For the initialisation of the forecast model the global model initialisation data must be maintained with the customising path *APO → Supply Chain Planning → SPP → Forecast → Initialise Base Values*. Within the 'initialisation'-view of the forecast profile it is possible to maintain the parameters for the determination of the upper and the lower MAD limit.

• *Parameter Overview*
Depending on the forecast model different parameters are required. These parameters are maintained in the 'model parameters'-view of the forecast model, and only those parameters are displayed which are relevant for the chosen forecast model. Some of these parameters are only used by a specific forecast model, others – like smoothing parameters – are used by several forecast models. Table 5.5 provides an overview of the more common parameters.

Table 5.5. Common Forecast Model Parameters

Parameter	A1	B1	C1	D1	E1	F1	G1	H1	I1
Alpha	X	X			X				
Beta		X			X				
Gamma					X				
Smoothing Par. Set	X	X			X				
Time Smoothing							X		
MAD Smoothing							X	X	
Trend Delimiter		X		X	X				
Per. for Trend Line				X	X				
Periods for Std. Dev.	X	X	X	X	X	X	X	X	X

• *Smoothing Factors*
The factors alpha, beta and gamma are smoothing factors for the calculation of the base value, the trend and the seasonality when using exponen-

tial smoothing (first order, second order or trend seasonal model) For the rough tuning of these smoothing parameters a smoothing parameter set is required. If fine tuning is used, not only the value of these parameters but also the start value, the end value and the increment have to be maintained (see chapter 5.4).

For the intermittent model (G1) a smoothing factor is used to calculate the periods between the order items, and another smoothing factor for the mean average deviation (MAD). The latter is also required for the dynamic moving average.

• *Forecast Trend Delimiter*

The forecast models 2nd order exponential smoothing (B1), linear regression (D1) and seasonal trend (E1) do calculate a trend. After some periods this trend might result in very high or very low forecast values, which does not necessarily represent a likely forecast. Extreme forecast values can be avoided by using the forecast trend delimiter which cuts off the trend - either after a certain number of periods (parameter 'forecast trend delimiter (temporal)') or if the forecast value exceeds the current value by a certain percentage. Figure 5.32 shows these settings in the 'model parameter'-view of the forecast profile for a restriction after 50 % or 12 periods.

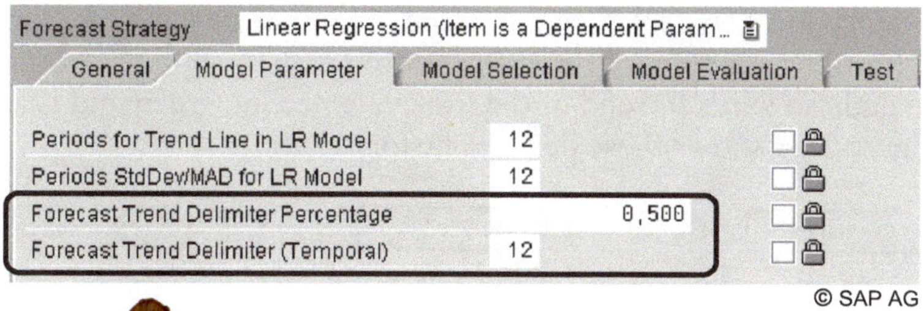

Fig. 5.32. Forecast Trend Delimiter

The impact of the forecast trend delimiter is shown in figure 5.33 – at the left without trend delimiter and at the right with trend delimiter.

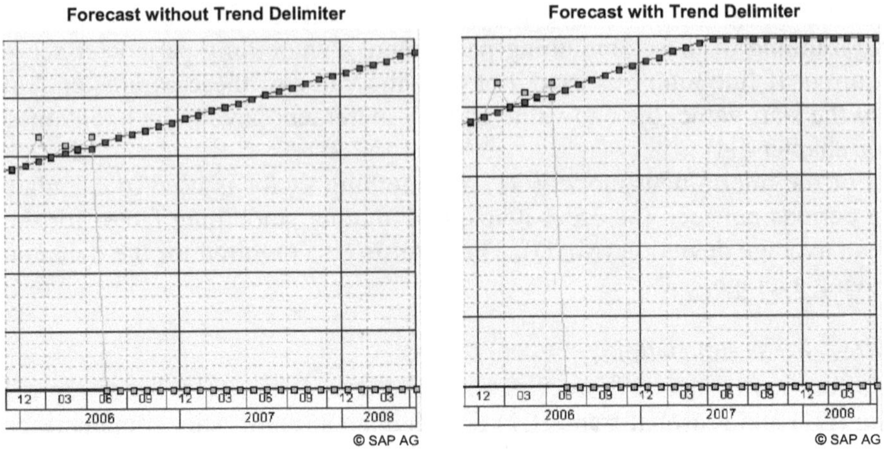

Fig. 5.33. Forecast Without and with Trend Delimiter

• *Forecast Model Selection*

The selection of the appropriate forecast model is of crucial importance for the quality of the forecast. The most important factor to determine the forecast model is the type of the demand history. Typical types of the demand history are constant demand, trend, seasonal demand, seasonal demand with trend – and very often for service parts – sporadic or intermittent demand. Towards the end of the life cycle declining demand is another type. Figure 5.34 shows these demand history types.

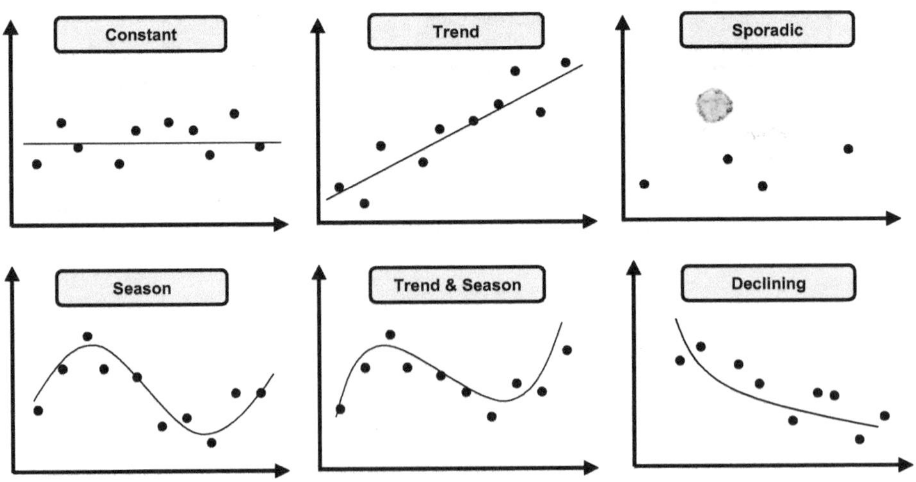

Fig. 5.34. Demand History Types

The selection of the forecast model is usually based on an analysis of the demand history – either interactively or automated as described in chapter 5.4. In the following we describe very briefly the nine different forecast models for service parts planning. The purpose is rather to give an idea about the rough properties of each model than to describe in detail how they calculate the forecast. The latter is found e.g. in the SAP online help.

• *First Order Exponential Smoothing*
First order exponential smoothing (FOES) is often used as a default for a constant forecast. Depending on the alpha smoothing factor the more recent demand has a bigger influence on the forecast – the higher the alpha factor the bigger the influence of the more recent values. Common values for alpha are between 0.1 and 0.3. In service parts planning it is possible to use this model with the demand quantity (A1) or with the demand items as leading parameter (A2). In the latter case zero-demand periods (with an undefined average demand per order item) are skipped for calculation. Figure 5.35 shows an example for the forecasting with a first order exponential smoothing model. In this case four years of demand history are used and the forecast is calculated for two years.

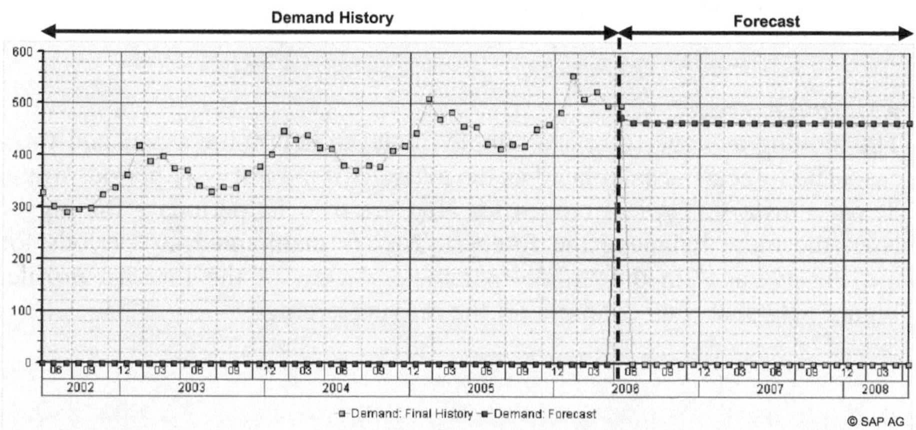

Fig. 5.35. Forecasting with First Order Exponential Smoothing

This example shows very clearly that the result of the first order exponential smoothing is a constant value and that more recent values have a bigger impact.

• *Second Order Exponential Smoothing*

If the demand history suggests a trend, second order exponential smoothing (SOES, B1) is a very common forecast model. Additionally to the 1st order exponential smoothing a term for the trend is added. This term is smoothed by the beta factor – the higher the beta factor the bigger the influence of the more recent values. Figure 5.36 shows the forecast with second order exponential smoothing for the same history as in figure 5.35.

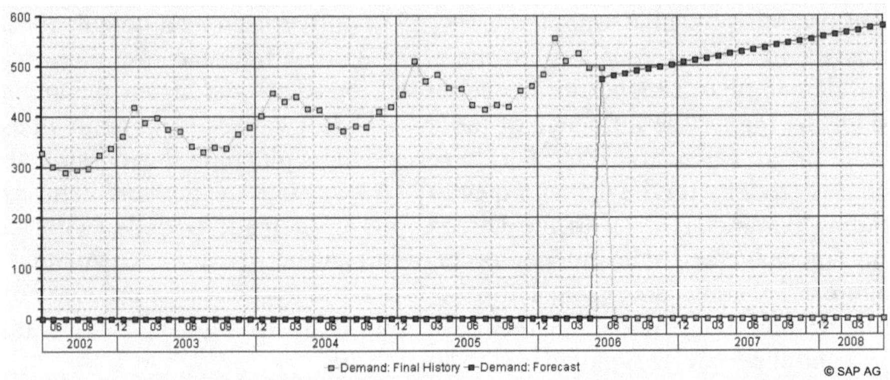

Fig. 5.36. Forecasting with Second Order Exponential Smoothing

• *Moving Average*

The moving average (C1) is a simple model to determine a constant forecast. The forecast is calculated as the average of the last N_{MA} periods of the demand history. Typical ranges for N_{MA} are 6 to 12 periods – the bigger N_{MA}, the more balanced the forecast. N_{MA} is maintained as 'periods for moving average' in the 'model parameters'-view of the forecast profile. Figure 5.37 shows an example for the moving average.

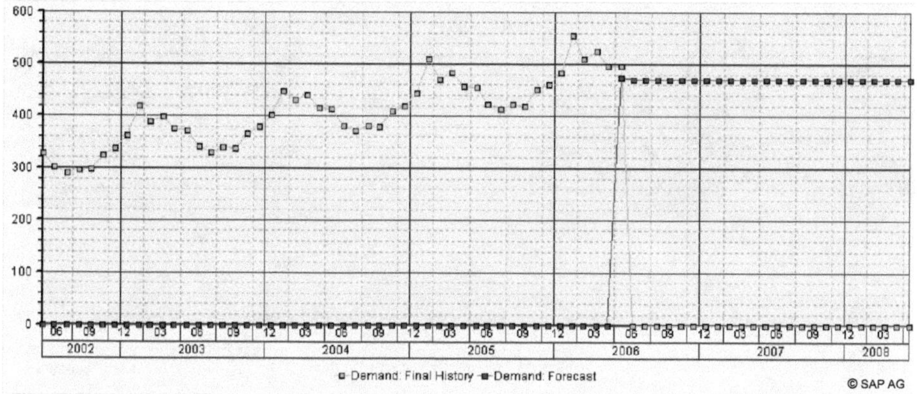

Fig. 5.37. Forecasting with Moving Average

• *Linear Regression*

Linear regression (D1) extrapolates the demand history with a straight line using the method of the least squares as shown in figure 5.38. The number of historical periods to determine the straight line is maintained as 'periods for trend line' in the 'model parameters'-view of the forecast profile.

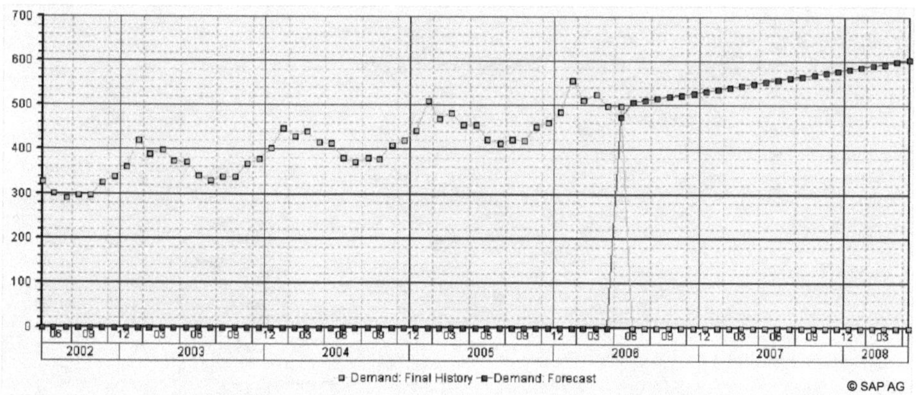

Fig. 5.38. Forecasting with Linear Regression

• *Seasonal Trend Model*

The seasonal trend model (E1) works similar like the second order exponential smoothing but considers also seasonal patterns. The seasonal patterns are not adapted from the demand history but modelled by seasonal coefficients which are maintained explicitly – which is an advantage if only few periods of demand history are available. Figure 5.39 shows an example for forecasting with the seasonal trend model.

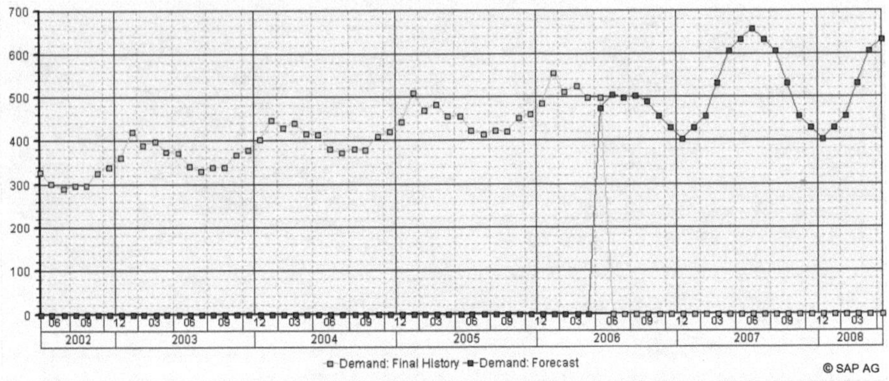

Fig. 5.39. Forecasting with the Seasonal Trend Model

A prerequisite for the execution of the seasonal trend model is that a seasonal coefficient group is assigned to the forecast profile. The seasonal coefficient group is created with the customising path *APO → Supply Chain Planning → SPP → Forecasting → Define Seasonal Coefficients* and contains seasonal indices for 12 periods, figure 5.40. These seasonal coefficients define the shape of the seasonality. In order not to smooth these coefficients the gamma factor should be zero.

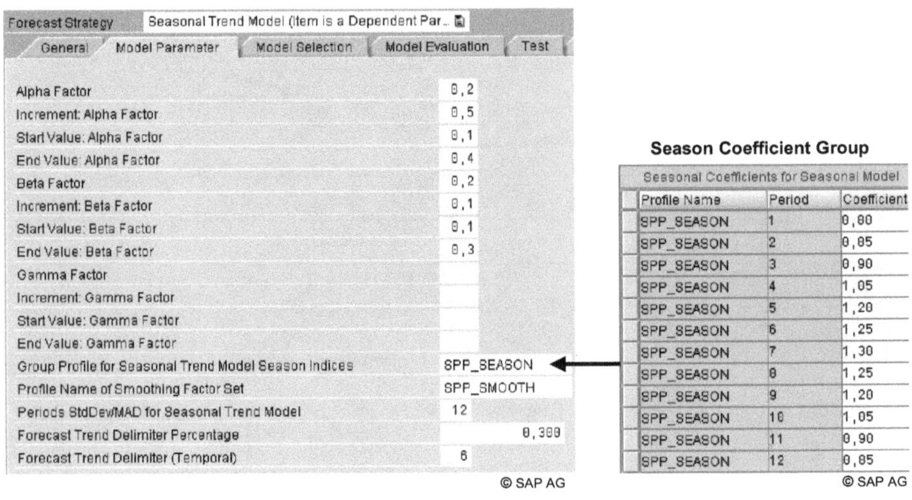

Fig. 5.40. Season Coefficient Group

• *Seasonal Trend Model with Fixed Periods*
The seasonal trend model with fixed periods (F1) is the default model for service parts with seasonal demand behaviour. At least 24 months of demand history are required for this forecast model. The annual trend is determined and the past seasonality applied on top. The seasonal coefficients are calculated as an average from the past years. If 36 periods of demand history are available, the trend is calculated as the weighted average of the three years. The annual weighting factor is defined in the forecast profile. Figure 5.41 shows an example for this forecast model.

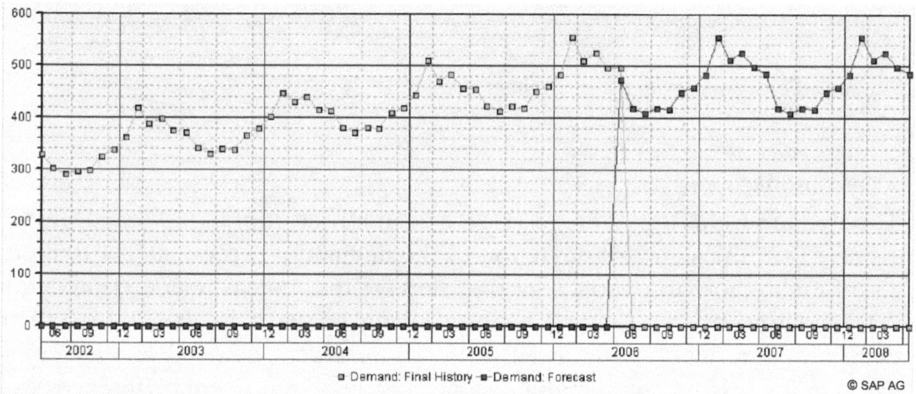

Fig. 5.41. Forecasting with Seasonal Trend Model with Fixed Periods

• *Intermittent Model*
The model for intermittent demand (H1) is designed for sporadic demand. Similar to the Croston model, it calculates the demand quantity based on non-zero periods and the duration between the demand periods. Exponential smoothing is applied to calculate the durations between the demand periods, and – differing from the Croston model – the demand quantities are determined as an average of the non-zero periods. The result of the forecasting with the intermittent forecast model is a constant forecast as shown in figure 5.42.

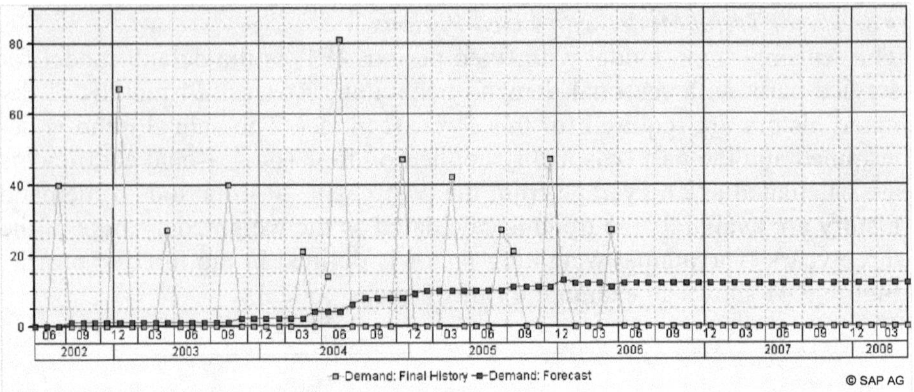

Fig. 5.42. Forecasting with the Intermittent Model

• *Dynamic Moving Average*

The dynamic moving average (H1) is a modified moving average model especially if the standard deviation of the demand is large – as is often the case for slow moving parts. The first step for the forecast calculation is the determination of the demand history. Using t-tests it is checked whether there are significant differences in the more recent demand history compared to the less recent demand history. The less significant differences exist, the more periods are used. After outlier correction the forecast is calculated for the order items as an average of the demand history. Figure 5.43 shows an example for forecasting with the dynamic moving average model.

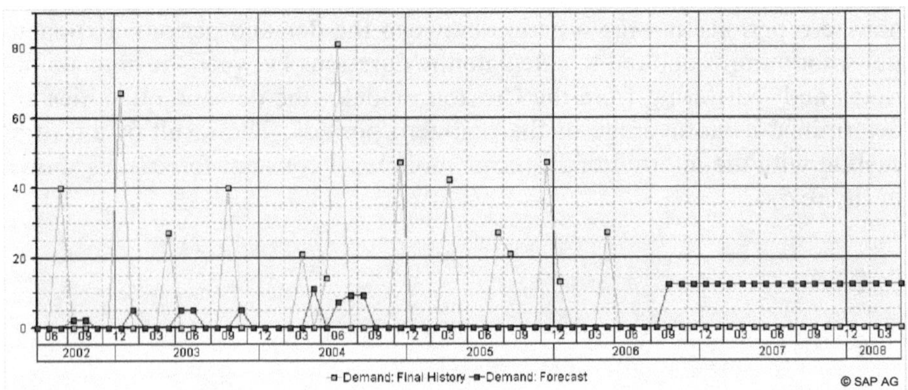

Fig. 5.43. Forecasting with the Dynamic Moving Average Model

The dynamic moving average model uses the weekly forecast values. These values are available even if the periodicity for forecasting was set to month or posting periods.

• *Declining Demand*
The declining demand forecast is used for the end of a service part's life cycle. Assuming a constantly declining demand for a service part an exponential curve is used for the future projection of the demand. The prerequisite for the model is that there is a declining growth rate.

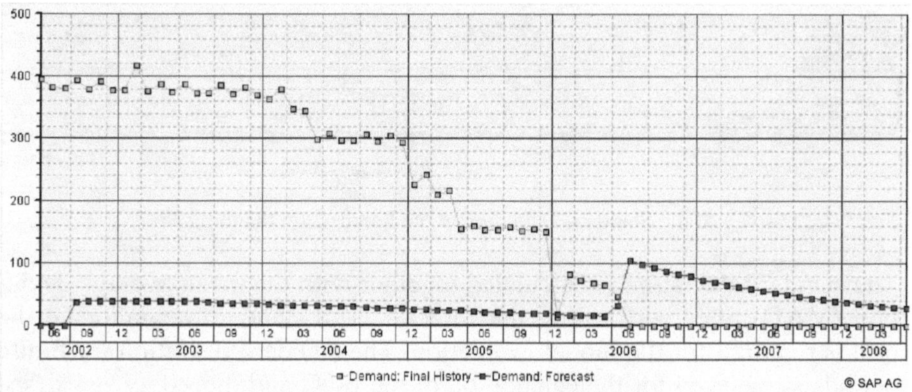

Fig. 5.44. Forecasting with the Declining Demand Forecast Model

Other prerequisites are that the product is not marked as 'new product' and that forecast values exist for the current period.

A detailed description of the forecast model algorithms is found in the SAP online help for service parts planning.

5.5.3 Standard Deviation

The standard deviation σ is an indicator for the difference between the historical forecast and the demand history and is therefore an indicator for the quality of the forecast. The calculation of the standard deviation is based on a number of past periods. The number of past periods is defined in the 'model parameter'-view of the forecast profile.

Assuming that the number of past periods for the calculation of the standard deviation is smaller than the number of periods for the demand history, different values exist for the standard deviation in the past periods. Therefore the value of the standard deviation depends on the period. For future periods the last value of standard deviation is applied and the standard deviation is constant (except for the seasonal trend model with fixed periods). The standard deviation is calculated for the demand quantities, the number of order items and the average demand per order item, and for the (detailed) forecast and the disaggregated forecast respectively. The standard deviation for the final forecast is either the standard deviation of the detailed forecast or the disaggregated forecast – depending whether 'use statistical forecast' is selected. Figure 5.45 shows the standard deviation for the demand quantity in the forecasting planning book.

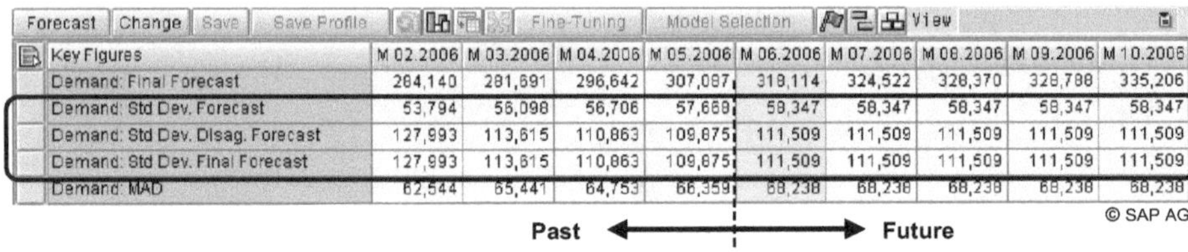

Key Figures	M 02.2006	M 03.2006	M 04.2006	M 05.2006	M 06.2006	M 07.2006	M 08.2006	M 09.2006	M 10.2006
Demand: Final Forecast	284,140	281,691	296,642	307,087	318,114	324,522	328,370	328,788	335,206
Demand: Std Dev. Forecast	53,794	56,098	56,706	57,669	58,347	58,347	58,347	58,347	58,347
Demand: Std Dev. Disag. Forecast	127,993	113,615	110,863	109,875	111,509	111,509	111,509	111,509	111,509
Demand: Std Dev. Final Forecast	127,993	113,615	110,863	109,875	111,509	111,509	111,509	111,509	111,509
Demand: MAD	62,544	65,441	64,753	66,359	68,238	68,238	68,238	68,238	68,238

Fig. 5.45. Display of the Standard Deviation in the Forecasting Planning Book

The standard deviation is calculated together with the mean average deviation (MAD) after performing the forecast. The standard deviation in the past is required for the model evaluation. The standard deviation for future periods is required for the calculation of the EOQ and the safety stock (see chapter 6).

5.5.4 Outlier Correction

The purpose of the outlier correction is to avoid that untypical values of the demand history mess up the forecast. Therefore the demand history is adjusted automatically before calculating the forecast. This adjustment is only temporary and not saved – the original demand history remains unchanged. For most of the forecast models outlier correction is an optional step, only for the intermittent model (G1), the dynamic moving average (H1) and the declining demand forecast (I1) the outlier correction is inherent and differs a little from the 'normal' procedure. For the seasonal trend model (E1) outlier correction is not possible. The 'normal' outlier correction for the forecast models A1 to D1 and F1 is described in the following.

Whether a historical demand value is considered as an outlier depends on its difference to the historical forecast of that period. If this difference exceeds a threshold, the demand history is adjusted (temporarily) to the boundary value. Outlier correction is only performed for demand values that are exceptionally high. Low values are not adjusted because periods with zero demand are common for service parts. Figure 5.46 shows the effect of outlier correction.

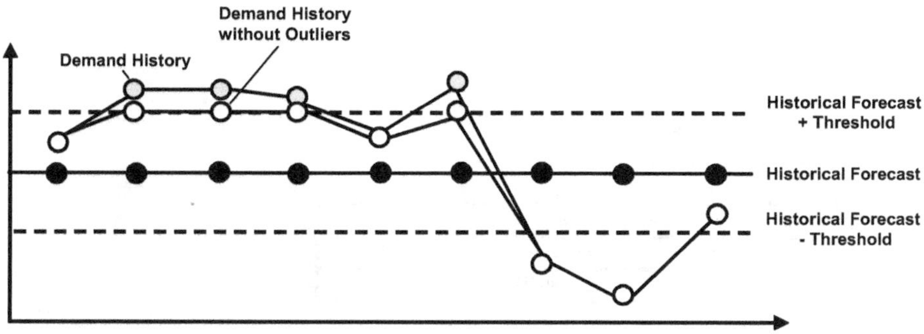

Fig. 5.46. Outlier Correction

Differing from Demand Planning in SAP APO™, the historical forecast is used and not the ex-post forecast.

Outlier correction is performed for the demand quantity and the average demand per order item. The threshold depends on the standard deviation σ and a factor – α for the demand quantity and β for the demand per order item. Formula 5.3 describes the condition for an outlier (for the demand quantity):

$$(\text{Demand }(t) - \text{Forecast }(t)) > \alpha * \sigma\ (t) \qquad (5.3)$$

Whether outlier correction is performed or not depends on the settings in the 'general'-view of the forecast profile (except for the models G1, H1 and I1 where outlier correction is inherent and therefore always performed). Figure 5.47 shows the indicator for automatic outlier correction which controls that outlier correction is performed (value 'Z'). Outlier correction is performed before forecasting. The parameters for the threshold definition (in relation to the standard deviation) – the α and the β factor – are defined in the forecasting profile as well.

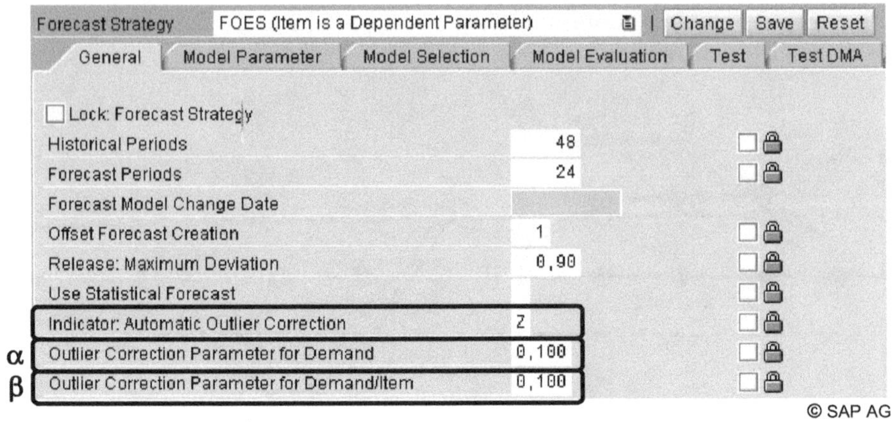

Fig. 5.47. Parameter for Outlier Correction in the Forecast Profile

With the parameter 'offset forecast creation' it is possible to shift the reference period for the forecast. The standard setting for this offset is 1.

5.6 Forecast Approval

The purpose of the forecast approval is to determine the final forecast for the facing locations. There are two forecasts available:

- the statistical forecast that was calculated based on the demand history of the location and
- the disaggregated forecast that was calculated based on the aggregated demand of all locations and disaggregated according to the individual statistical forecasts of the locations.

Which of these forecasts is used as final forecast depends on the setting 'use statistical forecast' in the tab 'general settings' of the forecast profile of the parent location ('X' – statistical forecast, blank – disaggregated forecast), figure 5.48. Interactively maintained forecast values always overwrite the calculated forecasts.

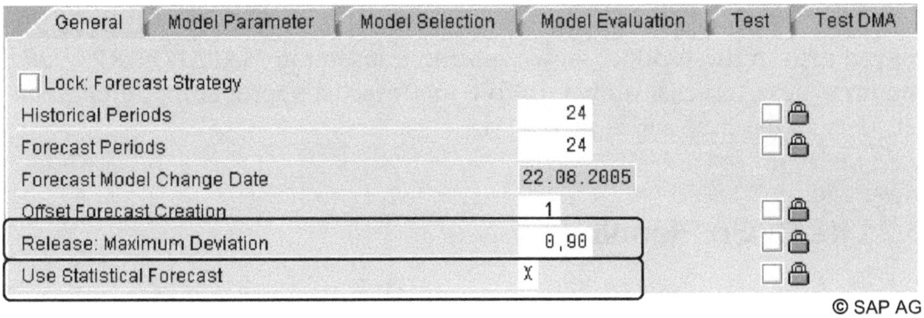

Fig. 5.48. Settings for the Forecast Release in the Forecast Profile

For each period the new forecast is compared with the pervious forecast. If the biggest deviation exceeds the threshold that is defined in the forecast profile (tab 'general settings', parameter 'release: maximum deviation'), no final forecast is calculated. In this case the final forecast of the previous planning run remains active until the forecast values are manually approved. The planning log issues a warning for this case.

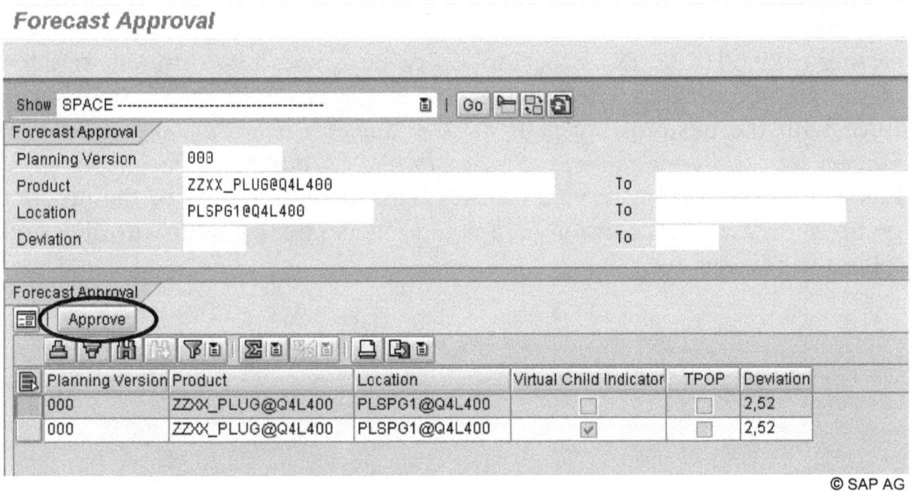

Fig. 5.49. Forecast Approval

The manual approval is performed with the transaction /SAPAPO/SPPFCSTAPPR. For each of the location products (in figure 5.49 product ZZXX_PLUG@Q4L400 in location PLSPG1@Q4L400 and its virtual child location) the deviation is displayed (in this case 2.52). Entries are only displayed if there are forecasts to be approved.

During the forecast approval forecast orders are created – these are displayed also in the product view with the transaction /SAPAPO/RRP3. DRP requires these forecast orders. Before the forecast approval the forecast exists only in the time series in TSDM.

5.7 Life Cycle Planning

5.7.1 Phase-In Forecasting

The idea of phase-in forecasting is to use the demand history of other products which have been recently introduced as a basis to determine the forecast for a new product. The product group determines which products are used for a reference demand history.

The phase-in forecasting for new products is done in two steps. In the first step the demand history is scaled and stored in the phase-in profile, and in the second step the scaled demand curve of the phase-in profile is applied for the new product. Accordingly the service for new product forecasting (SPP_PHASE_IN) is performed twice – with two different settings of the service profile. The service profile for phase-in forecasting is defined with the customising path *APO → Supply Chain Planning → SPP → Forecasting → Define Forecast Service Profile* as described in chapter 5.2. Figure 5.50 shows the service profiles with the assignment of the product group type and the control parameters 'generate phase-in profile' and 'phase-in forecasting'.

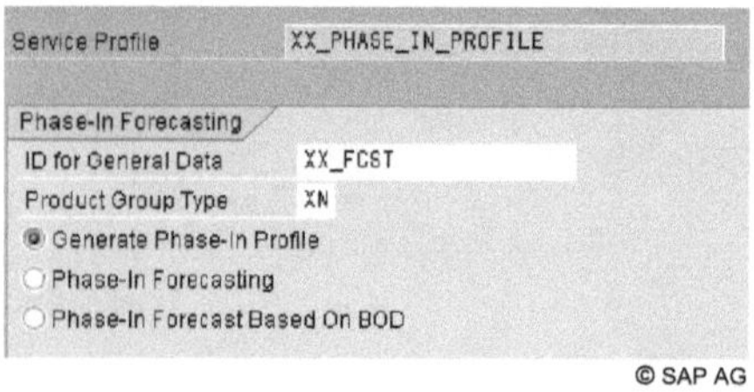

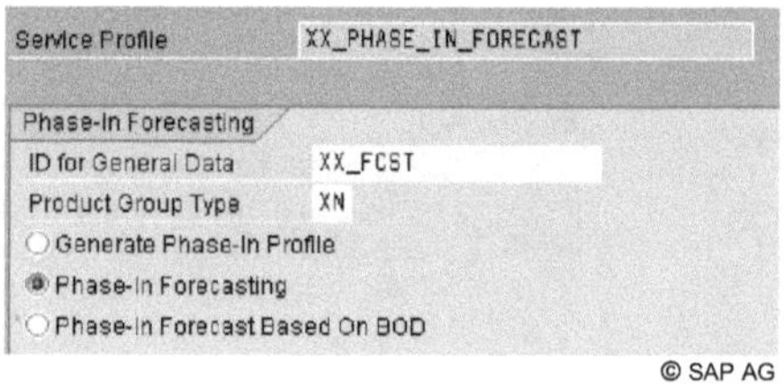

Fig. 5.50. Service Profile for Phase-In Forecasting

Note that this service requires a package creation method of the type PRODUCT_SIMPLE and not LOCATIONPRODUCT_PRODUCT.

The phase-in group defines how the demand curve in the phase-in profile is created – the number of phase-in forecast values ('length'), the maximum number of demand history periods and the minimum number of reference products to create the phase-in profile. The phase-in group is maintained with the customising path *APO → Supply Chain Planning → SPP → Forecasting → Define Phase-In Group*, figure 5.51.

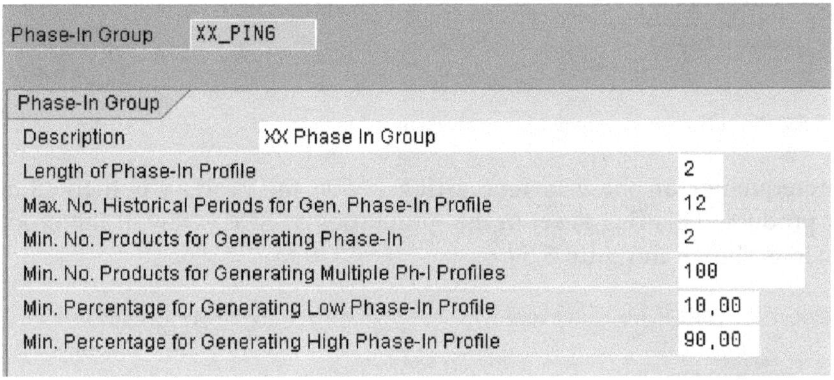

Fig. 5.51. Phase-In Group

The phase-in group is linked to the service part by using the same name for the product group. Figure 5.52 provides an overview of the settings for phase-in forecasting.

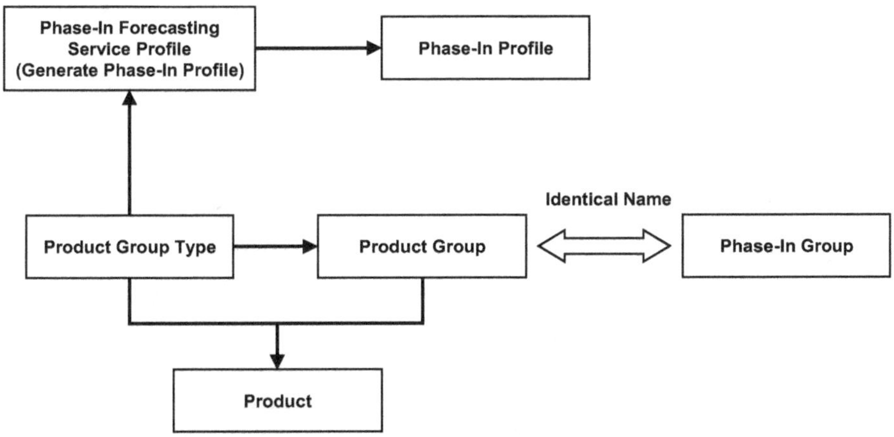

Fig. 5.52. Structure for Phase-In Forecasting

The connection between the phase-in group and the product is displayed in the forecast profile, figure 5.53. This assignment is done automatically and can not be changed interactively.

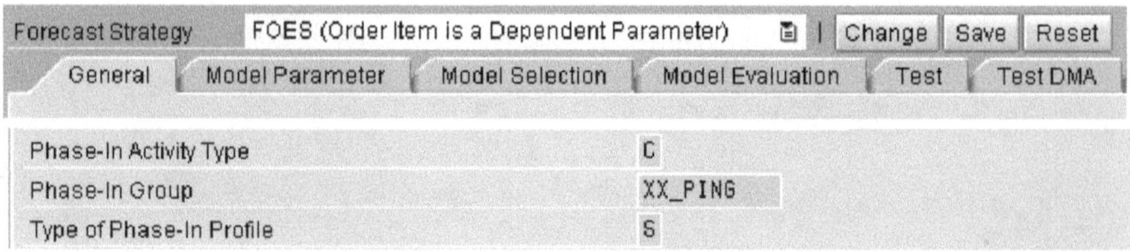

© SAP AG

Fig. 5.53. Phase-In Settings in the Forecast Profile

A prerequisite for phase-in forecasting is that the product is marked as a new product. This flag is set in the 'properties of SPP'-view of the product master as shown in figure 5.54.

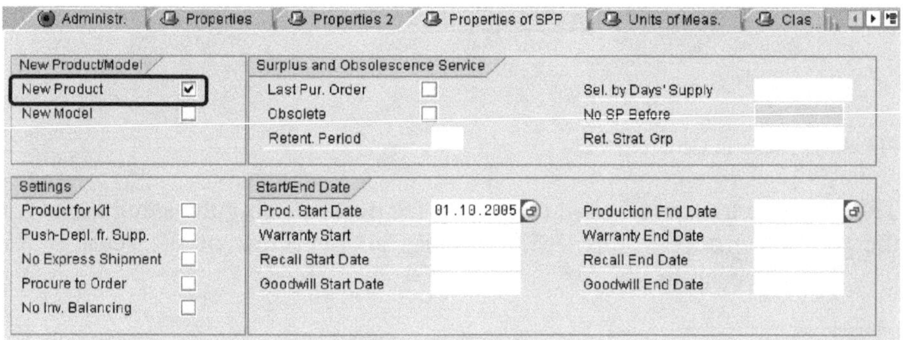

© SAP AG

Fig. 5.54. Indicator for New Product in the Product Master

5.7.2 Phase-Out Forecasting

Even if the production for the primary product has ceased, demand for the service part might occur quite some time later. For legal but also for commercial reasons it might therefore be required to keep the service part available for the customer.

The purpose of phase-out forecasting is to provide a reliable forecast for the service part at the end of the life cycle. Similar to phase-in forecasting the phase-out forecast is performed based on the demand history of reference products with the following three steps:

1. The phase-out profile is calculated based on the historical demand of the members of the phase-out group. The phase-out group contains percentages for the declining of the forecast.

2. The demand history of the final year – i.e. the year when the production of the primary product ended – is extrapolated by applying the percentages of the phase-out profile.
3. The phase-out forecast is compared with the actual history on a regular basis. If the threshold for the deviation is surpassed, an adjustment of the demand is performed. The percentage for the adjustment is the mean of the deviation of the last years.

The phase-out forecast is performed in yearly buckets. Therefore the time series for yearly buckets have to be used in the 'general data'-profile. Figure 5.55 shows the 'general data'-profile and the phase-out forecasting profile.

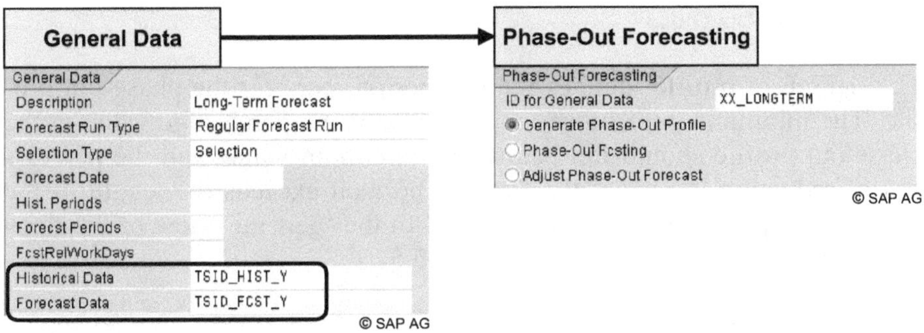

Fig. 5.55. Phase-Out Forecast Service

The forecast is only performed at the entry location of the respective product with the planning service SPP_PHASE_OUT. It is also possible to perform the phase-out forecasting and the adjustment interactively with the transaction /SAPAPO/SPPLONGFCST. The phase-out profile is displayed in this transaction as well. The generation of the phase-out profile however is only possible as a planning service.

The phase-out group is defined with the customising path *APO → Supply Chain Planning → SPP → Forecasting → Define Phase-Out Group*, figure 5.56.

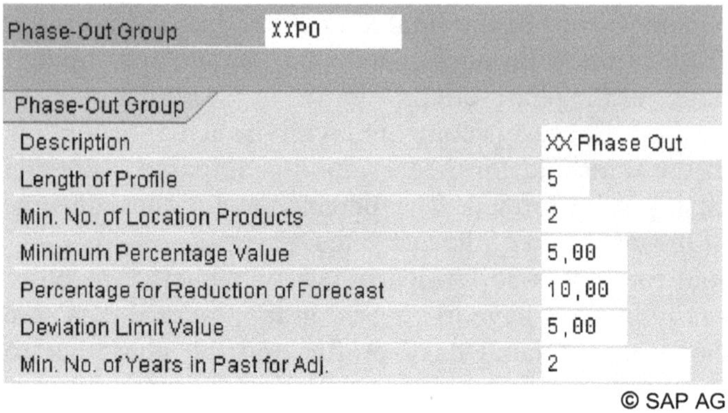

Fig. 5.56. Phase-Out Group

The 'length of profile' defines the number of years for the phase-out profile. The minimum percentage value is used if the percentage value in the phase-out profile should fall below this minimum value, and the percentage of reduction is used if the forecast horizon exceeds the length of the profile. The phase-out group is assigned to the 'general'-view of the forecast profile for the entry location, figure 5.57.

Fig. 5.57. Assignment of the Phase-Out Group to the Forecast Profile

The prerequisite for phase-out forecasting is that the production end date of the primary product (as maintained in the 'SPP inventory balancing/surplus'-view of the product master) is already reached, figure 5.58.

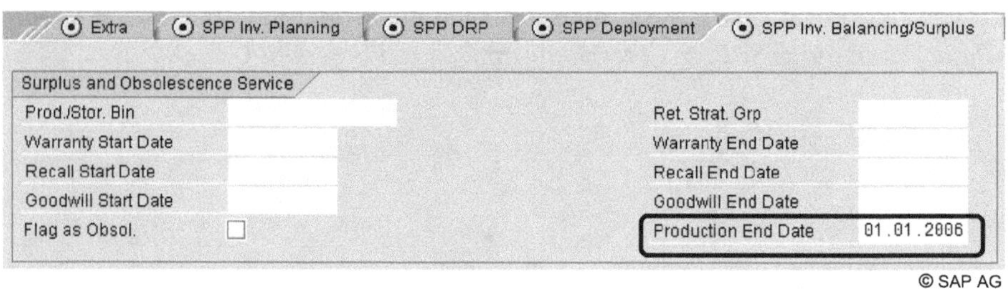

Fig. 5.58. Production End Date

6 Economic Order Quantity and Safety Stock

6.1 Process Overview

Most of the service parts – especially in the automotive and the engineering industry – have an immediate demand, i.e. the service part has to be available on stock. Since the forecast is always just an estimation of the future demand, it is necessary to compensate the deviations from the real demand (and the irregularities of the supply) by safety stock.

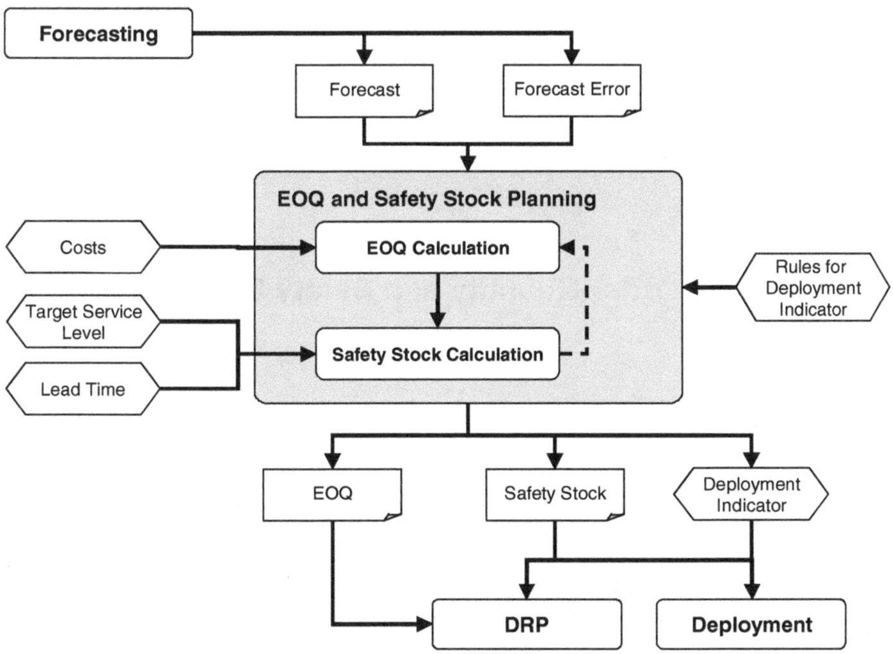

Fig. 6.1. EOQ and Safety Stock Planning Process Overview

The level of the safety stock depends primarily on the target service level – i.e. how much risk is taken to be unable to deliver – and the height and the reliability of the forecast as measured by the forecast error. The higher the target service level and the higher the forecast and the forecast error are, the higher the safety stock will be. Other factors that influence the safety stock quantity are the lead time for replenishment and the order quantity. Increasing lead time requires more safety stock as well as decreasing order quantity. Therefore the calculation of the economic order quantity (EOQ) and the safety stock are performed in one service. Figure 6.1 gives an overview of the EOQ and safety stock planning process.

EOQ and safety stock planning use only the forecast and the forecast error measured by the standard deviation (and not the demand history). Based on the forecast and the costs, first the EOQ is calculated and afterwards – taking the target service level and the lead time into account – the safety stock. If normal distribution is used to model the probability for customer orders (as opposed to Poisson distribution) the determination of EOQ and safety stock is an iterative process.

Another result of the EOQ and safety stock planning is the determination of the deployment indicator which decides whether the lead time for pull or for push deployment is used for planning. This decision is based on predefined rules and explained in chapter 10.2.

EOQ and safety stock are used by DRP in order to determine the requirements for procurement. Deployment considers the safety stock also for the calculation of the replenishment quantities and EOQ for rounding. The deployment indicator is an important parameter for both DRP and deployment.

6.2 Economic Order Quantity and Safety Stock

6.2.1 Economic Order Quantity

Each order costs money – not just the price for the goods but also transaction costs related with placing the order and handling costs in the warehouse. From this point of view it would be beneficial to place as little orders as possible, which would lead to high ordering quantities and subsequently to high average storage levels. High inventory levels are however undesired as well, mainly because of the capital commitment. The economic order quantity determines the order quantity where the total annual costs – i.e. the sum of the order quantity dependent annual stockholding costs C_{ANNSTH} and order quantity independent order costs C_{ANNORD} is minimal, figure 6.2.

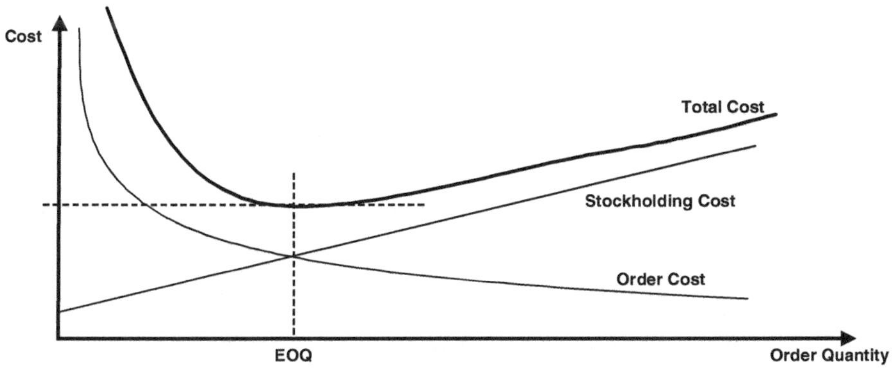

Fig. 6.2. Economic Order Quantity Calculation

All the costs for the economic order calculation are maintained in the product master. These costs are – like all the costs in SAP APO™ – without any dimension and not integrated with mySAP ERP™. Therefore they represent rather weighting factors than real costs.

• *Stockholding Costs*
The annual stockholding costs C_{ANNSTH} are calculated as the capital commitment per unit times the average stock on hand, formula 6.1. The average stock on hand is the safety stock and half of the order quantity Q.

$$C_{ANNSTH} = (\text{Safety Stock} + Q/2) * F_{HC} * C_P \quad (6.1)$$

Figure 6.3 shows the procurement cost C_P which is maintained in the view 'procurement' and represents the price of the service part.

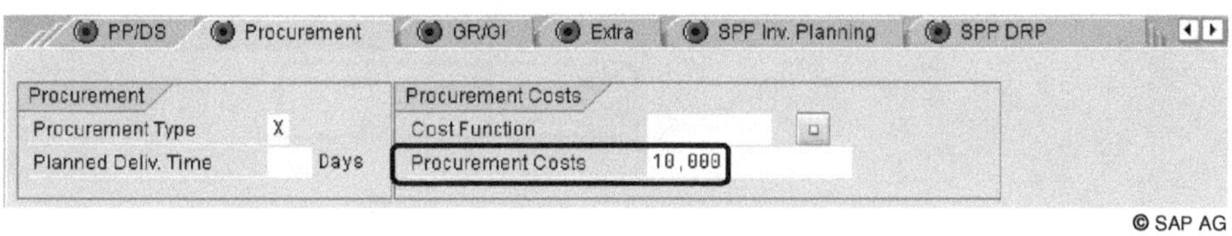

Fig. 6.3. Procurement Costs in the Product Master

The capital commitment per unit is represented by the procurement cost times the holding cost factor F_{HC}. The holding cost factor is maintained in the 'SPP DRP'-view of the product master. Figure 6.4 shows a holding cost factor of 0.5.

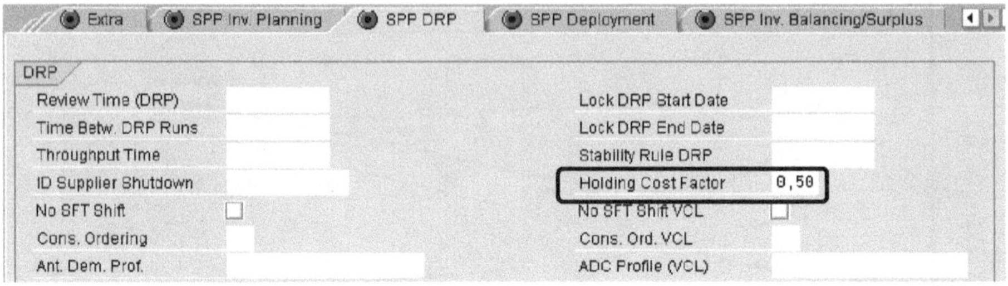

Fig. 6.4. Stock Holding Costs in the Product Master

• *Order Costs*

The fixed order cost C_{ORD} represents the transaction costs and the handling costs in the warehouse. Depending whether the product is procured via pull or via push deployment, the cost might be different. If for example push deployment sends the service part immediately to the next distribution centre, the effort for warehouse management is lower than for a service part that is stored into the warehouse and issued from the warehouse again. Figure 6.5 shows the maintenance of the fixed order costs for pull and for push deployment in the 'SPP inventory planning'-view of the product master.

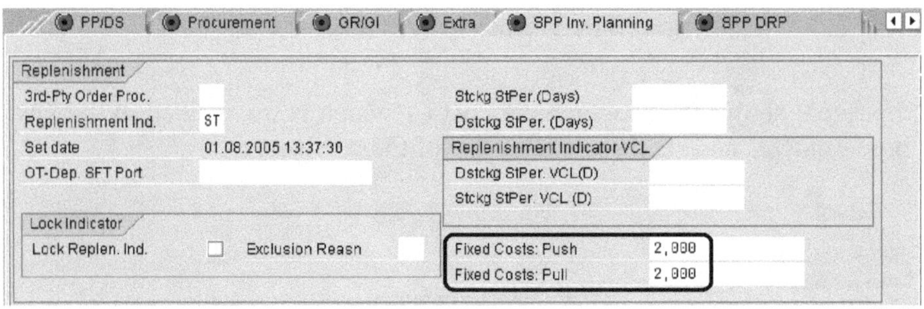

Fig. 6.5. Fix Order Costs in the Product Master

The annual order cost C_{ANNORD} however depends on the order quantity Q as well because the lower the order quantity, the more often it is necessary to order and the higher the annual order costs. For the calculation of the annual order cost C_{ANNORD} the annual forecast Q_{ANNFC} is used, formula 6.2.

$$C_{ANNORD} = C_{ORD} * Q_{ANNFC} / Q \tag{6.2}$$

• *Determination of the Economic Order Quantity*
The economic order quantity is calculated by applying the differential calculus to the formulas 6.1 and 6.2. Formula 6.3 shows the result.

$$Q_{EOQ}^2 = 2\ C_{ORD} * Q_{ANNFC} / (F_{HC} * C_P) \tag{6.3}$$

Accordingly, the EOQ increases with rising fix order costs and decreases with rising procurement cost and the stock holding factor, table 6.1.

Table 6.1. Dependency of the Economic Order Quantity

EOQ Increases with Rising...	EOQ Decreases with Rising...
Fix Order Cost	Procurement Costs
	Holding Cost Factor

The procurement costs for the EOQ calculation are applied for each location from the location specific product master. At the entry location it is possible to consider costs of scales as well.

6.2.2 Safety Stock

The purpose of the safety stock is to cover deviations of the demand and the supply. The assumption for service parts planning is that the supply side is monitored very carefully in order to keep the deviations to planning low and that the uncertainty on the supply side is low compared to the uncertainty on the demand side. Since the forecast is based on estimations, there is always a certain probability that the real customer demand exceeds the forecast. This probability is the higher the bigger the forecast error is. The basic idea of the safety stock is to cover for a certain probability of increased customer demand. Covering 100 percent would require infinite safety stock but covering e.g. 95 percent is possible and common with reasonable safety stock. The percentage that defines which probability of increased customer demand should be covered by safety stock is called target service level (TSL). Figure 6.6 visualises the forecasted demand and the probability of deviating customer demands – in this case represented by the standard distribution. The width of this graph is related to the forecast error. For a target service level of e.g. 90 percent the forecast has to be increased to a value where the area below that graph contains 90 percent of the area of the total graph for the distribution.

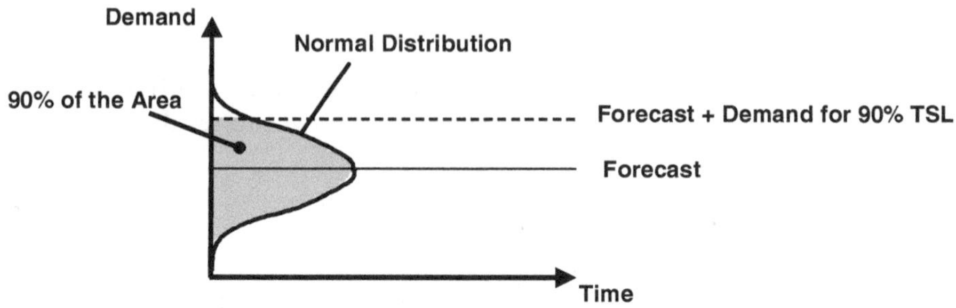

Fig. 6.6. Standard Deviation, Target Service Level and Demand

Assuming a constant demand, the reorder point for the forecast is calculated as the stock level that will just cover the demands for the lead time of the new supply. In this case the new supply arrives just at the time of the stock-out. To determine the safety stock for a target service level, the additional demand (forecast + demand for 90% TSL) is applied, which leads to an earlier projected stock-out and therefore to an earlier respective higher reorder point. The safety stock is the projected stock using the forecast (without additional demand) at the point in time when the projected stock using the forecast and additional demand becomes zero, figure 6.7.

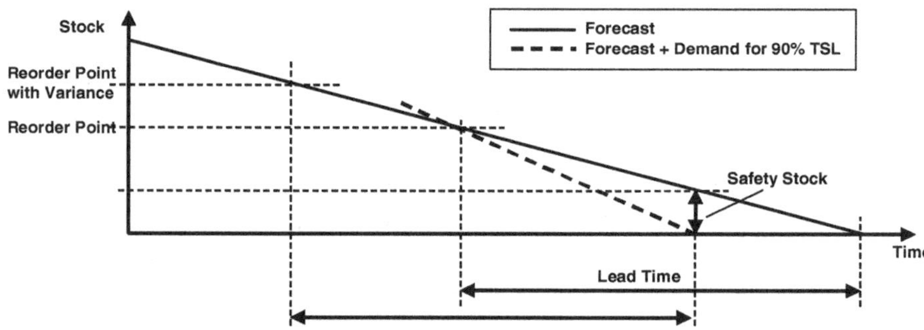

Fig. 6.7. Impact of the Additional Demand on the Reorder Point

The lead time consists of different master data parameters and is different for push and for pull deployment. Chapter 8.3 describes how the lead times are calculated.

6.2.3 Interdependency of EOQ, Safety Stock and TSL

The total target service level contains the horizon T before the reorder point (i.e. outside the lead time) and the horizon T_{LT} after the reorder point (i.e. within the lead time). Therefore the total target service level is higher than the previously calculated target service level within the lead time.

The bigger the EOQ, the longer the horizon outside the lead time and therefore the higher the total target service level with the same safety stock – or the less safety stock is required to meet the defined target service level. Figure 6.8 shows how an increased EOQ – represented by a higher stock level at the start – leads to a longer horizon outside the lead time and therefore to a higher total target service level.

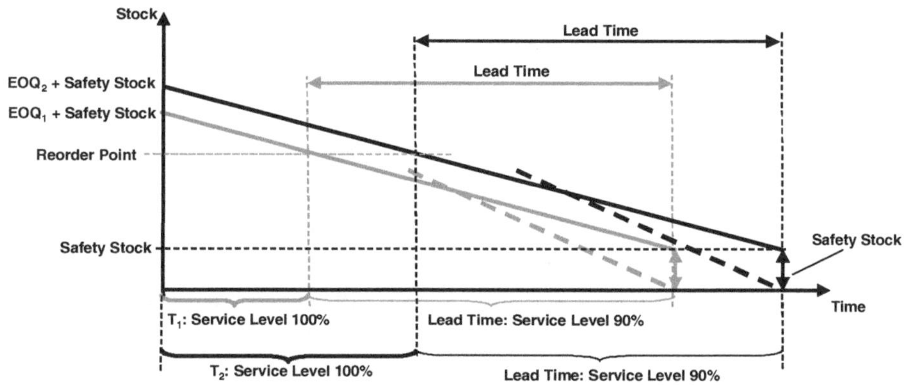

Fig. 6.8. Impact of the EOQ on the Target Service Level and the Safety Stock

Table 6.2 lists the impact of the factors TSL, lead time, standard deviation (forecast error) and EOQ on the safety stock.

Table 6.2. Dependency of the Safety Stock

Safety Stock Increases with Rising…	Safety Stock Decreases with Rising…
Target Service Level	Economic Order Quantity
Lead Time	
Standard Deviation	

Note that the absolute value of the forecast does not influence the safety stock but the absolute value of the standard deviation. The lead time calculation is explained in chapter 8.3 about DRP.

• *Target Service Level Maintenance*

For service parts planning the alpha target service level is used, i.e. the percentage of orders that are fulfilled completely. The target service level is defined with the transaction /SAPAPO/PINV_TL_MAIN. It is possible to define the target service level on different levels – if no definition on product, location or product group level exits, the fallback values are used.

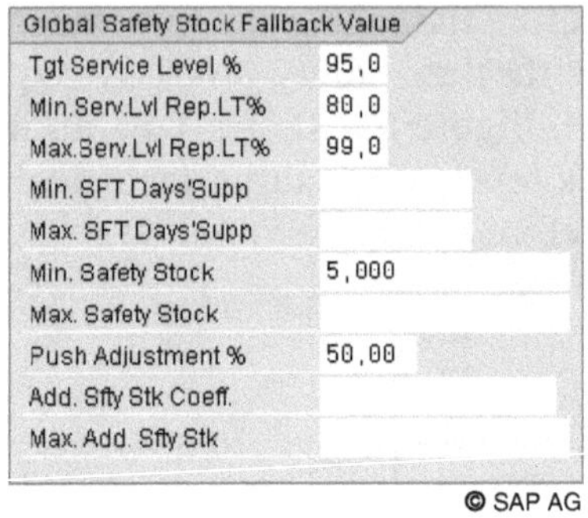

Fig. 6.9. Target Service Level Definition

First the definition on location product level is checked. In this case an entry with a blank product is ignored. In this table the entries are stored that were changed in the interactive inventory planning. If no values are maintained here, the check is continued at the product group level and from there to the global/local target safety stock rules. These settings are on version and location level, and it is possible to leave the location blank. The last check is for the global fallback values.

The target service level is the total target service level. The minimum TSL represents the TSL within the lead time. It is also possible to limit the safety stock values explicitly either by absolute values or by safety days' supply – both as minimum safety stock to ensure that a certain safety stock level is always kept as well as maximum safety stock.

• *Normal Distribution vs. Poisson Distribution*

The demand for service parts is usually caused by the failure of the original part. The failure of a part is a rather seldom and discrete event, and the appropriate distribution for seldom events is the Poisson distribution. Therefore the Poisson distribution is often considered to be more appropriate for service parts (Muckstadt 2005). Whether the normal distribution or the Poisson distribution is used is defined with the transaction /SAPAPO/PINV_MS_MAIN, figure 6.10.

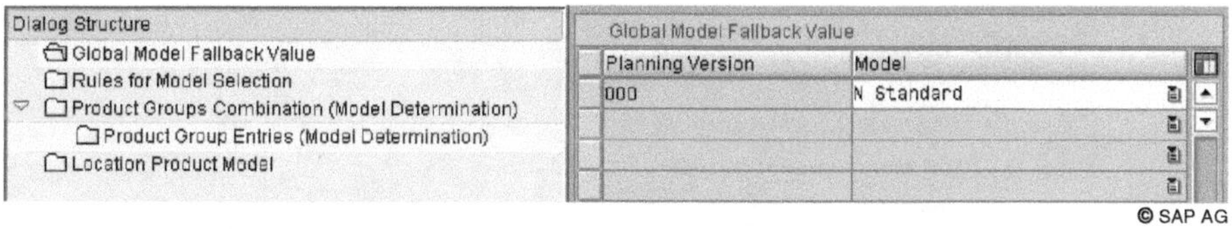

Fig. 6.10. Model Determination for the Safety Stock Calculation

Using the normal distribution the safety stock is calculated as a buffer for increased total order quantities, whereas with the Poisson distribution the safety stock is calculated as a buffer for an increased number of order items (assuming that each order item requests the average order quantity).

6.2.4 EOQ and Safety Stock Planning Service

The procedure for the calculation of EOQ and safety stock starts with the EOQ calculation, and rounding is applied for the EOQ. The safety stock is calculated based on the rounded EOQ. If normal distribution is applied the final determination of the EOQ and the safety stock is an iterative process with gradually increasing or decreasing values – depending on the rounding profile (else increment of 1).

EOQ and safety stock planning is performed with the planning service SPP_EOQSFT_SERVICE and is controlled by the planning service profile (customising path *APO → Supply Chain Planning → Service Parts Planning → Inventory Planning → Define Service Profile for EOQ/SFT calculation*), figure 6.11.

The service profile contains the parameters for rounding – the rounding profile and the indicator to round to the biggest pack size. The percentage for 'reduce order costs' controls that rounding to the biggest pack size reduces the order costs by this percentage.

Another parameter is the maximum difference between the current and the previous value for the safety stock ('maximum safety stock difference'). If this threshold is surpassed an interactive approval of the new values is required.

The option 'use additional safety stock' increases the calculated safety stock – e.g. to buffer for the deviation of the average demand. The additional safety stock is maintained in the target service level or in the 'SPP inventory planning'-view of the product master.

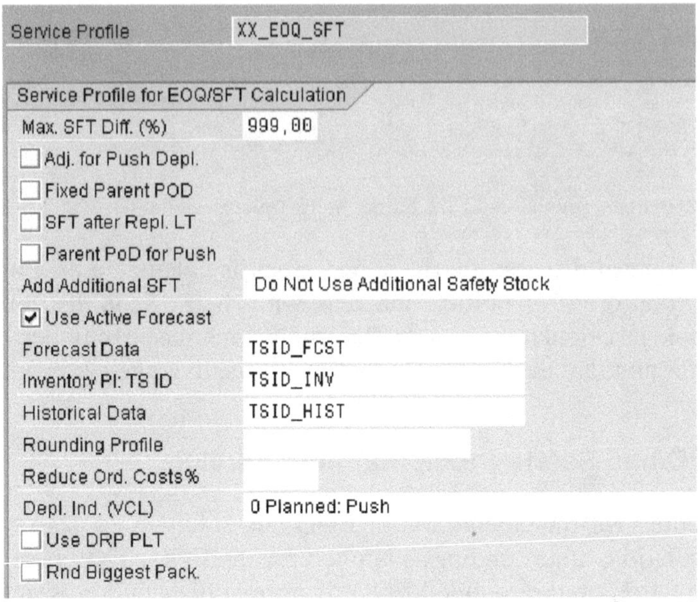

Fig. 6.11. Service Profile for EOQ and Safety Stock Calculation

• *Adjust Safety Stock in the Network for Push Deployment*

Safety stock is usually kept at all locations of the supply network. Even at the parent locations safety stock is kept in order to buffer for deviations of the customer demand at their child locations. This means that the safety stock at the parent location is composed of safety stocks for each of its child locations. The advantage of this is that the safety stock at the parent can be used more flexibly – e.g. the safety stock for child location SPB1 could be used to supply child location SPG2 if required. The disadvantage is that there is a lead time between parent and child.

Service parts planning offers two modes of replenishment, pull deployment and push deployment (see chapter 10.2). The assumption for push deployment is that the parts are not stored into the warehouse at the parent location but sent immediately to the child location. This procedure reduces the lead time compared to push deployment, where the parts have to be fetched from the warehouse first. Accordingly, a different lead time is used for pull and for push deployment.

If the safety stock stored at the child location is not sufficient, some of the safety stock at the parent location has to be transferred to the child location. This includes all the warehouse related activities at the parent location and therefore requires the lead times for pull deployment. If the child location is usually supplied via push deployment there will be a difference between the lead times. To compensate this increased lead time, it is possible to transfer a percentage of the parent's safety stock to the child location. This percentage is maintained in the target level settings (parameter 'push adjustment %' in figure 6.9) and applies only to the portion of the parent's safety stock that was calculated for this child location. As an extreme, if all child locations are replenished by push deployment and the percentage is set to 100, no safety stock remains at the parent location. The parameter 'adjust for push deployment' in the service profile controls whether the safety stock is actually adjusted for push deployment or not.

• *Constant and Non-Constant Safety Stock Models*

If there are huge changes in the demand of a product – e.g. because of seasonality – the safety stock must be adjusted in order to provide the same security for deviances in the demand. Whether the safety stock planning calculates a constant or a non-constant safety stock (and EOQ) depends on the forecast model. With the customising path *APO → Supply Chain Planning → Service Parts Planning → Inventory Planning → Assign Inventory Planning Type to Forecast Strategy* the dependency of the safety stock model to the forecast model is defined, figure 6.12.

Forecast Types

Model Types in Inventory Planning

FcstType	Description
A	FOES
B	SOES
C	GLEITENDER DURCHSCHNITT
D	LINEARE REGRESSION
E	TREND-SAISON-MODELL
F	TREND-SAISON-MODELL MIT F
G	SPORADISCHES MODELL
H	DYNAMISCH GLEITENDER MITT
I	FCST FOR DECLINING

© SAP AG

Inventory Planning Type per Forecast Type

Assignment of Forecast Strategies

F	FcstType	IP Type	Seasonal
A1	A	K Constant	☐
A2	A	K Constant	☐
B1	B	N Not Constant (Such as Seas	☐
B2	B	K Constant	☐
C1	C	K Constant	☐
D1	D	N Not Constant (Such as Seas	☐
E1	E	N Not Constant (Such as Seas	☑
F1	F	N Not Constant (Such as Seas	☑
G1	G	K Constant	☐
H1	H	K Constant	☐

© SAP AG

Fig. 6.12. Safety Stock Model

The parameter 'seasonal' is used by DRP for pre-season safety stock shift (see chapter 8.6.2).

• *Price Quantity Scales*

When ordering huge quantities from a supplier it is common to get a lower price per unit. These decreasing costs (price quantity scales) are not continuous but depend on thresholds. For EOQ and safety stock planning the cost function in the 'procurement'-view of the product master is used, figure 6.13.

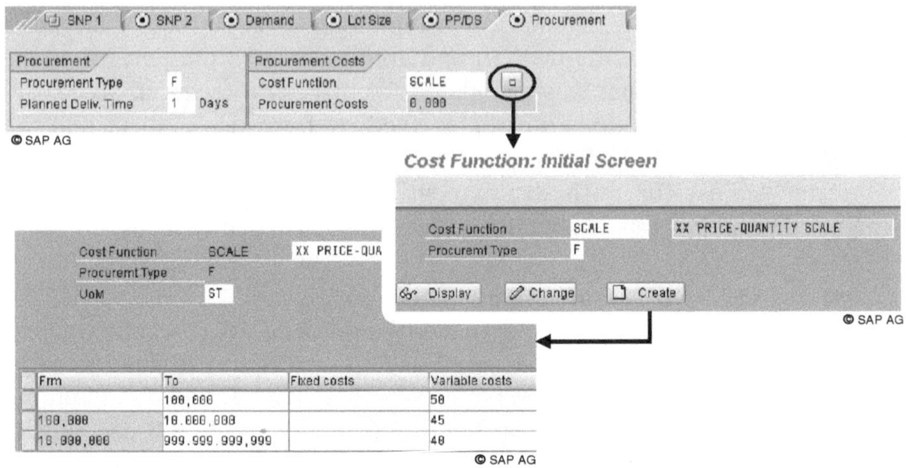

Fig. 6.13. Cost Function for Price-Quantity Scales in the Product Master

Note that the price quantity scales which are maintained in the info record in mySAP ERP™ and transferred to SAP APO™ in the procurement relationship are not used.

If price-quantity scales are used, the planning service calculates the EOQ and the safety stock for each price quantity scale and selects the solution with the least annual costs.

6.3 Planning Book for Inventory Planning

For interactive planning the planning book for inventory planning is used. It is called with the transaction /SAPAPO/SPPINVP and offers a detailed view on the input (e.g. standard deviation final forecast) and the output (e.g. EOQ and location's own safety stock). Figure 6.14 shows the planning book for inventory planning for the product ZZXX_ENGINE@Q4L400 at the location PLSPG2@Q4L400. In this case a constant safety stock model was used without any rounding because the economic order quantity of 64.035 pieces and the safety stock of 15.959 pieces do not vary in future time buckets.

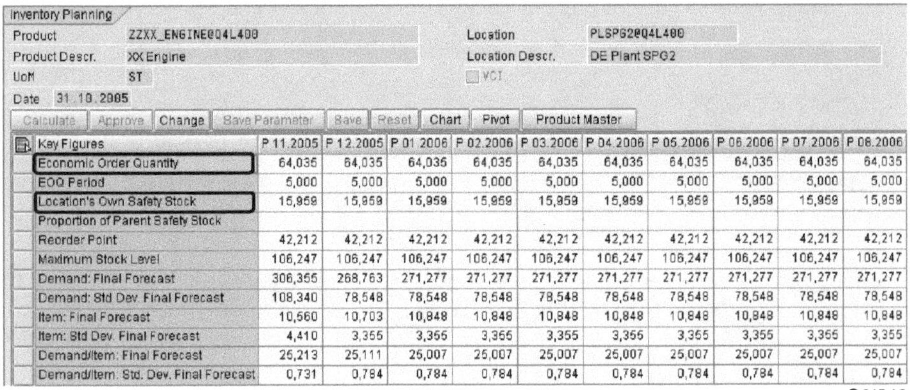

Inventory Planning

Product ZZXX_ENGINE@Q4L400 — Location PLSPG2@Q4L400

Product Descr. XX Engine — Location Descr. DE Plant SPG2

UoM ST — VCI

Date 31.10.2005

Calculate | Approve | Change | Save Parameter | Save | Reset | Chart | Pivot | Product Master

Key Figures	P 11.2005	P 12.2005	P 01.2006	P 02.2006	P 03.2006	P 04.2006	P 05.2006	P 06.2006	P 07.2006	P 08.2006
Economic Order Quantity	64,035	64,035	64,035	64,035	64,035	64,035	64,035	64,035	64,035	64,035
EOQ Period	5,000	5,000	5,000	5,000	5,000	5,000	5,000	5,000	5,000	5,000
Location's Own Safety Stock	15,959	15,959	15,959	15,959	15,959	15,959	15,959	15,959	15,959	15,959
Proportion of Parent Safety Stock										
Reorder Point	42,212	42,212	42,212	42,212	42,212	42,212	42,212	42,212	42,212	42,212
Maximum Stock Level	106,247	106,247	106,247	106,247	106,247	106,247	106,247	106,247	106,247	106,247
Demand: Final Forecast	306,355	268,763	271,277	271,277	271,277	271,277	271,277	271,277	271,277	271,277
Demand: Std Dev. Final Forecast	108,340	78,548	78,548	78,548	78,548	78,548	78,548	78,548	78,548	78,548
Item: Final Forecast	10,560	10,703	10,848	10,848	10,848	10,848	10,848	10,848	10,848	10,848
Item: Std Dev. Final Forecast	4,410	3,355	3,355	3,355	3,355	3,355	3,355	3,355	3,355	3,355
Demand/Item: Final Forecast	25,213	25,111	25,007	25,007	25,007	25,007	25,007	25,007	25,007	25,007
Demand/Item: Std. Dev. Final Forecast	0,731	0,784	0,784	0,784	0,784	0,784	0,784	0,784	0,784	0,784

Fig. 6.14. Planning Book for Inventory Planning

The parameters – costs, lead times and TSL – are displayed at the detailed section of the screen, figure 6.15.

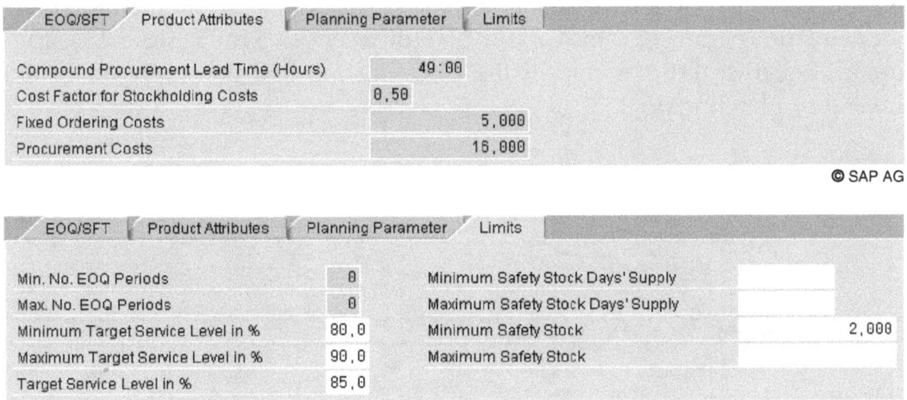

Fig. 6.15. Inventory Planning Details

The TSL can be changed there and will result in an entry in the TSL definition on location product level as shown in figure 6.9. It is possible to simulate the inventory planning and to save the results. Interactive inventory planning is however limited to an interactive change of the parameters (e.g. the target service level) and does not allow to change the EOQ and the safety stock directly.

The current period's EOQ and safety stock are saved in the 'SPP inventory planning'-view of the product master, figure 6.16. If a constant safety stock model is used, these values are applied by DRP and deployment (else the time series for EOQ and safety stock are used).

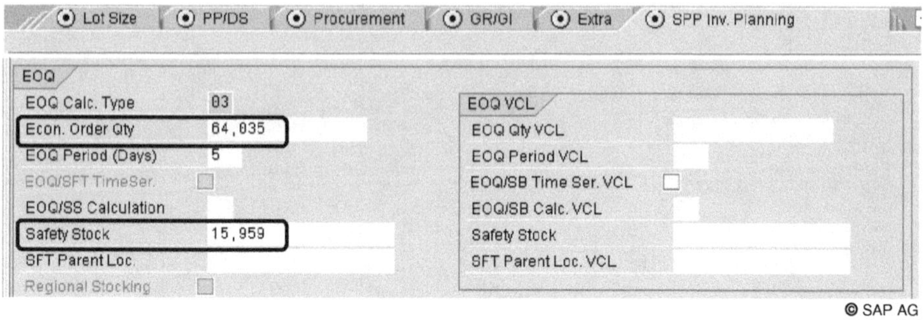

Fig. 6.16. Economic Order Quantity and Safety Stock in the Product Master

• *EOQ and Safety Stock Approval*
In case that the values for the EOQ and the safety stock differ largely from their previous values it is necessary to approve the new values in the planning book. The threshold for the approval is defined in the planning service profile (parameter 'maximum SFT difference', see figure 6.11). Figure 6.17 shows the message in the planning log and the approval in the inventory planning book.

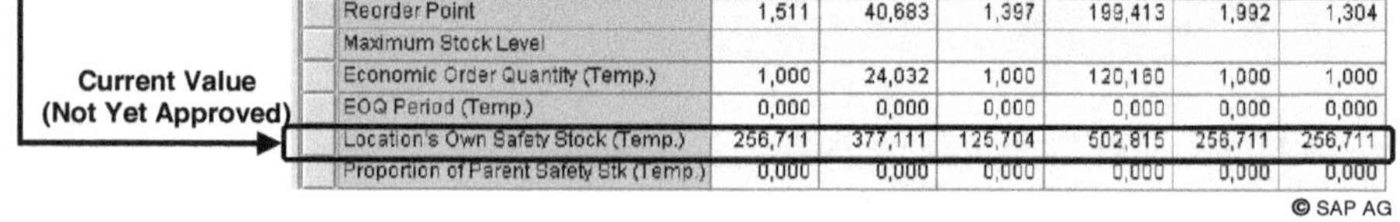

Key Figures	P 11.2005	P 12.2005	P 01.2006	P 02.2006	P 03.2006	P 04.2006
Economic Order Quantity	1,000	24,032	1,000	120,160	1,000	1,000
EOQ Period	0,000	0,000	0,000	0,000	0,000	0,000
Location's Own Safety Stock	1,000	1,000	1,000	1,000	1,000	1,000
Proportion of Parent Safety Stock	0,000	0,000	0,000	0,000	0,000	0,000
Reorder Point	1,511	40,683	1,397	199,413	1,992	1,304
Maximum Stock Level						
Economic Order Quantity (Temp.)	1,000	24,032	1,000	120,160	1,000	1,000
EOQ Period (Temp.)	0,000	0,000	0,000	0,000	0,000	0,000
Location's Own Safety Stock (Temp.)	256,711	377,111	125,704	502,815	256,711	256,711
Proportion of Parent Safety Stk (Temp.)	0,000	0,000	0,000	0,000	0,000	0,000

Fig. 6.17. Approval in the Inventory Planning Book

6.4 Additional Services

6.4.1 Deployment Indicator Determination

The deployment indicator controls whether a location is replenished by pull deployment (based on periodical deployment runs) or by push deployment (based on goods receipt). Chapter 10.2 explains the difference in detail. However, during the EOQ and safety stock calculation the deployment indicator is determined as well based on rules that relate to the EOQ, the product group or the forecast. These rules are defined with the transaction /SAPAPO/DEPL_IND_DEF and explained in chapter 10.2 as well.

6.4.2 ABC Classification

The ABC classification is performed by a separate service and sets the ABC indicator in the 'procurement'-view of the product master, figure 6.18.

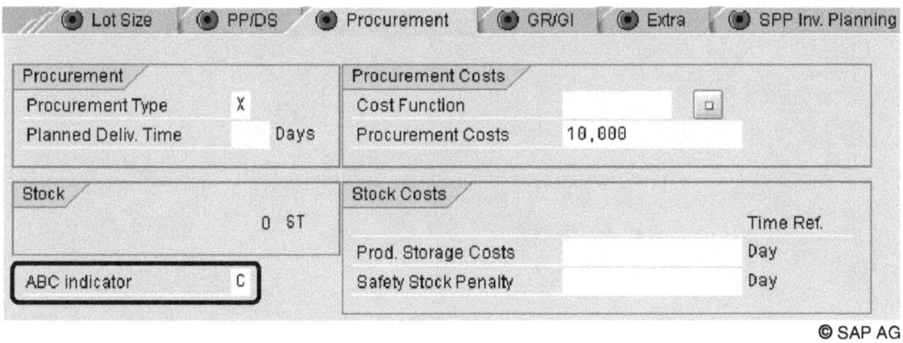

Fig. 6.18. ABC Indicator in the Product Master

The limits for the ABC classification are defined per location in the service profile, figure 6.19.

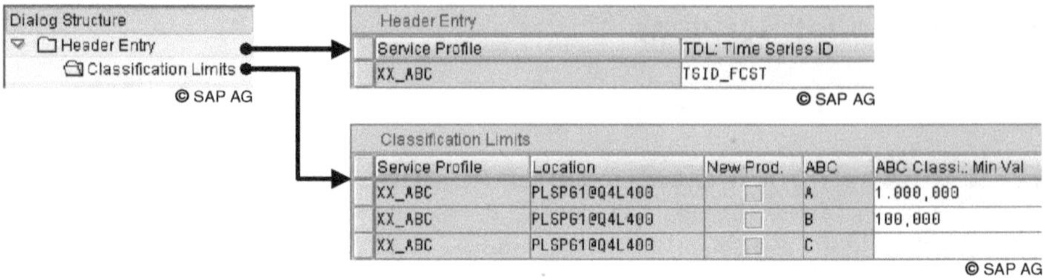

Fig. 6.19. Service Profile for ABC Classification

The ABC classification service is SPP_INVP_ABCCLASS. The ABC classification is however not used by service parts planning but by SAP EWM™.

7 Surplus and Obsolescence Planning

7.1 Process Overview

The goal of surplus and obsolescence planning is to identify inventory within the supply network – i.e. the BOD – which exceeds the projected demand and therefore only consumes warehouse space. In order to identify the surplus and remove it from the concerned warehouses, first the total surplus within the supply network is determined. This is done based on the total expected demand (including a safety buffer) and the total available stock and the stock in transit. In a second step the total surplus is disaggregated – in other words, the surplus quantities for the individual locations are determined. If the value of the surplus is within the predefined limits, orders for scrapping the surplus are created automatically. In the other case the scrap orders need to be approved interactively. Figure 7.1 shows the overview of the surplus and obsolescence planning process.

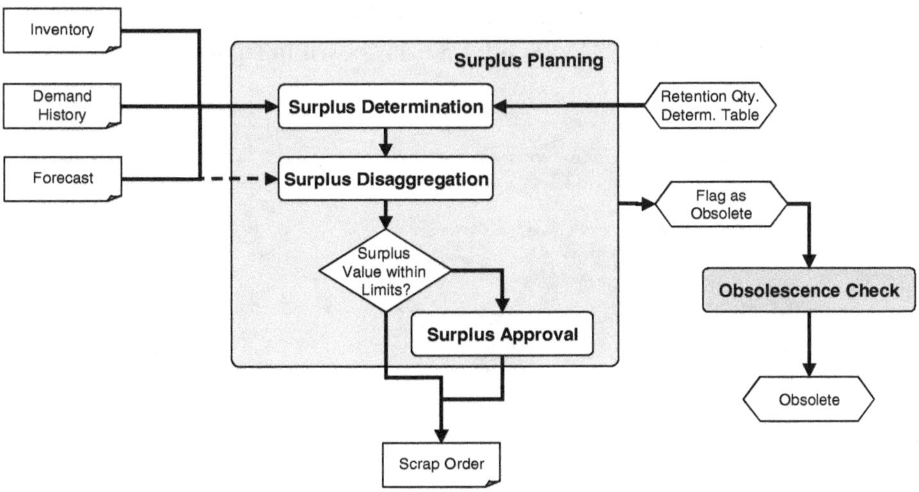

Fig. 7.1. Surplus Planning and Obsolescence Check Process Overview

The procedure for surplus determination differs depending on whether the service part belongs to a primary product that is still produced or whether the primary product is already out of production. If the primary product for the service part is not produced any more and the retention date for this product is reached, this product will become obsolete after the stock is used up. In this case the parameter 'flag as obsolete' is set per location product by the surplus planning service. The obsolescence check service checks whether there is no more stock or stock in transit and whether all location products are marked as 'flag as obsolete'. In this case another parameter – 'obsolete' – is set at product level and the service part can be removed from the system.

• *Surplus Planning and Obsolescence Check Services*

The planning service SPP_SOS_SURPLUS_DETERMINATION is used for surplus planning and it requires the package creation method PRODUCT_SOR_SRPL_DET. The planning service profile is defined with the customising path *APO → Supply Chain Planning → SPP → Surplus and Obsolescence Planning → define Service Profile for Surplus and Obsolescence Planning* and contains most of the planning parameters.

The obsolescence check requires a separate planning service with the technical name SPP_SOS_OBSOLESCENCE_CHECK. This planning service is used with the package creation method PRODUCT_SIMPLE. No service profile is required for this service.

• *General Settings*

The general settings for surplus and obsolescence planning are defined with the transaction /SAPAPO/SORCUST as shown in figure 7.2.

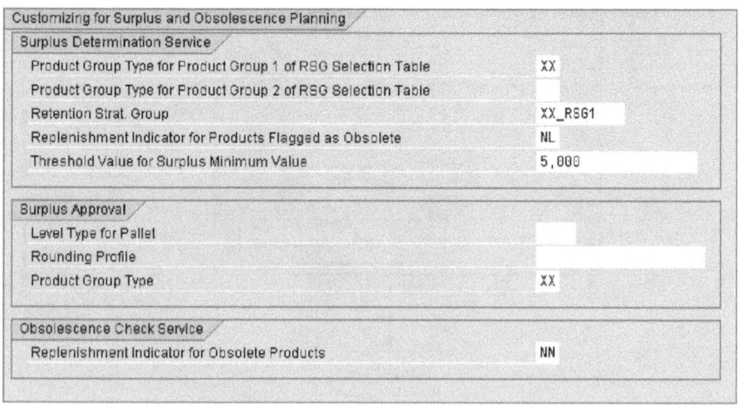

© SAP AG

Fig. 7.2. General Settings for Surplus and Obsolescence Planning

The general settings contain mainly fallback values for parameters like the retention strategy group. Another parameter is the replenishment indicator value in case of surplus and of obsolescence.

7.2 Surplus Quantity Determination

7.2.1 Overview and Common Steps

The first step for surplus planning is to determine the relevant products. Like the other planning services, surplus planning uses selection profiles. Additionally it is possible to add or remove individual products from the selection with the transaction /SAPAPO/SORSELMOD, figure 7.3.

Selection Change Table

Pl.Version	Selection Name	Product	Sel.Change
000	SPP_HAWA_ALL	SPE_HAWA_0007@RME801	Add to Selection
000	SPP_HAWA_ALL	SPP_HAWA_0013@RME801	Remove from Selection

Fig. 7.3. Change Selection

For the determination of the surplus quantity three different procedures exist, depending whether the service part is still produced and whether it is a high volume or a low volume part.

• *Current Model Part vs. Past Model Part*

The service part is considered as a past model part if the primary product that requires this service part is not produced any more. This is the case if the field 'production end date' in the product master is set and the year (and not just the date) is elapsed. The production end date is first checked location specifically in the 'SPP inventory balancing/ surplus'-view at the entry location. If this is empty, the production end date in the 'properties of SPP'-field is checked, figure 7.4.

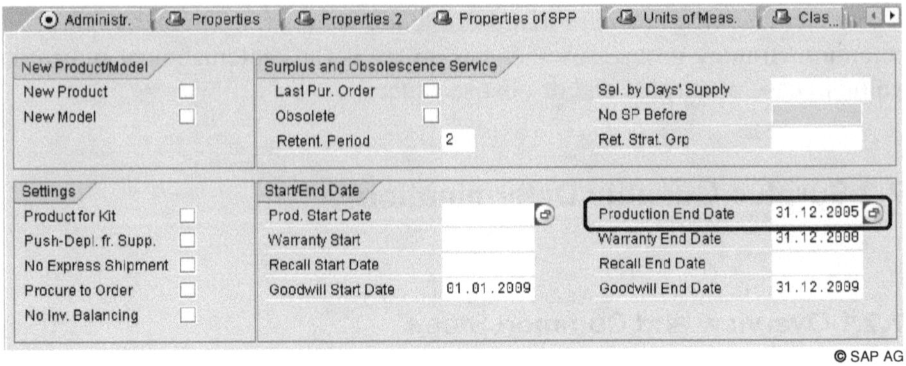

Fig. 7.4. Production End Date in the Product Master

If the service part is a past model part, the demand is calculated using phase-out forecasting. The end of the service part's planned availability is marked by the end of the retention period – which is not a static value but determined in a previous step.

For current part models either exponential smoothing is used – if it is a high volume part – or the surplus is determined using values from the retention quantity determination table. Exponential smoothing within surplus planning is performed as an extrapolation of the last five periods' demand (and does not use the algorithms for forecasting) Figure 7.5 shows these three options for the determination of the surplus quantity.

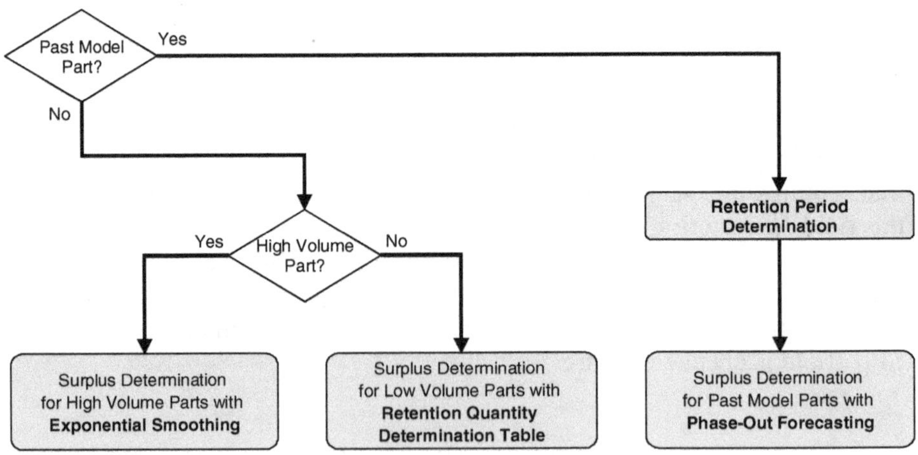

Fig. 7.5. Process Overview for Surplus Quantity Determination

Each of these methods – exponential smoothing, retention quantity determination table and phase-out forecasting – calculates the medium- to long-term requirements for the service part within the supply network. Only this amount – the retention quantity – needs to be kept, and the surplus is calculated as the difference between the stock and the stock in transit on one hand and the retention quantity on the other.

• *Planning Mode*

If a BOD has more than one entry location, either the whole supply network is planned together or each network of an entry point individually. For example, if different entry locations exist per region, this decision depends on the legal requirements and the model policy. Technically this decision is modelled by the parameter 'planning mode' in the service profile, figure 7.6.

Fig. 7.6. Planning Mode (Service Profile)

The two alternatives for the planning mode are 'plan for each BOD of an entry location individually' and 'plan whole BOD together'.

7.2.2 Surplus Quantity Determination for Current Model Part

The surplus quantity is calculated as the total stock plus the stock in transit minus the retention quantity, formula 7.1.

$$\text{Surplus} = \text{Stock} + \text{Stock in Transit} - \text{Retention Quantity} \tag{7.1}$$

Different procedures are used for the determination of the retention quantity, depending whether the service part is a high volume part or a low volume part – and if it is a low volume part, whether it is a very low volume part or a not quite so low volume part. Figure 7.7 shows the three checks how to determine which is which. In total four horizons (Y into the future and X, W, Z into the past) are used and three threshold values for the forecast and/or the demand history within these horizons (A, B, C). Only the (released) final forecast is considered.

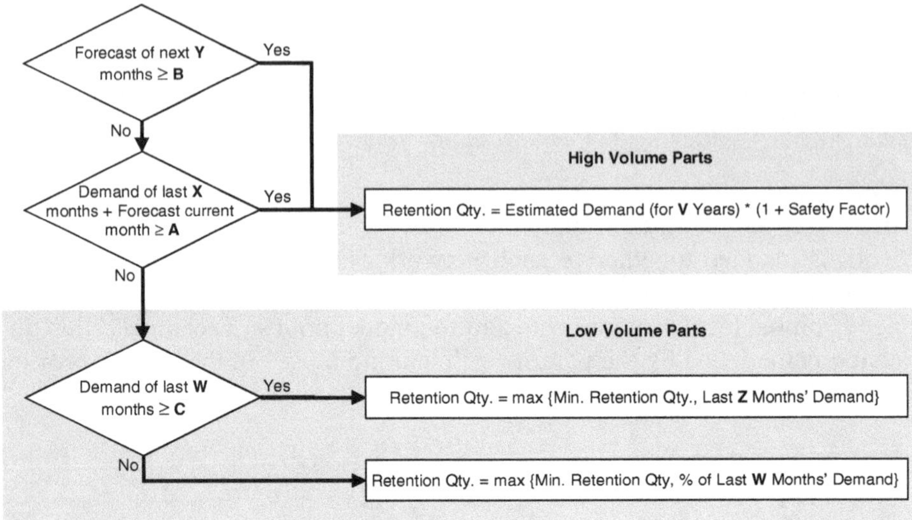

Fig. 7.7. Surplus Quantity Determination for Current Parts

If the service part is a high volume part, exponential smoothing is performed in order to determine the forecast for the retention period (parameter V). The retention period is maintained in years in the 'properties of SPP'-view of the product master, figure 7.8.

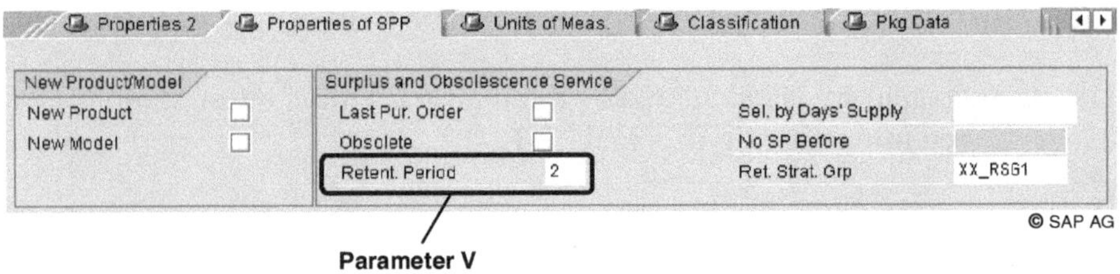

Fig. 7.8. Retention Period for Current Model Parts in the Product Master

The other parameters are maintained in the service profile as shown in figure 7.9.

Calculation of Surplus Quantity with Exponentially Smoothed Forecast		
Threshold Value for Forecast-Relevant Demand History	A	5.000,000
Horiz. f. Thr. Val. for Fcst-Rel. Demand Hist. (Mon.)	X	9
Threshold Value for Forecast-Relevant Demand	B	8.000,000
Horiz. for Threshold Val. for Fcst-Relevant Demand(Mon)	Y	12
RQDT: Threshold Value for Forecast-Rev. Demand Hist.	C	1.000,000
RQDT: Horiz. f. Thr. Val. f. Fcst-Rel. Dem.Hist. (Mon.)	W	2
Horizon for Forecast-Relevant Demand History (Months)	Z	4

Fig. 7.9. Parameters for Surplus Quantity Determination with Exponential Smoothing

• *Retention Quantity Determination Table*
The safety factor for the high volume parts, the minimum retention quantity and the percentage of the demand history for the low volume parts are maintained in the retention quantity determination table (RQDT). The RQDT is maintained with the transaction /SAPAPO/SORRETQTYDET, figure 7.10.

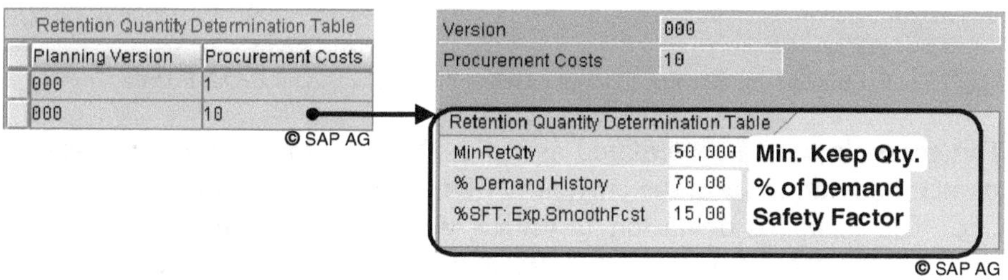

Fig. 7.10. Retention Quantity Determination Table

The RQDT is a global setting and is selected according to the procurement costs of the service part and the planning version.

7.2.3 Surplus Quantity Determination for Past Model Part

The prerequisites for the surplus quantity determination with phase-out forecasting are that

- the year of the production end date for the service part has passed and that
- phase-out forecasting was performed.

The surplus quantity is determined as the available stock plus the stock in transit minus the corrected gross demand (CGD), formula 7.2.

$$\text{Surplus} = \text{Stock} + \text{Stock in Transit} - \text{CGD} \tag{7.2}$$

The corrected gross demand (CGD) is calculated as the maximum of the 'gross demand' and the scaled demand of the past year as described in formula 7.3.

$$\text{CGD} = \max\{\text{Gross Demand}\ ;\ F_1 * \text{Demand of Last Year}\} \tag{7.3}$$

Only the forecast relevant demand of the last year is used (e.g. no future dated orders). The factor F_1 is maintained in the service profile as 'factor for forecast-relevant demand history of previous year', figure 7.11.

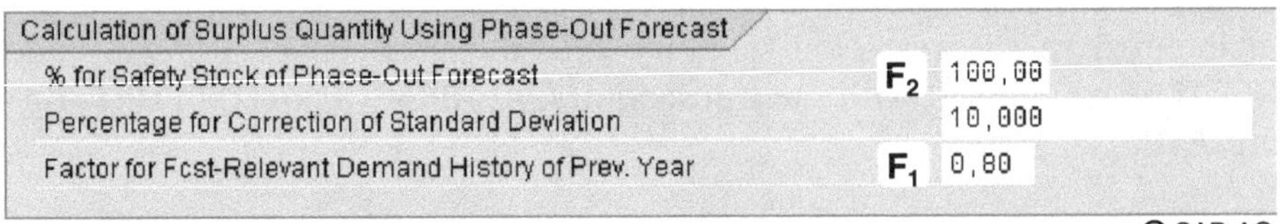

Fig. 7.11. Parameters for Surplus Quantity Determination with Phase-Out Forecasting

The gross demand is calculated as the sum of the forecast and the scaled standard deviation from the current period until the end of the retention period. The standard deviation is scaled with the parameter '% of safety stock of phase-out forecast' (F_2). Formula 7.4 describes the calculation of the gross demand.

$$\text{Gross Demand} = \Sigma_i\,(\text{Forecast}[i] + F_2 * \sigma[i])\ \forall\ i \in (0, \text{RP}) \tag{7.4}$$

If the parameter 'last purchase order' is set in the 'properties of SPP'-view of the product master, additionally the factor 'percentage for correction of standard deviation' is applied.

• *Retention Period*

The retention period describes the horizon for the availability of a service part after the production end date of its primary product. Even after the primary product is not produced any more, there are legal requirements to keep the service part available for a mandatory retention period. Often the service part is kept available for additional periods.

The retention period contains several parts – the mandatory retention horizon and one or more additional retention horizons. The relevant retention period depends on the forecasted demand. If the forecasted demand falls below a predefined threshold (the minimum demand of the retention strategy group), it is not economic any more to keep the service part available. For each additional retention horizon a different minimum demand can be defined. Figure 7.12 visualises the calculation of the retention period.

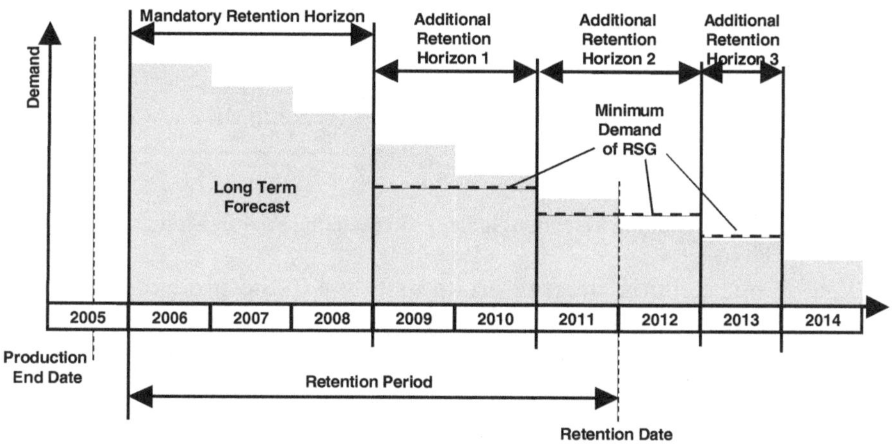

Fig. 7.12. Determination of the Retention Period

In this example the retention period ends at the end of year 2011 because in year 2012 the forecasted demand is below the minimum demand.

The parameters for the calculation of the retention period – the mandatory retention horizon, the additional maximum retention horizons and the minimum demands – are maintained in the retention strategy group (RSG). The retention strategy group is maintained with the transaction /SAPAPO/SORRETGRP, figure 7.13.

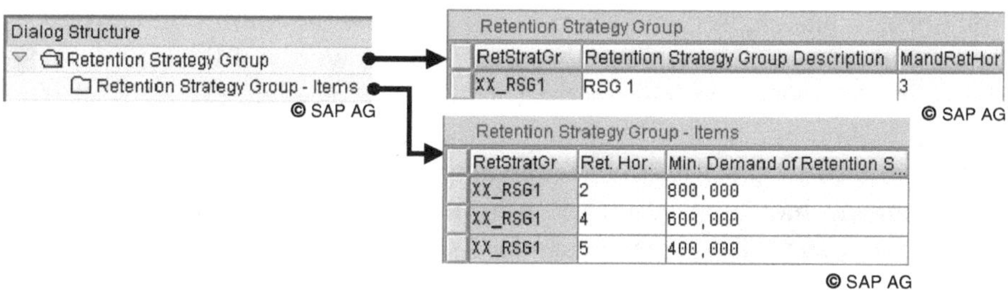

Fig. 7.13. Retention Strategy Group

The additional maximum retention horizon starts at the end of the mandatory retention horizon. The horizons within the additional maximum retention horizon are maintained as cumulative values, i.e. the additional maximum retention horizon defined in figure 7.13 is 5 years.

The retention strategy group is assigned to the product master in the location specific 'SPP inventory balancing/ surplus'-view or in the general 'properties of SPP'-view of the product master, figure 7.14.

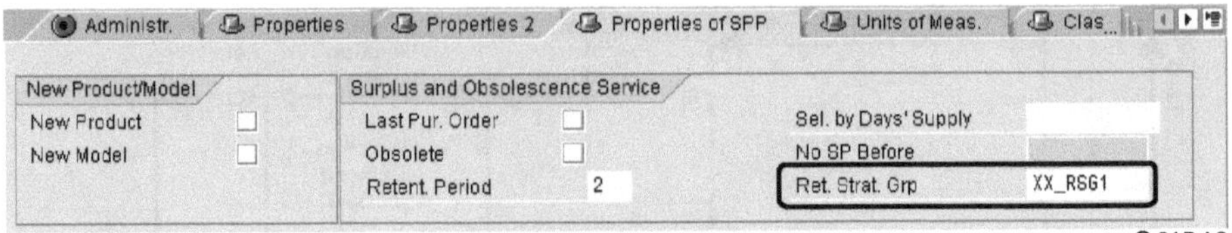

Fig. 7.14. Assignment of the Retention Strategy Group to the Product Master

If there is no retention strategy group assigned to the product master, the retention strategy group is selected by location and product group as defined in the retention strategy group selection table with the transaction /SAPAPO/SORRETGRPSEL, figure 7.15.

Retention Strategy Group Selection Table

Plannin...	Location	Recall	Haz.Subs.	Product Group	Product Group	RetStratGr
000	PLSPB1@Q4L400	☐	☐	NEW1		XX_RSG1

Fig. 7.15. Selection of the Retention Strategy Group

As a last fallback the retention strategy group that is assigned to the general settings is used.

- *Flag as Obsolete*

If surplus is determined with phase-out forecasting, the mandatory retention horizon has elapsed and the forecast is below the minimum demand as defined in the retention strategy group – in other words: if the retention period has elapsed – the parameter for 'flag as obsolete' is set (see figure 7.22). Another action is changing the replenishment indicator as defined in the general settings. In the example that is shown in figure 7.2 the replenishment indicator would be set to 'non-stocked, locked' (NL).

The parameter 'flag as obsolete' does not mean that service part is obsolete yet but is used as an input for the obsolescence check service.

7.3 Surplus Disaggregation

The surplus is determined for the whole BOD (or for the sub-BOD below the entry point). In order to remove the surplus, it is necessary to determine the surplus per location. This is called surplus disaggregation.

The surplus disaggregation starts with the determination of the keep quantity per location, and determines based on this the surplus quantity per location. It always starts with the locations which are not stocked. For these the retention quantity is zero. The stocked locations are sorted according to one of the following criteria:

- demand history (ascending)
- forecast (ascending)
- potential surplus quantity (descending)
- potential days' supply for surplus (descending)

A sorting of the locations by ascending demand history implies that the location with the lowest demand history is the first to remove its surplus.

The sorting is defined in the service profile as shown in figure 7.16. For the sorting according to the demand history or the forecast the considered horizon is specified in the service profile as well – in this example 12 months each.

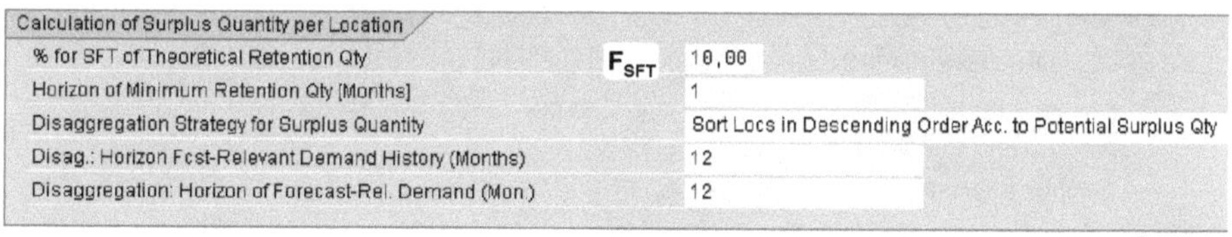

Calculation of Surplus Quantity per Location		
% for SFT of Theoretical Retention Qty	F_{SFT}	10,00
Horizon of Minimum Retention Qty [Months]		1
Disaggregation Strategy for Surplus Quantity		Sort Locs in Descending Order Acc. to Potential Surplus Qty
Disag.: Horizon Fcst-Relevant Demand History (Months)		12
Disaggregation: Horizon of Forecast-Rel. Demand (Mon.)		12

Fig. 7.16. Sorting of the Locations for Disaggregation (Service Profile)

The minimum retention quantity (MRQ) of the stocked location is calculated as described in formula 7.5.

$$MRQ = \max\{(SFT + EOQ + D_{LT}) * (1 + F_{SFT}); D_{MRQ}\} \qquad (7.5)$$

SFT is the safety stock, D_{LT} the demand over the lead time and D_{MRQ} the demand over the horizon of the minimum retention quantity. The horizon for the minimum retention quantity and the safety factor F_{SFT} are defined in the 'calculation of surplus quantity per location'-fields of the service profile as shown in figure 7.16.

The surplus quantity per location is calculated location per location in their order (first the non-stocked, then the stocked according to their sorting) until the total surplus is reached. Other criteria to stop the further calculation of surplus quantities per location are if the remaining surplus is below the average bin size or if the value of the remaining surplus is below the minimum surplus value. The minimum surplus value is defined in the location master as shown in figure 7.17. By remaining surplus we understand the difference between the total surplus quantity and the sum of the – already calculated – surplus quantities per location.

7.4 Surplus Approval

If the value of the surplus order at a location is above the threshold for the surplus approval, an interactive surplus approval is required. The threshold for the surplus approval is maintained in the location master with the transaction /SAPAPO/LOC3 as shown in figure 7.17.

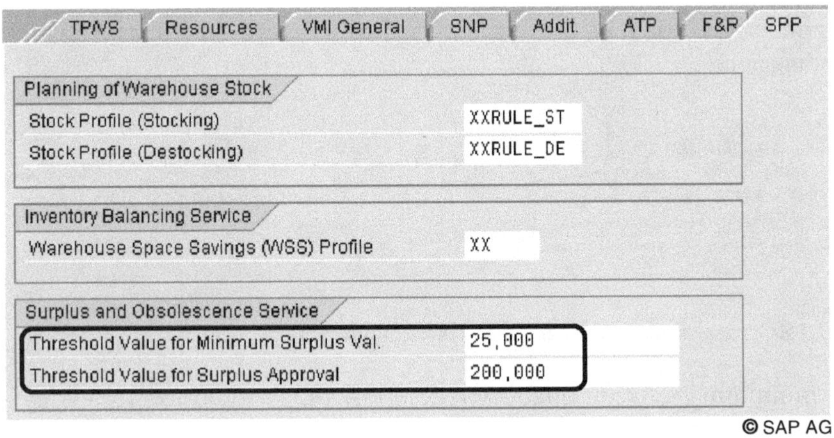

Fig. 7.17. Threshold Values for Surplus Approval in the Location Master

The interactive surplus approval is performed with the transaction /SAPAPO/SPPSOR. Figure 7.18 shows the screen for the approval of two surplus orders for the product ZZXX_SURPLUS@RME801.

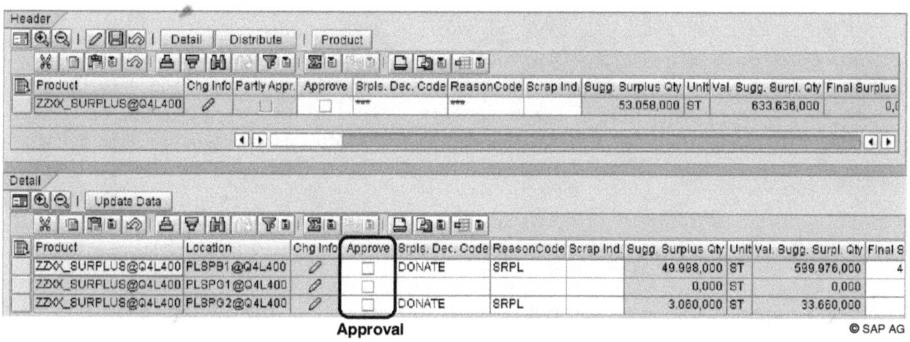

Fig. 7.18. Surplus Approval

For each suggested surplus order it is possible to change the quantity, the scrap indicator, the surplus decision code and the reason code. The order details show additional information, figure 7.19.

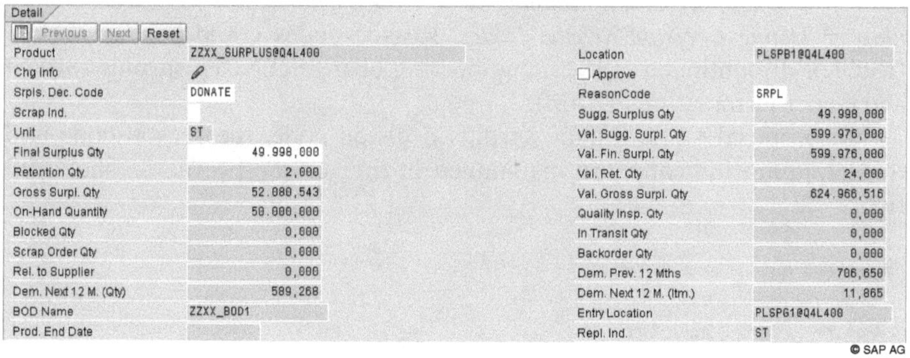

Fig. 7.19. Surplus Approval - Details

The approval is performed by setting the flag for 'approve' as shown in figure 7.18.

• *Surplus Decision Code, Scrapping Indicator and Reason Code*

The decision code is defined with the customising path *APO → Supply Chain Planning → SPP → Surplus and Obsolescence Planning → Define Decision Codes* and defines what to do with the surplus order – whether to remove the quantity from the available stock or not and whether to send the surplus order to mySAP ERP™ or not, figure 7.20.

Surplus Decision Code

SurDecCode	Surplus Decision Code	Action
DONATE	Donate	Take Quantity out of BOD, No Integration with ERP
PROD_R	Return to Production	Leave Quantity in BOD, No Integration with ERP
RETURN	Return to supplier	Take Quantity out of BOD, No Integration with ERP
SCRAP	Scrap	Take Quantity out of BOD, Integration with ERP

Fig. 7.20. Surplus Decision Code

If the decision code is to scrap the surplus quantity, the order is transferred to mySAP ERP™ as a scrap order.

The scrapping indicator defines the actions for scrapping – possible alternatives are to scrap entire stock, scrap the stock but retain remaining quantity or to scrap the stipulated quantity. If the scrapping indicator is blank, no action is taken for scrapping.

Reason codes are used for reporting and defined with the customising path *APO → Supply Chain Planning → SPP → Surplus and Obsolescence Planning → Define Decision Reason Codes*. Reason codes could be e.g. broken (BROK), discontinued (DISC), engineering change (ENGI), surplus (SRPL) and dealer termination (TERM).

The proposal value for the surplus decision code, the reason code and the scrapping indicator are maintained in the service profile as shown in figure 7.21.

Suggested Values for Surplus Approval

Surplus Decision Code	DONATE
Reason Code for Surplus Decision	SRPL
Scrapping Indicator	Not Relevant to Scrapping

Fig. 7.21. Proposal for Decision Code, Reason Code and Scrapping Indicator

As a result of the approval step a demand element of the ATP category SPPLIESCRT is created.

• *Processing of Surplus Orders*

Unless the decision code for the surplus order is SCRAP, the approved surplus order requires a subsequent processing step – e.g. to post a goods issue for the product. The logic for this subsequent processing is defined in the BAdI /SAPAPO/SOR_MANORD. The processing is triggered with the transaction /SAPAPO/SPPMSP as shown in figure 7.22.

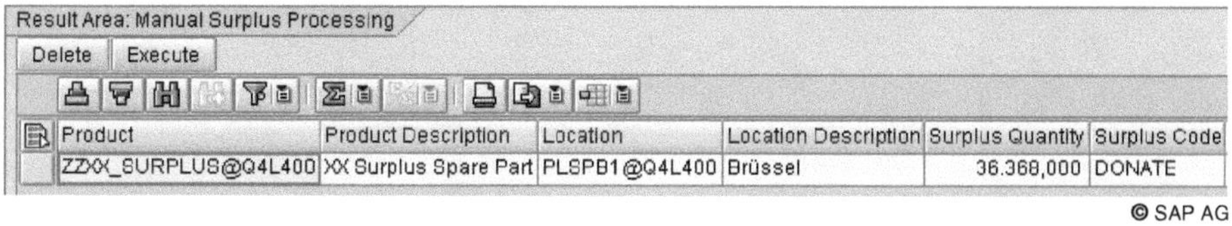

Fig. 7.22. Processing of Approved Surplus Orders

7.5 Obsolescence Check

The obsolescence check performs a check for all location products whether the parameter 'flag as obsolete' is set and whether no stock and no stock in transit exists any more. If both conditions are met, the parameter 'obsolete' is set for the product. Figure 7.23 shows this procedure.

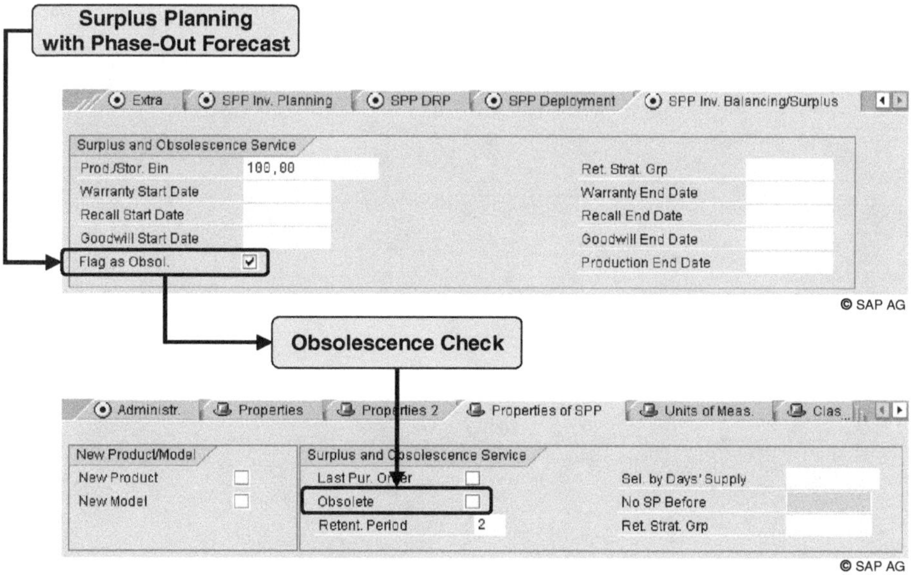

Fig. 7.23. Obsolescence Check

8 Distribution Requirements Planning

8.1 Process Overview

One characteristic of the service parts planning solution is the tree structure which is defined in the BOD. The implication of this structure is that the demand for the whole network is sourced via external procurement at the entry location (or at the entry locations, if the BOD has multiple entry locations). The purpose of DRP is to determine the procurement quantity taking the demands (forecast, safety stock, confirmed stock transfer demands and fixed demands), the inventory, the confirmed receipts, the lead times, the days of supply (i.e. the economic order quantity) and the pack stages of the whole supply network into account. Figure 8.1 shows the process overview of DRP.

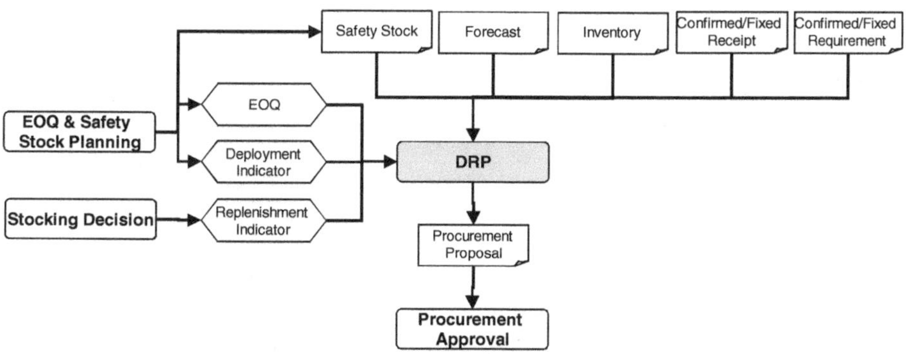

Fig. 8.1. DRP Process Overview

The result of the DRP process are procurement proposals – either schedule lines for scheduling agreements or purchase requisitions for contracts. Before the procurement proposal is released and sent to the supplier it needs to be approved as described in chapter 9.

• *DRP Planning Elements*
DRP is based on daily time buckets and orders (in contrast to forecasting and EOQ and safety stock planning). The forecast orders are created from the forecast time series during the forecast approval. The orders for the planned stock transfers are either just temporary or stored in live cache as orders – depending on the parameter 'save stock transport requisitions' in the DRP planning profile (see figure 8.71). For the planned stock transfer between two locations and for the planned stock transfer between a parent location and its virtual child location different ATP categories are used, table 8.1.

Table 8.1. DRP Planning Elements – ATP Categories

DRP Element	ATP Category	Category Text	Category Type
SPP Forecast	KA	SPP FCST	Forecast
SPP Stock Transfer (Receipt)	KB	SPPSTR IN	Receipt
SPP Stock Transfer (Demand)	KC	SPPSTR OUT	Reqmt.
SPP Stock Transfer VCL (Receipt)	KD	SPPSTR-VR	Receipt
SPP Stock Transfer VCL (Demand)	KF	SPPSTR-VD	Reqmt.

Neither the forecast nor the planned stock transfers are pegging relevant. The order types for procurement, for stock transfer orders and for sales orders are the same as in 'normal' SAP APO™.

8.2 DRP Logic

8.2.1 DRP Matrix

The purpose of DRP is to calculate the net requirements for the whole supply network (i.e. the BOD) and create procurement proposals. This is called 'roll-up the requirements' to the entry location.

The independent demand is mainly the forecast at the child locations – other demand elements are the future dated orders and the confirmed or fixed requirements. The difference between the independent (total) demand and the safety stock on one hand and the available stock and the fixed or confirmed receipts on the other hand is the net requirement of the child location. DRP covers this net demand by a planned stock transfer from the parent location. However, this planned stock transfer creates a demand at the parent location – shifted by the lead time. After performing a net requirements calculation for the parent location (planned stock transfer requirements, fixed requirements and stock transfer orders minus available stock and fixed receipts) the net requirement of the parent location is covered by a planned stock transfer from the next level (the parent location's parent location) and so on until the entry location is reached. The net requirement of the entry location is covered by a procurement proposal – either a schedule line or a purchase requisition. Figure 8.2 shows the demand and the material flow and the roll-up of the requirements for a two-level BOD.

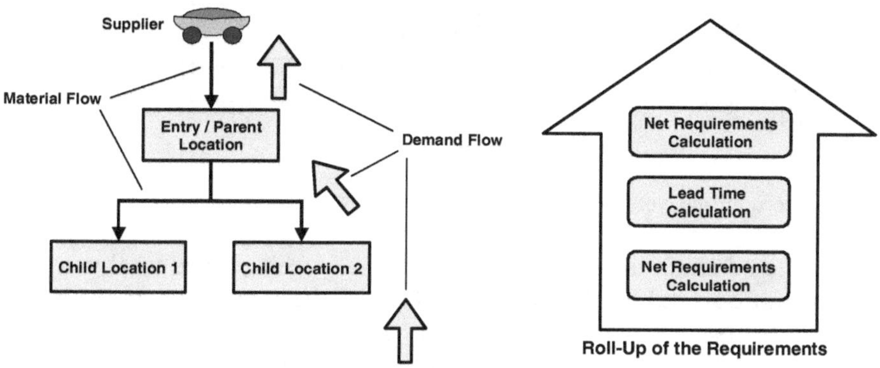

Fig. 8.2. Roll-Up of the Requirements in DRP

All planning data within the BOD including the inventory, the forecast and the external procurement is stored and displayed in the DRP matrix.

• *Net Requirements Calculation*

The net requirements calculation is performed for all stocked locations, and within each location for all time buckets of the planning horizon. Based on the projected stock of the previous period, the fixed gross receipts (e.g. stock in transit) of the current period are added and the gross demands (e.g. forecast and stock transfer requirements) are subtracted. If the calculated remaining quantity is below the minimum safety stock level, the difference is the theoretical net demand. This net demand is scheduled outside the freeze horizon to become the unrounded net demand. This unrounded net demand is rounded according to the EOQ or the EOQ POD (periods of demand) and the pack stages, and additionally stability rules and supplier shut down is applied. The result is the constrained rounded net demand – which represent the planned receipt from the supplier or the parent location. The projected stock is the calculated remaining quantity (after subtracting the total demand) plus the rounded net requirement. Figure 8.3 visualises this procedure. Only for the first day the real stock is used instead of the projected stock.

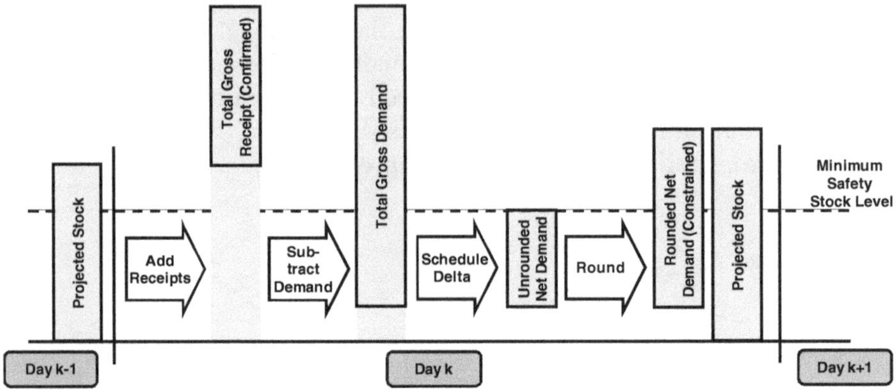

Fig. 8.3. Steps for the Net Requirements Calculation

The projected stock is either a positive value or zero. If the total gross demand is not covered by the projected stock of the previous period plus the confirmed gross receipts of the current period, a supply shortage occurs. This could be the case if the gross demand increases within the freeze horizon or if the stability rules prevent covering the demand. In this case the supply shortage of the previous period is used instead of the projected stock as shown in figure 8.4.

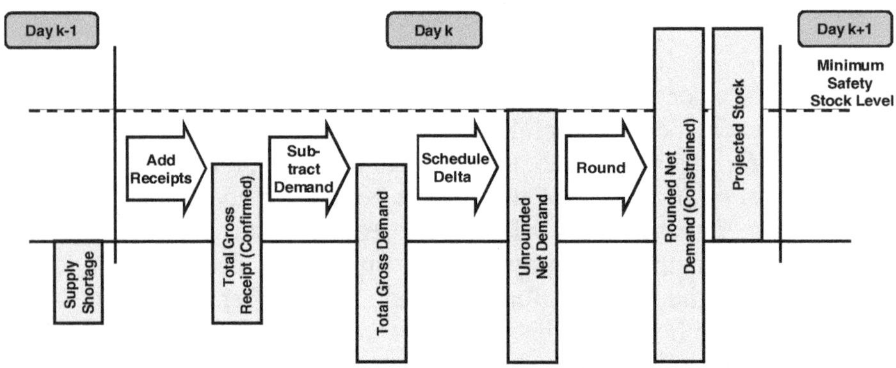

Fig. 8.4. Steps for the Net Requirements Calculation – Starting with a Supply Shortage

Each of the quantities in figure 8.3 and 8.4 is displayed in the DRP matrix as a separate key figure.

• *Key Figures*

The DRP matrix is displayed with the transaction /SAPAPO/SPPDRPM and provides an overview about the planning situation for a product in one location. The virtual child is considered as a different location to the parent location. The DRP matrix contains key figures with the demand, supply and inventory information as shown in figure 8.5.

Key figures	Overdue	12.09.2005	13.09.2005	14.09.2005	15.09.2005	16.09.2005	19.09.2005
+Total Gross Demand	39.910,000		230,000	18,000	4,000	4,000	
+Total Gross Receipt (Confirmed)							
Initial warehouse stock	40.000,000						
Projected Stock	90	90		382	378	374	374
Supply Shortage			140,000				
+Planned Minimum Safety Stock Level		254,387	254,387	254,387	254,387	254,387	254,387
Minimum Net Demand							
Unrounded Net Demand (Adapted)				412,387			
+Rounded Net Demand (Constrained)				540,000			
Economic Order Quantity	270,000	270,000	270,000	270,000	270,000	270,000	270,000

Fig. 8.5. DRP Matrix

The '*rounded ret demand (constrained)*' (RND) represents the supply – either as a schedule line from the supplier or as a planned distribution receipt. The 'rounded net demand (constrained)' is calculated by applying the rounding profile, the stability rules and the supplier shut down to the '*unrounded net demand (adapted)*' (UND). The 'unrounded net demand (adapted)' already considers the lead time and is calculated for the period k as the '*planned minimum safety stock level*' (MSSL) plus the '*total gross demand*' (TGD) and the '*supply shortage*' (SH) of the previous period (e.g. due to lead time) minus the '*projected stock*' (PS) of the previous period and the '*total gross receipts (confirmed)*' (TGR) as described in formula 8.1.

$$\text{UND}(k) = \text{MSSL}(k) + \text{TGD}(k) + \text{SH}(k-1) - \text{PS}(k-1) - \text{TGR}(k) \qquad (8.1)$$
$$\forall\, k \geq \text{Lead Time}$$

Either the projected stock or the supply shortage is zero. The 'unrounded net demand (adapted)' and therefore also the 'rounded net demand (constrained)' is placed at the last day of the lead time. Before that the 'unrounded net demand (adapted)' is zero. The reason for this is that the net demand has the meaning of a supply in the DRP matrix, and it is not possible to get a new supply within the lead time.

The total gross demand includes the forecast, fixed demands, substitution demand, distribution demand and customer demand, figure 8.6.

Key figures	Overdue	12.09.2005	13.09.2005	14.09.2005	15.09.2005	16.09.2005
-Total Gross Demand	39.910,000		230,000	18,000	4,000	4,000
-Corrected Forecast						
Forecast						
Fixed Demand (Overriding)						
-Substitution Demand						
1:1 Subsitution						
Substitution of Remanufactured Products						
Forwarding of Excess from/to CP						
-Fixed Demand (Non-Overriding)	10,000		230,000	18,000	4,000	4,000
Prioritized Fixed Demand (Non-Overrid.)						
Non-Prioritized Fixed Demand (Non-Over.)	10,000		230,000	18,000	4,000	4,000
Anticipated Demand						
+Planned Distribution Demand						
Confirmed Distribution Demand						
Open Customer Demand	39.900,000					

© SAP AG

Fig. 8.6. DRP Matrix – Total Gross Demand

The fixed demands might override or add to the forecast – this depends on the category of the fixed demand (see chapter 8.2.4 about fixed requirements). The distribution demand contains both the planned distribution demand (as the result of the DRP run) and the confirmed distribution demand (as the result of deployment or inventory balancing). Customer demand is considered as open customer demand if it is in the past or if it is a future dated order (FDO, see chapter 8.2.2 about forecast vs. customer requirements).

-Total Gross Receipt (Confirmed)						
+Substitution Receipt						
Fixed Receipt						
Anticipated Demand Coverage						
Distribution Receipt fr. BOD (Confirmed)						
Distr. Receipt from Supplier (Frozen)						
In Transit						

© SAP AG

Fig. 8.7. DRP Matrix – Total Gross Receipt

The total gross receipts contain mainly the fixed receipts (these are negative fixed requirements), the confirmed distribution receipts ('distribution receipt from BOD'), the planned procurement from the supplier within the freeze horizon ('distribution receipt from supplier (frozen)'), interactively fixed receipts and the stock in transit – both from the supplier and from a supplying location within the network, figure 8.7.

• *DRP Matrix Usability*

Within the DRP matrix it is possible to simulate the DRP run, but the result can not be saved. It is not possible to perform an interactive planning in the DRP matrix – to add requirements or receipts the functionality for fixed requirements has to be used.

Using the push buttons shown in figure 8.8 it is possible to display the actual stock, the EOQ and the EOQ periods of demand which are used for the rounding to days of supply (see chapter 8.2.3).

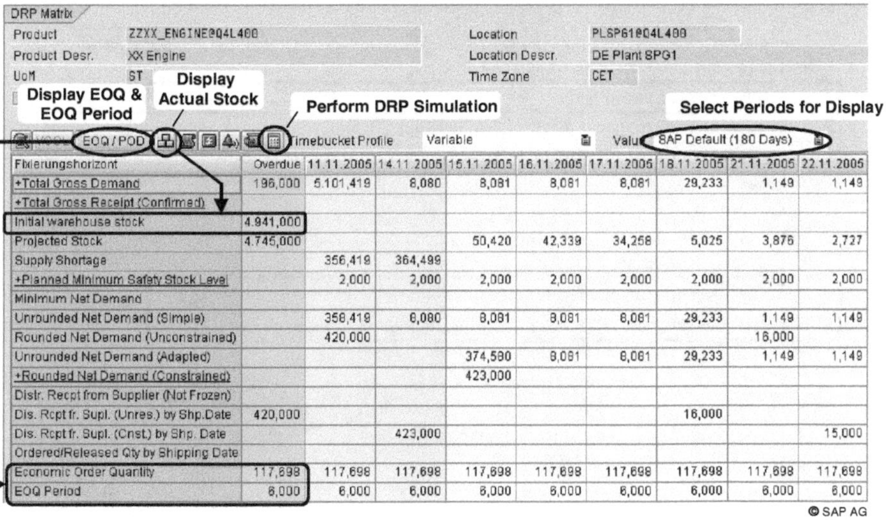

Fixierungshorizont	Overdue	11.11.2005	14.11.2005	15.11.2005	16.11.2005	17.11.2005	18.11.2005	21.11.2005	22.11.2005
+Total Gross Demand	196,000	5.101,419	8,080	8,081	8,081	8,081	29,233	1,149	1,149
+Total Gross Receipt (Confirmed)									
Initial warehouse stock	4.941,000								
Projected Stock	4.745,000			50,420	42,339	34,258	5,025	3,876	2,727
Supply Shortage		356,419	364,499						
+Planned Minimum Safety Stock Level		2,000	2,000	2,000	2,000	2,000	2,000	2,000	2,000
Minimum Net Demand									
Unrounded Net Demand (Simple)		358,419	8,080	8,081	8,081	8,081	29,233	1,149	1,149
Rounded Net Demand (Unconstrained)		420,000						16,000	
Unrounded Net Demand (Adapted)				374,580	8,081	8,081	29,233	1,149	1,149
+Rounded Net Demand (Constrained)				423,000					
Distr. Recpt from Supplier (Not Frozen)									
Dis. Rcpt fr. Supl. (Unres.) by Shp.Date	420,000						16,000		
Dis. Rcpt fr. Supl. (Cnst.) by Shp. Date			423,000						15,000
Ordered/Released Qty by Shipping Date									
Economic Order Quantity	117,698	117,698	117,698	117,698	117,698	117,698	117,698	117,698	117,698
EOQ Period	6,000	6,000	6,000	6,000	6,000	6,000	6,000	6,000	6,000

Fig. 8.8. DRP Matrix Usability

Using a different value for the variable time bucket profile it is possible to gain an aggregated view of the plan, figure 8.9.

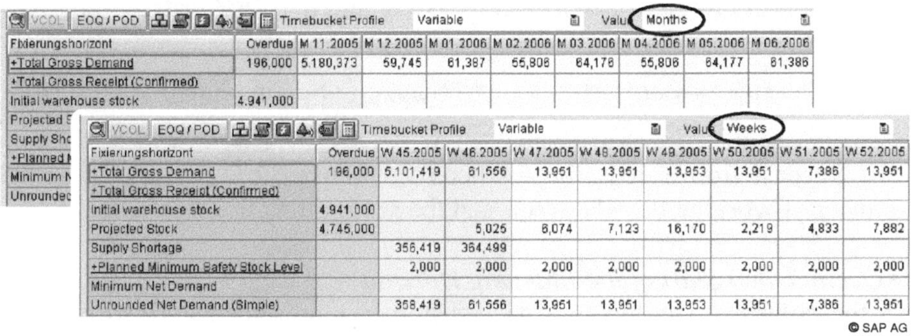

Fixierungshorizont	Overdue	M 11.2005	M 12.2005	M 01.2006	M 02.2006	M 03.2006	M 04.2006	M 05.2006	M 06.2006
+Total Gross Demand	196,000	5.180,373	59,745	61,387	55,808	64,178	55,806	64,177	61,386
+Total Gross Receipt (Confirmed)									
Initial warehouse stock	4.941,000								

Fixierungshorizont	Overdue	W 45.2005	W 46.2005	W 47.2005	W 48.2005	W 49.2005	W 50.2005	W 51.2005	W 52.2005
+Total Gross Demand	196,000	5.101,419	61,556	13,951	13,951	13,953	13,951	7,386	13,951
+Total Gross Receipt (Confirmed)									
Initial warehouse stock	4.941,000								
Projected Stock	4.745,000		5,025	6,074	7,123	16,170	2,219	4,833	7,882
Supply Shortage		356,419	364,499						
+Planned Minimum Safety Stock Level		2,000	2,000	2,000	2,000	2,000	2,000	2,000	2,000
Minimum Net Demand									
Unrounded Net Demand (Simple)		358,419	61,556	13,951	13,951	13,953	13,951	7,386	13,951

Fig. 8.9. Time Bucket Profiles for the DRP Matrix

When comparing the monthly values for the forecast in the DRP matrix with the forecasting planning book, it is likely to notice differences. These are due to the scaling of the forecast – forecasting assumes a constant number of working days per month (or per fiscal year period). This scaling factor is defined with the customising path *APO → Supply Chain Planning → SPP → Forecasting → Make General Settings Demand History* (see also chapter 3.2). The default scaling factor for months and fiscal year periods is 21 as shown in figure 8.10 (see also chapter 3.2.2).

General Settings for Demand History

Parameters	Parameter Value
Rules-Based ATP: Action Type	A
Calendar for Scaling	DP
Indicator: Lock Logic for BI InfoProvider	X
Indicator: Lock Logic for Creation/Maintenance of Hist. Dat	X
Indicator: Master Data Check (Boolean: ' ' Off / 'X' - On)	
Number of Re-Trys for Lock Logic	5
Pack Size for Reading/Writing InfoProv. (No. of Entries)	10000
Fiscal Year Variant	SP
Scaling Factor for Months (Number of Workdays)	21
Scaling Factor Business Year/Period (Number of Workdays)	21
Scaling Factor for Weeks (Number of Workdays)	5
Rules-based ATP: Technical Scenario	AA
Waiting Time: Lock Logic for BI InfoProvider (in Seconds)	10
Waiting Time: Lock Logic for Historical Data (in Seconds)	10
WDAYS_REQ	30

Fig. 8.10. Scaling Factor for Number of Workdays in Forecasting

The forecast from forecasting is divided by this scaling factor and transferred as daily forecast to the DRP matrix – but now for each working day according to the calendar for scaling. Formula 8.2 describes the difference in the monthly forecast between forecasting and the DRP matrix.

$$\text{Forecast}_{\text{DRP}} = \text{Forecast}_{\text{Forecasting}} * (\text{N}_{\text{Workdays}} / \text{Scaling Factor}) \qquad (8.2)$$

The forecast from forecasting is therefore adjusted by the ratio of actual number of working days $\text{N}_{\text{Workdays}}$ and the scaling factor.

• *Overdue and Start of the Planning Horizon*

In the column 'overdue' the past customer requirements, fixed requirements that are not yet expired, past distribution demand and confirmed receipts are displayed. Since there is no forecast consumption in service parts planning, past forecast does not contribute to the overdue requirements. Whether the current date is displayed as 'overdue' or as the first future (i.e. planned) column depends on the start of the planning horizon, figure 8.11.

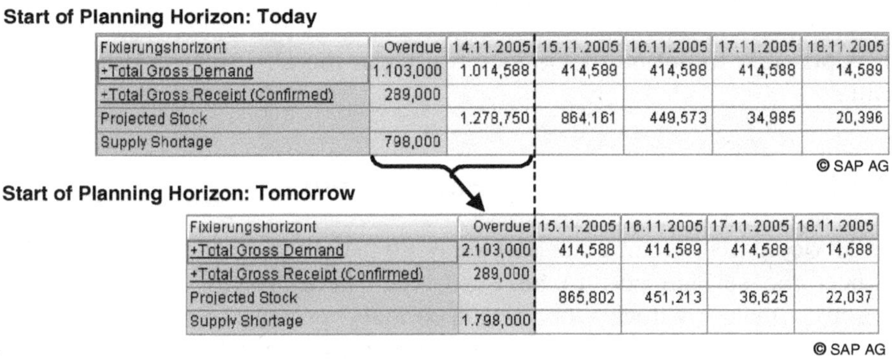

Start of Planning Horizon: Today

Fixierungshorizont	Overdue	14.11.2005	15.11.2005	16.11.2005	17.11.2005	18.11.2005
+Total Gross Demand	1.103,000	1.014,588	414,589	414,588	414,588	14,589
+Total Gross Receipt (Confirmed)	289,000					
Projected Stock		1.278,750	864,161	449,573	34,985	20,396
Supply Shortage	798,000					

Start of Planning Horizon: Tomorrow

Fixierungshorizont	Overdue	15.11.2005	16.11.2005	17.11.2005	18.11.2005
+Total Gross Demand	2.103,000	414,588	414,589	414,588	14,588
+Total Gross Receipt (Confirmed)	289,000				
Projected Stock		865,802	451,213	36,625	22,037
Supply Shortage	1.798,000				

Fig. 8.11. Overdue and Start of the Planning Horizon

In the example shown in figure 8.11 the current day is 14th of November. For this day a demand of 1014.588 is due and a demand of 1103 is already overdue. If the start of the planning horizon is set to 'tomorrow', the current day is considered already as past and the demands for the current day are considered as overdue. Therefore the overdue demand increases to 2103 (the missing 14.588 are the forecast for the current day, and the 'past' forecast does not contribute to the overdue demand).

The start of the planning horizon is defined in the DRP service profile (customising path *APO → Supply Chain Planning → SPP → DRP → Define Service Profile for DRP*), figure 8.12.

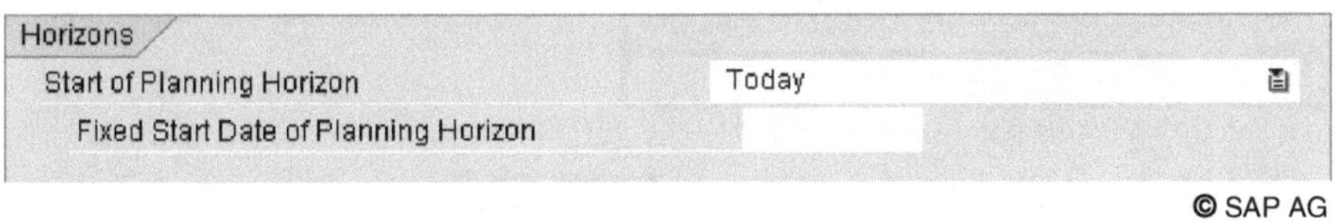

Fig. 8.12. Parameter for the Start of the Planning Horizon in the DRP Service Profile

The DRP service profile which is relevant for the DRP matrix is defined with the customising path *SCM Basis → Planning Service Manager → Assign Standard Service Profiles for UI*, figure 8.13.

Assign Standard Service Profiles for UI

User	Planning Service	Mode	Service Profile
DICKERSBACH	SPP_DRP		XX_DRP_WO_APPROVAL

© SAP AG

Fig. 8.13. Service Profile for the DRP Matrix

It is possible to define the service profile in the DRP matrix user specifically.

8.2.2 Forecast vs. Customer Requirements

In service parts planning the customers do usually not order in advance but expect the service part to be available. Therefore the SPP solution is mainly a make-to-stock – or more accurately: procure-to-stock – business, and the driver for the execution is the forecast and not the sales order. As a first approximation sales orders are irrelevant for service parts planning.

There are however some exceptions where customers place orders quite some time in advance. The approach of the service parts planning solution is to consider these separately: These 'future dated orders' (FDO) are not considered in the demand history and are therefore not covered by forecasting. Instead these orders add to the total gross demand. Whether a sales order is considered as a future dated order depends on the difference between the required delivery date and the order date. The threshold in days for this difference is defined with the customising path *APO → Supply Chain Planning → SPP → Basic Settings → Make Settings for Customer Demand*, figure 8.14 (see also chapter 3.2.2).

© SAP AG

Fig. 8.14. Consideration of Customer Requirements

The flag for FDO is set to the sales order by the ATP check during the transfer to SAP APO™.

8.2.3 Rounding to Days of Supply

The order quantity is rounded to days of supply using the economic order quantity (EOQ) or the EOQ periods of demand (POD). Though the EOQ is an absolute value and is used in DRP to determine the order quantity, it is derived from a days of supply calculation in inventory planning. Both EOQ and EOQ periods of demand are calculated by the EOQ and safety stock service and stored in the 'inventory planning'-view of the product master, figure 8.15. If a non-constant safety stock model is used, only the values for the first period are stored in the product master. In this case the planning book for inventory planning (transaction /SAPAPO/SPPINVP) has to be used in order to get an overview of the time dependent values (see chapter 6.3).

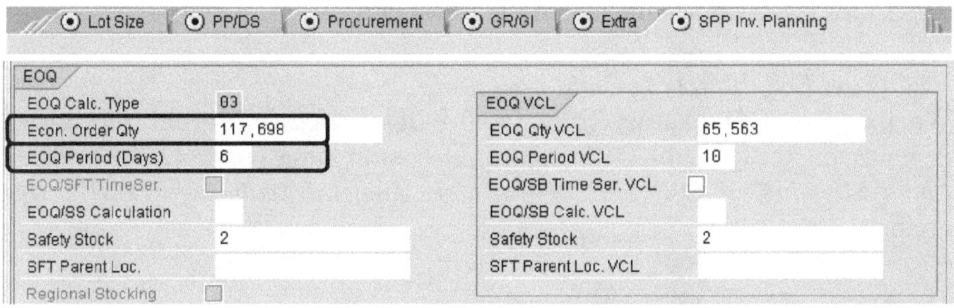

Fig. 8.15. EOQ and EOQ Periods of Demand (POD) in the Product Master

The lot size information in the 'lot size'-view of the product master is ignored. Whether the EOQ quantity or the EOQ POD is used depends on different settings for the entry location and the child locations.

• *EOQ vs. EOQ POD for Entry Locations*

Whether the EOQ quantity or the EOQ POD is used for the child locations depends on the setting in the 'SPP inventory planning'-view of the product master at the entry location, figure 8.16.

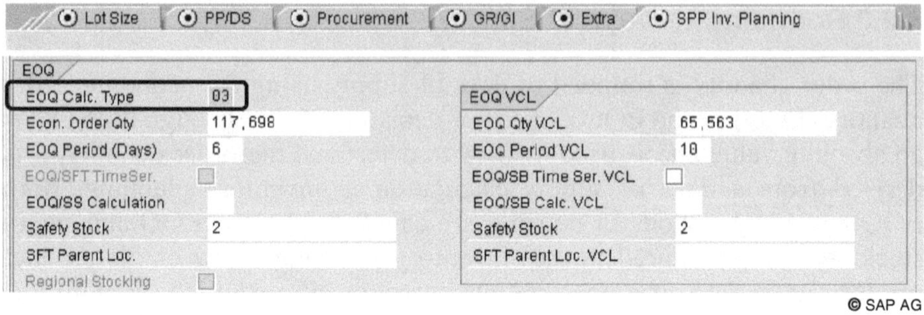

Fig. 8.16. Use of EOQ or EOQ POD for the Entry Location

The value '01' (EOQ manually locked) causes that the EOQ is used at the entry location, while the values '02' (EOQ period manually locked) and '03' (not locked) cause the use of the EOQ POD.

• *EOQ vs. EOQ POD for Child Locations*
Whether the EOQ quantity or the EOQ POD is used for the child locations depends on the general DRP setting in customising (path *APO → Supply Chain Planning → SPP → DRP → Make General Settings for DRP*), figure 8.17.

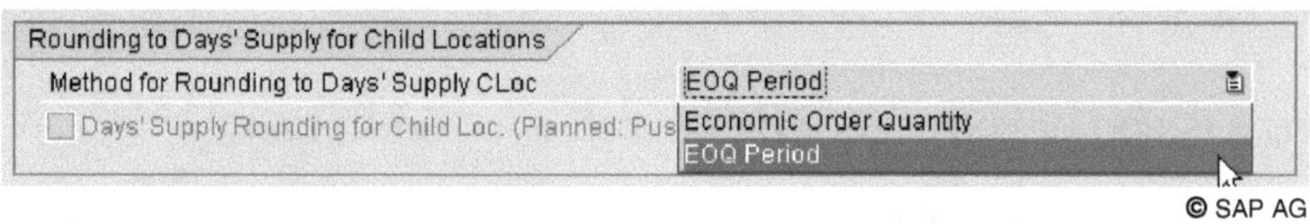

Fig. 8.17. Use of EOQ or EOQ POD for Child Locations

Figure 8.18 shows an example for the planning result when using the EOQ POD for rounding to days' supply. The first net demand occurs on the 15.11.2005. Since the EOQ POD at that date is 5, the net demand of the next 5 days is ordered. The EOQ quantity and the EOQ POD are displayed in the DRP matrix with the button 'EOQ/POD'.

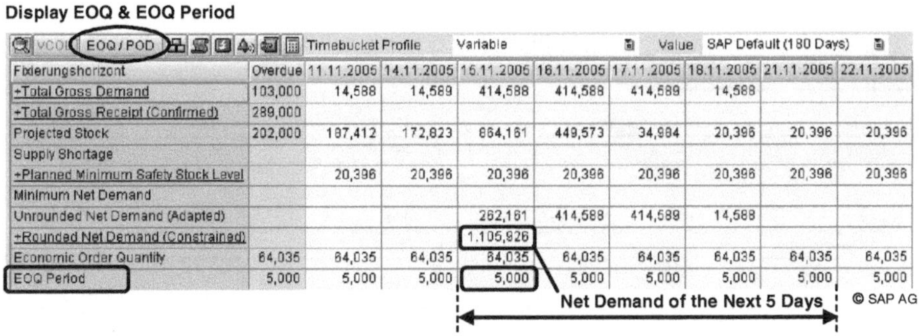

Fixierungshorizont	Overdue	11.11.2005	14.11.2005	15.11.2005	16.11.2005	17.11.2005	18.11.2005	21.11.2005	22.11.2005
+Total Gross Demand	103,000	14,588	14,589	414,588	414,588	414,589	14,588		
+Total Gross Receipt (Confirmed)	289,000								
Projected Stock	202,000	187,412	172,823	864,161	449,573	34,984	20,396	20,396	20,396
Supply Shortage									
+Planned Minimum Safety Stock Level		20,396	20,396	20,396	20,396	20,396	20,396	20,396	20,396
Minimum Net Demand									
Unrounded Net Demand (Adapted)				262,161	414,588	414,589	14,588		
+Rounded Net Demand (Constrained)				1.105,926					
Economic Order Quantity	64,035	64,035	64,035	64,035	64,035	64,035	64,035	64,035	64,035
EOQ Period	5,000	5,000	5,000	5,000	5,000	5,000	5,000	5,000	5,000

Fig. 8.18. Result of the DRP Run with Rounding to the EOQ Periods of Demand

8.2.4 Fixed Requirements

It is not possible to perform an interactive planning in DRP in the sense of changing the orders proposed by DRP in the DRP matrix. Planned distribution orders can not be changed at all, but it is possible to create additional fixed requirements with the transaction /SAPAPO/SPPFIXREQ, figure 8.19.

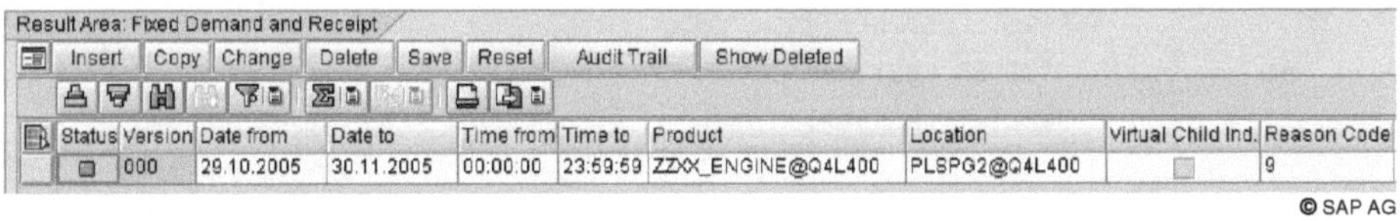

Status	Version	Date from	Date to	Time from	Time to	Product	Location	Virtual Child Ind.	Reason Code
	000	29.10.2005	30.11.2005	00:00:00	23:59:59	ZZXX_ENGINE@Q4L400	PLSPG2@Q4L400		9

Fig. 8.19. Fixed Requirement

The fixed requirement contains information e.g. about the quantity and the dates (from and to), the reason code and the demand type as shown in the details of the fixed requirement, figure 8.20. Two dates are maintained: the 'date from' is the due date and the 'date to' controls how long the fixed requirement will remain in the 'overdue'-column.

There are three fixed demand types: No priority, priority and override. The difference between a 'priority' and a 'no priority' fixed requirement is its prioritisation during tier processing in deployment, see chapter 10.4. Both types add to the existing demands. A fixed requirement of the type 'override' however will replace the forecast demand.

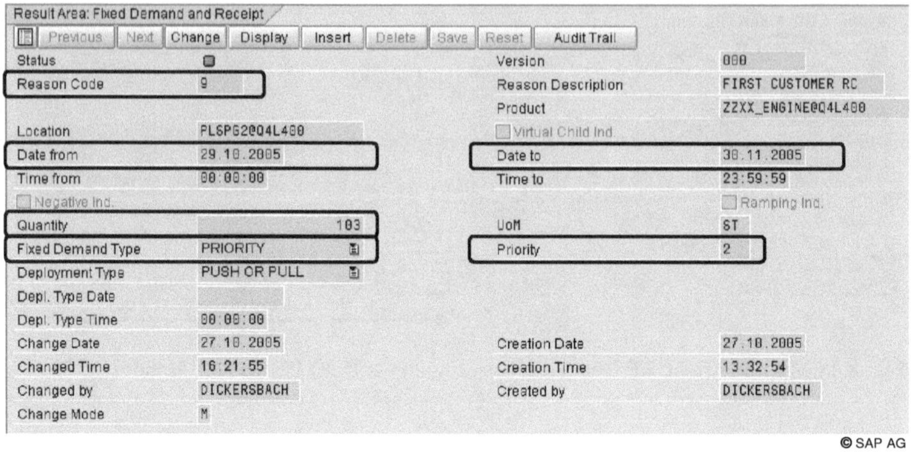

Fig. 8.20. Details of the Fixed Requirements

The reason code is a mandatory field for the creation of a fixed requirement. It is defined with the customising path *APO → Supply Chain Planning → SPP → DRP → Define Reason Codes for Fixed Demand*, figure 8.21.

SPP: Reason Code for Fixed Demands

Reason Code	Description	Non-Changeable Fixed Demand / Receipt
9	FIRST CUSTOMER RC	☐
91	ANOTHER CUSTOMER RC	☐
96	QUALITY INSPECTION	☐

© SAP AG

Fig. 8.21. Reason Code for Fixed Requirements

The fixed requirements can be changed in date and quantity. To track these changes an audit trail exists for each fixed requirement, figure 8.22.

Audit Trail

Date from	Date to	T	T	Quantity	UoM	R...	Ne...	Fixed Dem...	Priority	Deployment Type	D...	De...	Changed by	Change Date	Changed Time
29.10.2005	30.11.2005	0(	2:	103	ST	☐	☐	PRIORITY	2	PUSH OR PULL		00:0	DICKERSBA	27.10.2005	16:21:55
29.10.2005	30.11.2005	0(	2:	93	ST	☐	☐	PRIORITY	2	PUSH OR PULL		00:0	DICKERSBA	27.10.2005	14:29:52
29.11.2005	30.11.2005	0(	2:	93	ST	☐	☐	PRIORITY	2	PUSH OR PULL		00:0	DICKERSBA	27.10.2005	14:29:38
02.11.2005	30.11.2005	0(	2:	93	ST	☐	☐	PRIORITY	2	PUSH OR PULL		00:0	DICKERSBA	27.10.2005	13:32:54

© SAP AG

Fig. 8.22. Audit Trail for Fixed Requirements

8.3 Scheduling

The tasks for the scheduling in DRP are the determination of the lead times between the supply chain partners (e.g. between supplier and location or between two locations) and the consideration of calendars. Capacity constraints are not considered.

• *Scheduling Settings in the DRP General Settings*
In the general settings for DRP (customising path *APO → Supply Chain Planning → SPP → DRP → Make General Settings for DRP*) it is defined which calendar is used for the scheduling of the planned stock transfers and schedule lines, and whether a total procurement lead time or a more detailed component procurement lead time is used for the scheduling of stock transfers, figure 8.23.

With the definition of calendars it is defined whether the planning calendar for SPP is used or separate calendars, i.e. the shipping calendar or the source locations, the transportation calendar of the transportation lane and the receiving calendar of the target location. The definition of the different calendars for the location is described in chapter 2.1.4.

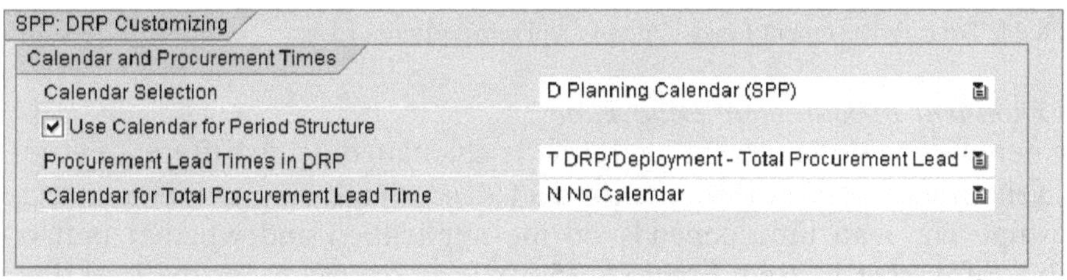

© SAP AG

Fig. 8.23. General DRP Settings for Scheduling

There are two ways how to calculate the lead times in DRP. One is to use the total procurement lead time in the transportation lane, the other is to calculate the lead time based on different entries of the transportation lane, the product master and the procurement relationship (component lead time). The setting 'procurement lead times in DRP' defines which is used. This definition is per client.

• *Total Procurement Lead Time*
The total procurement lead time is maintained in the transportation lane (transaction /SAPAPO/SCC_TL1) on the 'means of transport'- level, figure 8.24.

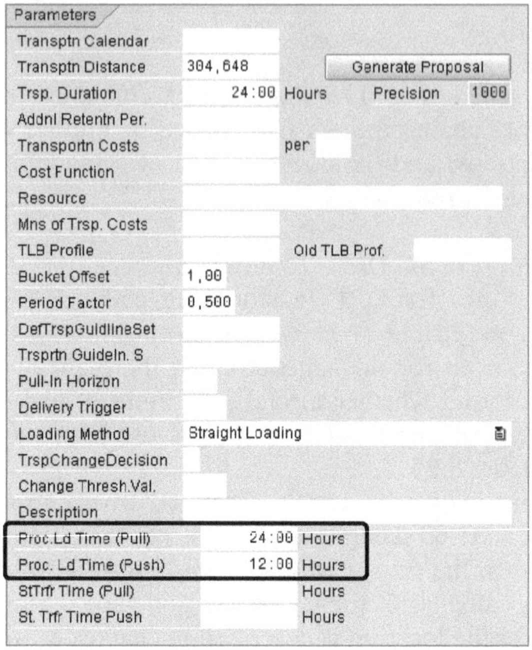

Fig. 8.24. Total Procurement Lead Time in the Transportation Lane

• *Component Procurement Lead Time*

The component procurement lead time is calculated using different entries from the transportation lane, the product master and the procurement relationship. The lead time depends on the application and whether pull or push deployment is used. Figure 8.25 gives an overview for the lead time elements from a supplier to the entry location and between a parent and a child location for the pull and the push deployment case.

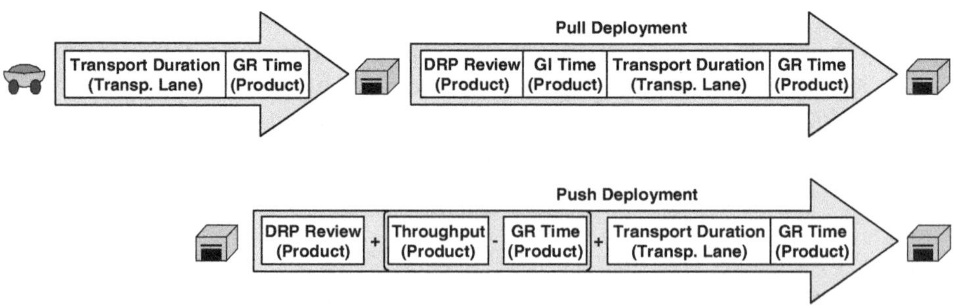

Fig. 8.25. Lead Time Components for Pull Deployment and for Push Deployment

In this figure we presume that the default scheduling settings are used. Though it is possible to configure the lead times in customising, it is strongly recommended not to make any changes. For each lead time between two partners of the supply chain (e.g. location to location, supplier to location, …) a scheduling scenario exists (to be precise, one scenario for pull deployment and one for push deployment). To this scheduling scenario a procurement lead time group ID is assigned. This procurement lead time group ID is freely defined and contains one or more elements ('sequence') which define the lead time. Figure 8.26 shows the structure of the lead time customising.

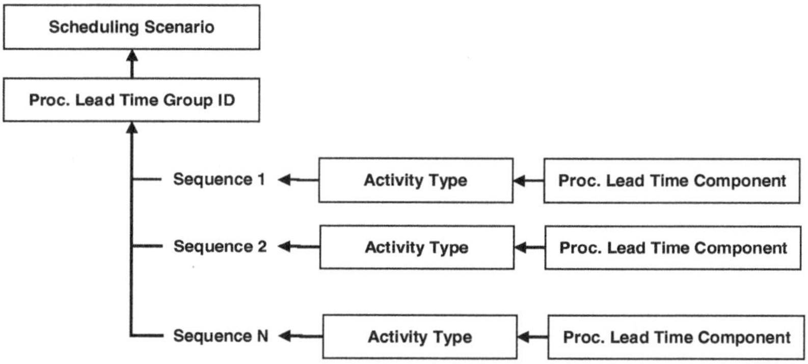

Fig. 8.26. Structure of the Lead Time Customising

The activity type defines which kind of activity contributes to the lead time. Possible values are order processing, goods receipt, shipment, goods issue and production. The procurement lead time component defines which master data entry is used or whether a synchronisation with a calendar is performed. The customising settings are maintained with the path *APO → Supply Chain Planning → SPP → Basic Settings → Configure Scheduling*, figure 8.27.

Scheduling Scenarios

Scheduling Scenario	Status	Procurement Lead Time Group ID
DRP/Depl. Matrix: Supplier to Entry Location	SAP Standard	SYNC,C6,C8
DRP/Depl. Matrix Location to Location (Push)	SAP Standard	C2DEPL+(C7-C8),C6,C8
DRP/Depl. Matrix: Location to Location (Pull)	SAP Standard	C2DEPL+C4,C6,C8
DRP/Depl. Matrix: Location for Virtual Child Loc	SAP Standard	NULL
DRP/Depl. Matrix: Location for Virtual Child Loc	SAP Standard	NULL

Fig. 8.27. Configuration of the Scheduling Scenarios

For the procurement lead time group there is a naming convention: the components – i.e. the master data fields – are abbreviated as C2, C4 etc. The correspondences for the master data fields are listed in table 8.2. The procurement lead time group IDs are named with the content of their components.

Figure 8.28 shows the activity types and the procurement lead time components for the example of the location to location lead time in case of pull deployment (procurement lead time group ID ‘C2DEPL+C4, C6, C8’).

Procurement Lead Time Groups

Procurement Lead Time Group ID	Sequence	Activity Type	Procurement Lead Time Component
C2DEPL+C4,C6,C8	1	Goods Issue	Plan Approval and Review (Depl.) + GI; Ship-From Location
C2DEPL+C4,C6,C8	2	Shipment	Transport Duration
C2DEPL+C4,C6,C8	3	Goods Receipt	Goods Receipt Processing Time; Ship-To Location

Fig. 8.28. Configuration of the Component Lead Times

The elements C2, C2DEPL, C3, C4, C6, C7, C8, F and PLIFZ correspond to fields in the master data. Table 8.2 lists the correspondence between the elements and the master data fields. The elements C3, F, PH and PLIFZ are used for the calculation of horizons for DRP (see chapter 8.4). The component lead time consists of different terms that are separated by commas. Each term is scheduled according to its own calendar (e.g. shipping calendar, receiving calendar) and is either a positive value or zero. SYNC means that the scheduled date of the previous term is synchronised with the calendar and might be rescheduled. The terms are added.

Table 8.2. Lead Time Relevant Fields

Element	Field Name	Master Data	View
C2	Review-Time (Depl.)	Product	SPP Deployment
C2DEPL	Review-Time (DRP)	Product	SPP DRP
C3	Communication Duration	Transport Lane	Header
C4	GI Processing Time	Product	GR/GI
C6	Transport Duration	Transport Lane	Means of Transport
C7	Throughput Time	Product	SPP DRP
C8	GR Processing Time	Product	GR/GI
F	Correct. Of Fix Period	Transport Lane	Header
PH	Partner Horizon	Transport Lane	Product
PLIFZ	Planned Delivery Time	Procurement Relationship	

Figure 8.29 shows the lead time relevant fields of the product master.

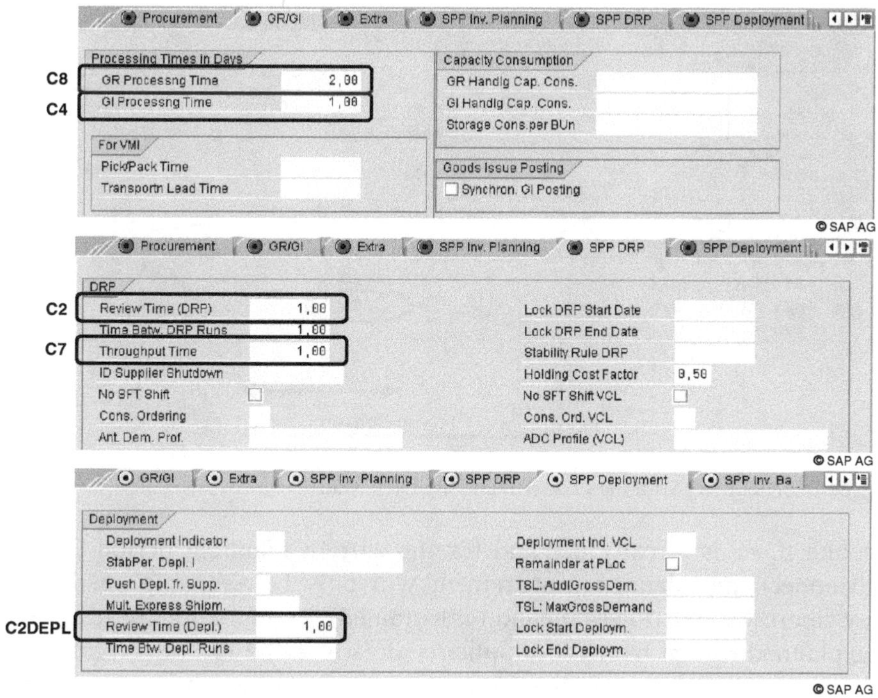

Fig. 8.29. Lead Time Relevant Fields in the Product Master

The transport duration in the transportation lane is maintained in the view for the means of transport as shown later in figure 8.35.

• *Scheduling and Demand Date*

Scheduling is required in order to determine the demand date of a planned stock transfer at the entry location. This applies both to a planned stock transfer or a planned procurement. Figure 8.30 shows an example for a planned procurement from a supplier.

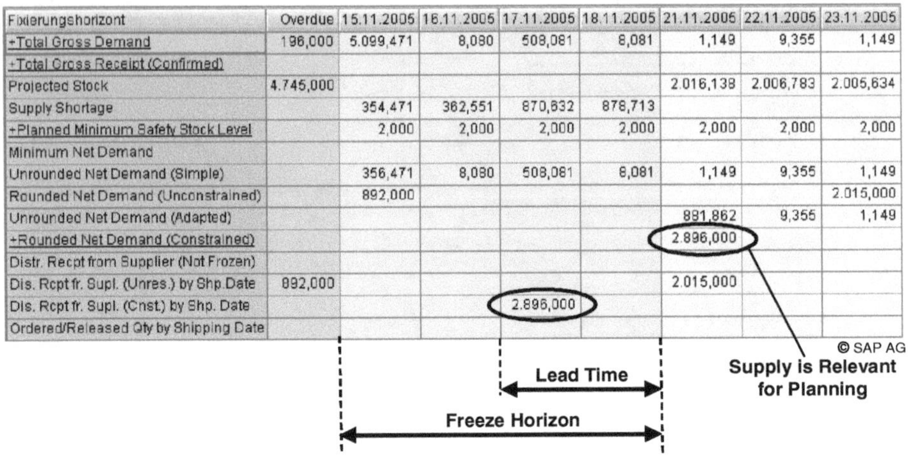

Fixierungshorizont	Overdue	15.11.2005	16.11.2005	17.11.2005	18.11.2005	21.11.2005	22.11.2005	23.11.2005
+Total Gross Demand	196,000	5.099,471	8,080	508,081	8,081	1,149	9,355	1,149
+Total Gross Receipt (Confirmed)								
Projected Stock	4.745,000					2.016,138	2.006,783	2.005,634
Supply Shortage		354,471	362,551	870,632	878,713			
+Planned Minimum Safety Stock Level		2,000	2,000	2,000	2,000	2,000	2,000	2,000
Minimum Net Demand								
Unrounded Net Demand (Simple)		356,471	8,080	508,081	8,081	1,149	9,355	1,149
Rounded Net Demand (Unconstrained)		892,000						2.015,000
Unrounded Net Demand (Adapted)						881,862	9,355	1,149
+Rounded Net Demand (Constrained)						2.896,000		
Distr. Recpt from Supplier (Not Frozen)								
Dis. Rcpt fr. Supl. (Unres.) by Shp.Date	892,000					2.015,000		
Dis. Rcpt fr. Supl. (Cnst.) by Shp. Date				2.896,000				
Ordered/Released Qty by Shipping Date								

Fig. 8.30. Scheduling with the Lead Time in the DRP Matrix

Though there is already demand for the current planning period (15th of November), the planned procurement will only be available on the 21st (key figure 'rounded net demand (constrained)') – just after the lead time. The planned receipt from the supplier is already at the 17th (key figure 'distribution receipt from supplier (constrained)'), but does not yet resolve the shortage since goods receipt is not yet performed. The difference between the net demand and the supply quantity is due to the EOQ.

• *Scheduling Simulation and Explanation*

For a better understanding of the scheduling results it is possible to simulate scheduling for any scheduling scenario for a service part between two locations with the transaction /SAPAPO/SPP_SCHD_EXP. Figure 8.31 shows the result for the scheduling scenario 2 (DRP lead time location to location for pull deployment) between the locations PLSPG1@RME801 and PLSPG2@RME801. The individual parts of this scheduling scenario – C2DEPL + C4, C6, C8 as shown in figure 8.28 – are listed with their durations. In this example the duration of each part is 24 h.

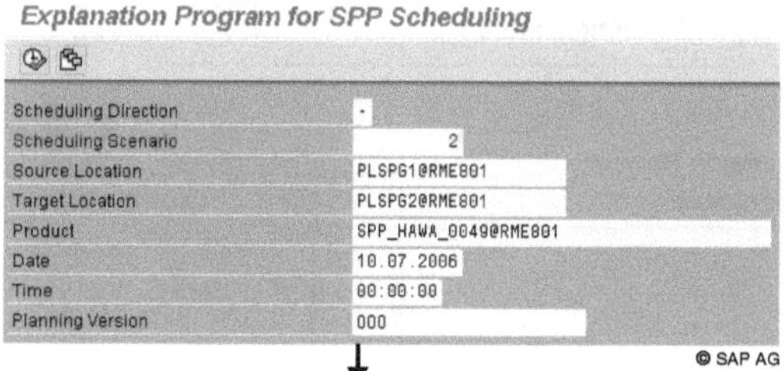

	Activity Type	Procurement Lead Time Component	Duration	Calendar	Time Stamp	PLSPG1@RME801 ==>>	PLSPG2@RME801
Entry Time Stamp					20.060.709.220.000	10.07.2006 00:00:00 (CET)	10.07.2006 00:00:00 (CET)
3	GR	C8R	24:00:00		20.060.708.220.000	9.07.2006 00:00:00 (CET)	9.07.2006 00:00:00 (CET)
2	TRAN	C6	24:00:00		20.060.707.220.000	8.07.2006 00:00:00 (CET)	8.07.2006 00:00:00 (CET)
1	GI	C2D+C4	24:00:00		20.060.706.220.000	7.07.2006 00:00:00 (CET)	7.07.2006 00:00:00 (CET)
Result Time Stamp					20.060.706.220.000	7.07.2006 00:00:00 (CET)	7.07.2006 00:00:00 (CET)

Fig. 8.31. Scheduling Simulation and Explanation

The scheduling direction is set with '–' as backward and with '+' as forward.

8.4 Horizons

The DRP planning run creates, changes and deletes planned stock transfers and schedule lines (respectively purchase requisitions). Depending on how far in the future the order changes are due, not all changes are desired. Horizons are used to restrict the automatic planning changes. For DRP the following four horizons are relevant:

- Freeze horizon: The freeze horizon represents the physical lead time of the supplier plus the plan review time, the communication time and the buffer for the correction of the fixed period.
- Limited freeze horizon: The limited freeze horizon represents additionally the production time of the supplier without the buffer for the correction of the fixed period.
- Plan submission horizon: Within the plan submission horizon the scheduling releases are transferred to the supplier (BAdI required, see chapter 9.6)
- Planning horizon: DRP planning is only performed within this horizon.

These horizons are determined by different master data settings – similar to the lead time. Figure 8.32 shows these four horizons.

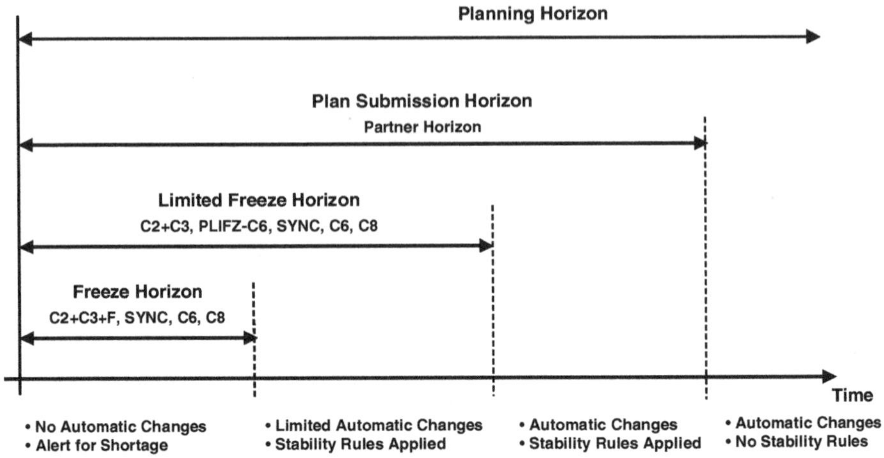

Fig. 8.32. Horizons and Stability Rules

The planning horizon is restricted using the parameter 'planning horizon' in the product specific view of the transportation lane. Given the default customising, the three horizons are defined by the master data entries shown in figure 8.33.

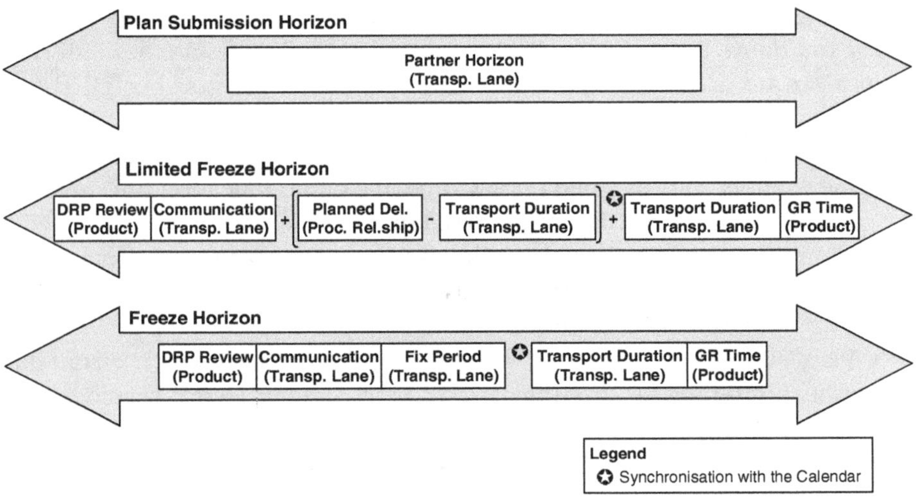

Fig. 8.33. Lead Time Components for the Horizons

The notation for the limited freeze horizon differs from the other ones. The term 'planned delivery time (procurement relationship) – transport duration (transportation lane)' is a positive value or zero, and it is scheduled separately. Therefore it is not possible to simplify the formula for the limited freeze horizon.

In the DRP matrix the freeze horizon and the limited freeze horizon are displayed in grey resp. yellow, figure 8.34.

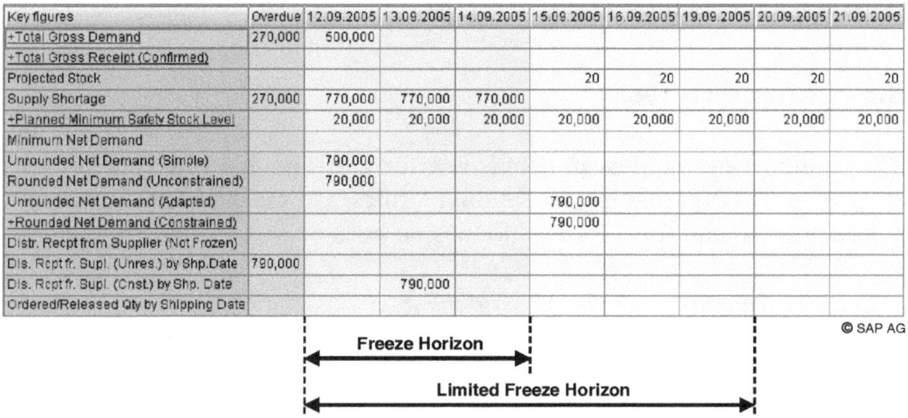

Key figures	Overdue	12.09.2005	13.09.2005	14.09.2005	15.09.2005	16.09.2005	19.09.2005	20.09.2005	21.09.2005
+Total Gross Demand	270,000	500,000							
+Total Gross Receipt (Confirmed)									
Projected Stock					20	20	20	20	20
Supply Shortage	270,000	770,000	770,000	770,000					
+Planned Minimum Safety Stock Level		20,000	20,000	20,000	20,000	20,000	20,000	20,000	20,000
Minimum Net Demand									
Unrounded Net Demand (Simple)		790,000							
Rounded Net Demand (Unconstrained)		790,000							
Unrounded Net Demand (Adapted)					790,000				
+Rounded Net Demand (Constrained)					790,000				
Distr. Recpt from Supplier (Not Frozen)									
Dis. Rcpt fr. Supl. (Unres.) by Shp.Date	790,000								
Dis. Rcpt fr. Supl. (Cnst.) by Shp. Date			790,000						
Ordered/Released Qty by Shipping Date									

Fig. 8.34. Horizons in the DRP Matrix

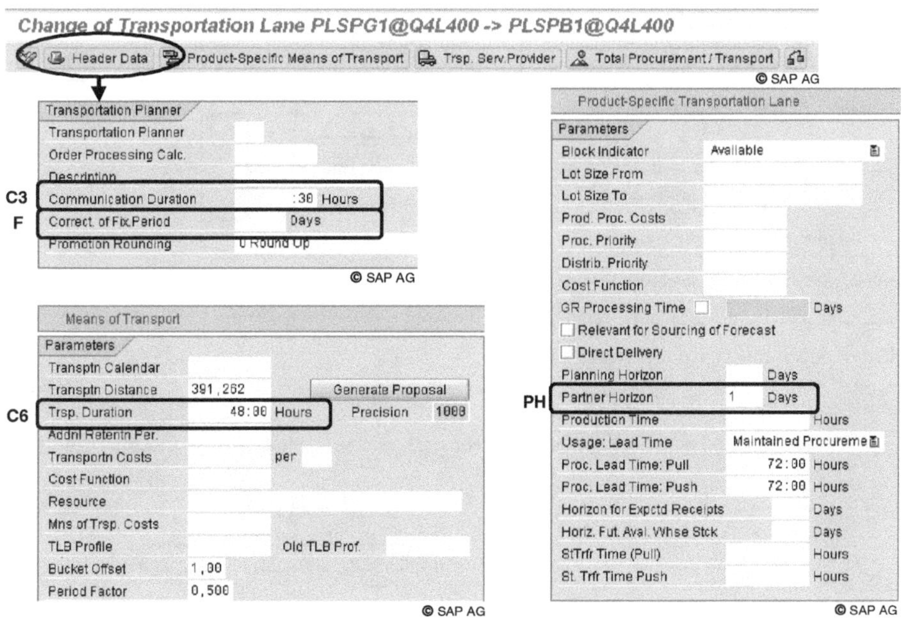

Fig. 8.35. Lead Time Relevant Fields in the Transportation Lane

Table 8.2 lists the master data fields which correspond to the elements for the calculation of these horizons. Some of these are new fields in the transportation lane. Figure 8.35 shows these fields for the sake of better recognition. Note that the 'header data'-view in the transportation lane is new.

8.5 Stability Rules

The stability rule defines in detail how far it is allowed to change the results of a DRP planning run. Stability rules are defined for the limited freeze horizon and for the plan submission horizon.

• *Stability Rule Structure and Assignment*
The stability rule for DRP is maintained with the customising path *APO → Supply Chain Planning → SPP → DRP → Define Stability Rules for DRP Horizons* and contains four different rules: for expedite and de-expedite orders within the limited freeze horizon and the plan submission horizon. Figure 8.36 shows the structure of the stability rule.

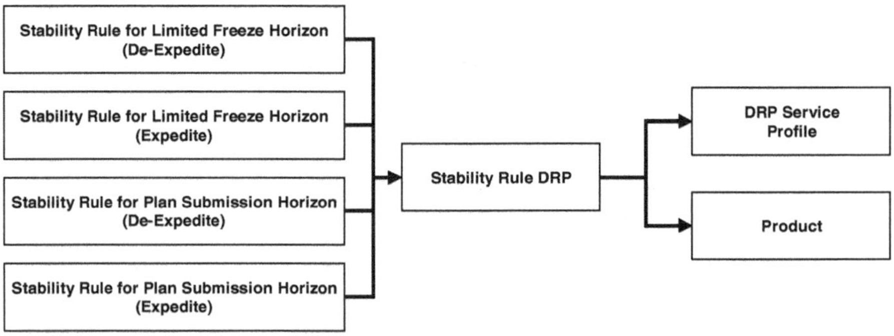

Fig. 8.36. Stability Rule Assignment

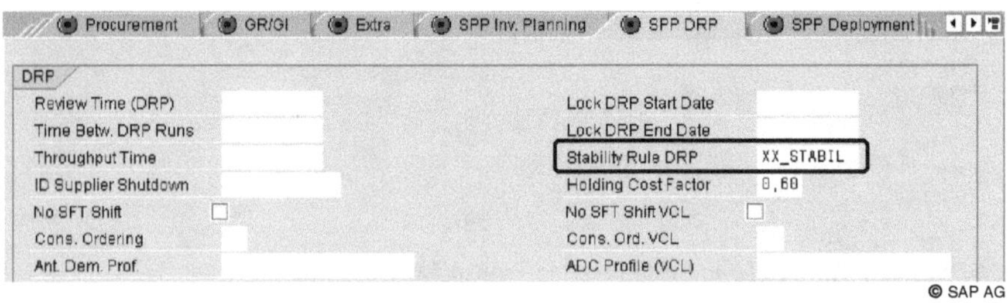

Fig. 8.37. Assignment of the Stability Rule to the Product Master

The stability rule is assigned to the product in the 'SPP DRP'-view or to the DRP service profile. The standard stability rule of the DRP service profile is used if no stability rule is assigned to the product, figure 8.37.

To take the stability rules into account, the parameter 'apply stability rules' must be set in the DRP planning profile. Figure 8.38 shows this setting and the standard stability rule.

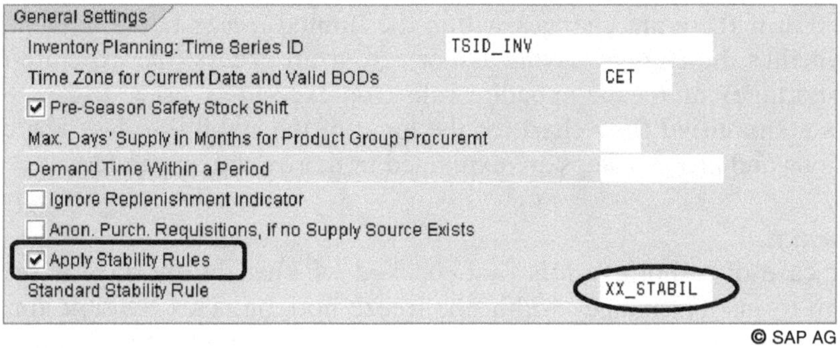

Fig. 8.38. Apply Stability Rules and the Standard Stability Rule in the DRP Service Profile

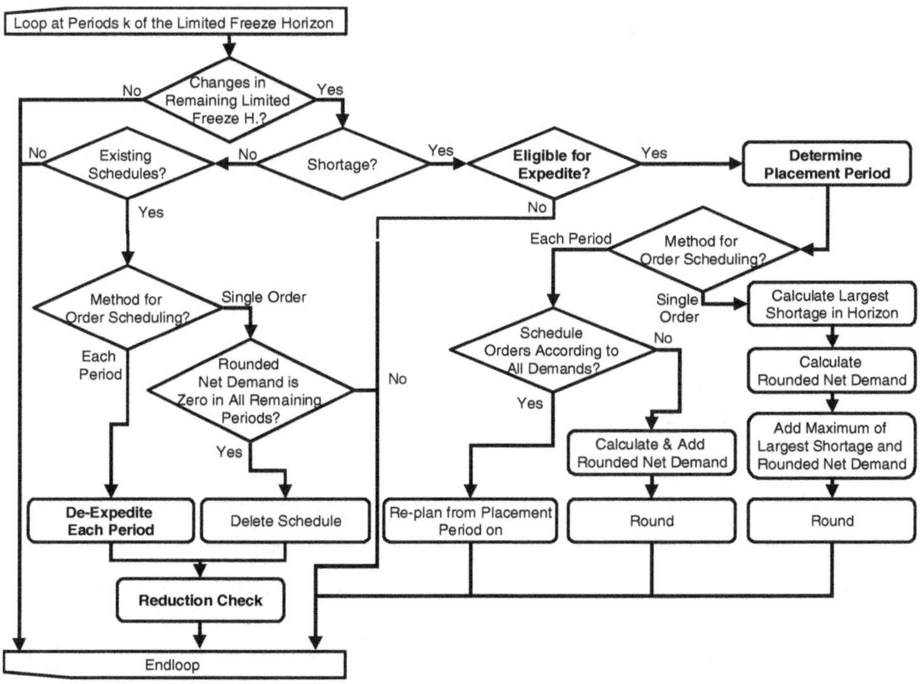

Fig. 8.39. Stability Rule Logic for the Limited Freeze Horizon

• *Stability Rule Logic*
In comparison to the settings in the release creation profile in mySAP ERP™ and SAP APO™ procurement, the logic of the stability rules in DRP is far more complicated. In order not to overstrain this topic, we are looking only at the functionality of the stability rules within the limited freeze horizon.

The stability rules (for the limited freeze horizon) only come into consideration if there are changes within the limited freeze horizon. Depending whether the change means a shortage or an excess, the expedite rule (for shortage) or the de-expedite rule (for excess) is used. Figure 8.39 shows a simplified flow chart for the logic of the stability rules. The bold decisions and process steps are explained in more detail separately.

• *Expedite*
In the case of a shortage it is first checked whether the shortage is severe enough to justify changes within the freeze horizon. This 'eligible for expedite'-check compares the shortage within the limited freeze horizon to the demand of the next 21 days, whether the shortage is not too close at the end of the freeze horizon and whether some days in the future there is still a shortage, figure 8.40.

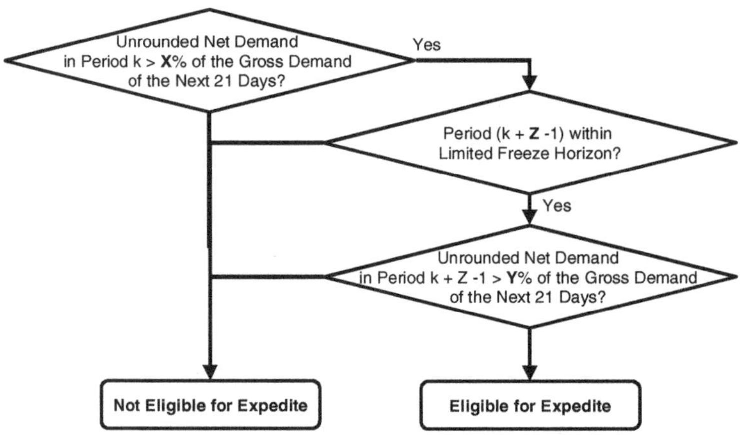

Fig. 8.40. Eligibility Check for Expedite

The parameters X, Y and Z are maintained in the stability rule for the limited freeze horizon (expedite), figure 8.41. Note that only the flagged demand elements are considered for the shortage calculation – if for example the forecast is not flagged, a shortage due to uncovered forecast demand will not cause eligibility and therefore no new order will be created within the limited freeze horizon. Another point regarding the calculation of the shortage is that only the unrounded demand is used, not the rounded demand.

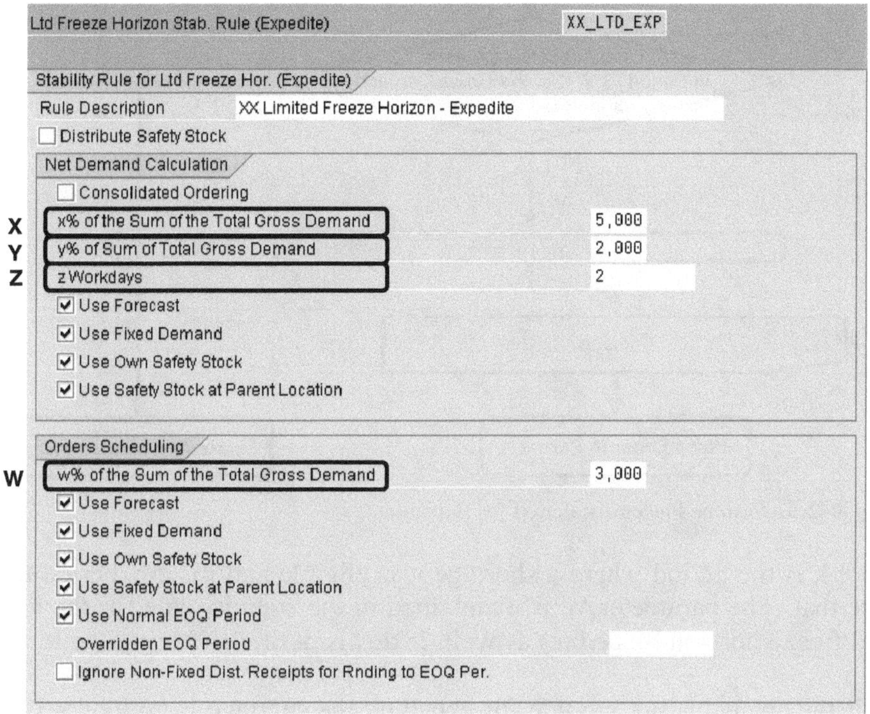

Fig. 8.41. Stability Rule for the Limited Freeze Horizon (Expedite)

If a shortage within a period of the limited freeze horizon is eligible, the next step is to determine the date of the schedule line. The quantity of the schedule line depends on the 'orders scheduling' parameters of the stability rule (see figure 8.41). The period where the order is scheduled is not necessarily the same period where the first shortage was eligible but might be earlier. The idea for this is that if the additional effort respectively cost is accepted to order within the limited freeze horizon, one might as well order early enough to cover an earlier shortage which did not qualify for expedite orders. If there is an earlier period with a shortage that exceeds W percent of the next 21 days' gross demand, the order is placed in that period, figure 8.42.

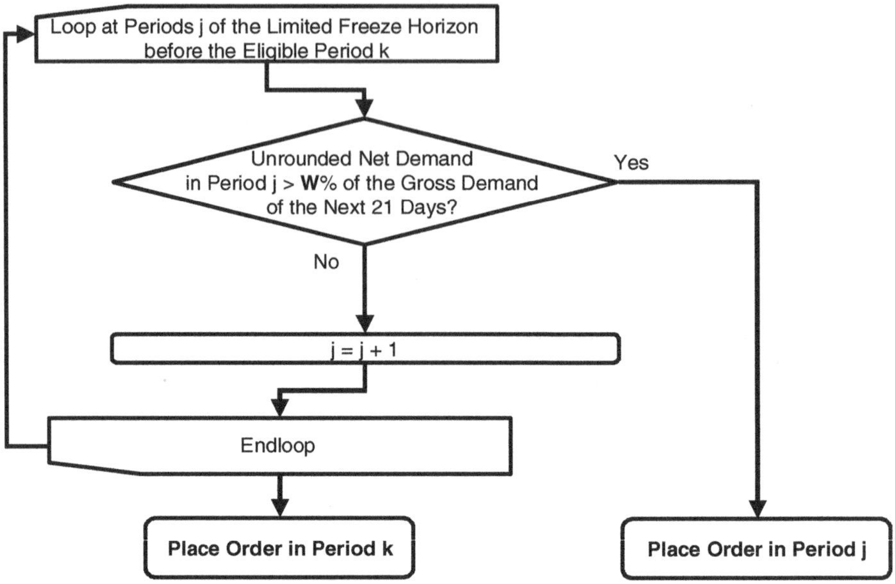

Fig. 8.42. Determine Placement Period for Expedite

Here k is the period where a shortage was eligible and j is any period before that. The parameter W is maintained in the stability rule for the limited freeze horizon (expedite) as well. If this is desired, W has to be lower than X.

If the change is not eligible for expedite, the shortage is not covered in the limited freeze horizon. Figure 8.43 shows an example for this case.

Freeze Horizon	Overdue	16.11.2005	17.11.2005	18.11.2005	21.11.2005	22.11.2005	23.11.2005
+Total Gross Demand	113,537	118,696	6,697	506,697	4,688	4,688	4,688
+Total Gross Receipt (Confirmed)							
Projected Stock							20,309
Supply Shortage	113,537	232,233	238,930	745,627	750,315	755,003	
+Planned Minimum Safety Stock Level		20,000	20,000	20,000	20,000	20,000	20,000
Minimum Net Demand							
Unrounded Net Demand (Simple)		252,233	6,697	506,697	4,688	4,688	4,688
Rounded Net Demand (Unconstrained)		253,000	6,000	507,000	5,000	5,000	4,000
Unrounded Net Demand (Adapted)				765,627	770,315	775,003	779,691
+Rounded Net Demand (Constrained)							780,000
Distr. Recpt from Supplier (Not Frozen)							
Dis. Rcpt fr. Supl. (Unres.) by Shp.Date	253,000	6,000	507,000	5,000	5,000	4,000	5,000
Dis. Rcpt fr. Supl. (Cnst.) by Shp. Date						780,000	5,000
Ordered/Released Qty by Shipping Date							

No Supply Due to Stability Rules

Fig. 8.43. Effect of Stability Rules in the DRP Matrix

The rounded net demand (constrained) – which represents the planned receipts from the supplier – does not react to the change in the demand and remains zero until the end of the limited freeze horizon on the 22.11.3005.

• *Method for Order Scheduling*
The stability rules offer three methods for order scheduling: Single order, each individual period and no change of order quantity. Using 'no change of order quantity' the stability rules prevent DRP from changing the orders – only alerts are created. With the 'each period'-method the additional order quantity is the rounded net demand of the placement period, whereas the additional order quantity with the 'single order'-method is the maximum of the rounded net demand and the biggest shortage within the limited freeze horizon.

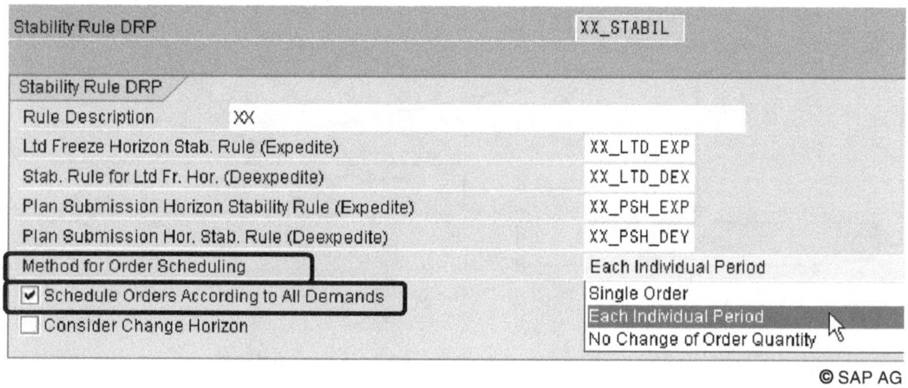

Fig. 8.44. Method for Order Scheduling

Given the multitude of parameters it is not easy to understand the results. Using the method 'each period' and the setting 'schedule orders according to all demands' one has the best chances.

The flag for the change horizon controls that if there is no change within the change horizon, no further action is taken. The reason is not to 'disturb' the supplier unnecessarily. However, this flag might add to confusion when interpreting the result of the DRP run.

• *De-Expedite*
In case of an excess, the de-expedite branch of the flow chart in figure 8.39 becomes relevant. If there is a schedule line to be reduced/deleted, one of the following procedures is taken: If the method for order scheduling is 'single order', the schedule line is deleted if the rounded net demand in all

remaining periods is still zero without the excess schedule line. For the 'each period'-method figure 8.45 shows the process flow.

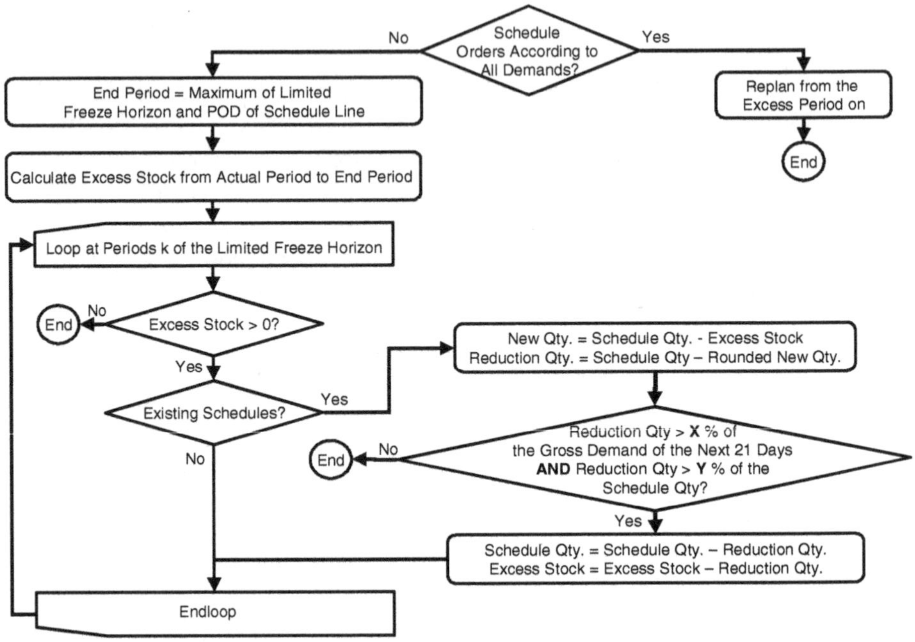

Fig. 8.45. De-Expedite for 'Each Period'-Order Scheduling

The parameters X and Y are maintained in the stability rule for the limited freeze horizon (de-expedite), figure 8.46.

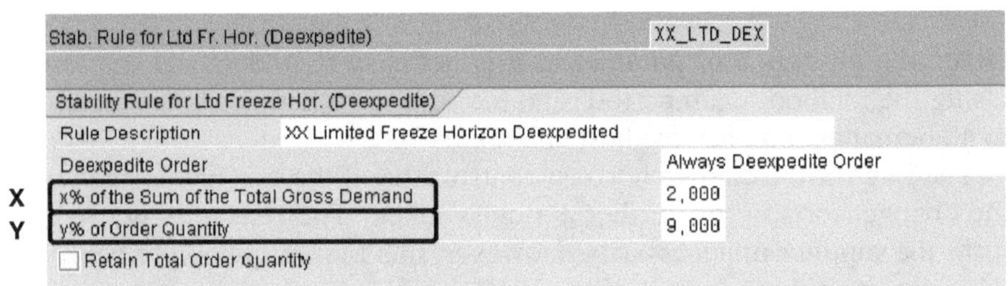

© SAP AG

Fig. 8.46. Stability Rule for the Limited Freeze Horizon (De-Expedite)

If the total order quantity in the limited freeze horizon is reduced, an alert is created. The prerequisite is that the checkbox 'retain total order quantity' in the stability rule for de-expedite is marked.

8.6 DRP Features for Seasonality

8.6.1 Anticipated Demand Coverage

If a seasonal forecast model is used, the value of the forecast changes from month to month (or from fiscal year period to fiscal year period). The forecast value is equally distributed in DRP along the daily buckets in DRP. This might lead to a huge and sudden increase of the demand from one day to the other.

The purpose of the anticipated demand coverage is to smooth the increase of the demand by placing fixed requirements. The anticipated demand coverage works only for the increase of the demand, not for the decrease. To keep the demand balance, fixed receipts are placed a number of periods later, figure 8.47.

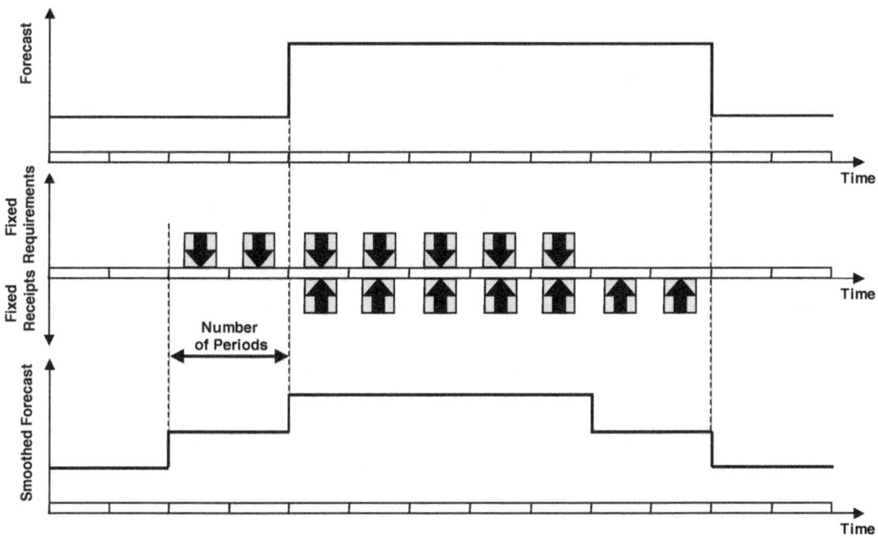

Fig. 8.47. Anticipated Demand Coverage

Both fixed requirements and fixed receipts are placed for the periods where no smoothing applies. The reason for this is that the difference between the 'valid from'-date and the 'valid to'-date of the fixed requirements spans the number of periods that are used for the anticipated demand coverage – in the example shown in figure 8.47 the fixed requirement has to be valid for two additional days until the according fixed receipt is placed.

The number of the periods, the quantity of the fixed requirements and the threshold for the anticipated demand coverage are defined with the customising path *APO → Service Parts Planning → SPP → DRP → Anticipated Demand Coverage → Create Profile for Anticipated Demand Coverage*, figure 8.48.

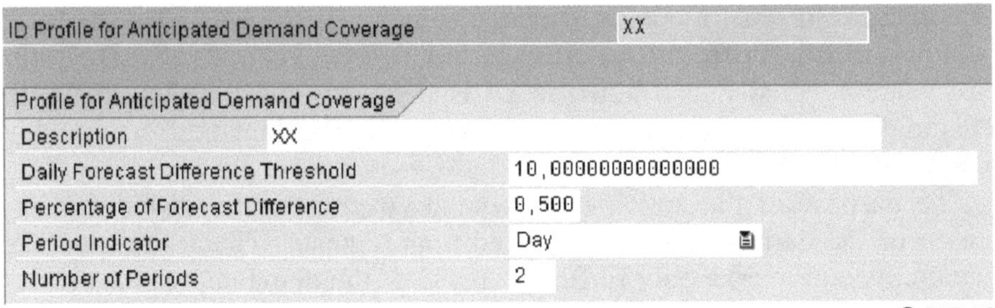

© SAP AG

Fig. 8.48. Profile for Anticipated Demand Coverage

The settings in figure 8.48 control that the increase in the daily forecast has to be above 10 to cause the anticipated demand coverage ('daily forecast difference threshold') and the fixed requirements and receipts will cover 50 % of the increase ('percentage of forecast difference'). The shift between fixed requirements and fixed receipts is 2 days – defined by the period indicator 'day' and the 'number of periods'. If another period indicator – e.g. 'week' – is selected, only one fixed requirement and/or fixed receipt is created for the whole week. If the period of coverage by the economical order quantity is below one week, this might not be sufficient to smooth the demand. The anticipated demand coverage profile is assigned to the product in the 'SPP DRP'-view, figure 8.49.

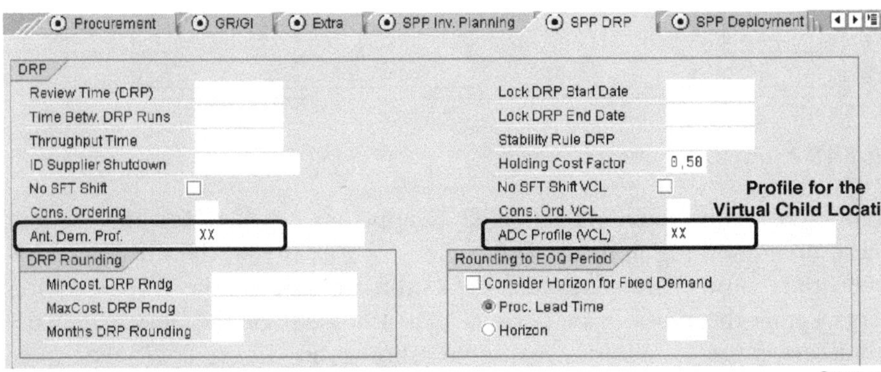

© SAP AG

Fig. 8.49. Assignment of the ADC Profile to the Product Master

Figure 8.50 shows an example in the DRP matrix for the smoothing of the increase. The 'fixed demand (non-overriding)' contains the fixed requirements for anticipated demand coverage. There might be a shifting of the demand due to non-working days (as on the 17th and 18th in figure 8.50).

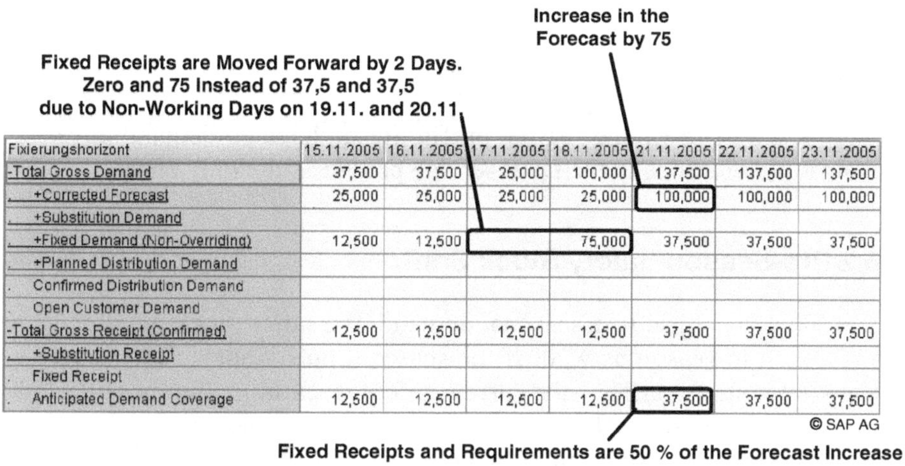

Fixierungshorizont	15.11.2005	16.11.2005	17.11.2005	18.11.2005	21.11.2005	22.11.2005	23.11.2005
-Total Gross Demand	37,500	37,500	25,000	100,000	137,500	137,500	137,500
+Corrected Forecast	25,000	25,000	25,000	25,000	100,000	100,000	100,000
+Substitution Demand							
+Fixed Demand (Non-Overriding)	12,500	12,500		75,000	37,500	37,500	37,500
+Planned Distribution Demand							
Confirmed Distribution Demand							
Open Customer Demand							
-Total Gross Receipt (Confirmed)	12,500	12,500	12,500	12,500	37,500	37,500	37,500
+Substitution Receipt							
Fixed Receipt							
Anticipated Demand Coverage	12,500	12,500	12,500	12,500	37,500	37,500	37,500

Fig. 8.50. Example for Anticipated Demand Coverage in the DRP Matrix

The reaction of the anticipated demand coverage at the end of the forecasting period is shown in figure 8.51 for the same example. In this case the decrease is smoothed.

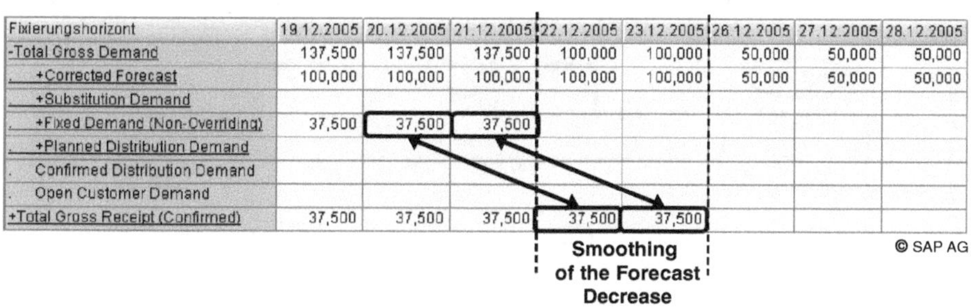

Fixierungshorizont	19.12.2005	20.12.2005	21.12.2005	22.12.2005	23.12.2005	26.12.2005	27.12.2005	28.12.2005
-Total Gross Demand	137,500	137,500	137,500	100,000	100,000	50,000	50,000	50,000
+Corrected Forecast	100,000	100,000	100,000	100,000	100,000	50,000	50,000	50,000
+Substitution Demand								
+Fixed Demand (Non-Overriding)	37,500	37,500	37,500					
+Planned Distribution Demand								
Confirmed Distribution Demand								
Open Customer Demand								
+Total Gross Receipt (Confirmed)	37,500	37,500	37,500	37,500	37,500			

Fig. 8.51. ADC – Smoothing of the Forecast Decrease at the End of the Forecast Period

The anticipated demand coverage is not part of the DRP planning service but requires the separate planning service SPP_PRF. The service profile is created with the customising path *APO → Service Parts Planning → SPP → DRP → Anticipated Demand Coverage → Define Service Profile for Anticipated Demand Coverage*, figure 8.52.

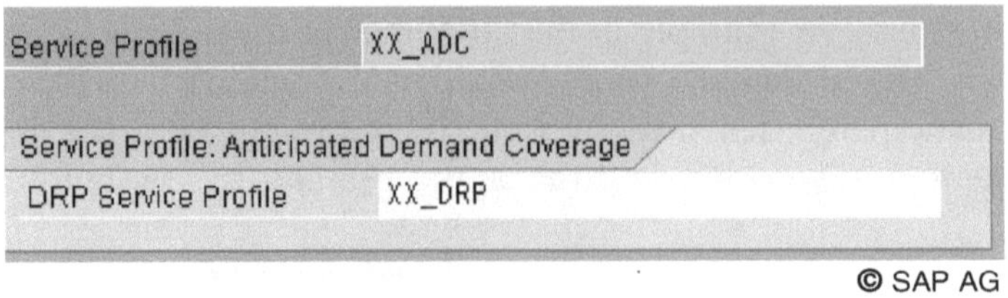

Fig. 8.52. Service Profile for Anticipated Demand Coverage

As figure 8.52 shows, the service profile for anticipated demand coverage contains the reference to the DRP service profile as the only entry.

8.6.2 Pre-Season Safety Stock Shift

If a product is subject to a seasonal demand, the safety stock might change from season to season as well. If the seasonal behaviour differs – e.g. because winter starts earlier – the current safety stock might not be sufficient. Using the pre-season safety stock shift DRP does not cover the actual safety stock but the maximum of the next N_{SS} periods, figure 8.53.

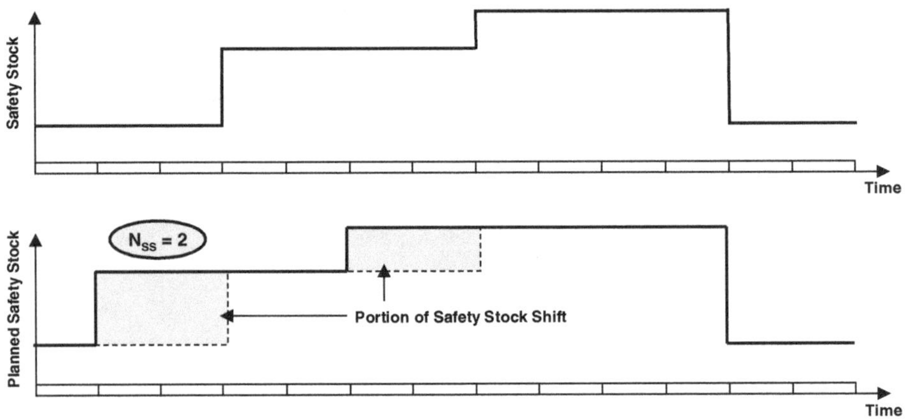

Fig. 8.53. Seasonal Safety Stock Shift

The number of periods N_{SS} depends on the procurement cost of the product and is defined in a table with the customising path *APO → Supply Chain Planning → SPP → DRP → Define Parameters for Pre-Season Safety Stock Shift*, figure 8.54.

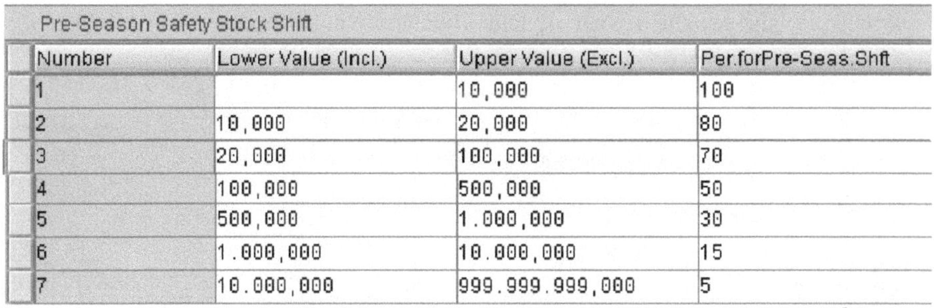

Pre-Season Safety Stock Shift

Number	Lower Value (Incl.)	Upper Value (Excl.)	Per.forPre-Seas.Shft
1		10,000	100
2	10,000	20,000	80
3	20,000	100,000	70
4	100,000	500,000	50
5	500,000	1.000,000	30
6	1.000,000	10.000,000	15
7	10.000,000	999.999.999,000	5

Fig. 8.54. Parameters for Pre-Season Safety Stock Shift

The first prerequisite for the pre-season safety stock shift is that a seasonal forecast model is used for the location product and that there is a seasonal behaviour of the safety stock – which is modelled by the parameter 'seasonal' in the safety stock model (see figure 6.12).

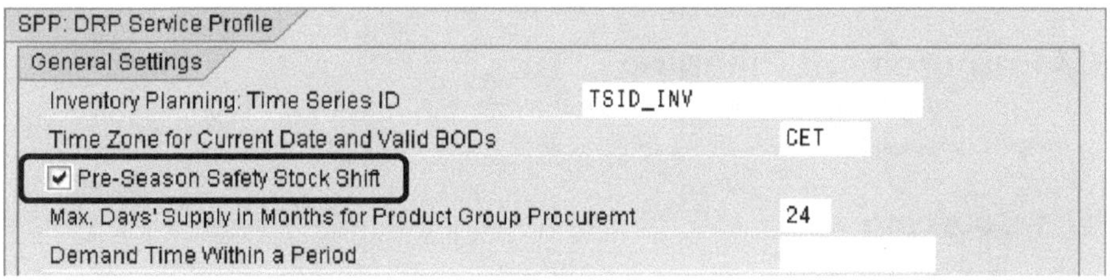

Fig. 8.55. Flag for Pre-Season Safety Stock Shift in the DRP Service Profile

The pre-season safety stock shift is applied if the according flag is set in the DRP service profile, figure 8.55. Another prerequisite is that the pre-season safety stock shift is not inhibited for the location product in the product master, figure 8.56.

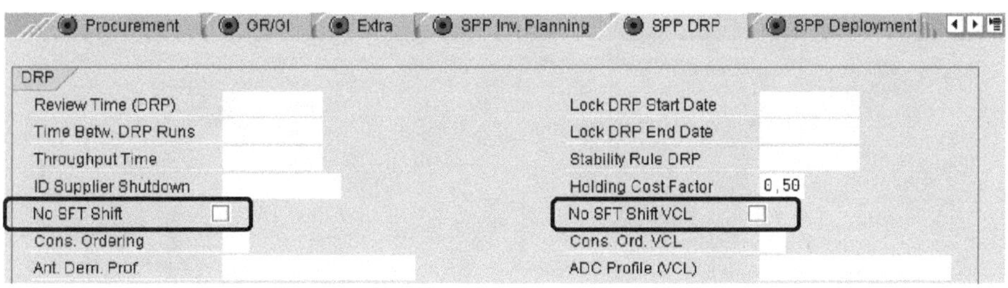

Fig. 8.56. Inhibit Pre-Season Safety Stock Shift in the Product Master

Figure 8.57 shows the result in the DRP matrix for a number of periods N_{SS} of two:

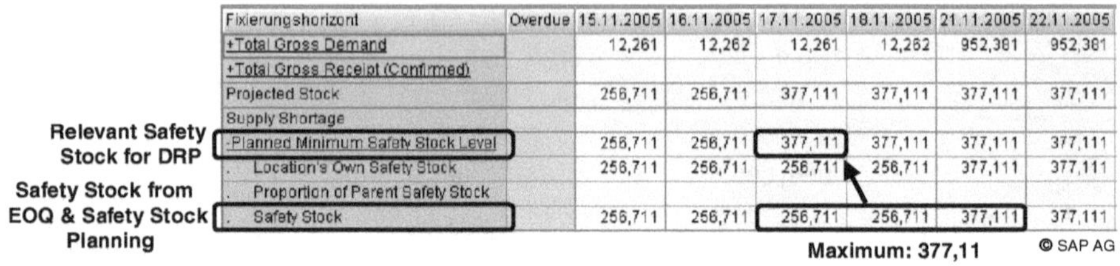

Fig. 8.57. Example for Pre-Season Safety Stock Shift in the DRP Matrix

The key figure 'safety stock' contains the safety stock that was calculated by the EOQ and safety stock service (see chapter 6). The planned minimum safety stock level – which is relevant for DRP – contains however the maximum safety stock of the actual period plus the next two periods.

8.7 Procurement Planning

8.7.1 Sourcing

The purpose of DRP is to create schedule lines or purchase requisitions at the entry location for the demand in the network. Contracts are the prerequisite for the use of purchase requisitions. Both scheduling agreements and contracts are created in mySAP ERP™ and transferred to SAP APO™ via CIF as procurement relationships. Figure 8.58 shows procurement relationships in SAP APO™ (transaction /SAPAPO/PWBSRC1) based on scheduling agreements and on contracts.

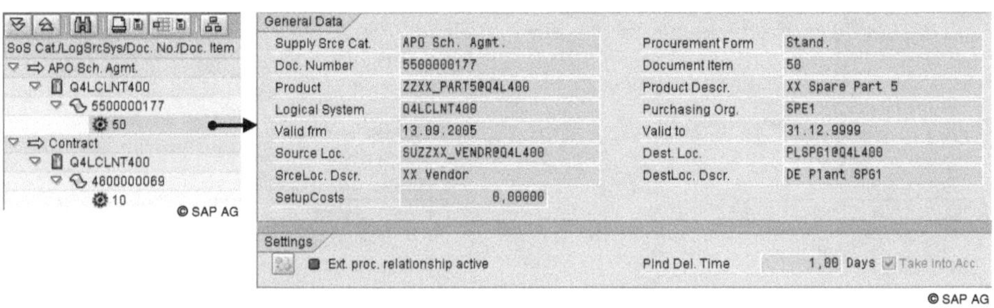

Fig. 8.58. Procurement Relationships

For external procurement it is possible to consider multiple sourcing using quota arrangements (transaction /SAPAPO/SCC_TQ1) as shown in figure 8.59.

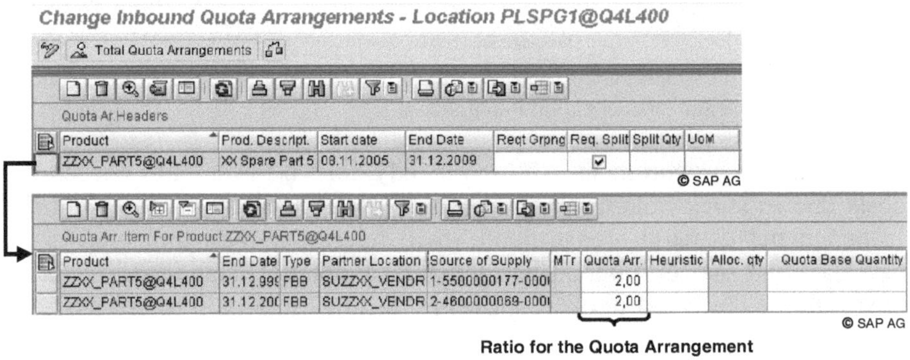

Fig. 8.59. Quota Arrangement

The processing of the procurement proposals is described in chapter 9.

8.7.2 Product Group Procurement

The idea of product group procurement is to reduce the fix order costs for slow moving parts. E.g. if some products require the same set-up at the supplier, savings are achieved by ordering these products together. The grouping for those products is done via product groups of a defined product group type. This product group type is defined in the general DRP settings with the customising path *APO → Supply Chain Planning → SPP → DRP → Make General Settings for DRP*, figure 8.60.

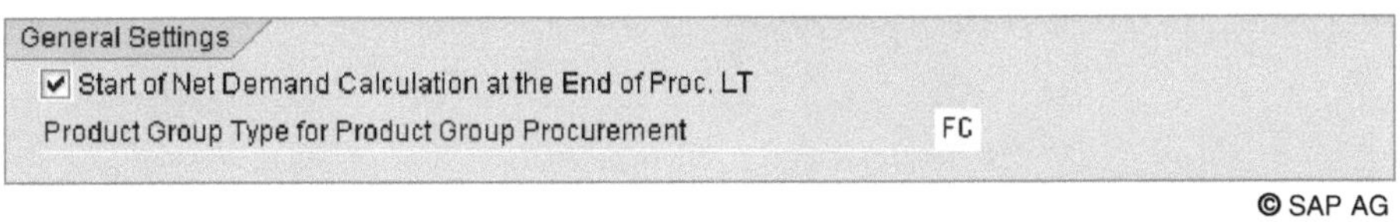

Fig. 8.60. Product Group Type for Product Group Procurement (General DRP Settings)

Figure 8.61 shows an example for product group procurement where part B is procured before its demand date.

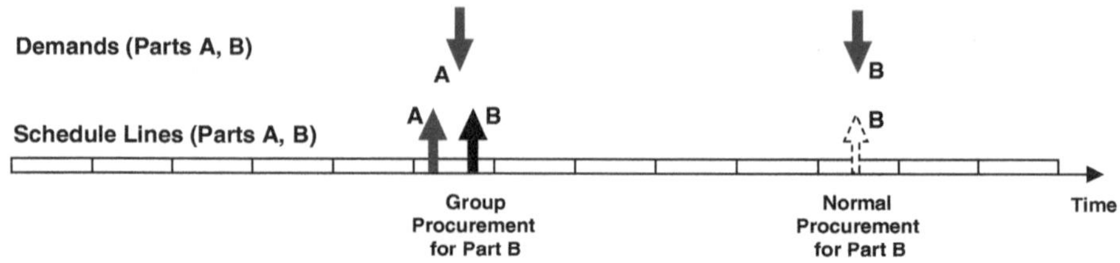

Fig. 8.61. Example for Product Group Procurement

Product group procurement is however only done if the savings exceed the costs due to stock holding. As a result of product group procurement the 'rounded net demand (constrained)' will be earlier than the 'total gross demand' and the 'unrounded net demand (adapted)'. This leads to an increase in the projected stock as shown in the DRP matrix in figure 8.62.

Fixierungshorizont	Overdue	W 45.2005	W 46.2005	W 47.2005	W 48.2005	W 49.2005	W 50.2005	W 51.2005
+Total Gross Demand							100,000	
+Total Gross Receipt (Confirmed)								
Projected Stock			100,000	100,000	100,000	100,000	100,000	
Supply Shortage								
+Planned Minimum Safety Stock Level								
Minimum Net Demand								
Unrounded Net Demand (Simple)							100,000	
Rounded Net Demand (Unconstrained)								
Unrounded Net Demand (Adapted)							100,000	
+Rounded Net Demand (Constrained)			100,000					

© SAP AG

Fig. 8.62. Example in the DRP Matrix for Product Group Procurement

To determine the optimal procurement interval for product group procurement, the total costs are calculated for all alternatives from monthly to yearly (increasing by monthly steps). The result of the product group procurement is displayed in the schedule board with the transaction /SAPAPO/SPPDRPSB, figure 8.63.

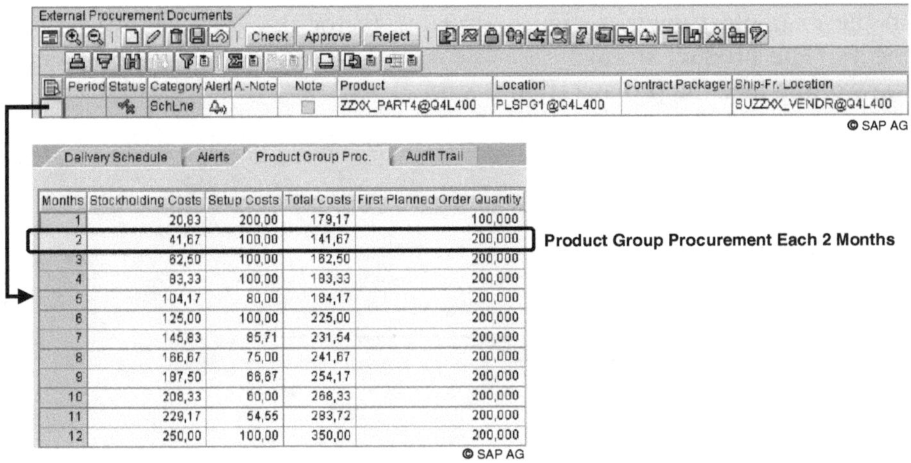

Months	Stockholding Costs	Setup Costs	Total Costs	First Planned Order Quantity
1	20,83	200,00	179,17	100,000
2	41,67	100,00	141,67	200,000
3	62,50	100,00	162,50	200,000
4	83,33	100,00	183,33	200,000
5	104,17	80,00	184,17	200,000
6	125,00	100,00	225,00	200,000
7	145,83	85,71	231,54	200,000
8	166,67	75,00	241,67	200,000
9	187,50	66,67	254,17	200,000
10	208,33	60,00	268,33	200,000
11	229,17	54,55	283,72	200,000
12	250,00	100,00	350,00	200,000

Fig. 8.63. Product Procurement Cost Alternatives

The total costs consist of the stockholding costs and the set-up costs. The stockholding costs are calculated as described in formula 8.4:

$$\text{Stockholding Costs} = 0.5 * (S_A + S_B) * C_{PS} * 365 * N_M / 12 \qquad (8.4)$$

Where N_M the number of month for product group procurement (2 months in figure 8.63), S_A is the stock after the procurement and S_B the stock before the next procurement, as shown in figure 8.64.

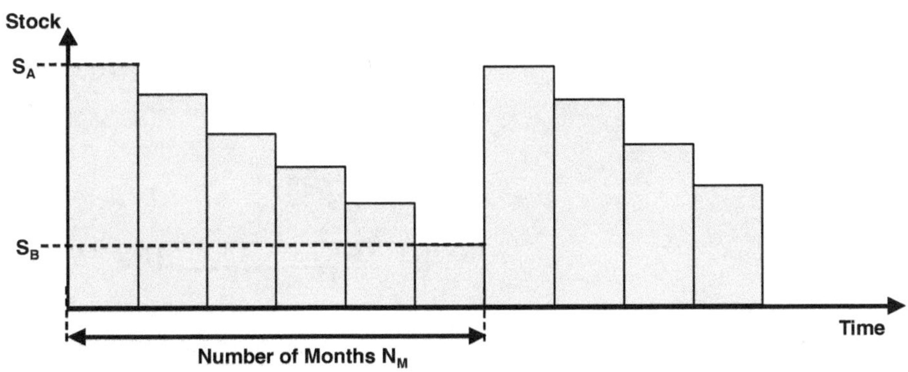

Fig. 8.64. Stock After and Before Product Group Procurement

In the example shown in figure 8.63 the factor $0.5 * (S_A + S_B)$ is 100 pieces. The product storage cost C_{PS} is maintained in the 'procurement'-view of the location product, figure 8.65.

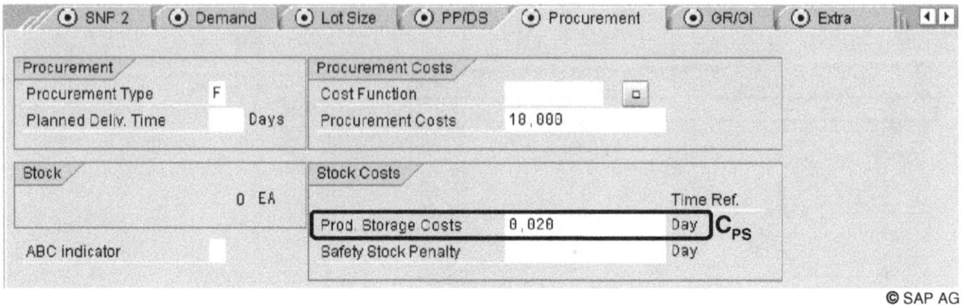

Fig. 8.65. Product Storage Cost per Day in the Product Master

If no product storage costs are maintained, the procurement costs times the stock holding factor is used instead, formula 8.5.

$$\text{Stockholding Costs} = 0.5 * (S_A + S_B) * C_P * F_{HC} * N_M / 12 \qquad (8.5)$$

The procurement costs C_P and the stock holding factor F_{HC} are maintained in the product master as shown in figure 8.66.

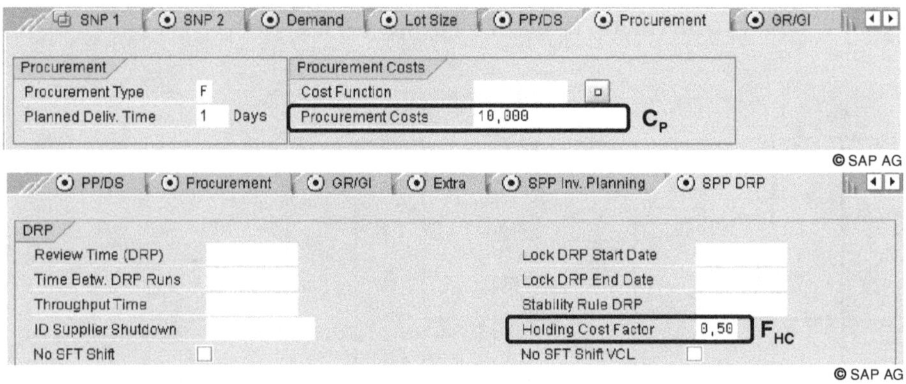

Fig. 8.66. Procurement Costs and Holding Cost Factor in the Product Master

The calculated stockholding costs are also displayed in the log. The set-up costs are maintained in the procurement relationship (transaction /SAPAPO/PWBSRC1), figure 8.67.

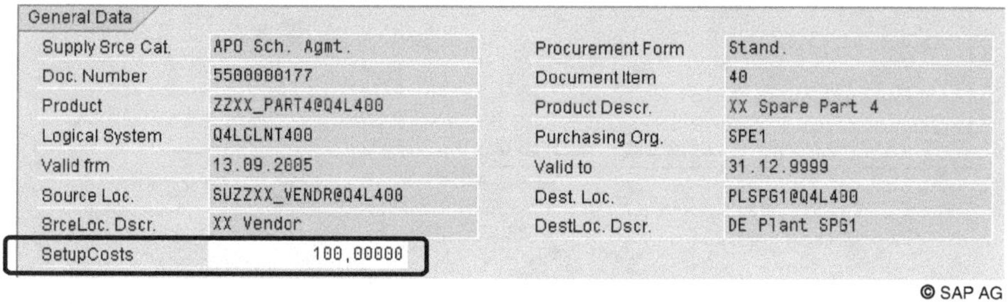

Fig. 8.67. Set-Up Costs in the Procurement Relationship

The set-up costs represent the costs for the whole product group, not just for the single product. For the calculation of the set-up costs of the product group the set-up cost of the service part is used which triggers the procurement. In order to avoid inconsistencies, the set-up costs should have the same value for all members of the product group.

8.7.3 Supplier Shutdown

In DRP it is possible to model shutdown times at the supplier – e.g. during summer vacation. In this case the demand is sourced earlier. The supplier shutdown is maintained as a master data with the transaction /SAPAPO/SPP_SSD, figure 8.68.

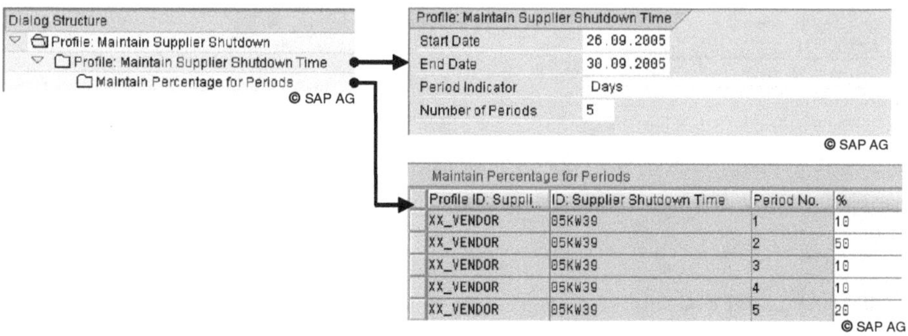

Fig. 8.68. Supplier Shutdown Maintenance

The demand for the shut down period is pulled forward according to the percentage of periods. Figure 8.69 visualises the way the percentage for periods is used.

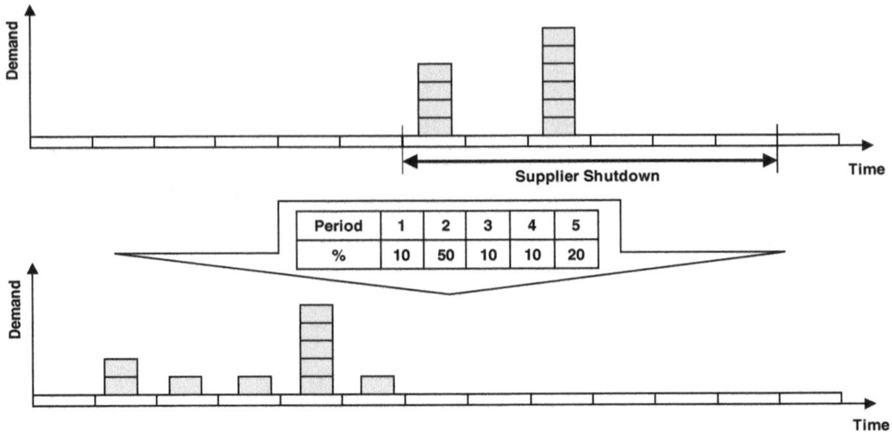

Fig. 8.69. Pull Forward According to the Percentage for Periods

For the pull forward the calendar is not considered. If the demand is pulled to a non-working day, it is added to the demand of the previous working day. The supplier shutdown is assigned to the product master in the 'SPP DRP'-view as shown in figure 8.70.

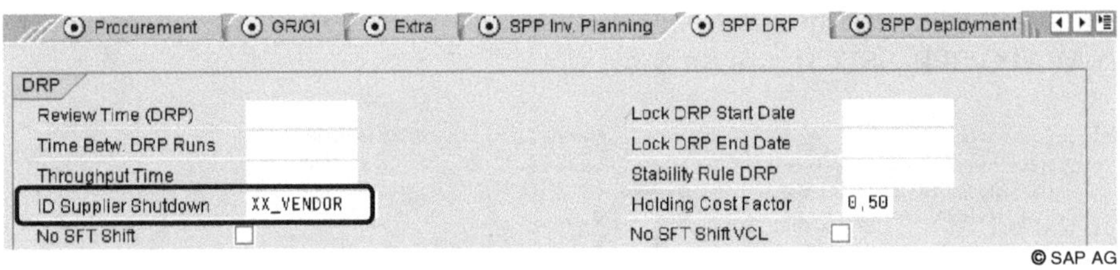

Fig. 8.70. Supplier Shutdown Assignment in the Product Master

8.8 DRP Service

The service profile for DRP (planning service SPP_DRP) is defined with the customising path *APO → Supply Chain Planning → SPP → DRP → Define Service Profile for DRP* as shown in figure 8.71. Most of the settings have already been explained. Other settings allow to ignore the replenishment indicator and to create purchase requisitions even if no procurement relationship is defined in DRP yet.

• *DRP Approval*
DRP approval is explained in chapter 9. Instead of performing the DRP approval as a separate service it is also possible to integrate it into the DRP planning service. For a separate DRP approval the entry 'separate DRP approval' must be selected. It is also possible to skip the DRP approval by the setting 'without DRP approval'.

From a performance perspective it is recommended to perform an integrated DRP approval instead of a separate DRP approval.

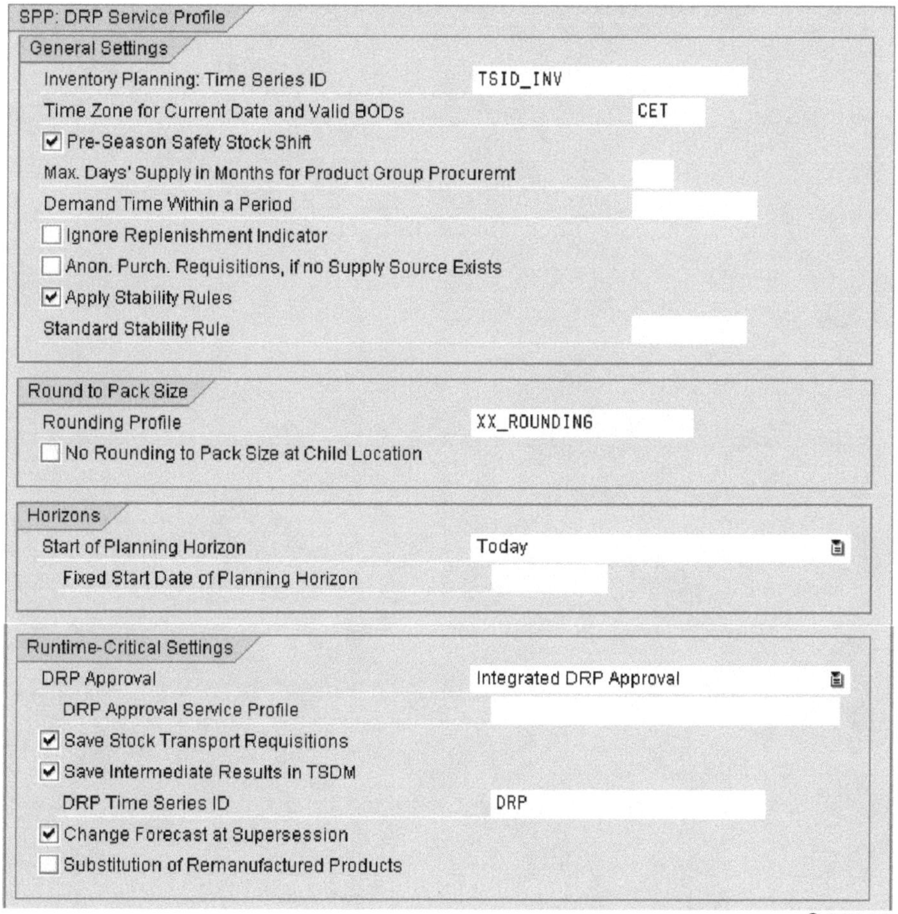

Fig. 8.71. DRP Service Profile

• *Standard Service Profiles*
The standard service profile for DRP GLOBAL_DEFAULT is created with the customising path *APO → Supply Chain Planning → SPP → DRP → Create*

Global Standard Service Profile for DRP and the standard profile for the automatic assignment of profiles with the path *APO → Supply Chain Planning → SPP → DRP → Anticipated Demand Coverage → Create Service Profile for Automatic Assignment of Profiles.*

9 Procurement Approval

9.1 Process Overview

The purpose of the procurement approval process is to prevent an unusually high procurement – quantity or value – without notice. The procurement approval process is subsequent to the DRP run, figure 9.1.

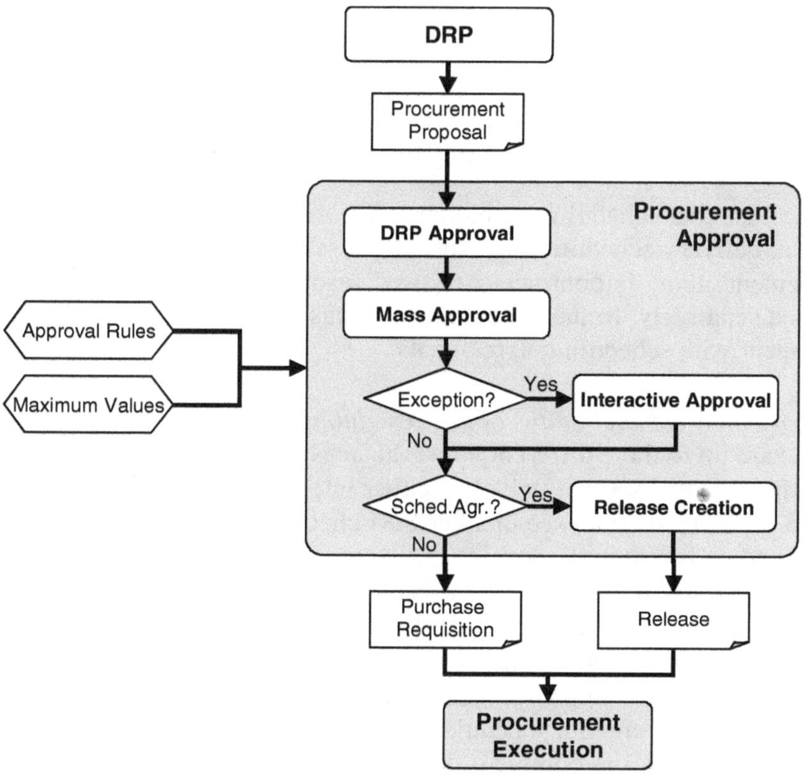

Fig. 9.1. Procurement Approval Process Overview

Releases are only created after the procurement is approved. Basis for the procurement approval are the approval rules and maximum values for some of the rules. The procurement approval is followed by the procurement execution, where the information is sent to the supplier via EDI or via SAP ICH™.

• *Procurement Order Types*

Service parts planning assumes that procurement using scheduling agreements is the common case. Alternatively it is possible to use purchase requisitions with reference to a contract. The objects and the process steps for approval differ only slightly.

Table 9.1. Procurement Order Types

Procurement Relationship with Supplier	Scheduling Agreement	Contract
Procurement Relationship per Service Part	Scheduling Agreement Item	Contract Item
Planning Result	Delivery Schedule	Purchase Requirements
Single Procurement Element	Schedule Line	Purchase Requirement
Release Creation	Release	n.a.
Purchase Order Creation	n.a.	Purchase Order Item

In the case that scheduling agreements are used, the approval is performed for the delivery schedule – i.e. for all the schedule lines – of a scheduling agreement item. If contracts are used, each purchase requisition is approved separately. In the following we focus on the description of the procurement with scheduling agreements.

• *Approval Steps and Status of the Scheduling Agreement Item*

There are up to three different approval steps:

- the approval service (which is either integrated into the DRP service or a separate service, see chapter 8.8) checks whether any rules are violated and creates alerts
- the mass approval allows to check the value (the total value and the difference to the last DRP run) for a selection of products and to approve or reject the whole selection
- the interactive approval is required for those scheduling agreement items which contain schedule lines with alerts.

Note that always the complete delivery schedule is approved and not the individual schedule line. Depending on the compliance with the rules and the approval step, the status of the scheduling agreement item changes.

Figure 9.2 provides an overview about the scheduling agreement item statuses (SAI) and the approval steps.

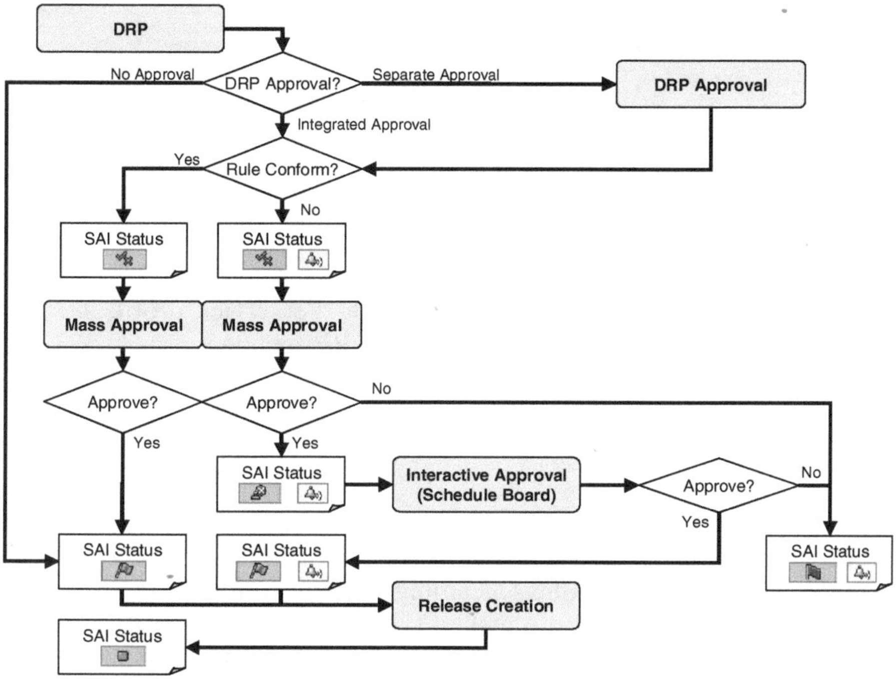

Fig. 9.2. Approval and Status of Scheduling Agreement Items

If a rule is violated an alert is created – this is visualised by the bell in the status. The status of the scheduling agreement item is displayed in the schedule board with the transaction /SAPAPO/SPPDRPSB, figure 9.3.

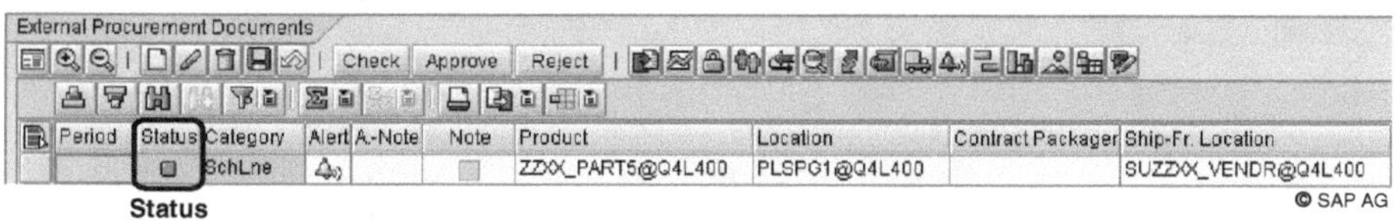

Fig. 9.3. Status of the Scheduling Agreement Item in the Schedule Board

The setting for the DRP approval (integrated, separate or no approval) is done in the DRP service profile, figure 9.4.

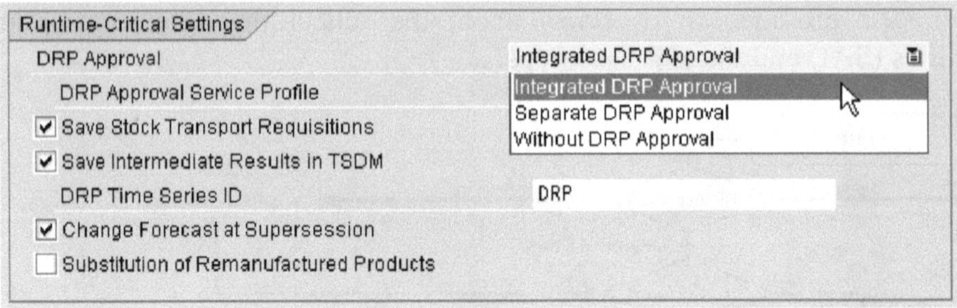

Fig. 9.4. DRP Approval Setting in the DRP Service Profile

If an integrated DRP approval is performed, the service profile for the DRP approval has to be referenced from the DRP service profile.

9.2 Approval Rules

The approval rules check whether the procurement proposal by DRP is within the defined limits. This determines the status of the procurement proposal – i.e. the status of the scheduling agreement item or the purchase requisition. The assignment of the alert type and whether the rule is active and used for the DRP result is defined with the customising path *APO → Supply Chain Planning → SPP → DRP → DRP Approval → Define DRP Approval Rules*, figure 9.5

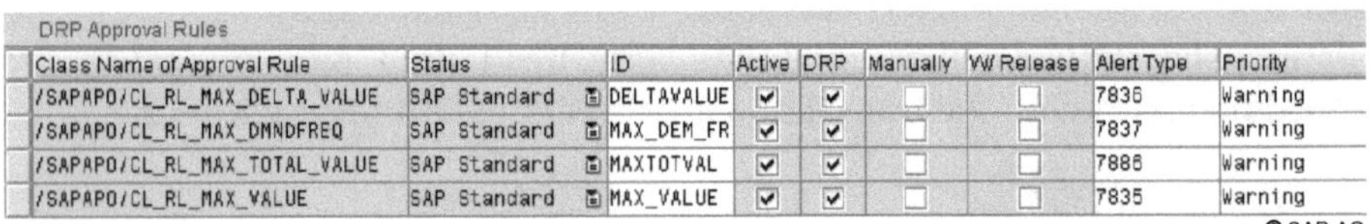

DRP Approval Rules

Class Name of Approval Rule	Status	ID	Active	DRP	Manually	W Release	Alert Type	Priority
/SAPAPO/CL_RL_MAX_DELTA_VALUE	SAP Standard	DELTAVALUE	☑	☑	☐	☐	7836	Warning
/SAPAPO/CL_RL_MAX_DMNDFREQ	SAP Standard	MAX_DEM_FR	☑	☑	☐	☐	7837	Warning
/SAPAPO/CL_RL_MAX_TOTAL_VALUE	SAP Standard	MAXTOTVAL	☑	☑	☐	☐	7886	Warning
/SAPAPO/CL_RL_MAX_VALUE	SAP Standard	MAX_VALUE	☑	☑	☐	☐	7835	Warning

Fig. 9.5. Approval Rules

The violation of a rule triggers an alert. Some of the rules – namely /SAPAPO/CL_RL_MAX_DELTA_VALUE, /SAPAPO/CL_RL_MAX_VALUE and /SAPAPO/CL_RL_MAX_DMNDFREQ – are related to maximum values. These values are defined in the maximum value profile with the transaction /SAPAPO/DRPC_EP, figure 9.6.

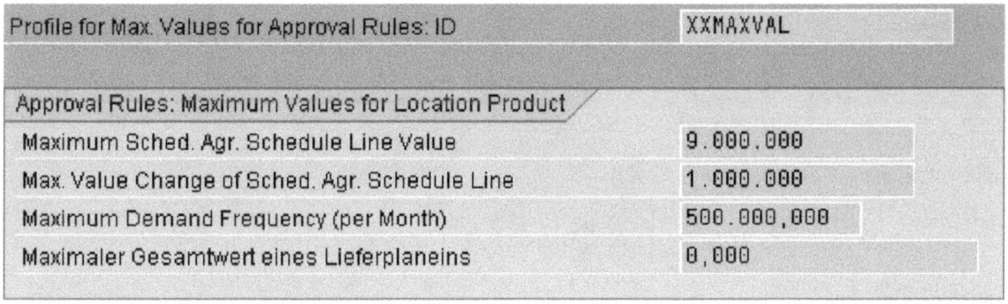

© SAP AG

Fig. 9.6. Profile for Maximum Values

The maximum value profile is assigned to the product master in the DRP view as shown in figure 9.7.

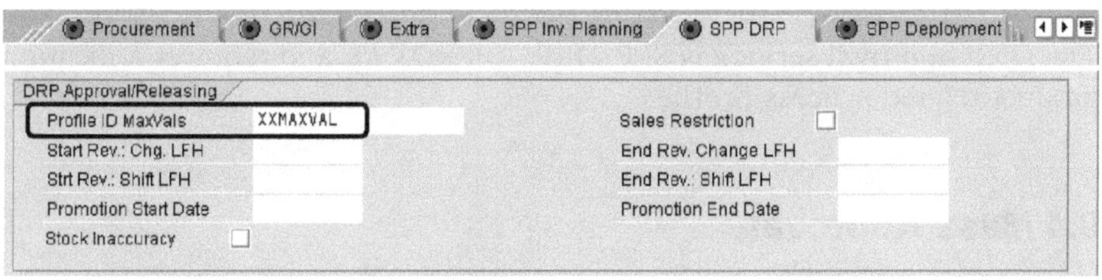

© SAP AG

Fig. 9.7. Assignment of the Maximum Value Profile to the Product Master

Note that there is no default maximum value profile. Notes 925171 and 929169 provide additional information for the creation of own approval rules.

9.3 Procurement Approval Service

The procurement approval service profile is defined with the customising path *APO → Supply Chain Planning → SPP → DRP → DRP Approval → Define Service Profile for DRP Approval* and contains the maximum procurement lead time, figure 9.8.

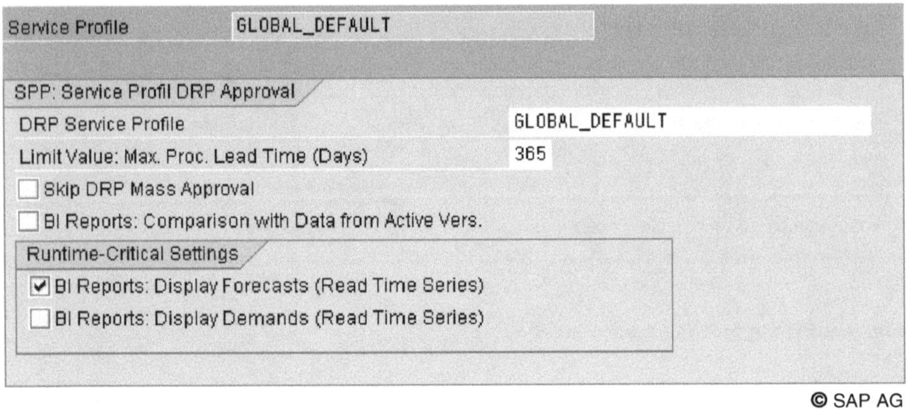

Fig. 9.8. Service Profile for Procurement Approval

The DRP approval service is SPP_DRP_APPROVAL and requires a location product related process profile.

9.4 Mass Approval

The purpose of the mass approval is to gain an overview of the procurement value for a group of products in order to avoid an unnoticed abnormal increase in the ordered value. The selection of the products is possible by product name, product group, supplier, BOD and others. The mass approval is performed with the transaction /SAPAPO/SPPDRPAPPR, figure 9.9.

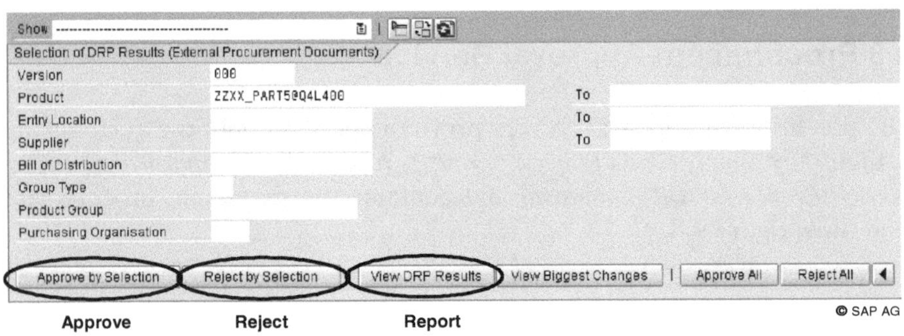

Fig. 9.9. Mass Approval

From the entry screen it is possible to call SAP BI™ reports and to approve or reject the procurement proposals for the selection. There are two reports to display the entire DRP results and the biggest changes. Figure 9.10 shows the report for the display of the DRP results.

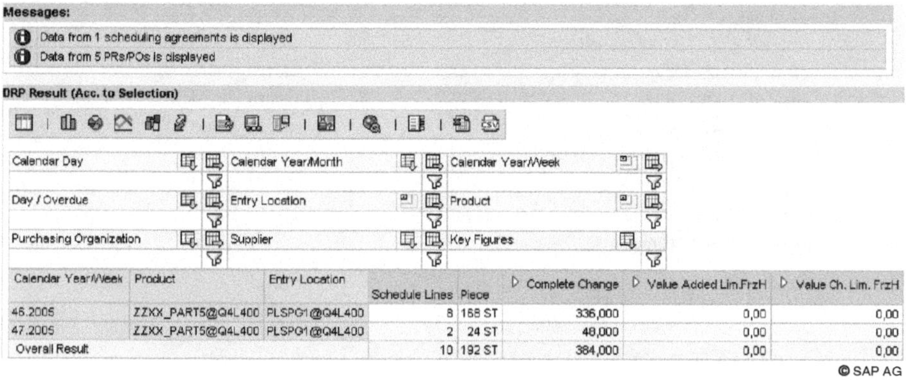

Calendar Year/Week	Product	Entry Location	Schedule Lines	Piece	Complete Change	Value Added Lim.FrzH	Value Ch. Lim. FrzH
46.2005	ZZXX_PART5@Q4L400	PLSPG1@Q4L400	8	168 ST	336,000	0,00	0,00
47.2005	ZZXX_PART5@Q4L400	PLSPG1@Q4L400	2	24 ST	48,000	0,00	0,00
Overall Result			10	192 ST	384,000	0,00	0,00

Fig. 9.10. SAP BI™ Report for the DRP Results

All newly created schedule lines and purchase requisitions are considered as DRP result. Since DRP performs a regenerative planning (in contrast to net change planning), all non-fixed receipts are considered here (i.e. purchase orders are excluded).

The report offers various options for visualisation – from swapping the axes to diagrams, figure 9.11.

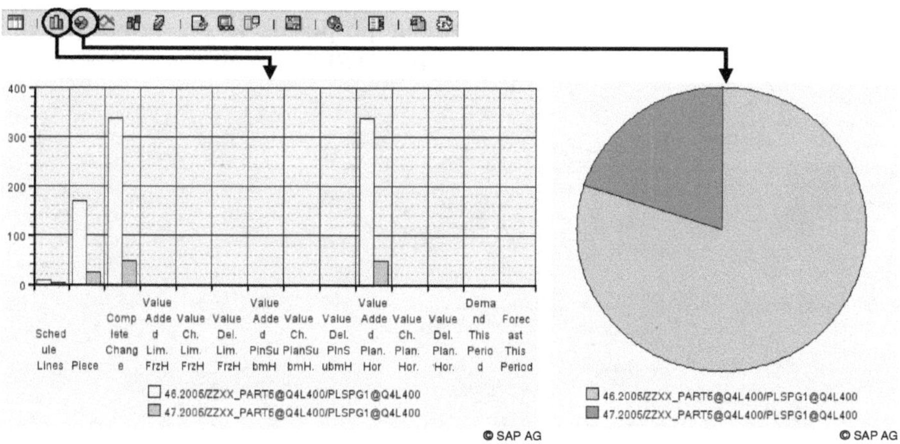

Fig. 9.11. Diagrams Within the DRP Result-Report

The prerequisite for the reporting is that the queries are defined in the global setting for DRP approval (customising path *APO → Supply Chain*

Planning → SPP → DRP → DRP Approval → Make General Settings for DRP Approval Parameters), figure 9.12.

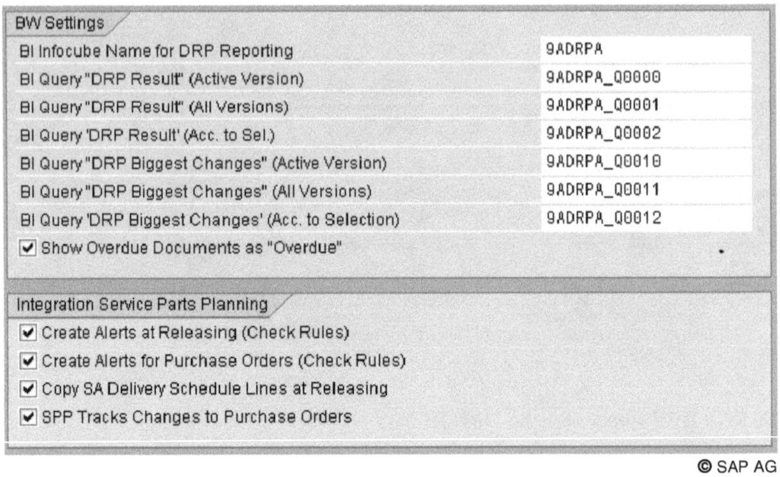

Fig. 9.12. General Settings for DRP Approval

9.5 Interactive Approval in the Schedule Board

The interactive approval of procurement proposals is performed in the schedule board with the transaction /SAPAPO/SPPDRPSB, figure 9.13.

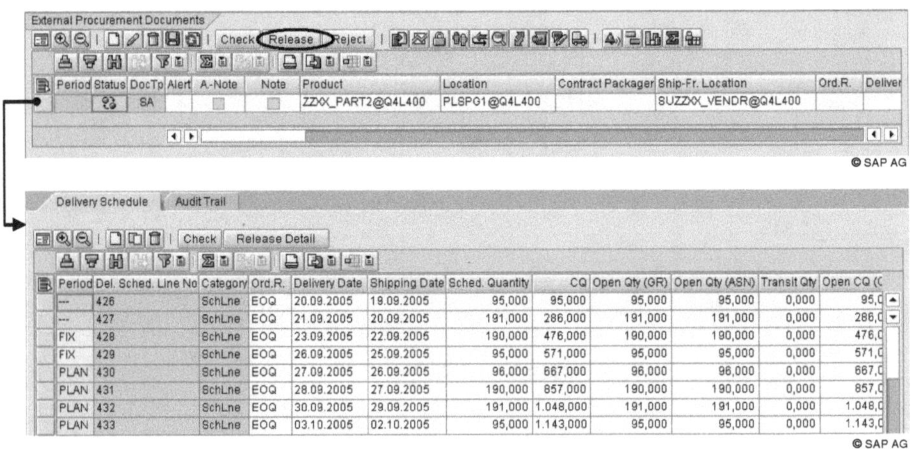

Fig. 9.13. Schedule Board for Interactive Approval

Note that the whole delivery schedule is approved, not an individual schedule line. It is possible though to create, change or delete schedule lines.

There are maximum limits for the individual approval. These limits are defined per user with the customising path *APO → SPP → DRP → DRP Approval → Define Management Approval* as shown in figure 9.14.

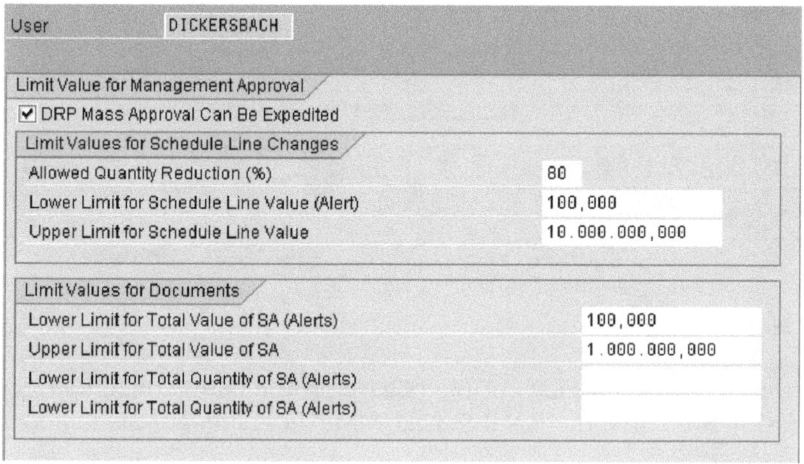

Fig. 9.14. Approval Limits per User

9.6 Release Creation

The release creation for service parts planning is performed like for standard procurement with scheduling agreements (see Dickersbach 2005). The only exception is that the status of the scheduling agreement item has to be 'approved' before the releases are created. The transaction for release creation is /SAPAPO/PWBSCH1 as shown in figure 9.15

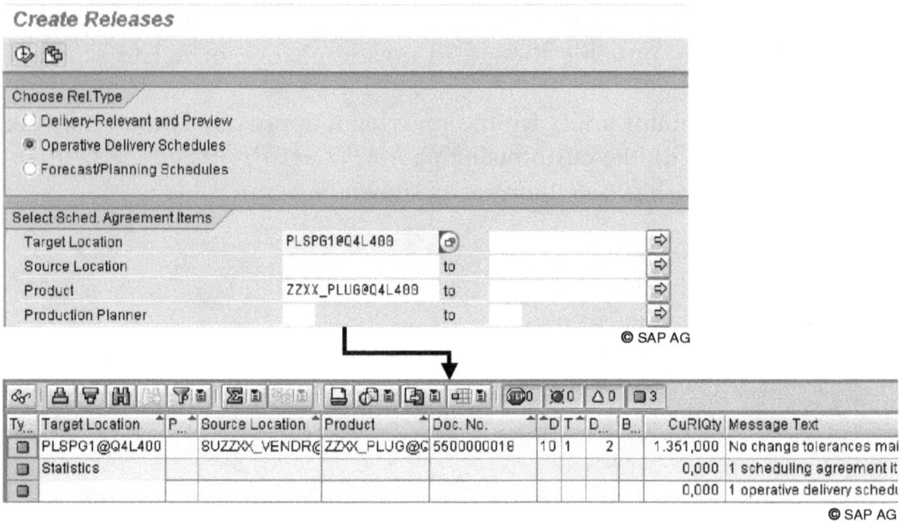

Fig. 9.15. Release Creation

The release creation horizon of the release profile is overruled by the plan submission horizon if the BAdI SMOD_MMPUR is implemented.

9.7 Procurement Execution

For the execution of the procurement the release is sent to the supplier. The common method is to use EDI for large suppliers and suppliers with a well developed IT landscape.

For small and medium suppliers it is however possible to apply SAP ICH™ in order to integrate them into the planning environment for service parts management with a comparatively low effort. In this case the release is sent as an IDOC from SAP APO™ via SAP XI™ – where it is converted to the XML format – to SAP ICH™. In SAP ICH™ the supplier creates an advanced shipping notification (ASN) which is sent via SAP XI™ to mySAP ERP™ as an inbound delivery. In mySAP ERP™ a validation of the ASN is performed, where its plausibility is checked (e.g. whether a scheduling agreement item for this product with the supplier exists). After the validation an acknowledgement is sent back to SAP ICH™ and the inbound delivery is sent to SAP EWM™ as an inbound delivery notification (IDN). This inbound delivery notification can be activated in the background to become an inbound delivery in SAP EWM™, and goods receipt can be posted. Figure 9.16 shows the document flow for procurement execution.

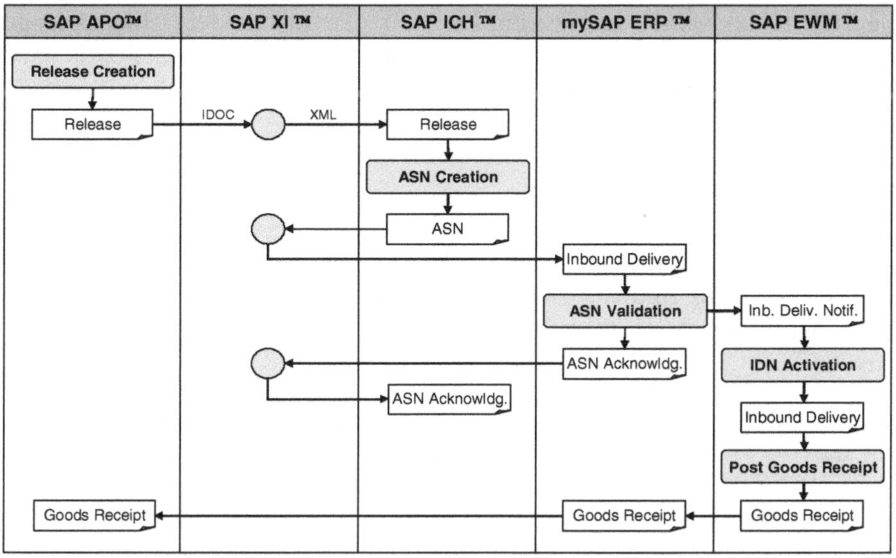

Fig. 9.16. Process Steps and Document Flow for Procurement Execution

Essential for the procurement execution process is that the supplier sends ASNs to mySAP ERP™.

• *Monitoring of the Release Transfer to SAP ICH™*

The transfer of the release from SAP APO™ to SAP XI™ and from SAP XI™ to SAP ICH™ is monitored in both systems (SAP XI™ for the transfer from SAP APO™ to SAP XI™, SAP ICH™ for the transfer from SAP XI™ to SAP ICH™) with the transaction SXMB_MONI.

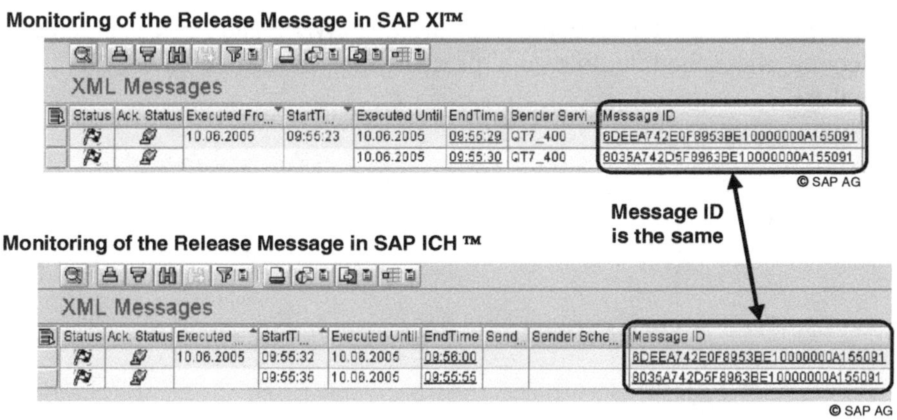

Fig. 9.17. Monitoring of the Release Message in SAP XI™ and SAP ICH™

Figure 9.17 shows the monitoring for a successful transfer – the message ID for a release is the same in both systems. The same transaction is used in SAP ICH™ to monitor the transfer of the message from SAP XI™ to SAP ICH™.

• *ASN Creation in SAP ICH™*

The supplier for service parts selects the scheduling agreement items with their releases using the menu path *Release Process → Release Overview Supplier* as shown in figure 9.18. The just-in-time (JIT) releases require the confirmation via ASN, therefore these are selected (1) and the details displayed (2).

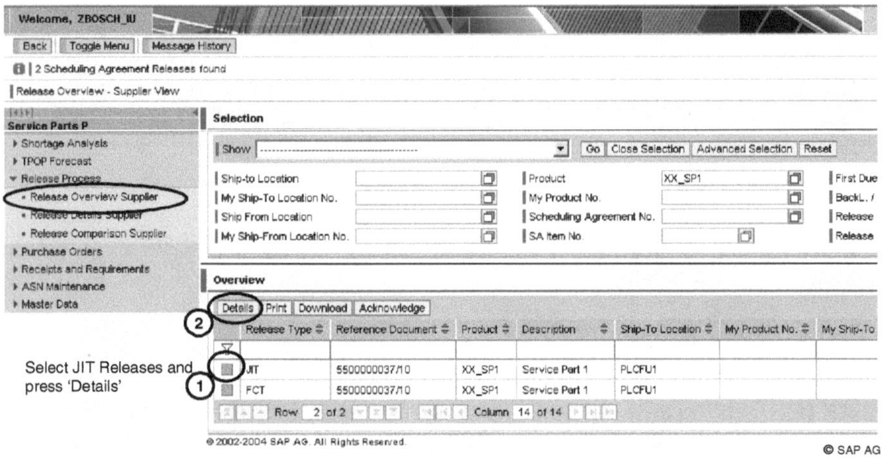

Fig. 9.18. Selection of the JIT-Releases

In the next screen the schedule lines are displayed. The ASN is created by selecting the schedule line and pressing the button 'create ASN', figure 9.19.

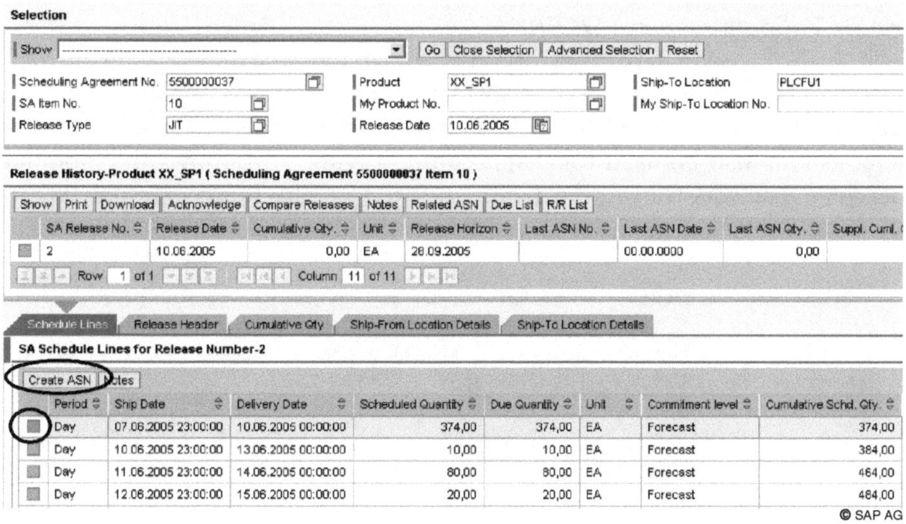

Fig. 9.19. Create ASN for Schedule Line

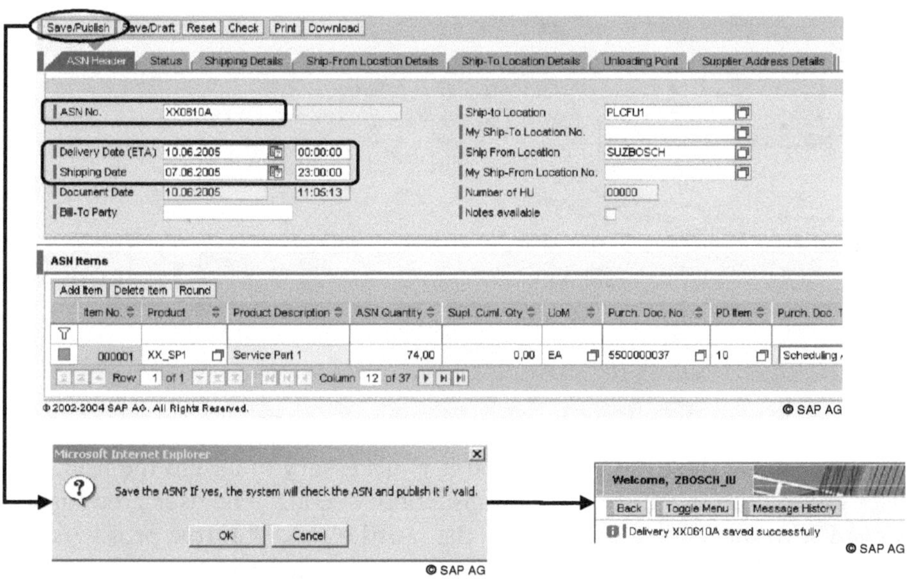

Fig. 9.20. Save and Publish ASN

In the next screen the shipping date and the delivery date can be adjusted if they differ from the dates in the schedule line. The supplier/external number for the ASN is maintained in this screen as well. As the last step the ASN is saved and published to mySAP ERP™ as shown in figure 9.20.

• *ASN Validation in mySAP ERP™*

The ASN in SAP ICH™ corresponds to an inbound delivery in mySAP ERP™. The inbound delivery is displayed, changed and copied in mySAP ERP™ with the transaction VL60. The transaction VL33N for inbound deliveries can also be used for display only. Figure 9.21 shows the inbound delivery that was transferred from SAP ICH™. The field 'external ID' in the header data shows the ASN number defined in SAP ICH™.

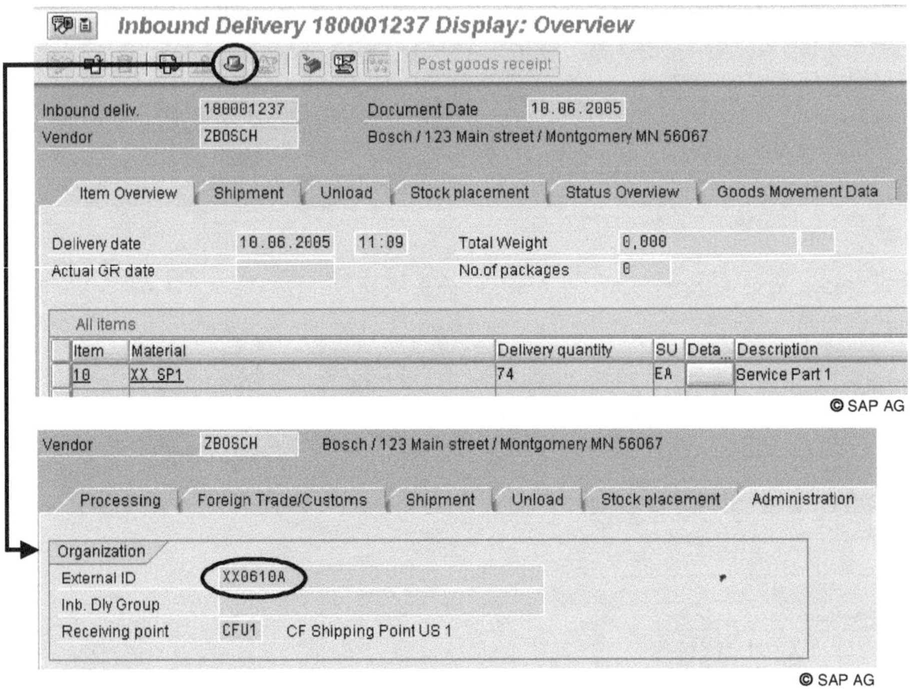

Fig. 9.21. Inbound Delivery (mySAP ERP™)

In order to use the transaction VL60 it is necessary to assign the user to a user group with the customising transaction VL60P2. The user group is assigned with the same transaction to the profile VL60ALL (the profile is defined with the customising path *Logistics Execution → SPM → Extended Inbound Delivery Processing (SPM) → UI Profiles → Maintain Profile → Assign Profile Modules to UI Profile*). It might also be necessary to activate the enhancements for service parts management with the customising path *Logistics Execution → SPM → Activate Enhancements for Service Parts Management (SPM) → Activate Enhancements for Service Parts Management.*

• *ASN Acknowledgement*

After the validation the order number of the mySAP ERP™ inbound delivery is sent as an acknowledgement to SAP ICH™. With the menu path *ASN Maintenance → ASN Overview Supplier* the order number of the mySAP ERP™ inbound delivery is displayed as 'internal ASN number', figure 9.22.

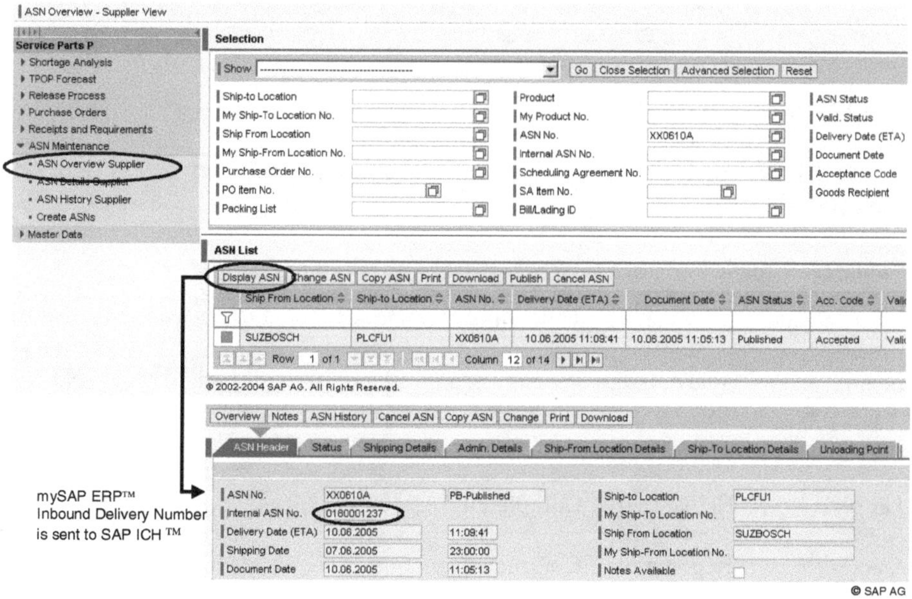

Fig. 9.22. ASN Acknowledgement – mySAP ERP™ Order Number in SAP ICH™

• *Goods Receipt*

After the validation the inbound delivery is sent to SAP EWM™ as an inbound delivery notification. This inbound delivery notification is activated in the background to become an inbound delivery as well. With the transaction /SCWM/PRDI goods receipt in SAP EWM™ is performed, figure 9.23. Before posting the goods receipt in SAP EWM™, first the inbound delivery has to be selected and changed (1), then it has to be posted that the delivery is 'in yard' (2) and it is unloaded ('unload', 3) before goods receipt can be posted (4).

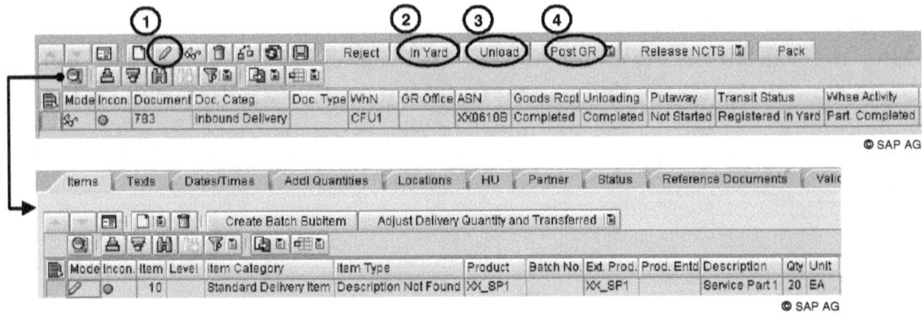

Fig. 9.23. Goods Receipt in SAP EWM™

Table 9.1 provides an overview about the inbound delivery status depending on the postings.

Table 9.2. Inbound Delivery Status

Status Posting	Transit Status	Unloading	Goods Receipt	Put Away	Warehouse Activity
None	In Transit	Not Started	Not Started	Not Started	Not Started
In Yard	Registered in Yard	Not Started	Not Started	Not Started	Not Started
Unload	Registered in Yard	Completed	Not Started	Not Started	Partially Completed
Goods Receipt	Registered in Yard	Completed	Completed	Not Started	Partially Completed

The goods receipt is finally published to mySAP ERP™ – usually in the background.

For test purposes it is also possible to post stock from a flat file using the transaction /SCWM/ISU.

10 Deployment

10.1 Process Overview

Deployment is concerned with the distribution of the goods along the BOD. While DRP calculates the requirements along the BOD in order to determine the procurement quantity at the entry location, deployment creates stock transfer orders from each parent location to its child locations. Figure 10.1 shows an overview of the process.

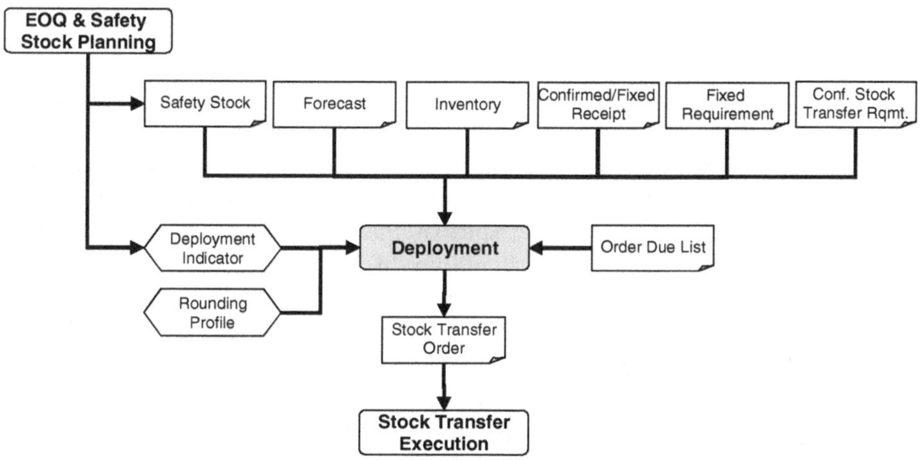

Fig. 10.1. Deployment Process Overview

The functionality for deployment in service parts planning differs in several points from deployment as in Supply Network Planning in SAP APO™. Two major differences are that the stock transfer order is always due today, i.e. there are no stock transfer orders created for future dates, and that the type of the demand (e.g. forecast or sales order) is grouped into tiers and is taken into consideration for the determination of the deployment quantities. Another feature is that deployment does not rely on the results of a previous DRP run but recalculates the requirements in the part of the BOD using the DRP algorithms. Therefore it is not necessary for deployment that planned stock transfer requirements exist.

Deployment is performed from the parent location to its direct child locations. If the BOD contains more than two levels, multiple deployment runs are required. For each parent location a deployment run is required to replenish the inventory from the entry location to the last customer facing location. Figure 10.2 shows this using the BOD from figure 2.2 as an example.

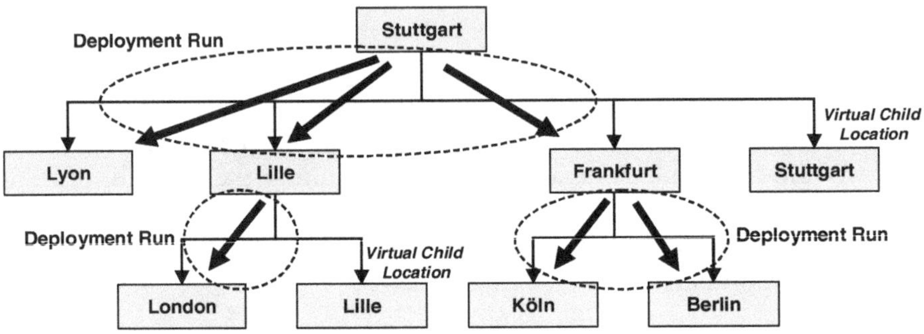

Fig. 10.2. Deployment Runs to Replenish the Entire BOD

In this case three deployment runs are required. Note that no stock transfer is created to the virtual child locations.

Figure 10.3 shows the flow chart for deployment. Depending whether the available quantity for deployment (ATD, available-to-deploy) at the parent location exceeds the demand of the child locations over the lead time or not, deployment proceeds in two different ways.

If the available quantity is above the demand over the lead time, a fair share calculation is performed to determine the deployment quantities for each location. These quantities might be reduced if they exceed the accepted storage quantity of the target location. The accepted storage quantity is represented by the time supply limit (TSL). As a last step rounding is performed according to the standard sequence rules.

In the other case the parent location does not have enough quantity available to cover the children's requirements over the lead time. The demand over the lead time at the child location is an overdue demand at the parent location. For this overdue demand tier processing is performed, where the demand elements are sorted according to their priority tiers. In the subsequent step the fair share calculation is applied to the priority tiers in order to determine the deployment quantities, and rounding is performed according to the sequence rules for the tiers.

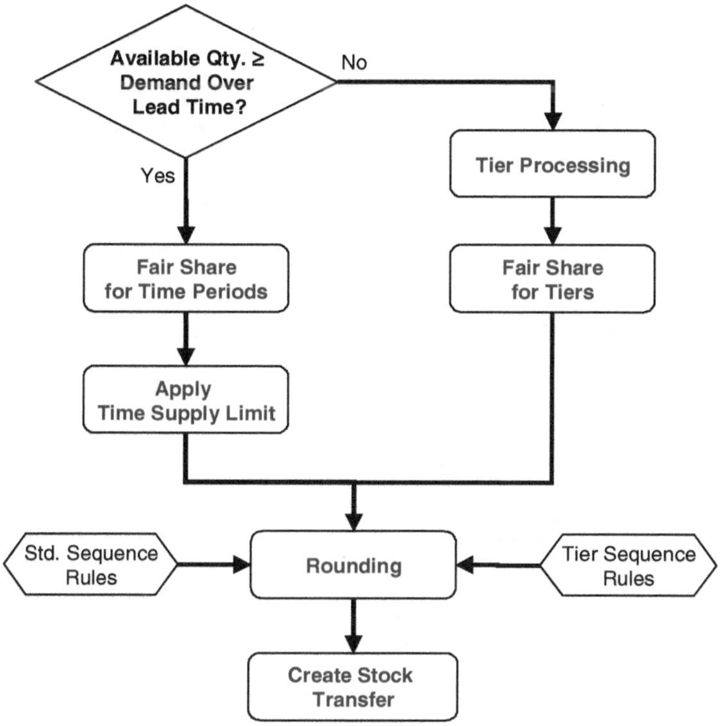

Fig. 10.3. Flow Chart for Deployment

10.2 Pull Deployment and Push Deployment

10.2.1 Difference Between Pull and Push Deployment

There are two different ways to perform deployment in service parts planning, these are pull deployment and push deployment. Pull deployment is performed by regular deployment planning runs and is triggered by a need at the child location – similar like the deployment in Supply Network Planning in SAP APO™. In contrast to this, push deployment is triggered by a goods receipt at the parent location, and the goods are not stored into the bins in the warehouse but sent to the child locations. Push deployment is intended for fast moving parts and has the advantage that it leads to a faster replenishment along the BOD.

• *Deployment Lead Time*
The lead time for deployment (and for DRP and inventory planning as well) differs depending on the use of pull or push deployment, because push deployment is usually faster. Therefore different scheduling scenarios are used for these two deployment strategies. The scheduling scenarios are described in chapter 8.3.

• *Deployment Indicator*
The deployment indicator is a setting in the 'SPP deployment'-view of the product master and defines whether pull or push deployment lead times are used for planning, figure 10.4. The deployment indicator of the product at the target location is the one which is used.

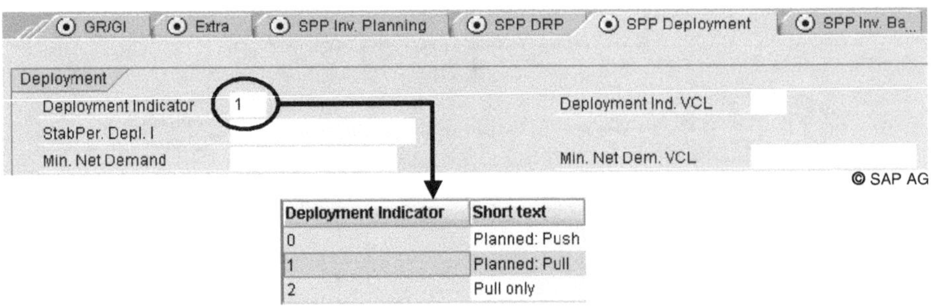

Fig. 10.4. Deployment Indicator in the Product Master

There are three values for the deployment indicator: Plan to push, plan to pull and pull only. Table 10.1 describes the implication of these values for the deployment strategy and the lead time for planning.

Table 10.1. Deployment Indicator

Deployment Indicator	Deployment Strategy	Lead Time for Planning
Plan to Push	Push or Pull	Push
Plan to Pull	Push or Pull	Pull
Pull Only	Pull	Pull

The lead times for pull or push deployment are used for planning purposes. Pull deployment creates stock transfers for all child locations which have an actual demand over lead time – independent of the deployment indicator. Push deployment might create stock transfers to child locations which are 'plan to push' or 'plan to pull'. For the scheduling of the stock transfer the lead times of the effective deployment mode is used – i.e. pull lead times if created by pull deployment and push lead times if created by push deployment.

Except for the difference in determining the available quantity for deployment (which is only the remainder of the goods receipt quantity after EDQA in the case of push deployment), the different lead times and the different triggers, pull and push deployment behave the same.

The deployment indicator is determined by the planning service for EOQ and safety stock (see chapter 6.4) based on the rules that are defined with the transaction /SAPAPO/DEPL_IND_DEF, figure 10.5.

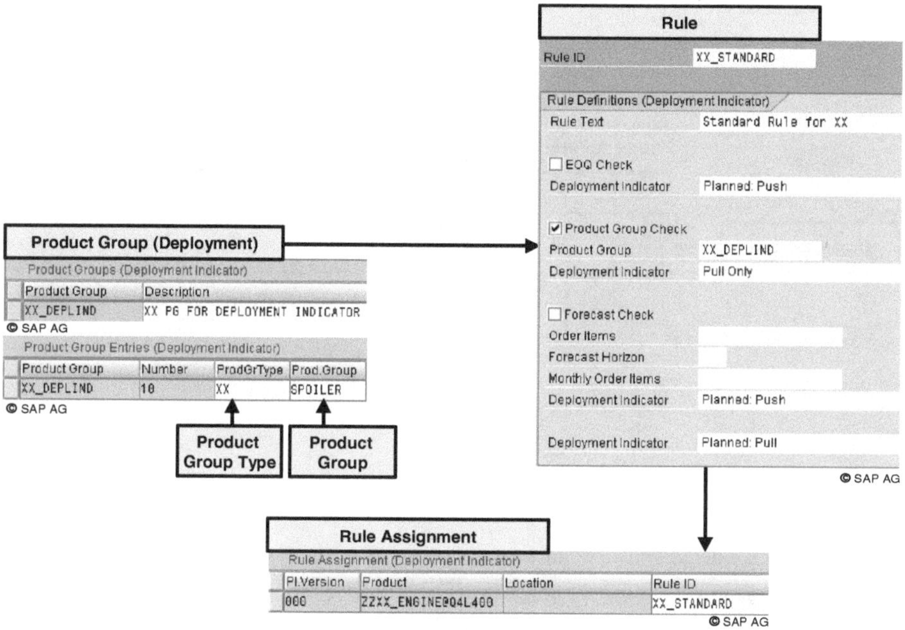

Fig. 10.5. Rules for Deployment Indicator Determination

The rule determines either based on the EOQ, the product group (as shown in figure 10.5) or the forecast the deployment indicator. The fallback indicator is defined at the bottom of the rule – in this case 'planned: pull'. The rule is assigned per location, per product or per location product in the same transaction.

10.2.2 Event Driven Quantity Assignment

Push deployment is triggered by goods receipt. This trigger is modelled using the functionality for event driven quantity assignment (EDQA). EDQA is used for other purposes as well, e.g. the change of ATP categories. The configuration of EDQA is done with the transaction /SAPAPO/EDQA_PD as figure 10.6 shows.

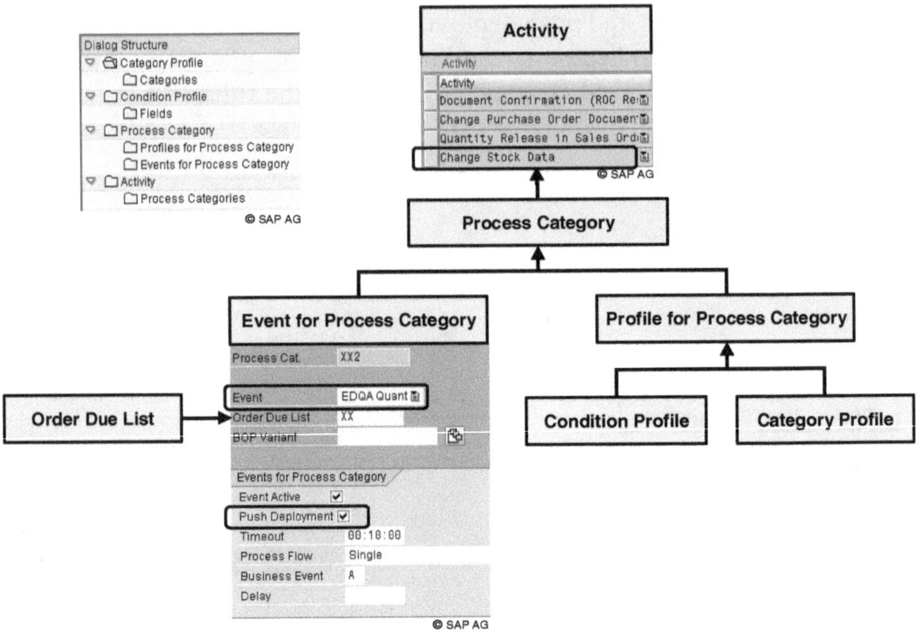

Fig. 10.6. Structure of the EDQA Configuration

• *Process Category*

Push deployment is configured in the process category – or to be more precise, in the 'event for process category' which contains settings defined with the process category as key. The event for the process category contains the event itself – in this case EDQA – and the order due list (ODL).

The process category contains as well a condition profile and – optionally – a category profile. The condition profile restricts the process category by fields from a field catalogue – e.g. material and plant. Push deployment is only performed for goods receipts which match this selection.

The category profile is used in order to change ATP categories. In the SPM solution the stock category is changed depending on the storage location – whether it is stored in the warehouse or still on a receiving dock. The process category itself is assigned to an activity – for push deployment to the activity 'change stock data'. These activities are pre-defined.

• *Order Due List*

Before deploying the receipt quantity it is checked whether there are customer orders with backlog. In this case the quantity is used to cover the open orders first. To determine these orders the order due list (ODL) is used.

The ODL processing is similar to the backorder processing (BOP) but leaner. It is based on the order due list where order priorities can be adjusted interactively. The ODL is defined with the customising path *APO → Global ATP → EDQA → Quantity Assignment to Order Due List → Configure Order Due List*, figure 10.7.

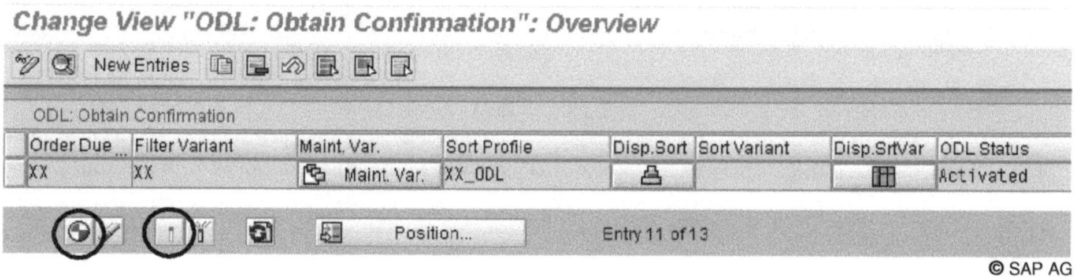

Fig. 10.7. Order Due List

Like backorder processing, the order due list requires a filter type and a sort profile. When defining the fields for the filter type and the sort profile for the ODL, the field catalogue for ODL and not for BOP should be used, figure 10.8.

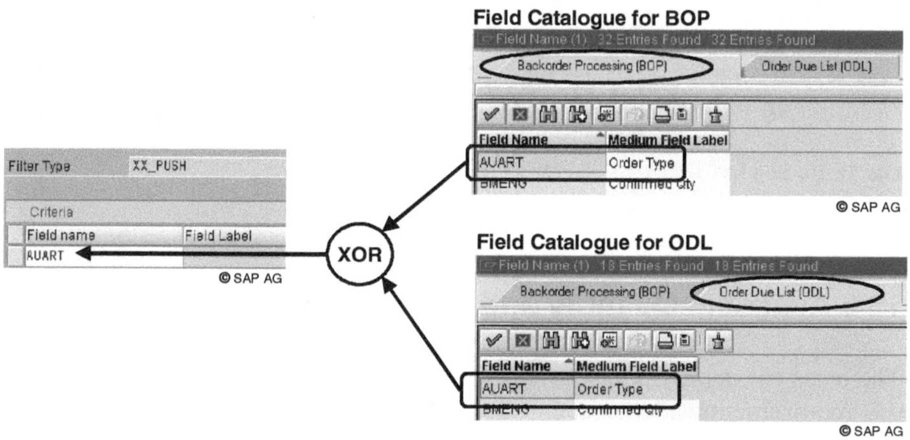

Fig. 10.8. Different Field Catalogues for BOP and ODL

A technical prerequisite for EDQA is that the event linkage (transaction /SAPAPO/EDQA_EC) is active, figure 10.9.

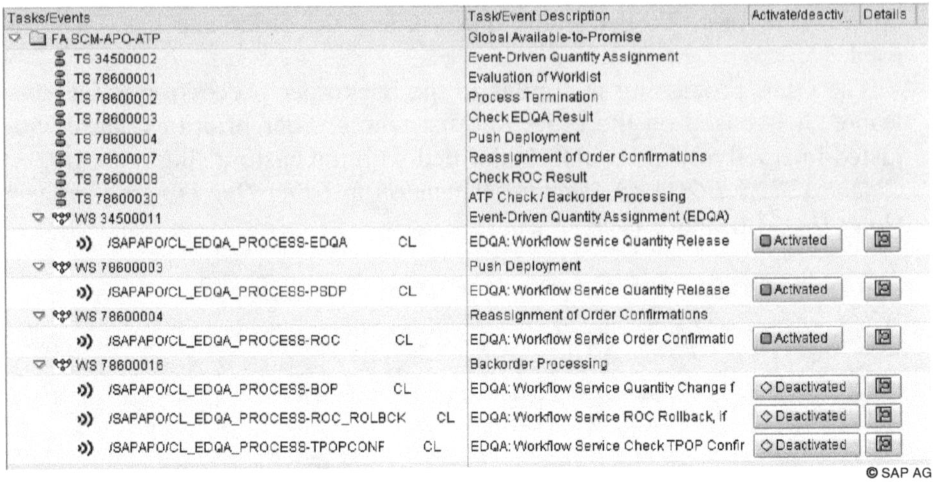

© SAP AG

Fig. 10.9. Event Linkage

Push deployment requires two functions: the deployment itself and the EDQA. EDQA creates a log of its own which is displayed with the transaction /SAPAPO/EDQA as figure 10.10 shows.

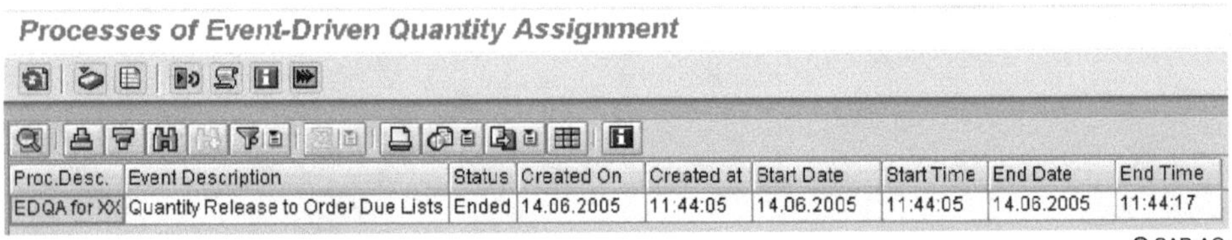

© SAP AG

Fig. 10.10. Log for EDQA

10.3 Available Quantity and Demands for Deployment

The basis for deployment is the determination of the available quantity and the requirements. Deployment does not rely on the results of previous planning processes but does both by itself.

• *Available Quantity*
When push deployment is used, the available quantity for deployment is the remainder of the goods receipt quantity which is not assigned to the order due list by EDQA. For pull deployment however it is necessary to determine the available quantity based on the inventory and the confirmed

customer orders. For this a product availability check is performed using the ATP group of the location product and the business event defined in the general settings for deployment (transaction /SAPAPO/DEPLCUST).

If no business event is maintained, no ATP check is performed but the initial stock as displayed in the DRP matrix is used. Note 902556 provides hints about the definition of the scope of check. The requirements for previously created stock transfer are already removed during the deployment internal net requirements calculation.

• *Deployment Matrix*

The deployment matrix is the basis for the determination of the demands for deployment and is calculated by deployment based on the DRP matrices. The deployment matrix differs slightly from the DRP matrix: the demands are cumulated, the available quantity is determined via ATP check and – this is probably the biggest difference – the demand of some of the child locations is netted with the parent location. This is the case if one of the following conditions applies:

- the location is a virtual child location
- the location does not have a compatible deployment indicator, e.g. if the deployment indicator is set to 'pull only' during push deployment
- the deployment indicator is set to 'plan to pull' or 'pull only' and the location does not have an actual demand over the lead time.

This netting makes the result sometimes a little bit hard to understand.

The relevant part of the deployment matrix is displayed in the deployment simulation UI (see figure 10.26) and in the planning log UI.

• *Deployment Flexibility in the Supply Chain*

As the real demand at the child locations might differ from the forecasted demand, a premature deployment to the child locations reduces the flexibility within the supply chain to supply the child locations according to their future needs. An example is shown in figure 10.11, where deployment distributes the all of the parent location's inventory – in this example 800 pieces – evenly to both child locations A and B. Because the real customer demand differs from the forecast, three days later it is obvious that child B will run out of stock while child A still has excess stock.

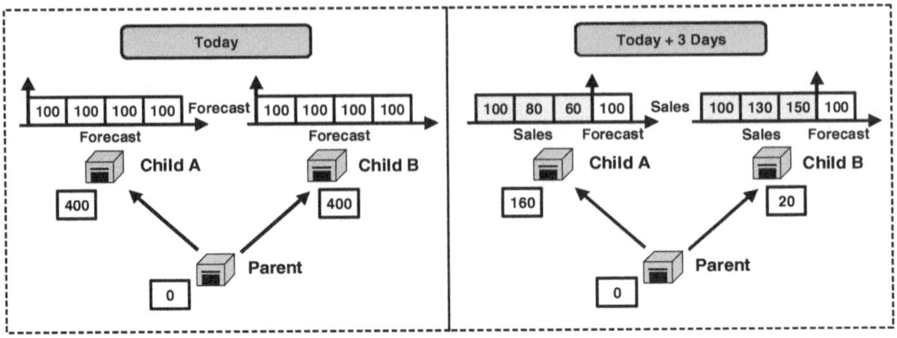

Fig. 10.11. Deployment of the Complete Stock at the Parent Location

Since there is no more stock left at the parent, a more costly lateral transfer from A to B is required. This situation can be avoided by retaining some stock at the parent. Figure 10.12 shows the same initial situation as in figure 10.11, but some stock is still kept at the parent location.

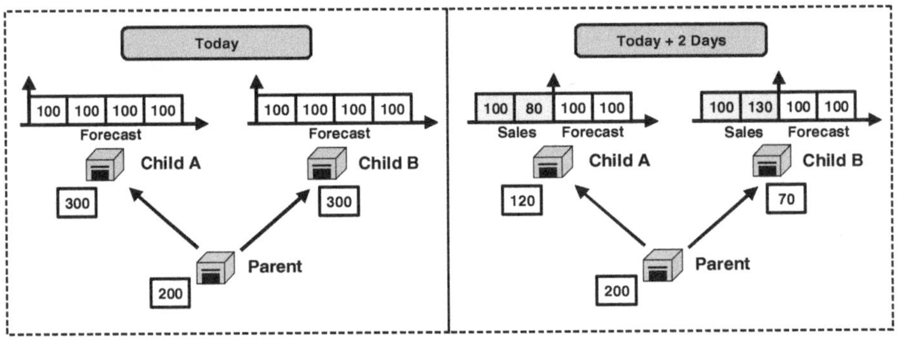

Fig. 10.12. Deployment with Retaining Stock at the Parent Location

Because stock is kept at the parent location, covering the difference between forecast and actual sales is possible with a new deployment from the parent location. There are two factors in favour of retaining inventory at the parent location: One is to limit the portion of the available deployment quantity at the parent location that is used to supply the child locations, and the other is to limit the supply quantity to the child location. The first is modelled by future due receipts and the second by the time supply limit.

• *Future Due Receipts*

When the deployment quantities are calculated, the demand of all child locations and the safety stock of the parent location are taken into consideration. However, stock transfer orders are not created for all locations, e.g.

- if the location is a virtual child location

- if the location does not have a compatible deployment indicator, e.g. if the deployment indicator is set to 'pull only' during push deployment
- if the deployment indicator is set to 'plan to pull' or 'pull only' and the location does not have an actual demand over the lead time

In this case the demand of these locations is netted with the parent location. Whether and how far future receipts are included into this netting depends on the parameter 'horizon for expected receipts' in the 'product'-view of the transportation lane, figure 10.13.

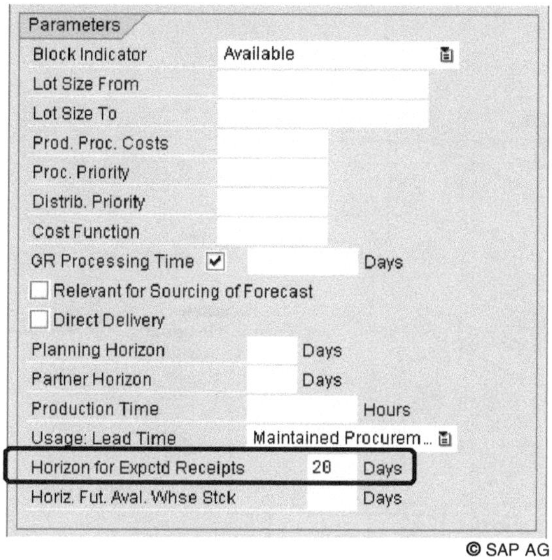

Fig. 10.13. Horizon for Expected Receipts in the Transportation Lane

If nothing is maintained, no future receipts are considered for the netting at the location. The consequence of this 'conservative' setting is that less stock is available for deployment to the child locations.

• *Time Supply Limit*

The time supply limit (TSL) determines how much stock is acceptable at the target location (from a deployment perspective). This value depends on the demand of the target location and is calculated as described in formula 10.1.

$$TSL = \min \{GR_{LT+AGD} + SS_{LT+AGD} + EOQ_{LT+AGD}; GR_{MGD}\} \qquad (10.1)$$

GR_{LT+AGD} denotes the gross demand over lead time plus the days defined in the parameter 'additional gross demand', SS_{LT+AGD} the safety stock and EOQ_{LT+AGD} the economic order quantity for the same time horizon. If the safety stock and the EOQ are time dependent, the highest values within the time period is used. GR_{MGD} is the gross requirement for the number of days as defined in the parameter 'maximum gross demand'. The parameters 'additional gross demand' and 'maximum gross demand' are defined in the service profile for deployment, in the location product and in the TSL parameter table. Figure 10.14 describes how the relevant setting is determined.

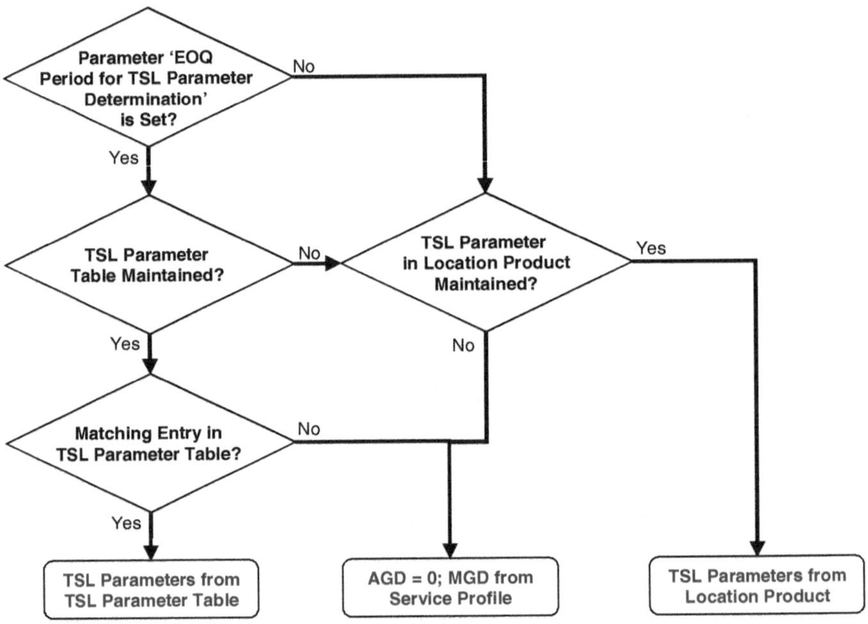

Fig. 10.14. Determination of the TSL Parameters

Figure 10.15 shows the parameter 'EOQ period for TSL parameter determination' and the TSL parameter 'maximum gross demand' in the service profile for deployment (transaction /SAPAPO/DEPLSPRF).

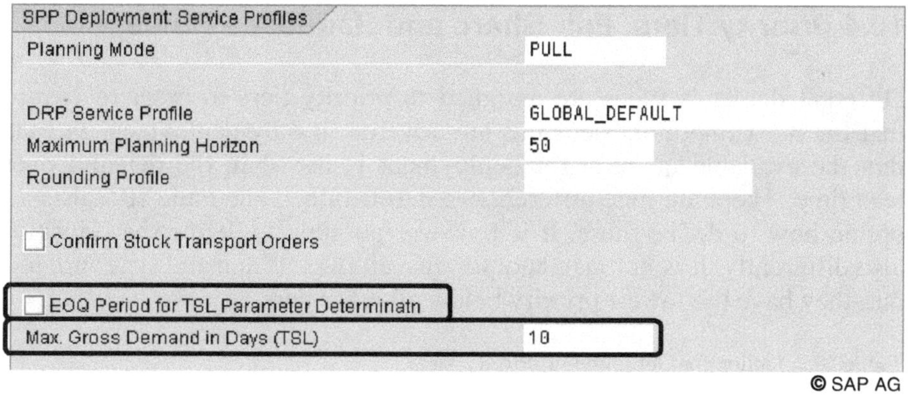

Fig. 10.15. TSL Parameter in the Service Profile

The table for TSL parameters is maintained with the transaction /SAPAPO/TSLPAR. Figure 10.16 shows the parameters 'additional gross demand' and 'maximum gross demand' in the product master of the child location.

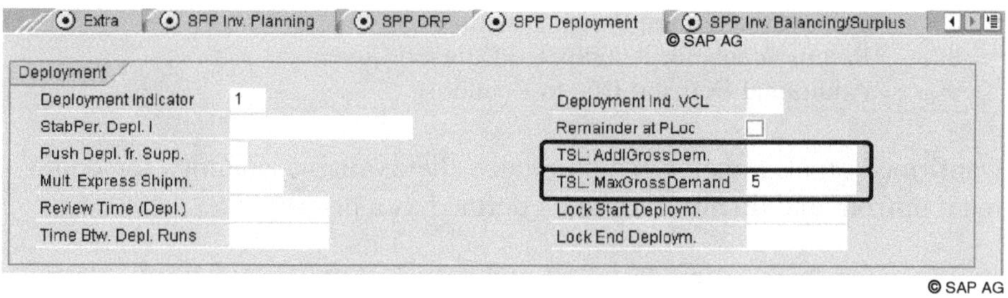

Fig. 10.16. TSL Parameters in the Product Master

Assuming that sufficient stock is available, only the maximum deployable quantity is sent to the child location. The maximum deployable quantity (MDQ) is the difference to the time supply limit (TSL), i.e. the TSL minus the stock at the child location and the stock in transit – unless the demand over lead time (DOLT) exceeds the TSL, formula 10.2.

$$MDQ = \max \{TSL - Stock_{Child\ Location} - In\ Transit;\ DOLT\} \qquad (10.2)$$

10.4 Priority Tiers, Fair Share and Sequence Rules

Different demands types are assigned to priority tiers in order to ensure that the most important demands are covered first by deployment in case that the available quantity for deployment is less than the demand over lead time. There are nine different pre-defined tiers, and table 10.2 lists an option how to define these. It is however possible to define the priorities also differently. It is not mandatory to use all tiers. If demand types are left out, they have the lowest priority below all other tiers.

Table 10.2. Option for Definition of Priority Tiers

Priority	Tier
1	Backorders
2	Prioritised Fixed Requirements
3	Demand Over Replenishment Lead Time: Forecast, Stock Transfer Requirements, Substitution Requirements
4	Safety Stock of the Child Location
5	Fixed Requirements (Non-Prioritised)
6	Proportion of the Parent's Safety Stock at the Child Location
7	Safety Stock of the Parent Location
8	Requirements for Anticipated Demand Coverage
9	Additional Demand Due to Rounding

Confirmed stock transfer orders reduce the available quantity for deployment upfront and do not have to be defined as a priority tier.

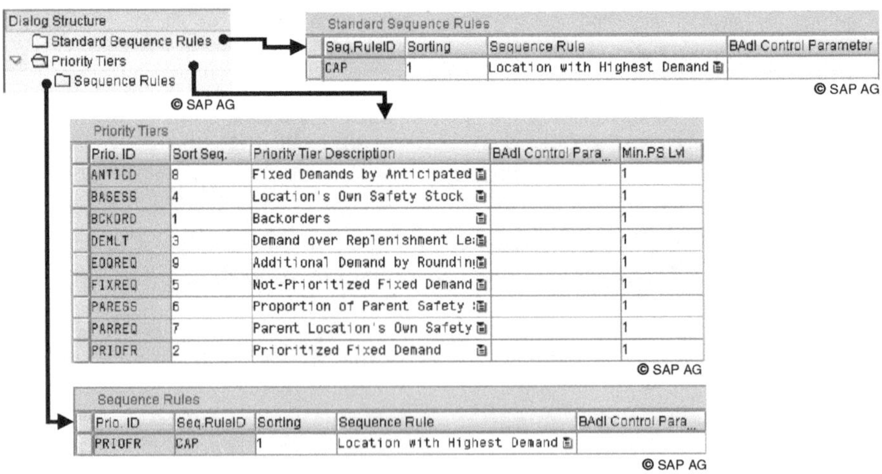

Fig. 10.17. Priority Tiers and Sequence Rules

The priority tiers are defined with the transaction /SAPAPO/TIERDEF, as shown in figure 10.17. Since deployment is performed from the parent to its direct children, the priority tiers apply also only to the demand types of the direct children.

In the same transaction sequence rules are defined and assigned to the tiers. The purpose of the sequence rules is to define the sequence of locations in which rounding of fair share quantities is performed. The standard sequence rules are applied if the available quantity for deployment is higher than the demand over lead time. In the other case the sequence rule is applied which is assigned to the tier where fair share is performed.

• *Example without Tier Processing*

The following example helps to understand how deployment calculates the deployment quantities using fair share and rounding in case that the available quantity for deployment is above the children's demands over the lead time. The initial situation for this example is shown in figure 10.18 where the locations A and B are supplied by the parent location C. The planning situation is simplified in order to make the example easier – e.g. the parent location does not have any own requirements in this case. Both locations have forecast demands and fixed requirements; location B has additionally a backorder (i.e. a customer order which is overdue for delivery). The net demand of the child locations is cumulated. The first date for the cumulated net demand is at the end of the lead time. Both child locations A and B have current stock of 10 pieces. The lead time from C to A is two days and from C to B three days.

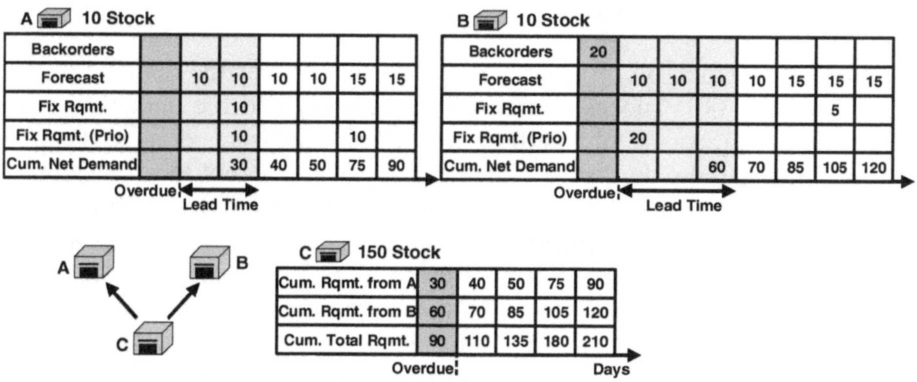

Fig. 10.18. Deployment Example – Initial Situation

The diagram at the bottom of figure 10.18 shows the demand situation at the parent location C. The cumulated net demand of the child locations is shifted by the lead time, therefore the demand over lead time at the child locations – in this a total of 90 pieces – is overdue at the parent location. For this example we assume 150 pieces of stock at the parent location C.

Deployment determines the order quantity for the stock transfer by allocating the available quantity to the child location according to the left branch of the flow chart shown in figure 10.3: Fair share, applying the TSL and rounding. Fair share determines the first proposal for the stock transfers. Figure 10.19 provides an overview about this procedure (assuming that no restrictions due to TSL apply).

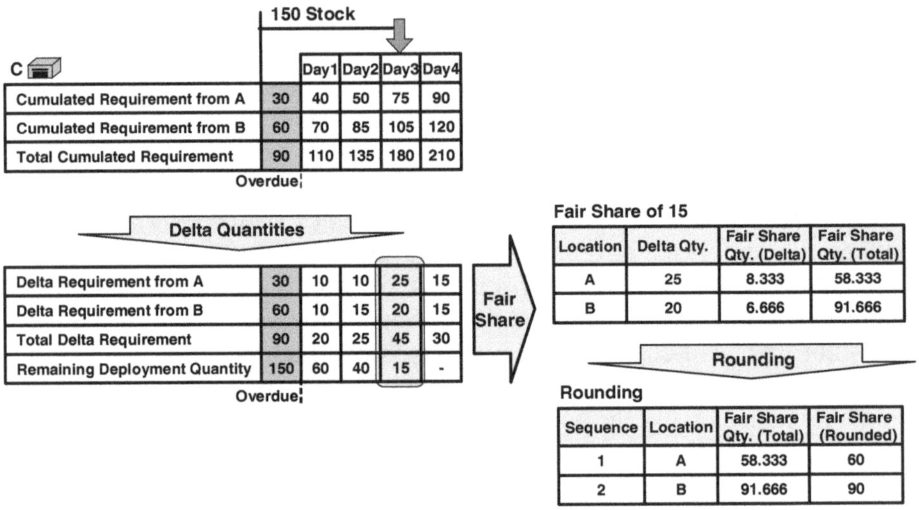

Fig. 10.19. Deployment Example Without Tier Processing

The available stock of 150 pieces is sufficient to cover the demand of the next two days (135 pieces cumulated) completely and the demand of the third day (180 pieces cumulated) partially. This analysis is done at the parent location, i.e. the demand for the next day at the parent location origins from a demand of the lead time plus one day at the child location. In the third day there are delta requirements of 25 pieces from location A and of 20 pieces from location B. However, there are only an additional 15 pieces stock left. The allocation of these 15 pieces to the child locations A and B is performed with fair share. The fair share quantity FS allocates the remaining deployment quantity (RDQ) proportionally to the delta requirement DR of the child locations in this time bucket, formula 10.3.

$$FS_{Child} = RDQ * DR_{Child} / \sum DR_{All\ Children} \tag{10.3}$$

In this example the fair share quantity for location A is calculated as

$$FS_A = 15 * 25 / (25 + 20) = 8.333 \tag{10.4}$$

and the fair share quantity for location B to 6.666 pieces accordingly. The total fair share quantity is determined by adding the cumulated demand of the previous days (which is covered by the available deployment quantity in any case). For location A the total fair share quantity becomes 58.333 pieces and for location B 91.333 pieces.

In the next step rounding is performed according to standard sequence rules – in this case first the location A is rounded to the pack stage of 10 pieces to a deployment quantity of 60 pieces. In order not to exceed the available quantity, the deployment quantity for location B is rounded downward to 90 pieces. Unless the maximum deployable quantity restricts these quantities, two stock transfers are created – to location A with 60 pieces and to location B with 90 pieces.

Note that as the result of deployment only one stock transfer is created per location, and that the stock transfer is always due today.

• *Example with Tier Processing*

For the same situation as shown in figure 10.18 we assume that only a stock of 60 pieces is available at the parent location C. Since the demand over lead time is 90 pieces, now tier processing is performed by splitting the demands over the lead time (which are overdue at the parent location) into the tier categories as defined in the table for priority tiers. Figure 10.20 shows this example for the tier definition as listed in table 10.2.

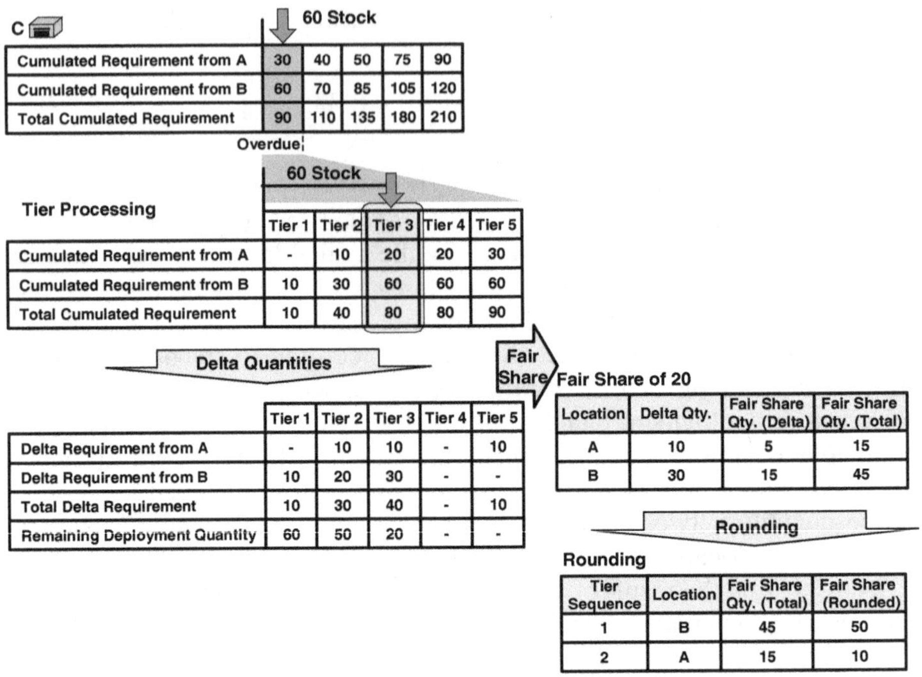

Fig. 10.20. Result of the Deployment Run

The procedure for determining the deployment quantity with tier processing is similar to the procedure shown in figure 10.19 – the main difference is that fair share is performed now for tiers instead of days.

10.5 Expedited Shipments

If it is possible to cover a demand in time or earlier by choosing a faster but more expensive means of transport, this shipment is called 'expedited'. The prerequisite for expedited shipments are:

- there is a faster but more expensive means of transport,
- the product is not excluded from expedited shipment (a setting in the 'properties of SPP'-view of the product master) and
- there are tier requirements eligible for expedited shipment.

Whether a tier requirement is eligible for expedited shipment or not is defined in the service profile for deployment, figure 10.21. In this case demands belonging to tier 1 or to tier 2 are eligible.

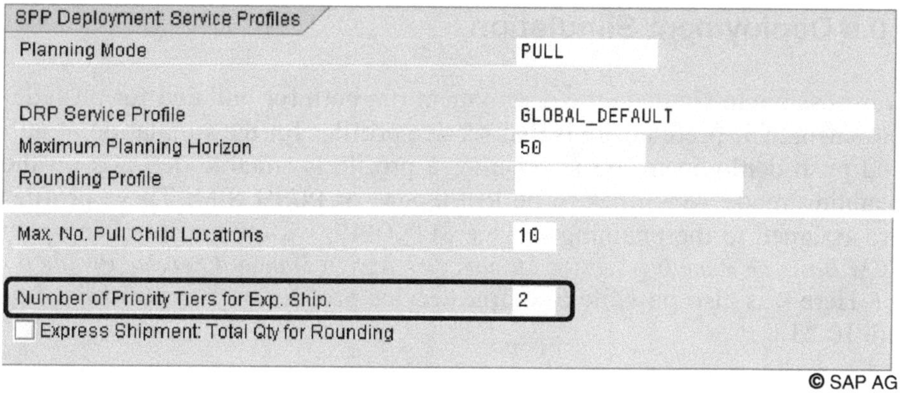

Fig. 10.21. Eligible Tiers for Expedited Shipment

If there are demands eligible for expedited shipment, the deployment run is performed first for the expedited shipments and then with the remaining quantity for the normal demands. Stock transfer orders for expedited shipment are displayed separately in the result screen of deployment simulation (see figure 10.26) and in the log for deployment.

Other parameters for expedited shipment are the settings for maximum weight, volume and dimension for expedited shipment in the header data of the transportation lane, figure 10.22. These are economical limits and not technical limits (since they are independent of the means of transport).

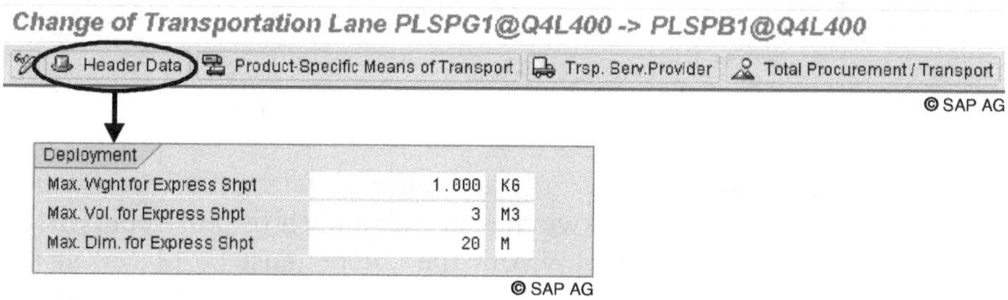

Fig. 10.22. Parameters to Limit the Expedited Shipment per Transportation Lane

The weight and volume for the requested quantity is taken from the product master. If the potential expedited shipment exceeds these limits, the expedited shipment is created only within these limits.

10.6 Deployment Simulation

It is possible to simulate the deployment run both for pull and for push deployment. The prerequisite is that service profiles for the simulation of pull and push deployment exist. Whether a profile is suitable depends on the planning mode which has to be PULL_SIM or PUSH_SIM. These profiles are assigned to the planning service SPP_DEPL with the customising path *SCM Basis → Planning Service Manager → Assign Standard Service Profile for UI*. Here it is also possible to define service profiles user specifically, figure 10.23.

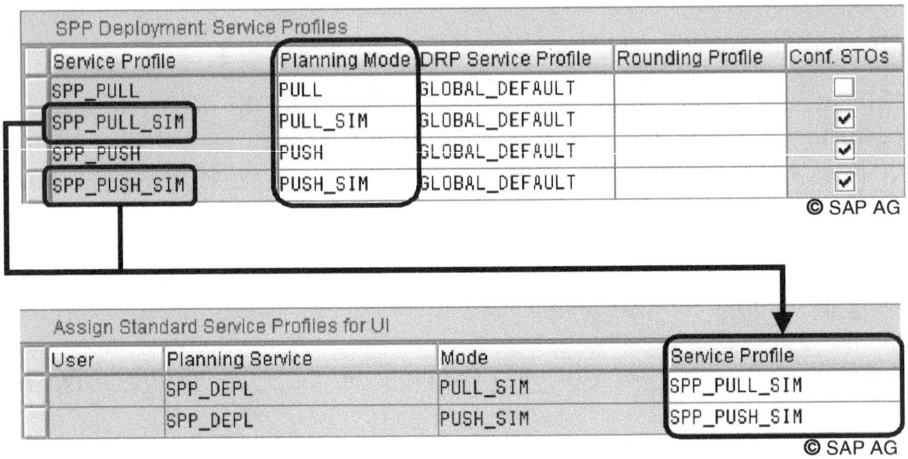

Fig. 10.23. Deployment Service Profile and Assignment for Simulation

The deployment simulation is performed with the transaction /SAPAPO/SPPDEPL. The mode switches between push or pull deployment. For the simulation of push deployment the cursor must be placed at the parent location and the available quantity – the quantity for the simulated goods receipt – has to be maintained interactively. For the simulation of pull deployment the cursor can be placed on any of the child locations, figure 10.24.

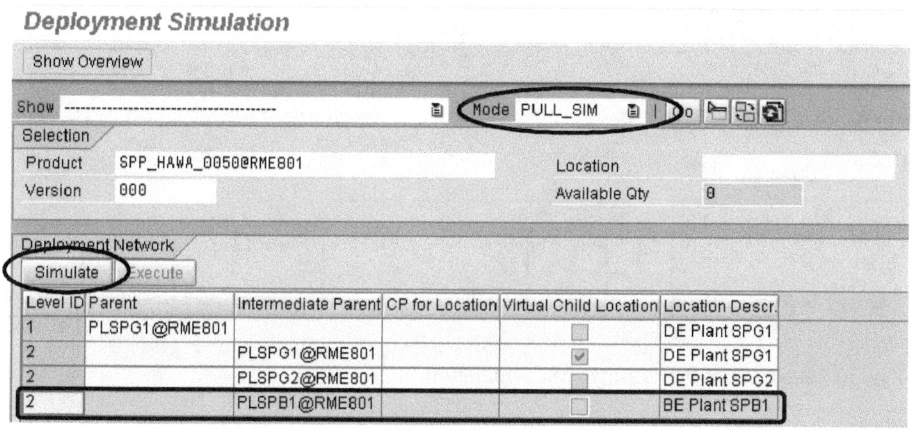

Fig. 10.24. Deployment Simulation

The result of the deployment simulation is displayed in different views. The stock transfer overview shows the available quantity for deployment and for each of the locations additional information, e.g.:

- whether the location is a parent location
- whether the demands of the location are netted with its parent location (see chapter 10.3)
- the calculated deployment quantities for the child locations ('deployed quantity')
- whether a stock transfer order would have been created (checkbox 'STO')
- the quantities of the stock transfer orders for expedited shipment and for normal shipment

Figure 10.25 shows an example, where out of the 80 available pieces only four are kept at the parent location SPG1, 40 pieces are sent to the location SPG2 and 36 pieces are sent to the location SPB1 – 10 pieces out of these as expedited shipment.

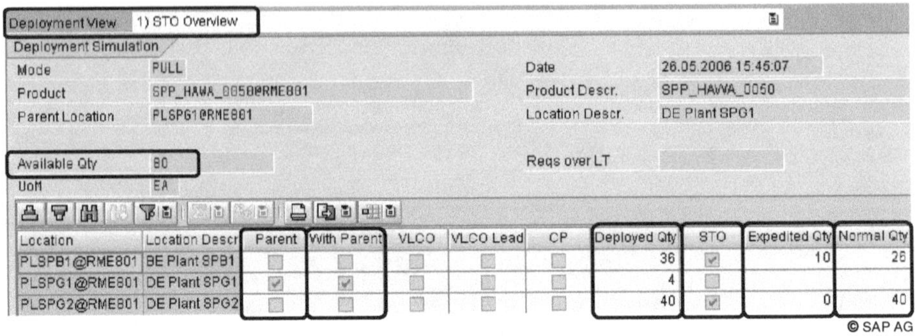

Fig. 10.25. Result of the Deployment Simulation

In this case stock transfer orders would have been created for SPG2 and SPB1 but not for SPG1, since this is the parent location.

More detailed information is available in the deployment views 'express shipment' (if expedited shipments are created) and 'normal shipping', figure 10.26. Here the part of the deployment matrix is displayed which is the basis for the calculation of the deployment quantities.

Deployment View: 2) Express Shipment

Location	Location Descr.	Deployed Qty	STO	Tier 2	Tier 2 (r)	Fair Share Qty	Reqs over LT	Max. Ship Qty.
PLSPG2@RME801	DE Plant SPG2	0	☐	0,000	0,000	0,000	40,000	40,000
PLSPB1@RME801	BE Plant SPB1	10	☑	10,000	10,000	10,000	39,000	39,000
PLSPG1@RME801	DE Plant SPG1	0	☐	0,000	0,000	0,000	127,000	

© SAP AG

Deployment View: 3) Normal Shipping

Location	Location Descr.	Deployed Qty	STO	Tier 6	Tier 6 (r)	Tier 7	Tier 7 (r)	Fair Share Qty	Reqs over LT	Max. Ship Qty.
PLSPB1@RME801	BE Plant SPB1	26	☑	25,084	26,000	25,084	26,000	26,000	29,000	29,000
PLSPG2@RME801	DE Plant SPG2	40	☑	39,461	40,000	39,461	40,000	40,000	40,000	40,000
PLSPG1@RME801	DE Plant SPG1	4	☐	0,000	0,000	126,226	127,000	4,000	127,000	

© SAP AG

Fig. 10.26. Detailed Views for the Deployment Simulation Result

In the 'express shipment'-view only plant SPB1 has tier requirements which are eligible for expedited shipment – in this case 10 pieces of tier 2. These 10 pieces are allocated first and reduce the available quantity as well as the demand – in the 'express shipment'-view the requirements over lead time for the location SPB1 are 39 pieces, whereas in the 'normal shipping'-view the requirements over lead time are reduced to 29 pieces.

The tiers – as displayed in the detailed views – contain the cumulated demands. In the 'normal shipping'-view the cumulated requirements of the locations SPB1 and SPG2 for tier 6 and tier 7 are displayed. The demand types are however of the tiers 3 to 5 and are covered by the available quantity. Only location SPG1 has requirements of tier 7. Since this requirement of 127 pieces is not covered by the available quantity any more, fair share is performed. In this case the fair share is very simple: SPG1 gets the remaining quantity of 4 pieces.

10.7 Stock Transfer Approval

If the flag for 'confirm stock transport orders' is set in the service profile, all the stock transfer orders are not released automatically but require an interactive approval, figure 10.27.

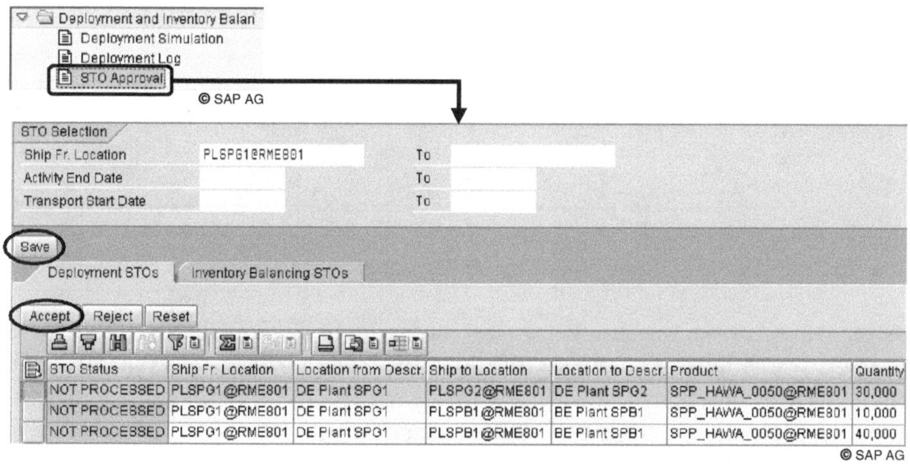

Fig. 10.27. Stock Transfer Approval

The stock transfer approval is performed with the same transaction /SAPAPO/SPPDEPL as the deployment simulation. After saving the approval the status of the order changes to 'approved' and the stock transfer order is sent to mySAP ERP™.

10.8 Stock Transfer Execution

The stock transfer execution involves three systems and two locations. The processing of the stock transfer order is done mainly in mySAP ERP™, SAP EWM™ posts the goods issue and the goods receipt and – after approving the stock transfer – SAP APO™ reflects the current data for planning purposes. Figure 10.28 provides an overview of the document flow across the three systems for the source and the target location.

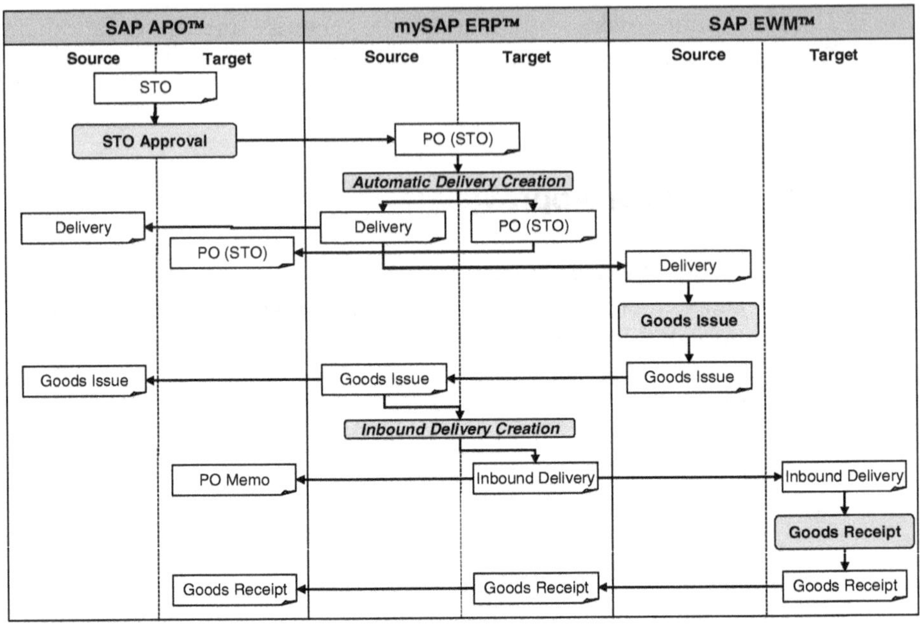

Fig. 10.28. Order Flow for the Stock Transfer Execution

After transferring the stock transfer order to mySAP ERP™ a delivery is created immediately at the source location. The delivery is transferred to SAP EWM™ – which is displayed in mySAP ERP™ by the status 'distributed' in the delivery, figure 10.29 (transaction VL03N).

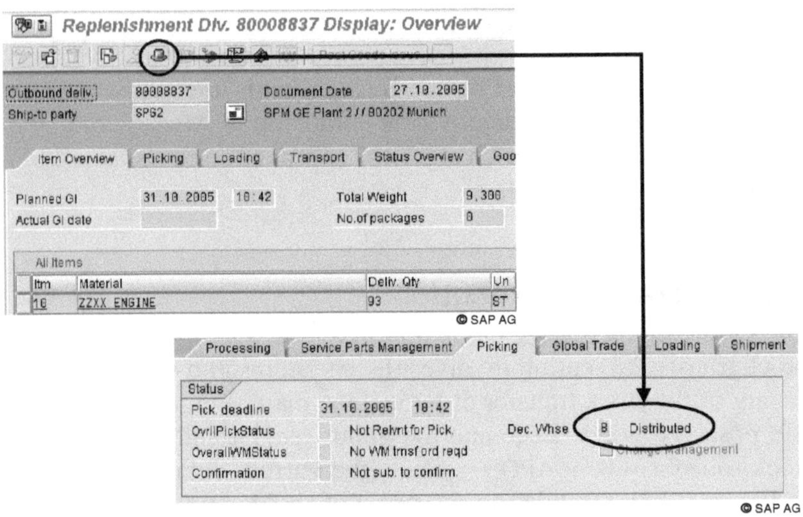

Fig. 10.29. Outbound Delivery with Status 'Distributed' in mySAP ERP™

Based on this delivery it is possible to post the goods issue in SAP EWM™. The goods issue will trigger in mySAP ERP™ the creation of an inbound delivery at the target location. SAP EWM™ finally posts the goods receipt based on the inbound delivery.

For stock transfers within a company the order type UBL is used, for cross company stock transfer the order type UB. The delivery type NL is assigned for the stock transfer within a company and delivery type NLCC for cross company stock transfer. Even for stock transfers within a company an info record is required because the confirmation control (0004) has to be maintained. The automatic creation of a delivery is defined with the customising path *Materials Management → Purchasing → Purchase Order → Set Up Stock Transport Order → Activate Automatic Delivery Creation and CRM Billing*, figure 10.30.

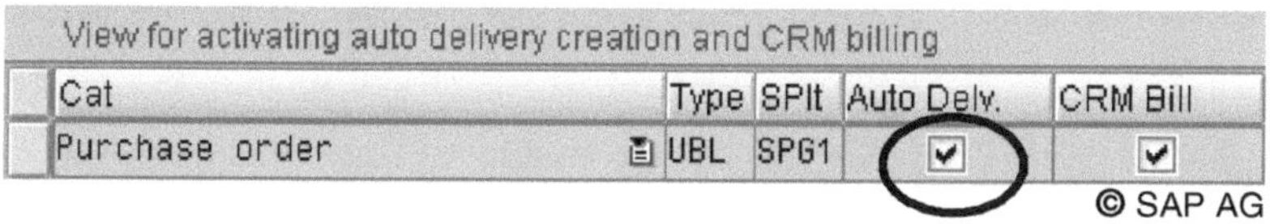

Fig. 10.30. Automatic Delivery Creation

11 Inventory Balancing

11.1 Process Overview

The supply of locations is done via deployment along the BOD. Lateral stock transfers are usually avoided because there are more costly: The service part has to transferred one more time, which means additional costs, and the lateral transfer itself might be less cost efficient due to low volume. In exceptional cases a lateral stock transfer is desired nevertheless.

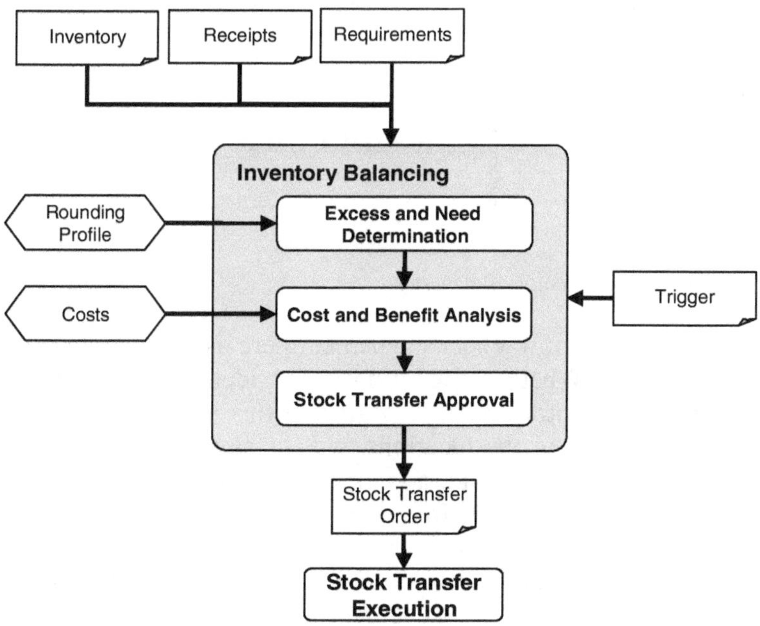

Fig. 11.1. Inventory Balancing Process Overview

The purpose of inventory balancing is to supply locations laterally – i.e. not along the regular paths of the BOD – in case of need at one location and surplus at the other location. The nature of inventory balancing is short term and is intended in most cases as an optional step if deployment fails to supply the needs.

• *Example*
A BOD with a very simple structure is used as an example for inventory balancing. This simple BOD contains the parent SPG1 and two children SPG2 and SPB1, figure 11.2. The normal way of supply is via deployment from the parent to the children along the BOD. In this example however, there is a shortage for the child SPB1 which can not be covered by the parent. Therefore the shortage at SPB1 will remain even after deployment.

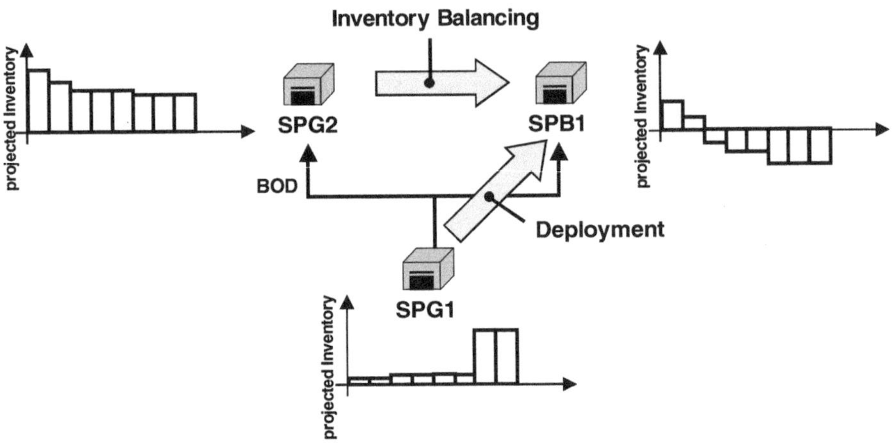

Fig. 11.2. Example for Inventory Balancing

Inventory balancing now checks whether there is another location with surplus in the near. Whether a location is considered to be 'in the near' is modelled by the inventory balancing area. If this is the case, a transportation lane exists between the locations and the savings by a stock transfer exceed the costs by a threshold, a lateral stock transfer is created – in this example from SPG2 to SPB1. Inventory balancing does only create stock transfers outside the 'normal' BOD relationship.

Inventory balancing might also be triggered by a de-stocking decision or by supersession in order to get rid of the predecessor product.

11.2 Inventory Balancing Area

The inventory balancing area contains those locations which are allowed to perform these lateral stock transfers. The inventory balancing area is modelled as a hierarchy. A dummy location (which is not used for any other purpose) defines the name of the inventory balancing area, and all locations of the inventory balancing area are assigned to this dummy location. The hierarchy structure for this hierarchy is assigned to the general settings for inventory balancing. Figure 11.3 gives an overview of these settings. Note that not the ID but the name (i.e. the short text) of the hierarchy is used in the assignments.

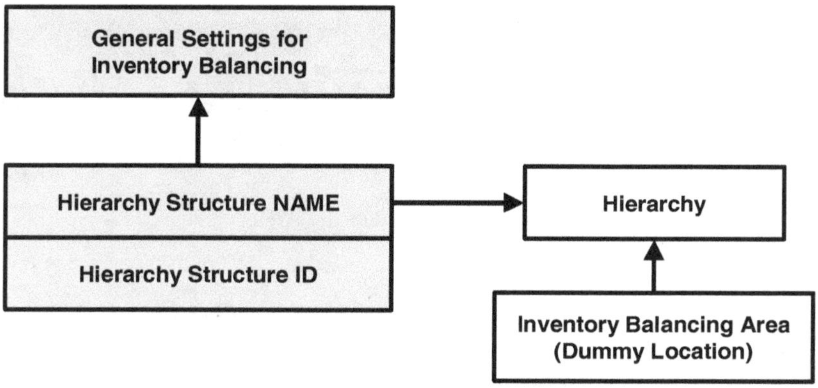

Fig. 11.3. Structure of the Settings for the Inventory Balancing Area

• *Dummy Location for Inventory Balancing Area*
The dummy location is created in SAP APO™ with the transaction /SAPAPO/LOC3 as shown in figure 11.4. Since the location is interactively created and not transferred from mySAP ERP™, it is necessary to assign the location explicitly to the active model 000.

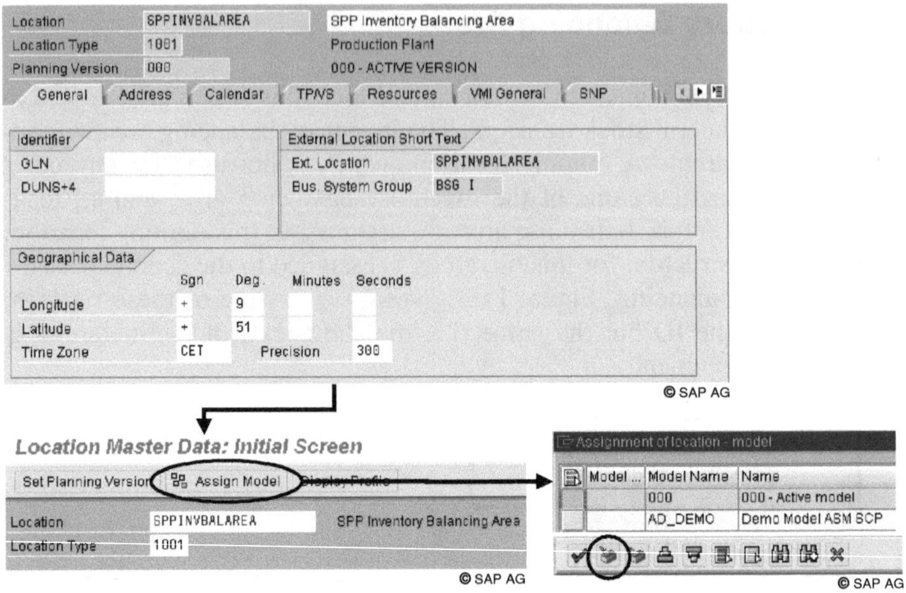

Fig. 11.4. Dummy Location for the Inventory Balancing Area

• *Hierarchy for Inventory Balancing*

The hierarchy for inventory balancing (here: SPP_INVBAL_AREAS) is maintained like any other hierarchy with the transaction /SAPAPO/RELHSHOW and with reference to the hierarchy structure for inventory balancing areas (here: SPP_INVBALANCING), figure 11.5. The inventory balancing area (here: SPPINVBALAREA) is the dummy location that is assigned at the first level of the hierarchy.

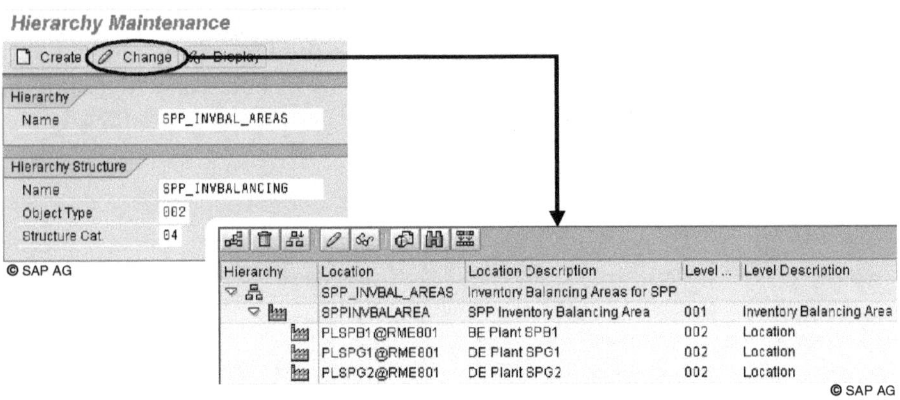

Fig. 11.5. Inventory Balancing Area

In this example the inventory balancing area SPPINVBALAREA is defined by the dummy location SPPINVBALAREA, and the locations PLSPB1@RME801, PLSPG1@RME801 and PLSPG2@RME801 are assigned to the dummy location (the parent location has to be assigned as well). This is one prerequisite for stock transfers between PLSPG2@RME801 and PLSPB1@RME801 – a transportation lane between the locations is the other. As a last step the hierarchy has to be assigned to the active model 000.

• *Hierarchy Structure*

The hierarchy structure for inventory balancing areas is defined with the customising path *APO → Master Data → Hierarchy → Define Hierarchy Structure* and relates to the object 'location' and has a link to the table /SAPAPO/RELEHLOC, figure 11.6.

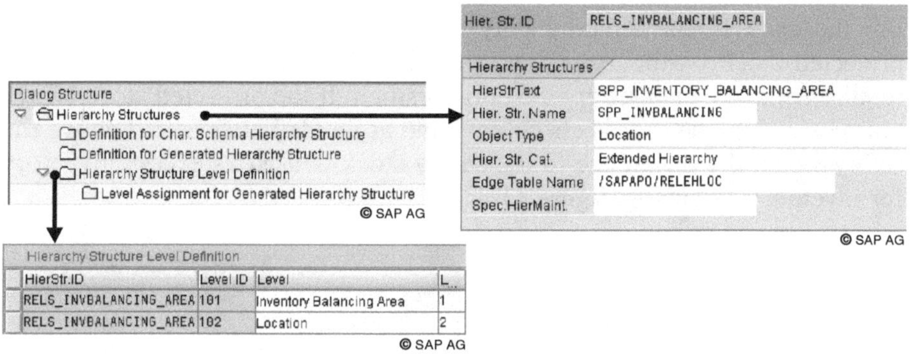

Fig. 11.6. Hierarchy Structure for Inventory Balancing

• *Assignment of the Hierarchy Structure for Inventory Balancing Area*

As a last step the hierarchy structure is assigned to the general settings for inventory balancing. Only one hierarchy structure can be used for inventory balancing. This is defined with the customising path *APO → Supply Chain Planning → SPP → Inventory Balancing → Make General Settings for Inventory Balancing*, figure 11.7.

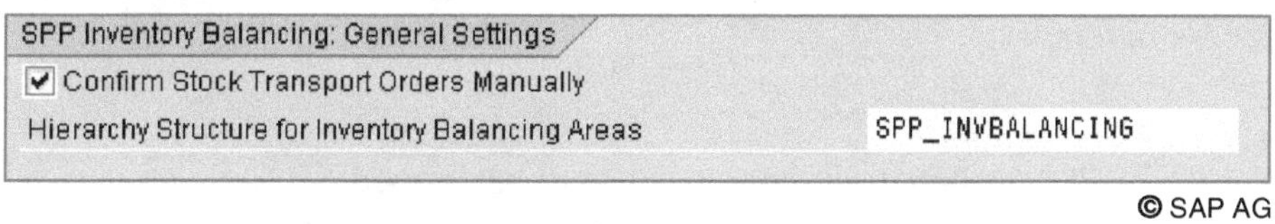

Fig. 11.7. Assignment of the Hierarchy Structure for Inventory Balancing

11.3 Excess and Need Determination

The prerequisite for a lateral stock transfer is that there is at least one location with excess inventory and one location with a shortage. Therefore the first step in inventory balancing is the determination of locations with need and locations with excess.

Lateral stock transfers are usually an additional effort. Therefore it is important to ensure that the excess inventory is not just a momentary state to cover requirements in the very near future. Before the location with excess inventory transfers its stock to the location with need it should also be checked that the parent location will not cover the need in the meantime. These checks are performed using three parameters for the excess check date, the need check date and the need verification date.

- *Excess Determination*

For the excess determination only the stock on hand is considered. The projected stock (without receipts) describes how much stock is left if all requirements are covered by the current stock. If the projected stock (without receipts) at the excess check date and at the day after is still above the safety stock, the difference to the safety stock is used as excess inventory for inventory balancing, figure 11.8.

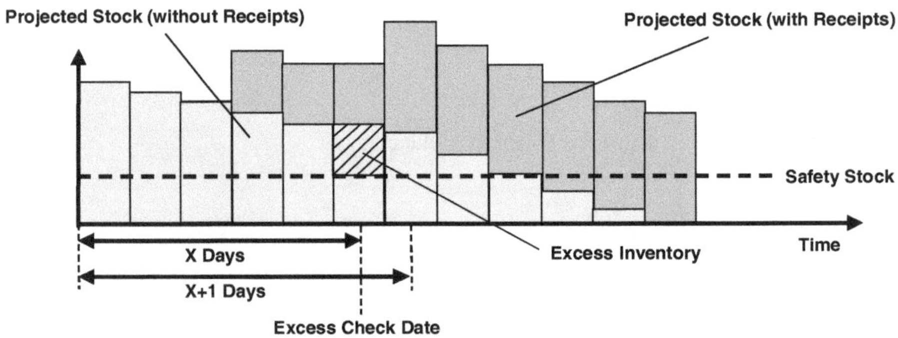

Fig. 11.8. Excess Determination

Figure 11.8 shows also that the later the excess check date, the smaller the excess inventory.

- *Need Determination*

For the need determination three checks are performed:

1. Is there a net requirement at the need check date?
2. Is there still a net requirement at the need verification date?

3. Does the parent also have a net requirement at the need check date?

Only if all three conditions are met a need is calculated at the location. The need is calculated as the net requirement at the need check date. Figure 11.9 shows the need determination (without the check at the parent location). The need quantity is the net demand at the need check date.

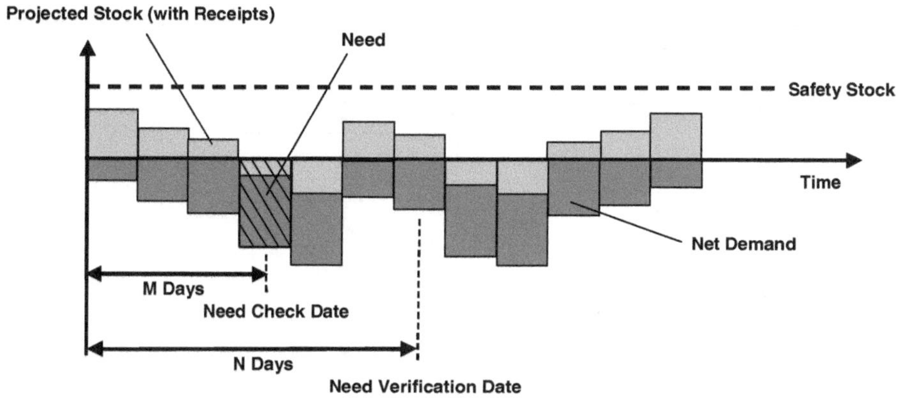

Fig. 11.9. Need Determination

• *Check Date Parameters*

The parameters for the dates are defined in the inventory balancing parameter profile with the transaction /SAPAPO/RDPLPRF. The inventory balancing parameter profile is assigned to the inventory balancing area with the transaction /SAPAPO/RDPLPRFA, figure 11.10.

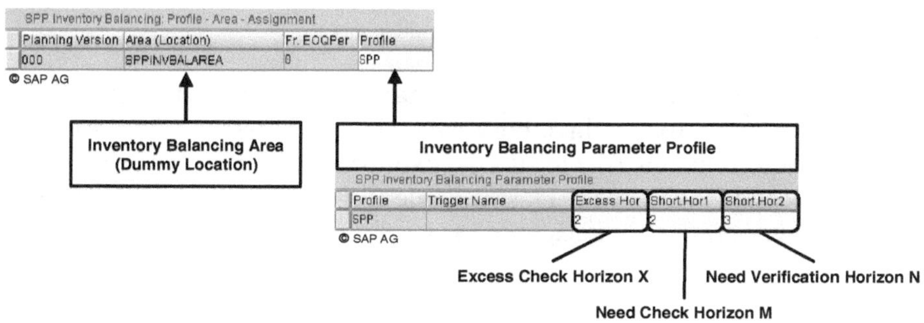

Fig. 11.10. Maintenance of Excess Check and Need Check Dates

• *Inventory Balancing Work Queue*

The excess and the need determination is performed for all locations within the inventory balancing area. The locations are sorted by their excess respectively their need, and the highest excess is matched with the highest need. If the cost and benefit analysis turns out to be favourable, a stock transfer is created, else the excess is matched with the next need – and cost and benefit analysis is performed again. After each stock transfer the locations are re-sorted by their excess and need. Figure 11.11 shows the flow chart for this procedure.

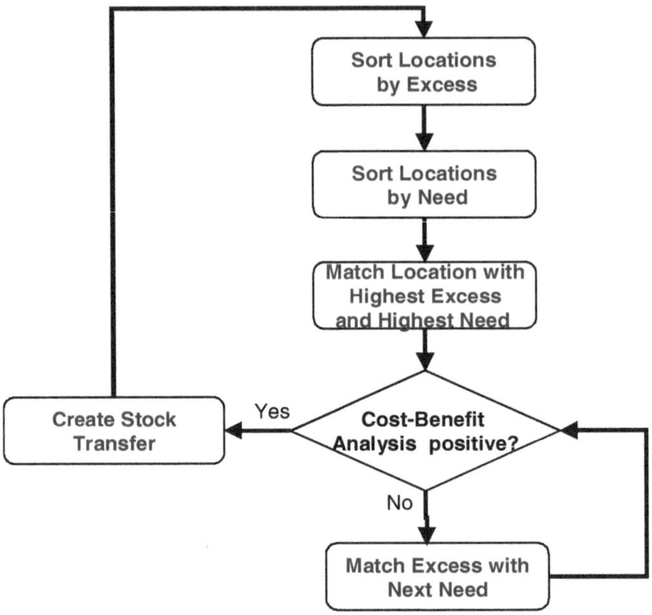

Fig. 11.11. Flow Chart for Matching of Excess and Demand

This flow is repeated until all excess locations are processed. Figure 11.12 shows an example for the inventory balancing work queue. The inventory balancing area contains five locations; two locations with excess inventory and two locations with need. This example assumes that the cost and benefit analysis supports all suggestions for stock transfers.

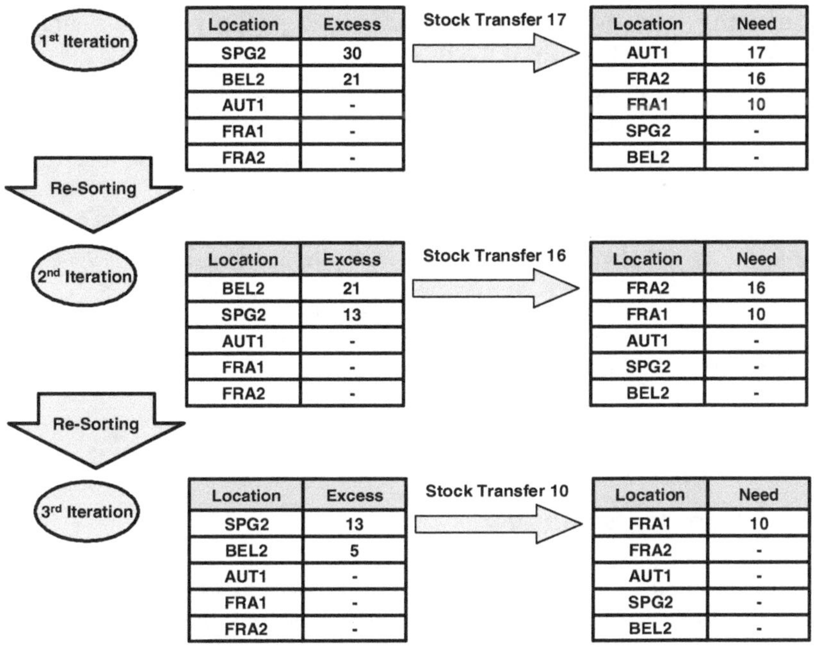

Fig. 11.12. Example for the Inventory Balancing Work Queue

In this example all locations belong only to one inventory balancing area. Since one location can belong to more than one inventory balancing area, all involved locations have to be considered. Before a stock transfer is created, additionally it must be checked whether the locations belong to the same inventory balancing area.

11.4 Cost and Benefit Analysis

11.4.1 Cost and Benefit Analysis Overview

If the difference between the savings and the move costs is above the threshold that is defined in the inventory balancing service, a stock transfer for inventory balancing is created. The savings contain the inventory savings S_{INV}, the warehouse space savings S_W, and the service benefit S_{SB}.

$$S_{INV} + S_W + S_{SB} - \text{Move Costs} \geq \text{Threshold} \tag{11.1}$$

The inventory and the warehouse space savings apply at the source location and the service benefit at the target location.

The threshold is defined in the service profile for inventory balancing with the customising path *APO → Supply Chain Planning → SPP → Inventory Balancing → Define Service Profile for Inventory Planning*, figure 11.13.

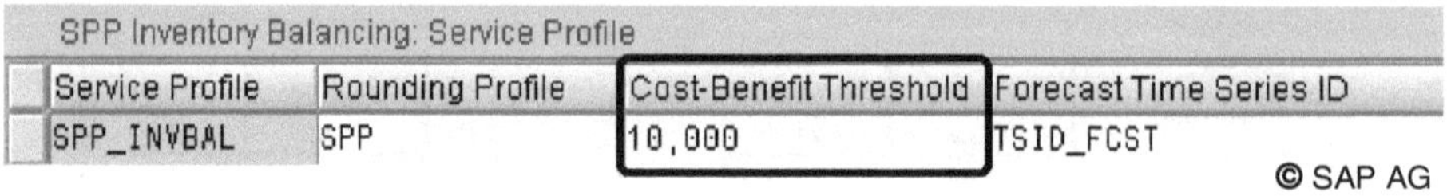

Fig. 11.13. Service Profile for Inventory Balancing

11.4.2 Inventory Savings

The annual inventory costs are the procurement costs C_P for the product times the annual forecast Q_{ANNFC} multiplied by the holding cost factor F_{HC}. The inventory savings at the source location are the portion of the deployed quantity Q_{INVBAL}, formula 11.2.

$$S_{INV} = F_{HC} * C_P * Q_{INVBAL}^2 / Q_{ANNFC} \tag{11.2}$$

The procurement costs are maintained in the 'procurement'-view of the product master. The holding cost factor F_{HC} represents the average inventory in the warehouse and is maintained in the product master, figure 11.14.

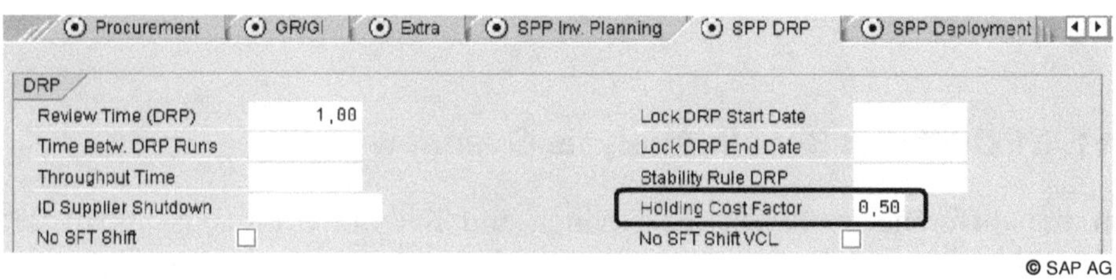

Fig. 11.14. Holding Cost Factor in the Product Master

11.4.3 Warehouse Space Savings

The warehouse space savings apply at the supplying location and represent the benefit by freeing up warehouse capacity. The warehouse space savings S_W are calculated as

$$S_W = S * TRUNC\ (Q_{INVBAL} / Q_{BIN}) * S_B \qquad (11.3)$$

where S is a factor, Q_{INVBAL} the quantity for inventory balancing, Q_{BIN} the average bin quantity and S_B the savings per bin. The warehouse space savings depend on the utilisation of the bins (Q_{BIN}) and the warehouse. This information is maintained as static parameters in the product master respectively in the WSS storage type settings. The warehouse utilisation is not directly used in formula 11.3 but for the determination of the savings factor S in the warehouse space savings profile. Figure 11.5 provides an overview of the involved entities and parameters.

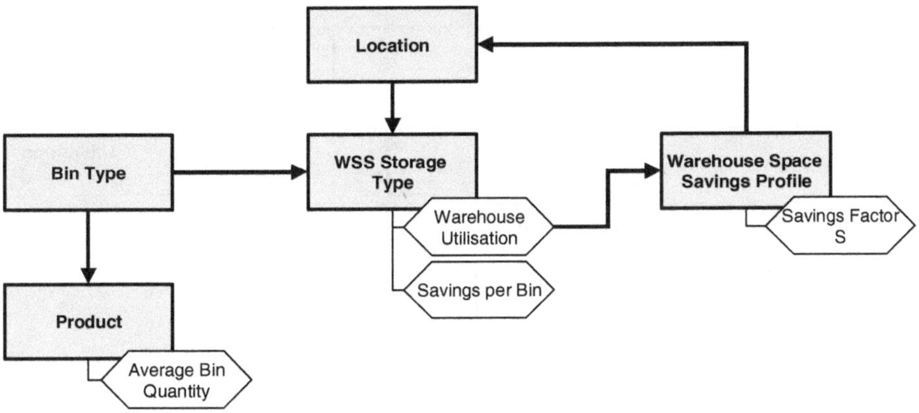

Fig. 11.15. Entities and Parameters for the Warehouse Space Saving

The average bin quantity for the bin type (parameter 'WSS storage type') is maintained in the product master as shown in figure 11.16.

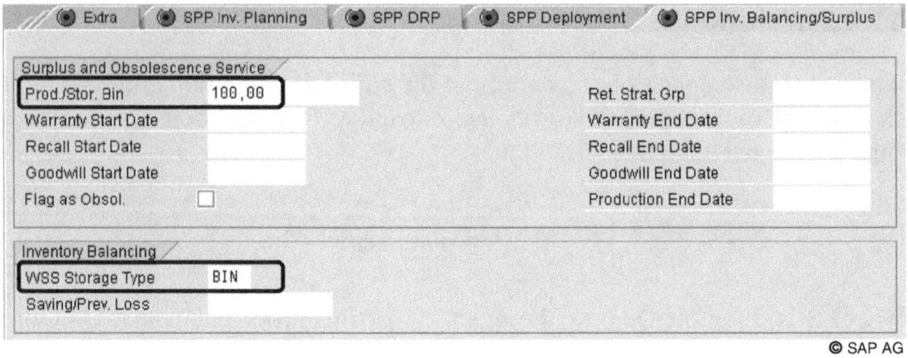

Fig. 11.16. Average Bin Quantity and Bin Type

The factor S is calculated using the warehouse space savings profile and the settings for the WSS storage type per location as shown in figure 11.17.

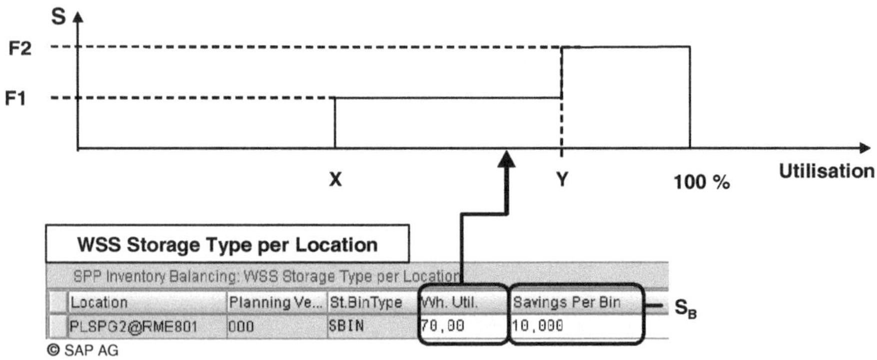

Fig. 11.17. Determination of the Factor S Based on the Estimated Utilisation

The WSS storage type settings contain the savings per bin S_B as well and are maintained with the transaction /SAPAPO/RDPLWSTYPLOC. Note that the storage bin type has to match the WSS storage type in the product master.

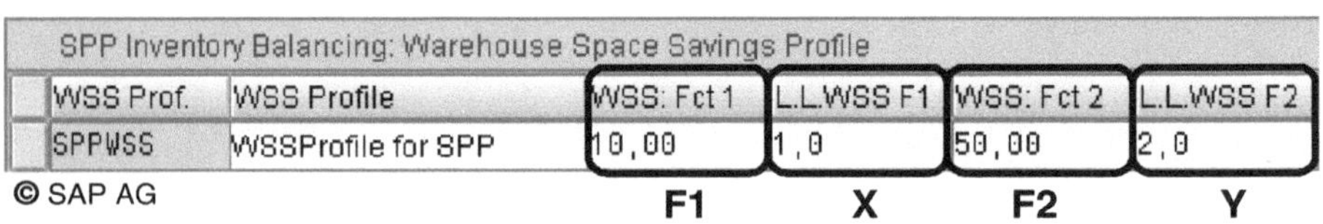

Fig. 11.18. Warehouse Space Savings Profile

The parameters F1, F2, X and Y are defined with the transaction /SAPAPO/RDPLWSSPRF in the warehouse space savings profile, figure 11.18. The warehouse space savings profile finally is assigned to the location in the 'SPP'-view, figure 11.19.

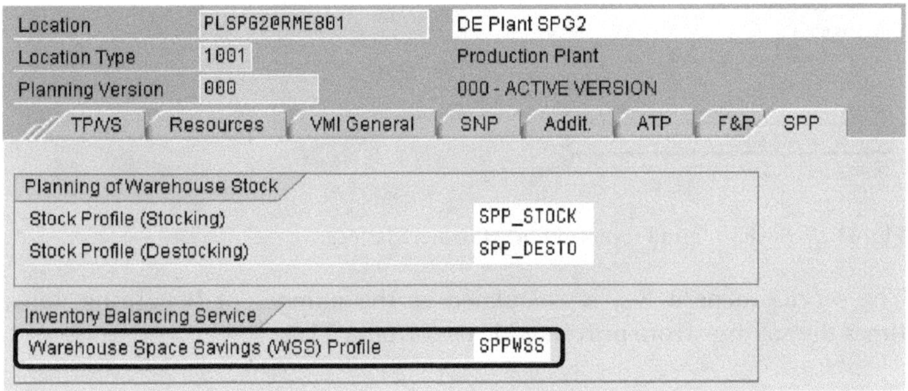

Fig. 11.19. Assignment of the Warehouse Space Savings Profile to the Location

11.4.4 Service Benefit

The service benefit takes the prevented loss of an order into account and is therefore only calculated if inventory balancing is triggered by an unsuccessful deployment run (trigger SPP_PULL_DEPL_NOSUCC) or by an expedited demand in the firmed horizon (trigger SPP_EXPEDITE_FIRMHOR). Another characteristic of the service benefit calculation is that the benefit from a prevented loss is maintained per order item and not per missing quantity. Figure 11.20 shows the maintenance of the savings from a prevented loss in the product master.

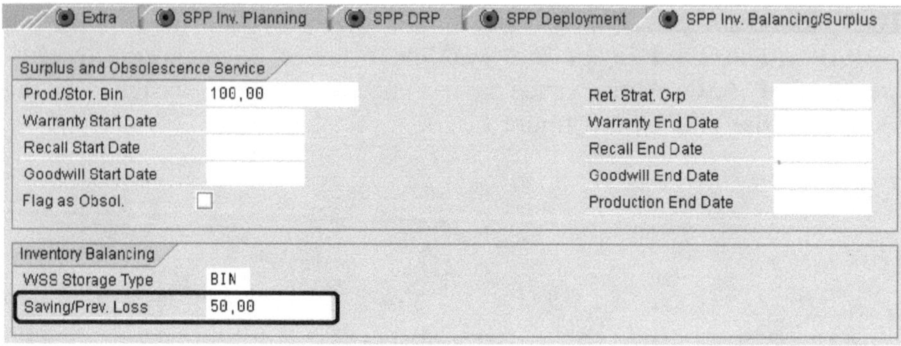

Fig. 11.20. Savings from Prevented Loss (Product Master)

The service benefit S_{SB} is calculated as the number of benefiting items times the savings from prevented loss, formula 11.4.

$$S_{SB} = N_{BI} * S_{PL} \tag{11.4}$$

S_{PL} are the savings from prevented loss as maintained in the product master and N_{BI} the number of benefiting items.

• *Number of Benefiting Items*
The number of benefiting items N_{BI} is calculated by dividing the quantity Q_{LP} that prevents a loss by the forecast for the average item quantity FC_{IQ}, formula 11.5.

$$N_{BI} = Q_{LP} / FC_{IQ} \tag{11.5}$$

The quantity Q_{LP} that prevents the loss is the minimum of the transferred quantity by inventory balancing Q_{INVBAL} and the shortage quantity $Q_{SHORTAGE}$, formula 11.6.

$$Q_{LP} = \min \{Q_{INVBAL}, Q_{SHORTAGE}\} \tag{11.6}$$

If the excess inventory within the inventory balancing area does not cover the complete shortage, the service benefit applies only to those items covered by the transferred quantity. Figure 11.21 shows the calculation of the loss prevention quantity Q_{LP} for the case that the shortage exceeds the excess inventory.

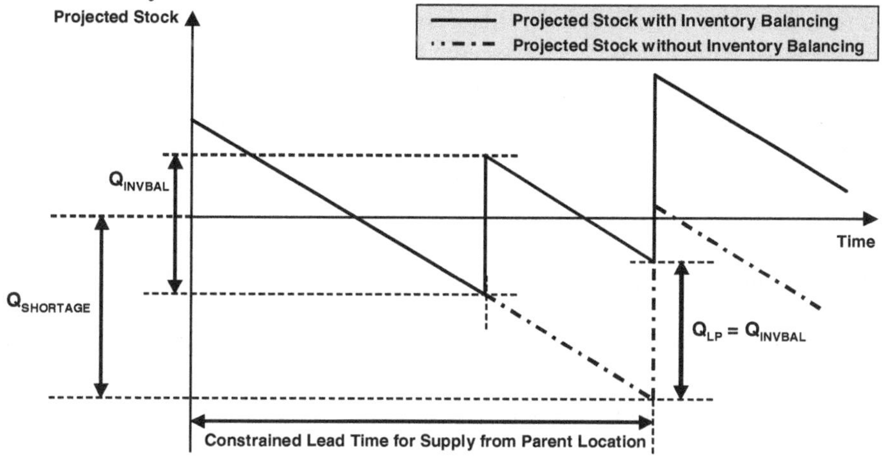

Fig. 11.21. Loss Prevention Quantity (Shortage Exceeds Excess Supply)

The dotted line shows the expected shortage quantity if the location has to wait until the parent location is able to send supplies. A lateral stock transfer within the inventory balancing area is faster and covers a portion of the shortage – nevertheless there will be a new shortage situation before the supply from the parent arrives. Therefore the whole stock transfer quantity Q_{INVBAL} contributes to the service benefit.

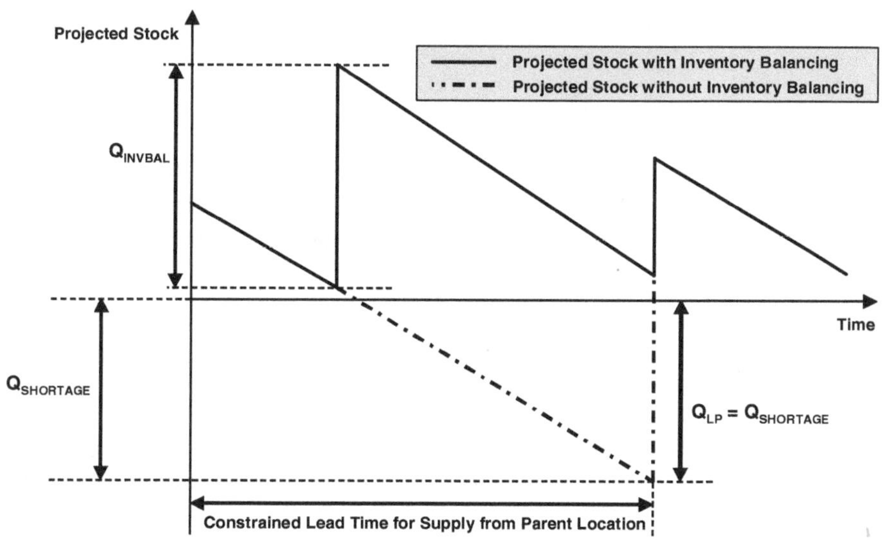

Fig. 11.22. Loss Prevention Quantity (Inventory Balancing Exceeds Shortage)

In the other case the stock transfer quantity Q_{INVBAL} exceeds the shortage. This might be the case if the safety stock is replenished as well or if the transfer quantity is rounded. In this case not the whole stock transfer quantity Q_{INVBAL} contributes to the service benefit but only the shortage quantity $Q_{SHORTAGE}$, figure 11.22.

Based on the loss prevention quantity Q_{LP} the number of benefiting items is calculated using the average demand quantity per item of the forecast.

11.4.5 Move Costs

The move costs consist of the goods issue costs at the source location, the transport costs and the goods receipt costs at the target location. These parameters are shown in figure 11.23.

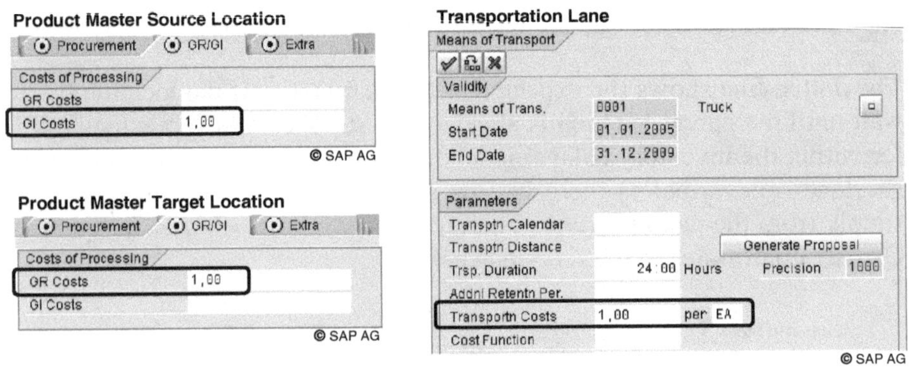

Fig. 11.23. Parameter for the Move Costs

The transport costs are maintained in the transportation lane per means of transport and not per product. The base unit of the transport cost must be maintained in the product master as well – either as base unit or as an alternative unit of measure.

11.5 Inventory Balancing Service

The service profile for inventory balancing is defined with the customising path *APO → Supply Chain Planning → SPP → Inventory Balancing → Define Service Profile for Inventory Planning* and contains the rounding profile, the threshold for the cost-benefit analysis and the time series for the forecast, figure 11.24.

SPP Inventory Balancing: Service Profile

Service Profile	Rounding Profile	Cost-Benefit Threshold	Forecast Time Series ID
SPP_INVBAL	SPP	10,000	TSID_FCST

Fig. 11.24. Service Profile for Inventory Balancing

11.6 Stock Transfer Approval

Depending on the general settings for inventory balancing (see figure 11.7) an interactive confirmation of stock transfer orders might be required. The stock transfer approval is performed with the transaction /SAPAPO/SPPDEPL as described in chapter 10.7

12 Supersession

12.1 Process Overview

The replacement of a service part with another service part (or with several other service parts) is called supersession. Reasons for supersession might be changes in the product, changes in the service parts portfolio or changes in the sales package – e.g. from a kit to separate service parts or the other way around. Therefore supersession is not an independent process but relies mainly on the service parts planning processes manage demand, forecasting, EOQ and safety stock planning, and DRP.

In service parts planning the supersession service calculates the key dates for planning with supersession. These dates are stored in service parts specific fields of the interchangeability master. Therefore the use of the interchangeability function differs significantly from standard SAP APO™.

Out of the five dates that service parts planning uses for supersession, two dates are required for the process overview: The pending obsolescence date (POD, in standard SAP APO™ known as the start date of the interchangeability) and the successor product planning date (SPPD) which describes the date where planning for the successor product must start.

If the POD is reached, the supersession service calculates the five dates for the supersession, among these the SPPD. Only after the SPPD is reached, realignment copies the demand history of the predecessor service part to the history of the successor service part. Forecasting then calculates the forecast for the successor product based on this transferred demand history. This forecast is additional, because the demand history of the predecessor remains and therefore a forecast is calculated also for the predecessor. The same applies to EOQ and safety stock calculation which is done for both the predecessor and the successor.

If everything runs smoothly, the demand for the predecessor is covered with the remaining stock and new supplies are already available to cover the demand for the successor. In case of an imbalance – either because the stock for the predecessor is not sufficient to cover the demand (for the predecessor) or because there is stock left – DRP creates substitution orders to cover the demand for the successor with supply elements of the predecessor or the other way around. Figure 12.1 shows the process overview of service parts planning with supersession.

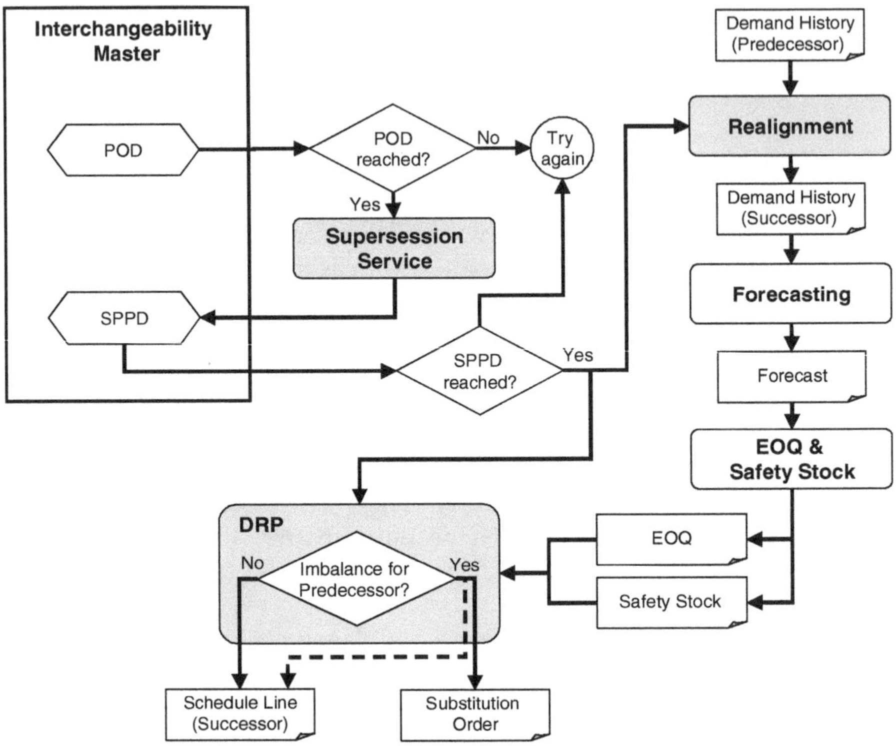

Fig. 12.1. Service Parts Planning with Supersession

The main features to consider supersession for service parts planning are the supersession service, the realignment of demand history and the interchangeability master. The forecasting and the EOQ and safety stock planning functionality is not affected by supersession at all. The only planning area which offers additional functionality is DRP with the creation of substitution orders.

Deployment does not include the substitution orders into the deployable quantity, therefore excess supplies of the predecessor at the entry location will not be transferred to cover a demand for the successor product at the child locations. This will cause an imbalance in the short-term planning, which will be resolved by the ATP check for the sales order. The prerequisite is that rules-based ATP is used with a location substitution procedure that checks the entry location and that the interchangeability master is used for product substitution.

12.2 Supersession Service and Interchangeability Master

The supersession functionality in service parts planning relies on dates for the use-up of the predecessor and the planning start date for the successor service part. Five dates are used for supersession:

- the pending obsolescence date (POD) is the earliest date that the successor product can be used
- the successor product planning date (SPPD) defines when planning for the successor product starts
- he successor product receipt date (SPRD) is the first date when the successor product is available at the entry location
- the stock exhaustion date (SED) is the projected stock-out for the predecessor
- the stock exhaustion warning date (SEWD) is used to check whether the calculation for the SED is still correct

The POD is maintained in the interchangeability master as 'valid from'-date. After the POD is reached, the supersession service calculates the other four dates as shown in figure 12.2. All the dates are stored in the interchangeability master.

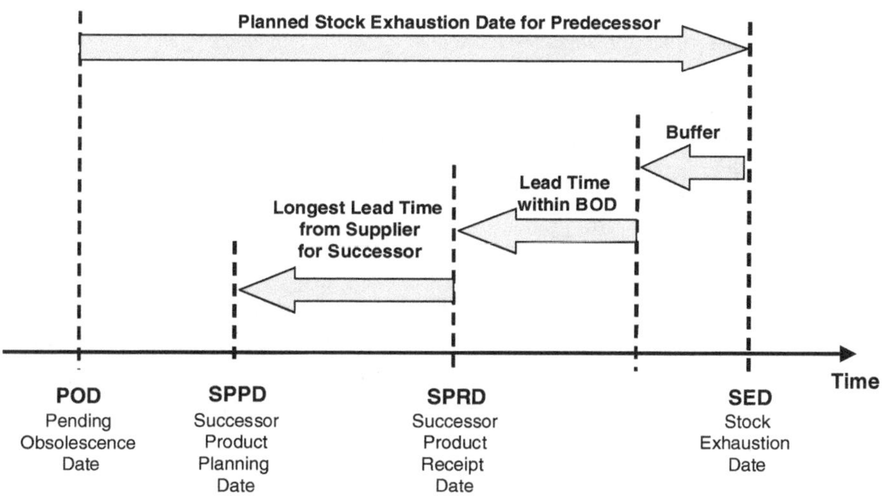

Fig. 12.2. Dates for the Supersession

The stock exhaustion date (SED) is the date where the stock for the predecessor product is used up. Based on this date the supersession service calculates the successor product planning date (SPPD) as the date where the planning for the successor product has to begin. The scheduling elements for this calculation are the (longest) lead time from the supplier to the entry location plus the lead time within the BOD – both for the successor product. Additionally a buffer can be considered. The buffer is defined with the customising path *APO → Supply Chain Planning → SPP → Supersession → Make Settings for Calculating Supersession Times* or with the transaction /SAPAPO/SPRSCUST in the general settings for supersession, figure 12.3.

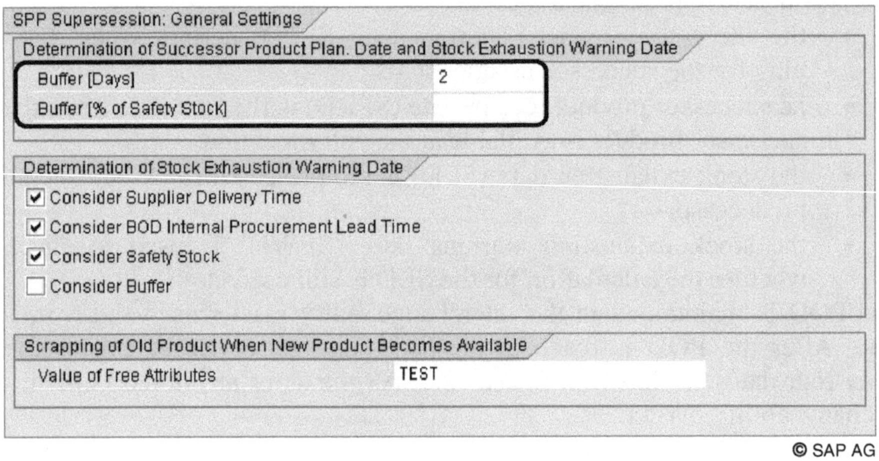

Fig. 12.3. General Settings for Supersession

The buffer consists of two elements, an absolute number of days defined in the general settings plus a percentage of the safety stock. The idea is that the supersession planning service is performed daily so that the dates (SED, SPPD and SPPRD) are updated.

• *Stock Exhaustion Warning Date*
The stock exhaustion warning date (SEWD) is used to monitor the current stock exhaustion date. The SED is recalculated until the SEWD is reached. If the current SED lies before the SEWD, an alert is raised. In the general settings for the supersession as shown in figure 12.3 it is defined which components are used to calculate the SEWD.

• *Supersession Service*
The aim of the supersession service is the calculation of the SPPD (successor product planning date) based on the SED (stock exhaustion date) and

the SEWD (stock exhaustion warning date). A prerequisite for the supersession service is that the POD (pending obsolescence date) is reached – else there will be no calculation.

The service profile for supersession is defined with the customising path *APO → Supply Chain Planning → SPP → Supersession → Define Service Profile for Supersession*, figure 12.4.

SPP Supersession: Service Profile

Service Profile	MxStkExHor	DRP Service Profile
XX_SUPERSESSION	180	XX_DRP

Fig. 12.4. Supersession Service Profile

The entry in the field 'maximum stock exhaustion horizon' is a threshold for the calculation of the supersession dates: if the calculated SED is above the threshold, no dates are saved to the interchangeability master.

The supersession service is called SPP_SUPERSESSION and requires a package creation method for location products.

• *Interchangeability Master*

Supersession in service parts planning requires the master data object 'interchangeability group' which is maintained with the transaction /INCMD/UI. The type of the interchangeability group has to be 'supersession' (form-fit-function classes are not supported), and for DRP the direction must be 'full'. The 'valid from'-date determines the date, from which the successor product should be used. This date is entered when creating the interchangeability group and corresponds to the POD. In the location dependent part of the interchangeability group the SED, SPPD and SPRD are stored as a result of the supersession service, figure 12.5. The interchangeability group can be changed only until realignment is run.

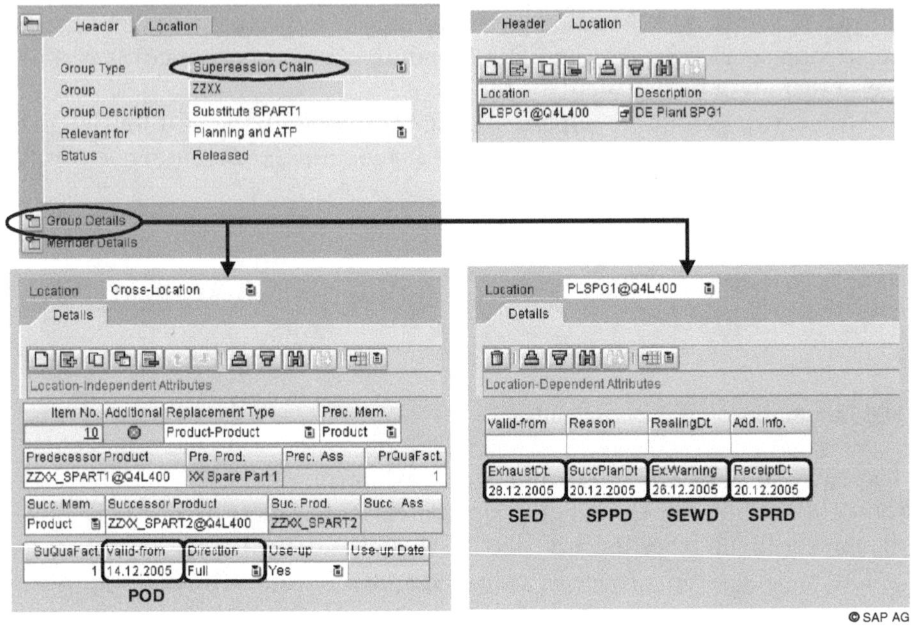

Fig. 12.5. Interchangeability Master

For service parts planning it is required to maintain the interchangeability group location dependent as well for the entry location. Most of the information is maintained without reference to the location as shown on the bottom left part of figure 12.5. In this case a substitution from the predecessor product ZZXX_SPART1@Q4L400 to the successor product ZZXX_SPART2@Q4L400 takes place with the quantity relation of 1 to 1. The quantities are defined by the preceding respectively succeeding quantity factor and the type of the substitution by the replacement type – in this case product-product. Note 832393 lists the restrictions regarding other supported replacement types.

12.3 Realignment for Supersession

The purpose of the realignment step within supersession is to provide the successor product with a data history in order to enable forecasting and inventory planning for the successor product. The service profile for realignment is defined with the customising path *APO → Supply Chain Planning → SPP → Forecasting → Define Service Profile for Reorganisation of Demand History*, figure 12.6.

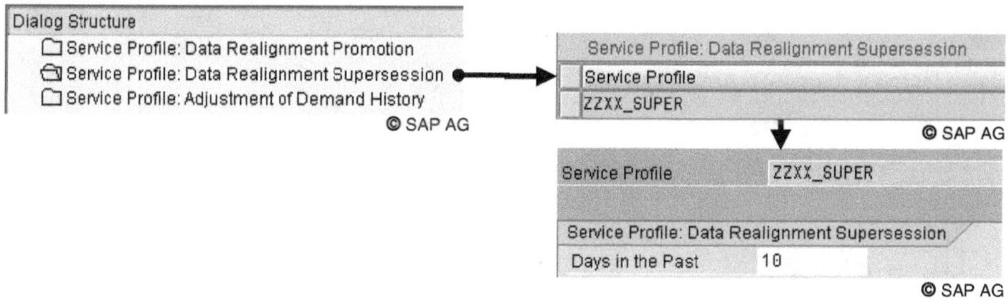

Fig. 12.6. Realignment Service Profile for Supersession

The entry 'days in the past' indicates how far the SPPD is allowed to be in the past in order to be still considered in realignment. If the SPPD is not reached, no realignment is performed.

As the result of the realignment step the history for forecasting is created for the successor product. This includes the changes for the demand history in 9ADEMMUL – which is used by forecasting – but not on the item level in 9ARAWMUL. The history is displayed with the transaction /SAPAPO/SPPDMDH.

12.4 DRP with Supersession

DRP starts with the procurement of the successor product at the SPPD. The idea of service parts planning with supersession is to determine this date in such a way that the supply for the predecessor product covers the demand for the predecessor product and the successor product is only procured for the demand of the successor product. Usually there are differences between the plan and the reality, and in this case it is desired to use the supply of the predecessor to cover the demand of the successor – or the other way around.

• *Substitution Orders*

To model the coverage of one product by the other substitution orders are created. The characteristic of substitution orders is that they are a supply for one product and a demand for the other. Figure 12.7 shows the substitution orders in the DRP matrix. In this case the substitution order uses stock of the predecessor product ZZXX_SPART1@Q4L400 to cover demand for the successor product ZZXX_SPART2@Q4L400.

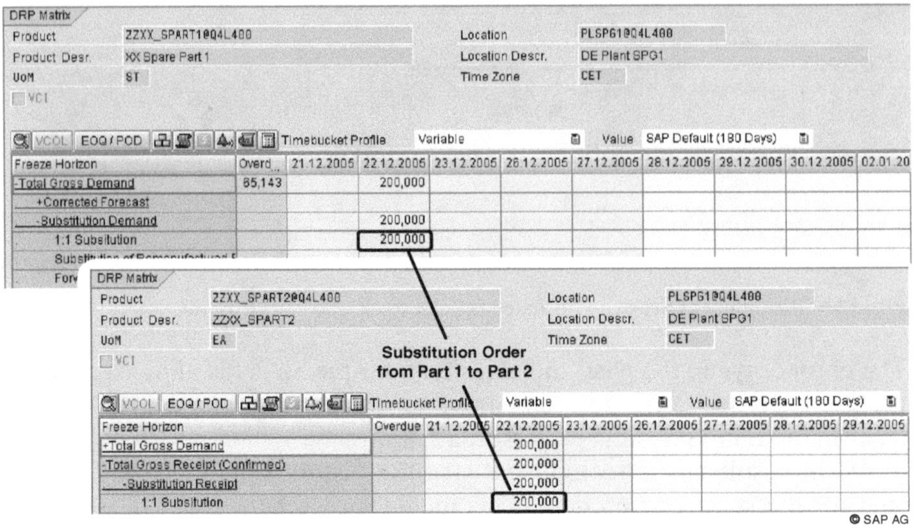

Fig. 12.7. Substitution Order in the DRP Matrix

Using the function for details it is possible to display the substitution order, figure 12.8.

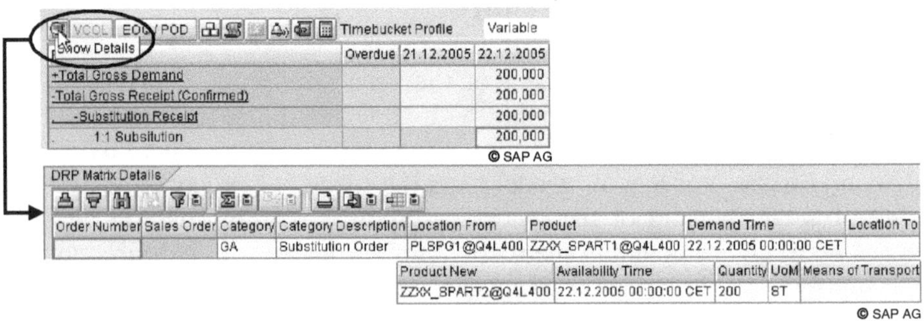

Fig. 12.8. Substitution Order Detail

The substitution orders exist solely in SAP APO™ and have no corresponding object in mySAP ERP™.

• *Horizons*

As result of the realignment the history of the preceding product was copied to the succeeding product. In the subsequent processes forecast and EOQ and safety stock planning have been performed for both the predecessor product and the successor product. In order to prevent an unlimited double procurement the net requirements planning is restricted for products involved in supersessions.

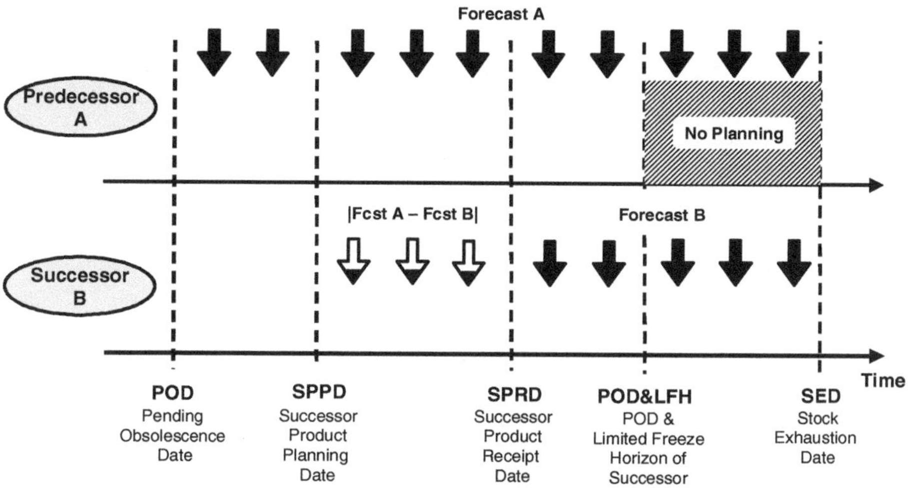

Fig. 12.9. Horizons for DRP with Supersession

After the POD plus the limited freeze horizon of the successor no planning is performed any more for the predecessor. Between the SPRD and the SPPD only the difference between the forecast of the predecessor and the successor is relevant for the planning of the successor product in order to avoid double procurement.

13 Sales Order Fulfilment

13.1 Process Overview

Within service parts management two scenarios for sales order fulfilment exist: sales from stock and third party order processing (TPOP). Sales from stock is the common scenario where a sales order is confirmed (and delivered from) based on available stock. If service parts planning has been performed properly, this should be possible – unless it was decided that the customer facing location should not contain any stock (see chapter 4). In this case – or if the customer demand exceeds the forecast and the safety stock – it is checked whether any other distribution centre within the supply network is able to confirm the sales order. For the check within the supply network (i.e. the BOD) rules-based ATP is used. In the second scenario, third party order processing, the service part is procured directly from the supplier to the customer. Neither scenario is part of service parts planning, but at least the more straightforward scenario of sales from stock is briefly introduced in order to complete the picture from a supply chain management point of view.

The order fulfilment process for service parts management includes the four systems mySAP CRM™ for sales, SAP APO™ for the rules-based ATP check, mySAP ERP™ for the processing of the deliveries and SAP EWM™ for goods issue. Figure 13.1 shows the process overview of sales order fulfilment and the document flow between the systems. The process starts with the creation of the sales order in mySAP CRM™ and the call of rules-based ATP in SAP APO™. Assuming that there is sufficient stock on hand, the sales order item is confirmed, and the sales order is saved in mySAP CRM™. This sales order is transferred to SAP APO™ and to mySAP ERP™. In SAP APO™ it is a sales order as well but in mySAP ERP™ it is reflected as an unchecked delivery. Changes in the sales order will be transferred to both SAP APO™ and mySAP ERP™. The next step is to process the unchecked deliveries in mySAP ERP™ – i.e. to create a (normal) delivery for the unchecked delivery. At this point in time the ATP check is performed again, but not necessarily in SAP APO™. As result a delivery is created and sent to SAP APO™ (where it replaces the sales order) and to SAP EWM™.

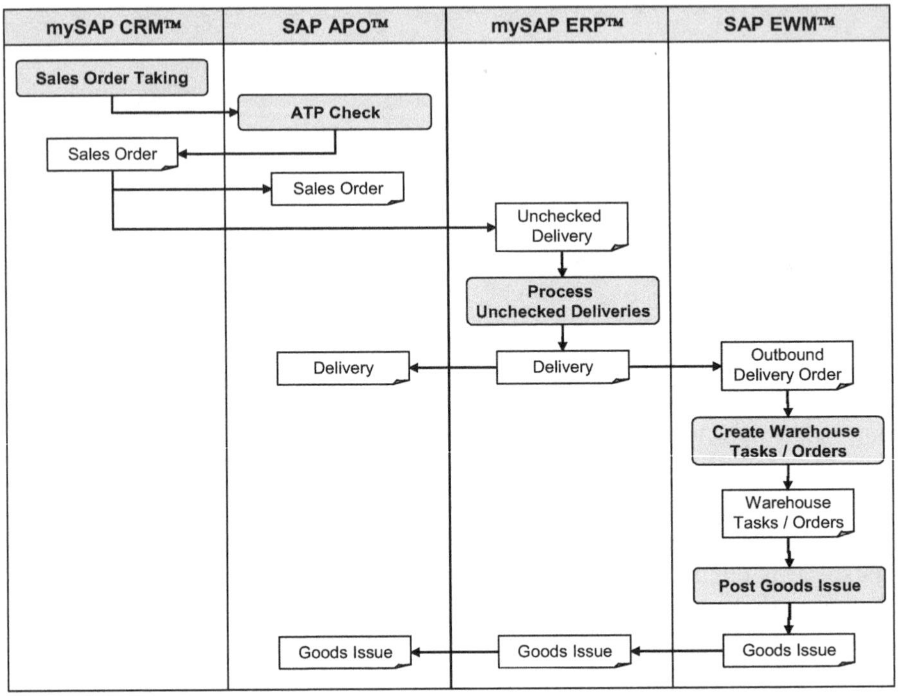

Fig. 13.1. Sales Order Processing – Process Overview

In SAP EWM™ the delivery is first reflected as an outbound delivery notification but can be activated in the background to become an outbound delivery order. For the outbound delivery order a warehouse task and subsequently a warehouse order is created and confirmed in SAP EWM™, and goods issue is posted. The posting of the goods issue is then transferred to mySAP ERP™ and from mySAP ERP™ to SAP APO™.

13.2 Sales Order Taking

13.2.1 Basic Sales Configuration for mySAP CRM™

The purpose of this paragraph is to provide a very rough overview about the entities which are required for sales order processing in mySAP CRM™ for someone who is only familiar with mySAP ERP™ and SAP APO™.

The organisation structure for sales, the order types and the item categories are created in mySAP ERP™ and transferred to mySAP CRM™. The order type in mySAP ERP™ corresponds to the transaction type in mySAP CRM™. Figure 13.2 shows the correspondence of these entities. In mySAP CRM™ up to three transaction types can be assigned per user in the user profile and are displayed in the icon bar.

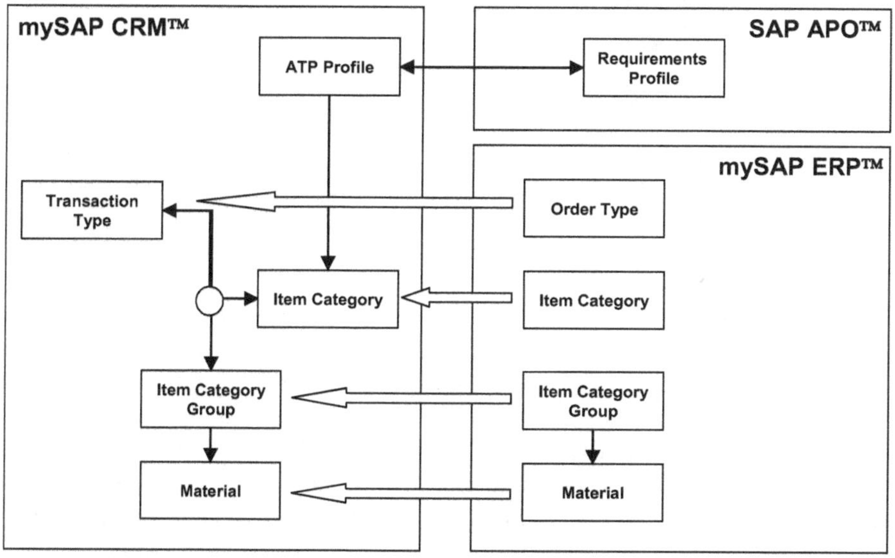

Fig. 13.2. Basic Configuration in mySAP CRM™

The ATP profile in mySAP CRM™ corresponds to the requirements profile in SAP APO™ (see chapter 13.3). There is however no integration for these settings, therefore it has to be ensured during the implementation that corresponding entities exist with the same name. The ATP profile is defined in mySAP CRM™ with the customising path *CRM → Basic Functions → Availability Check → Availability Check Using SAP APO → Define ATP Profile* and assigned to the item category with the customising path *CRM → Basic Functions → Availability Check → Availability Check Using SAP APO → Assign*

ATP Profile to Item Category, figure 13.3. The ATP profile in mySAP CRM™ does not contain any information and is only used to select the requirements profile in SAP APO™.

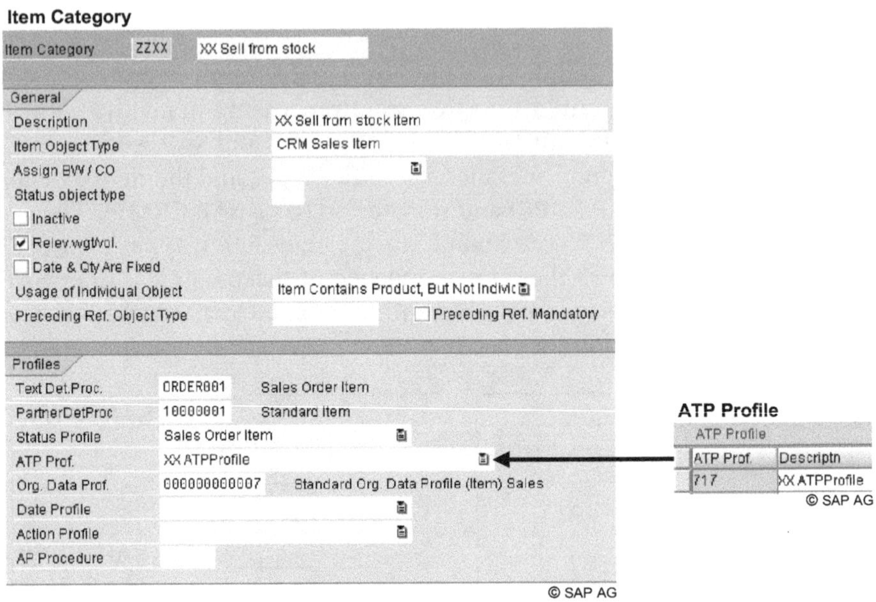

Fig. 13.3. Assignment of the ATP Profile to the Item Category

The transaction type in mySAP CRM™ – which corresponds to the order type in mySAP ERP™ – is maintained with the customising path *CRM → Transactions → Basic Settings → Define Transaction Types*, and the item category with the customising path *CRM → Transactions → Basic Settings → Define Item Categories*. Finally, the assignment of the item categories to the transaction type is performed with the customising path *CRM → Transactions → Basic Settings → Define Item Category Determination* as shown in figure 13.4.

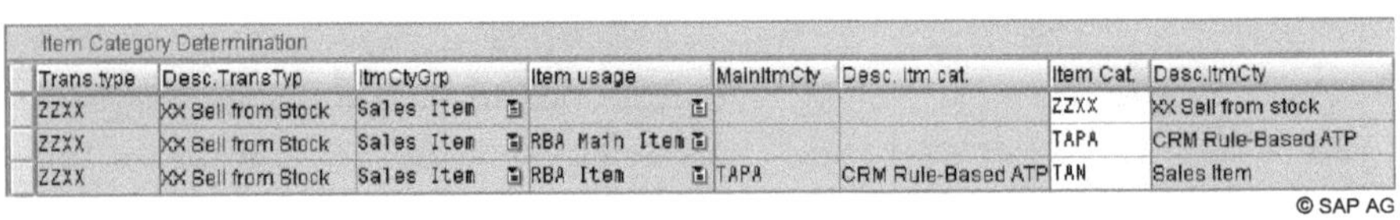
Item Category Determination

Trans.type	Desc.TransTyp	ItmCtyGrp	Item usage	MainItmCty	Desc. Itm cat.	Item Cat.	Desc.ItmCty
ZZXX	XX Sell from Stock	Sales Item				ZZXX	XX Sell from stock
ZZXX	XX Sell from Stock	Sales Item	RBA Main Item			TAPA	CRM Rule-Based ATP
ZZXX	XX Sell from Stock	Sales Item	RBA Item	TAPA	CRM Rule-Based ATP	TAN	Sales Item

© SAP AG

Fig. 13.4. Assignment of Item Categories to the Transaction Type

13.2.2 Sales Order Taking in mySAP CRM™

Sales orders in mySAP CRM™ are created with the transaction CRMD_ORDER as shown in figure 13.5. In this example the transaction type 'XX sell from stock' is used for a sales order of 10 pieces of the material ZZXX_SPARE. The confirmed quantity is the result of the rules-based ATP check in SAP APO™. Other results of the rules-based ATP check are the creation of a sub-item (for the same material) and that the delivering plant is entered in the field 'vendor'. This information is transferred from SAP APO™.

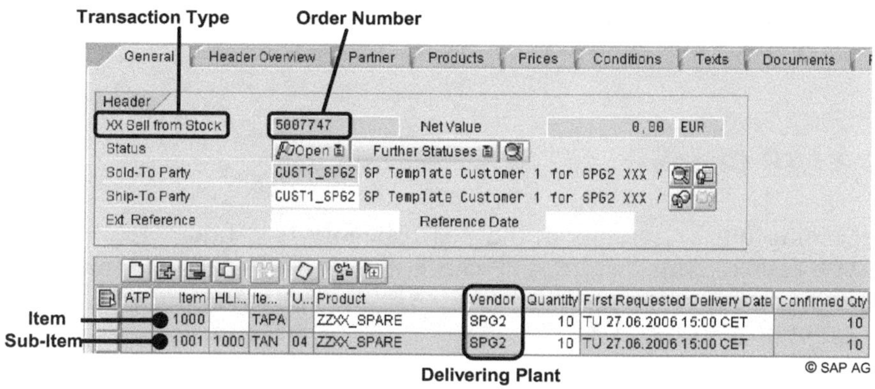

Fig. 13.5. Sales Order in mySAP CRM™

In the sales order not only the requested and confirmed dates are recorded but also the times – differing from mySAP ERP™. Figure 13.6 shows the schedule lines for this sales order.

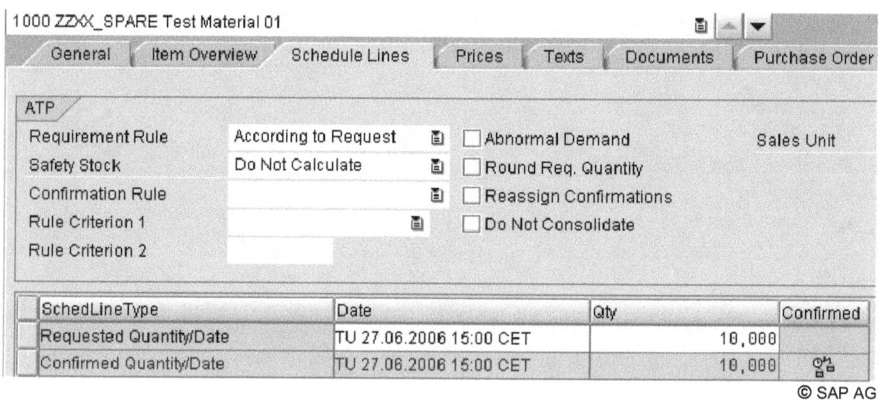

Fig. 13.6. Schedule Lines in the mySAP CRM™ Sales Order

• *Sales Order in SAP APO™*

The sales order is transferred to SAP APO™ and displayed in the product view (transaction /SAPAPO/RRP3) as shown in figure 13.7. Two lines are displayed for the sub-item, one with the request and one with the confirmation. The main item is not transferred at all.

ZZXX_SPARE@Q4L400 in PLSPG2@Q4L400 (Make-to-Stock Production)

Avail/ReqD	Avail/ReqT	Category	Receipt/Rqmt. Elemt.	Rec/ReqQty	Conf. Qty.	Available	Surp/short
27.06.2006	15:00:00	SalesOrder	5007747/001001/1	10-	0	75	0
27.06.2006	15:00:00	SalesOrder	5007747/001001/2	0	10-	75	0

Fig. 13.7. Sales Order in SAP APO™

13.3 ATP Check

Depending on the settings in the item category (see figure 13.3) mySAP CRM™ calls the rules-based ATP check in SAP APO™. In order to display the result of the ATP check the user parameter APO_ATP_PARA has to be set to '5' in mySAP CRM™.

Reqmts prfl	717 XX CRM Profile
Maintain Requirements Profile (ATP)	
Category	BM
Order Header Cat.	BM
Check Mode	X50
Business Event	A
Assignment Mode	No assignment
TQA Type	E Write both internal and external temporary objects
Validity TQAs	
Tech. Scenario	AA
Business Trans.	ZSFS
Rule Strategy	SP02
Scheduling Ind.	A Execute Scheduling
Preselection Substns	☐

Fig. 13.8. Requirements Profile in SAP APO™

• *Requirements Profile*
Since mySAP CRM™ does not have a requirements class, the parameters for the ATP check in SAP APO™ are defined in the requirements profile. The sales order in mySAP CRM™ contains only the ATP profile, and the name of the ATP profile is used to select the requirements profile in SAP APO™. Figure 13.8 shows the requirements profile which is defined in the SAP APO™ customising with the path *APO → Global ATP → General Settings → Maintain Requirements Profile.*

In mySAP CRM™ there is no connection between sales organisation and/or material to a delivering plant. Therefore the start location - the location where the first ATP check is performed – is determined by SAP APO™ using rules-based ATP. The rule strategy for the rule to determine this start location is also maintained in the requirements profile.

• *Rules-Based ATP with mySAP CRM™*
For the service parts management scenario two rules are required: one to determine the start location for the ATP check and another rule for location substitution (and product substitution if supersession is used). This makes the configuration of the rules-based ATP check more complex than usual. Figure 13.9 shows the settings for this configuration.

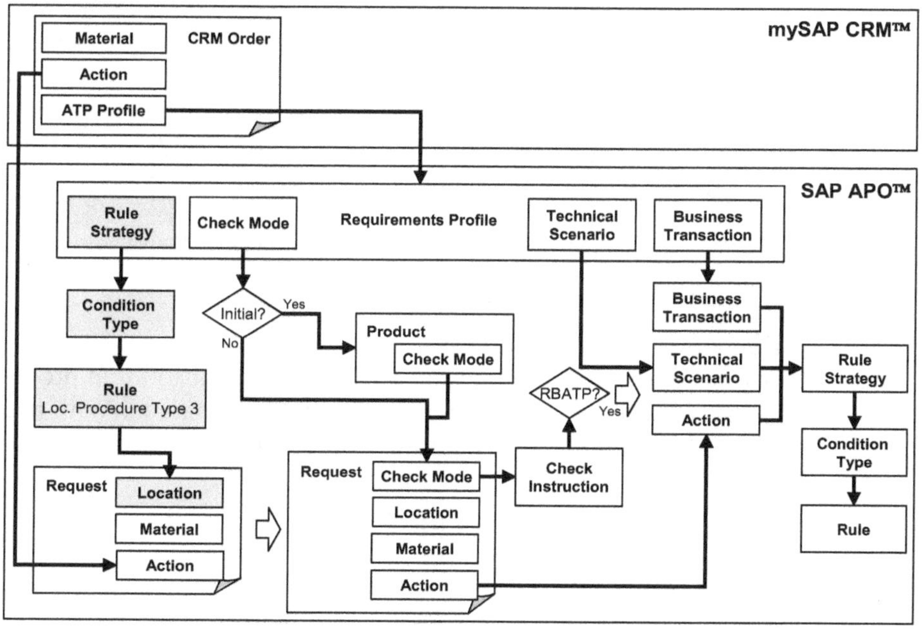

Fig. 13.9. Parameters for the Rules-Based ATP Check in SAP APO™

The sales order from mySAP CRM™ contains an ATP profile. With the ATP profile the requirements profile in SAP APO™ is found, and from the requirements profile the rule strategy and the first rule to determine the start location.

Now the information is complete to perform an ATP check in SAP APO™: Material and action from the sales order, start location from the first rule and check mode from the requirements profile or the product master. If it is defined in the check instructions to perform a rules-based ATP – as required for the service parts management scenario – additionally the technical scenario and the business transaction is taken from the requirements profile.

• *Rule for the Determination of the Start Location*
The rule for the determination of the start location contains a location substitution procedure which contains the start location as the only location. The difference to the 'normal' location substitution procedure as used in the rules-based ATP is that the type of the procedure has to be '3' (list for CRM). Figure 13.10 shows a location substitution procedure for the determination of the start location.

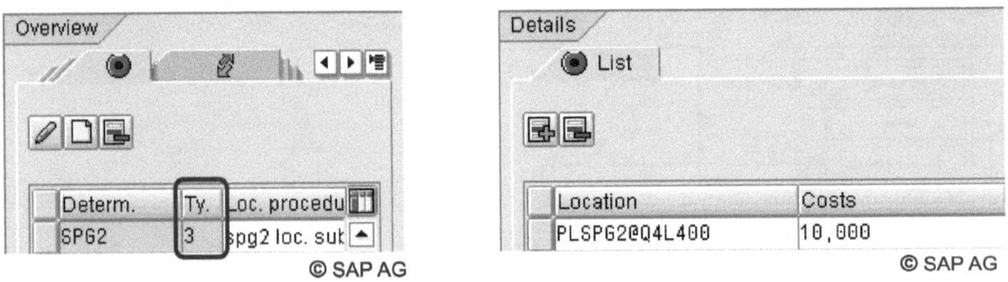

Fig. 13.10. Location Substitution Procedure for the Determination of the Start Location

• *Rule for Rules-Based ATP*
The rule for rules based ATP contains another location substitution procedure of the type '0' where a sequence of locations is maintained. With this type of location substitution procedures at least two locations are required, figure 13.11.

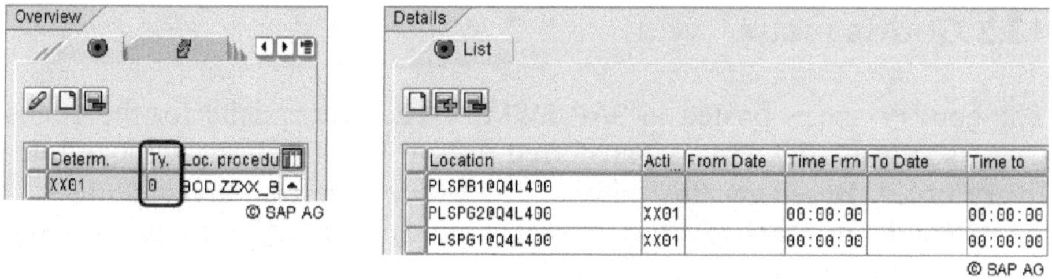

Fig. 13.11. Location Substitution Procedure for Rules-Based ATP

The properties and settings for rules-based ATP and location substitution are described in the literature (Dickersbach 2005).

- *Check Instructions*

Among the rules-based ATP settings within the check instructions the parameter 'create sub-item' has to be selected in order to ensure a smooth integration with mySAP CRM™, figure 13.12.

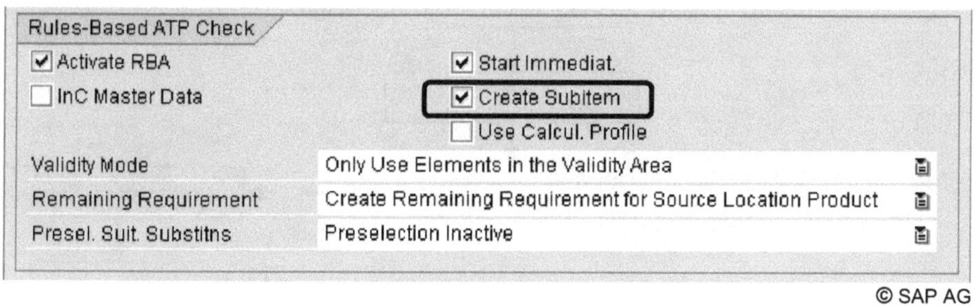

Fig. 13.12. Check Instructions for Rules-Based ATP

13.4 Processing of Unchecked Deliveries

The sales order is transferred from mySAP CRM™ to mySAP ERP™ as an unchecked delivery. This unchecked delivery is however not displayed in the stock/ requirements list. Therefore the stock/ requirements list does not show the correct requirements situation. These unchecked deliveries are only displayed with the transaction VL06U.

The delivery is created in mySAP ERP™ as a subsequent document to the unchecked delivery (instead from the sales order as in the straightforward mySAP ERP™ sales order fulfilment process). The transaction to check the unchecked deliveries and convert them to deliveries is VL10UC.

13.5 Goods Issue

The goods issue is posted in SAP EWM™. The prerequisite for the goods issue is that the delivery is transferred to SAP EWM™ as an outbound delivery order. Based on this outbound delivery order a warehouse task is created and a warehouse order is created and confirmed before goods issue is posted. Figure 13.13 shows these steps.

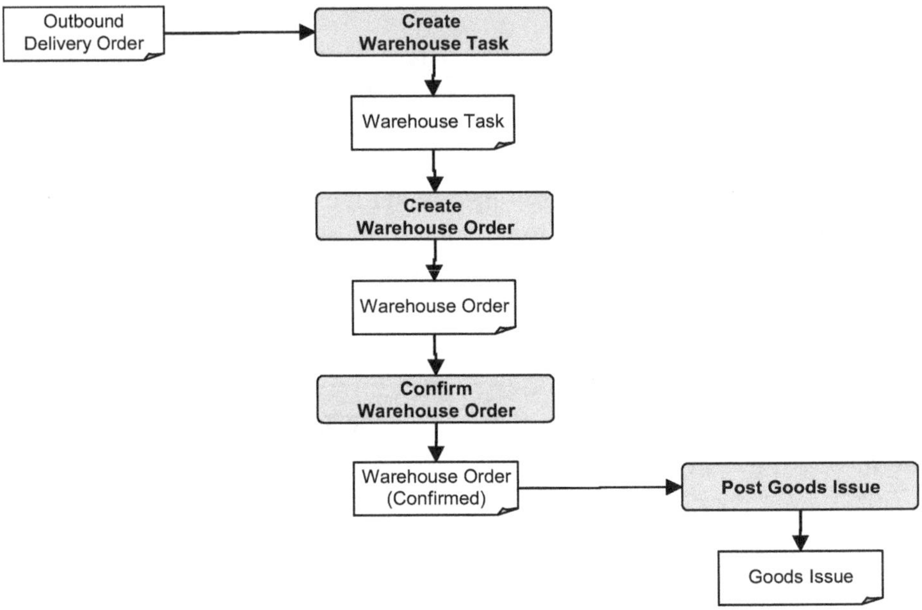

Fig. 13.13. Steps for Posting Goods Issue in SAP EWM™

The outbound delivery is displayed in SAP EWM™ with the transaction /SCWM/PRDO. It is possible to use the delivery number from mySAP ERP™ as a search criterion. Figure 13.14 shows the SAP EWM™ outbound delivery order to the mySAP ERP™ delivery 80008837

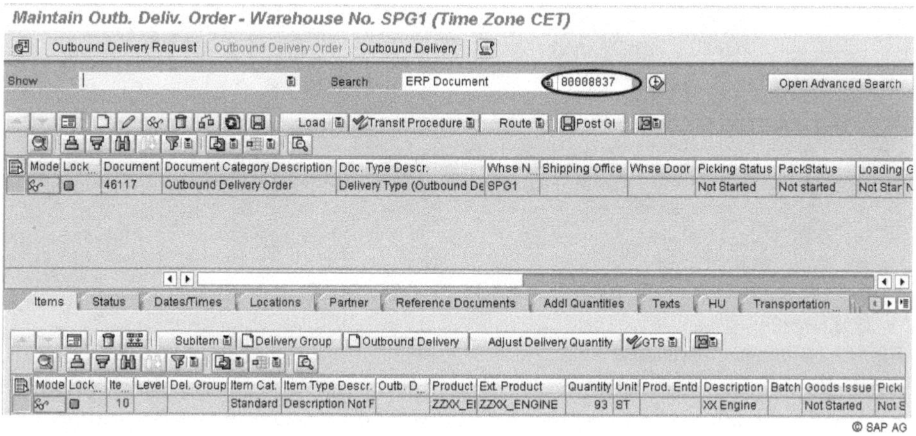

Fig. 13.14. Outbound Delivery Order in SAP EWM™

If the outbound delivery order is not found, one possible reason is that the wrong warehouse is selected. The warehouse is changed with the menu path *Settings* → *Default Values* as shown in figure 13.15.

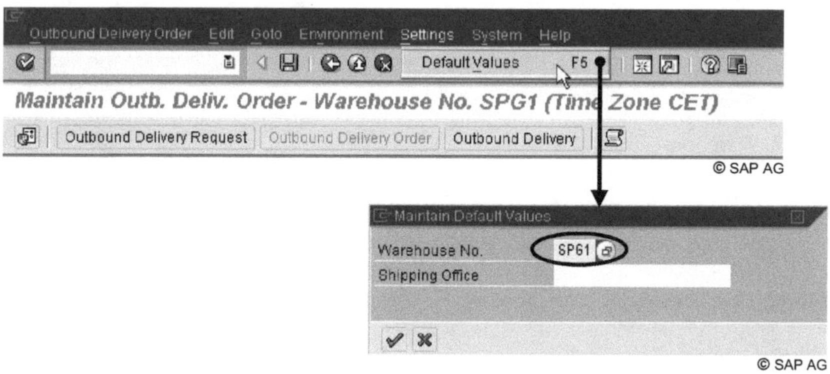

Fig. 13.15. Change the Warehouse

• *Warehouse Task*

In the next step a warehouse task is created for the outbound delivery order with the menu path *Outbound Delivery Order* → *Follow-On Functions* → *Warehouse Task*, figure 13.16.

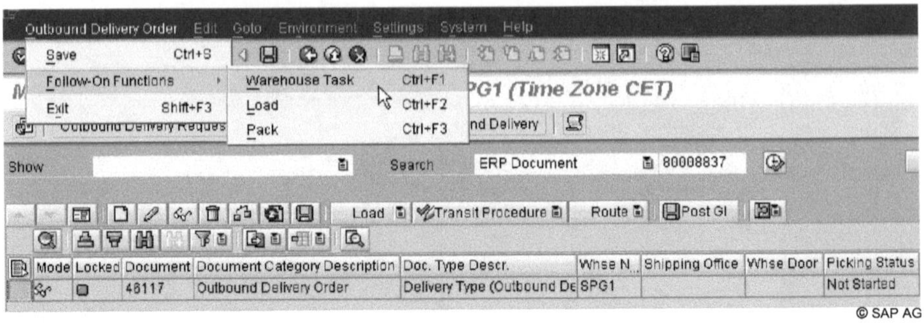

Fig. 13.16. Create Warehouse Task

Figure 13.17 shows the request for the warehouse task with the warehouse request number 46117.

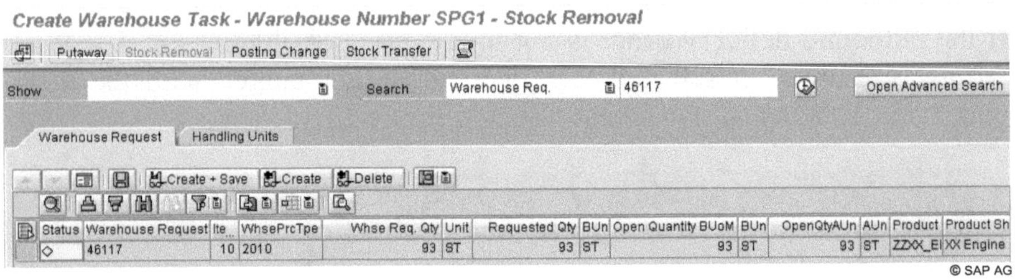

Fig. 13.17. Warehouse Task

In the details of the warehouse task the default values for the source bin and the destination bin are maintained, figure 13.18.

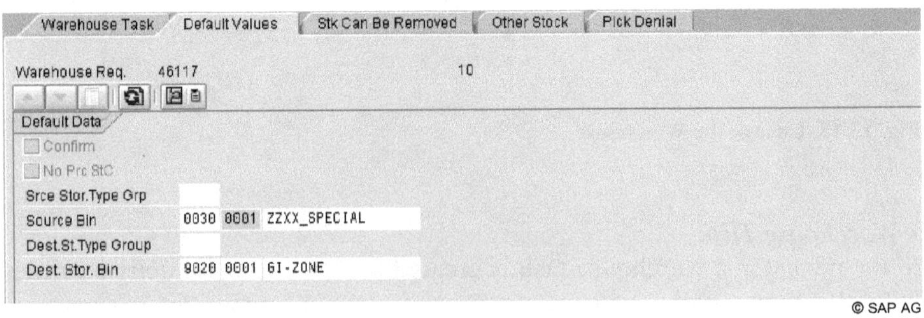

Fig. 13.18. Default Values for Warehouse Task

These default values are required for the creation of the warehouse task. Figure 13.19 shows the steps for the creation of the warehouse task.

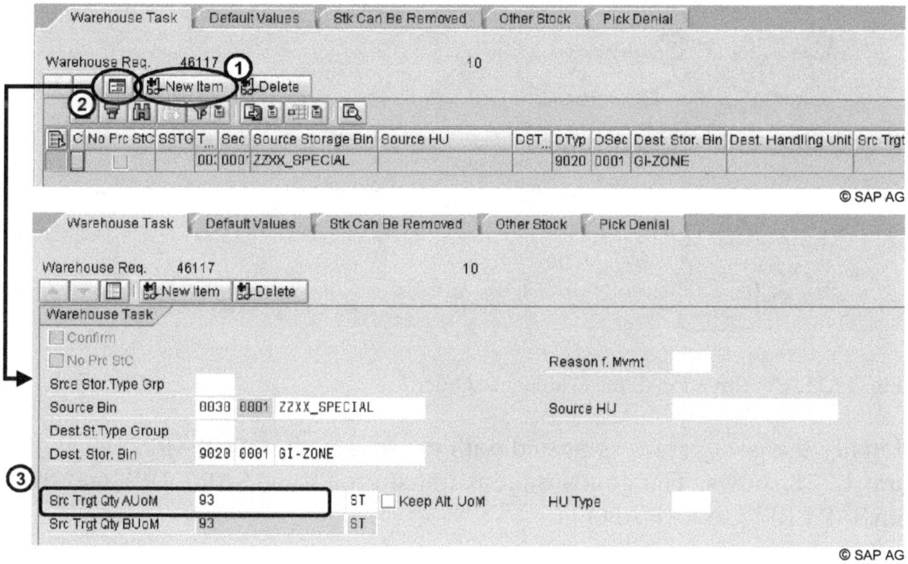

Fig. 13.19. Create Warehouse Task

• *Warehouse Order*
Based on the warehouse task it is possible to create a warehouse order as figure 13.20 shows.

Fig. 13.20. Create Warehouse Order

In the next step the warehouse order is confirmed with the transaction /SCWM/TO_CONF, figure 13.21.

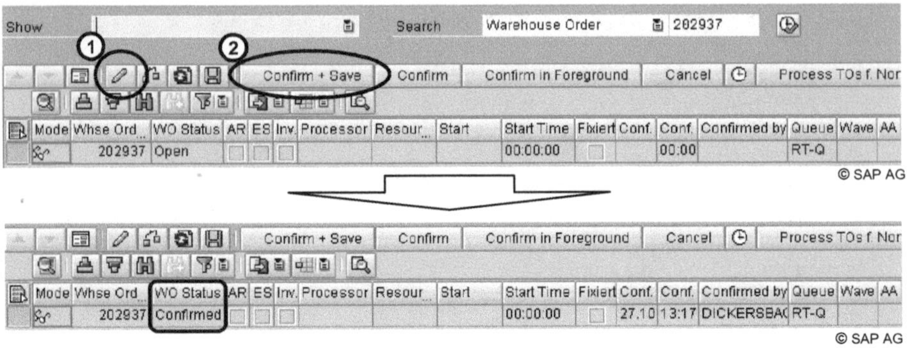

Fig. 13.21. Confirmation of the Warehouse Order

Finally the goods issue is posted with the transaction /SCWM/PRDO as figure 13.22 shows. The goods issue is transferred to mySAP ERP™ and from mySAP ERP™ to SAP APO™.

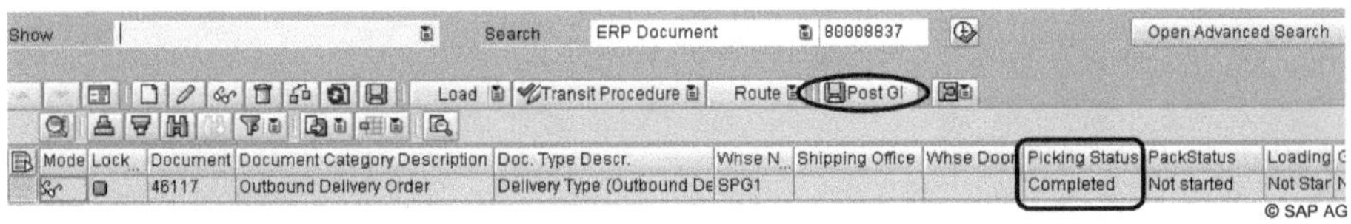

Fig. 13.22. Goods Issue

14 Monitoring and Reporting

14.1 Monitoring and Reporting Overview

Within the service parts management solution different tools exist for monitoring and reporting. Monitoring is used to observe the supply chain in order to help the planner intervening in case of imbalances and other problems. Imbalances are shown in the shortage monitor, and for other problems the alert monitor is used. Both tools are in SAP ICH™ and allow the supplier to have a look at the imbalances and other problems that concern him. As a third tool in SAP ICH™, the SPP cockpit provides an overview of the planning situation of a service part within the BOD – e.g. stock, stock in transit, forecast etc. The data for monitoring in SAP ICH™ is read mainly from tables that are used (and filled) by SAP APO™ applications.

Reporting on the other hand is used to evaluate the performance of the supply chain on a regular basis. The major information is the outbound performance towards the customers (here the service level is the most important KPI), the performance within the supply chain (e.g. whether the planned lead times are kept) and the performance of the suppliers. The information of the reporting is used for medium- or long-term structural and strategic decisions.

These reports are available as business content in SAP BI™. The data basis for these reports is pre-processed in mySAP SCM™ before it is transferred for reporting to SAP BI™.

14.2 Shortage Monitor

All monitoring tools in SAP ICH™ are accessible from mySAP SCM™ with the transaction /SAPAPO/SPP. For an external supplier it is possible to access SAP ICH™ via internet with a URL (Leitz 2005).

• *Planning Service for the Shortage Monitor*
The data for the shortage analysis is based on the service parts planning applications in SAP APO™. The prerequisite to view this data in the shortage monitor is the preparation of this data with the planning service SPP_SHORTAGE_MONITOR. This service does not require a service profile but a process profile with the package creation method PRODUCT_SIMPLE. This planning service needs to be performed with the planning service manager as for the other planning services and as described in chapter 2.3.

• *Shortage Overview*
The shortage overview shows at a glance the number of products with low safety days' supply ('critical products'), backorders and overdue schedule lines, figure 14.1.

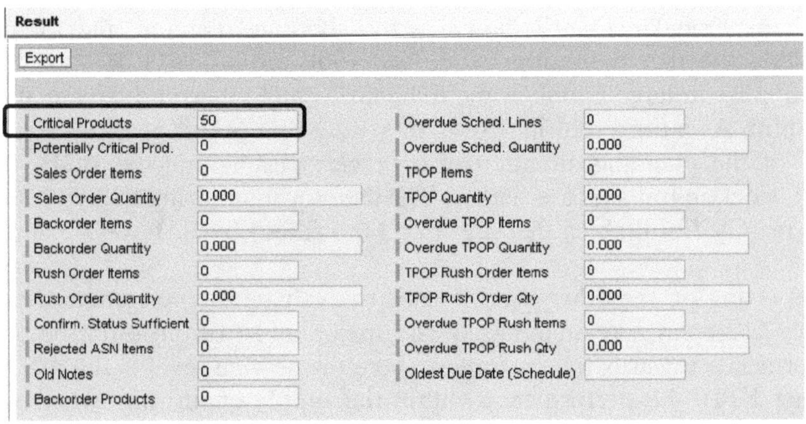

Fig. 14.1. Shortage Overview

The shortage overview is the default application when entering SAP ICH™ as a planner via the transaction /SAPAPO/SPP. For more details the shortage monitor is used.

• *Safety Days' Supply for the Shortage Monitor*
The shortage monitor is based on the safety days' supply. This safety days' supply is calculated by the planning service SPP_SHORTAGE_MONITOR as the minimum of two safety days' supplies:

- safety days' supply based on the average consumption of the last seven days

- safety days' supply based on the demand as shown in the DRP matrix

Only the stock on hand is used for this calculation, not the planned receipts. Figure14.2 shows an example for the calculation of the safety days' supply – in this case the safety days' supply based on the demand of the DRP matrix is the shorter and therefore used as the resulting safety days' supply.

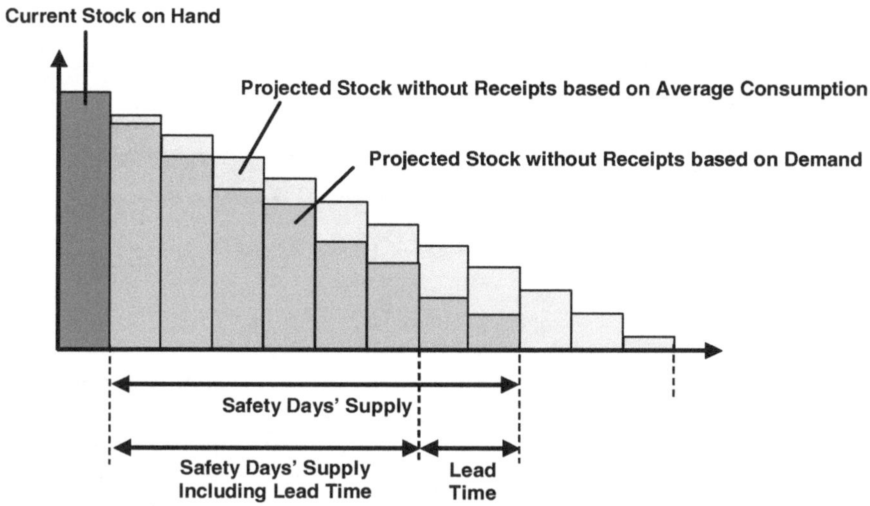

Fig. 14.2. Safety Days' Supply for the Shortage Monitor

Whether the lead time is subtracted from the safety days' supply or not depends on the parameter 'days' supply including procurement lead time' in the general settings for the shortage analysis (see figure 14.3).

• Criticality Status and Open Quantity

The shortage monitor classifies products into critical, potentially critical and non critical depending on their safety days' supply at the entry location. The limits for these categories are also maintained in the general settings for the shortage analysis (with the customising path *APO → Supply Chain Planning → SPP → Monitoring → Shortage Analysis → Make General Settings for Shortage Analysis*). Figure 14.3 shows an example with the thresholds of 5 days for critical products and 10 days for potentially critical products.

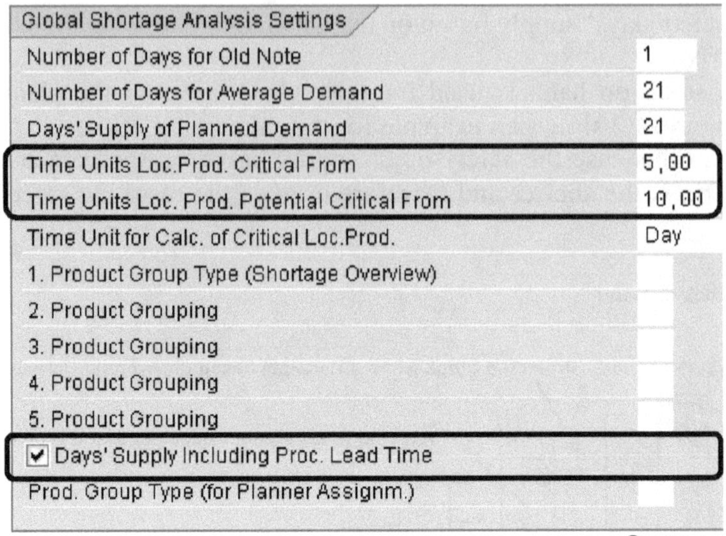

© SAP AG

Fig. 14.3. General Settings for the Shortage Analysis

The product is not critical any more if the safety days' supply is above the limit for the potentially critical product. In this example stock for 10 days is required in order to keep the product not critical. The open quantity is the missing quantity which is required additionally to the current stock in order to achieve that the product is not critical any more. Criticality, open quantity and stock on hand are displayed in the shortage monitor.

• *Shortage Monitor*

The navigation with transactions is not possible within SAP ICH™. Instead a navigation bar exists on the left side of the screen. Figure 14.4 shows this navigation bar and the shortage monitor. In this example the selection was restricted by planner.

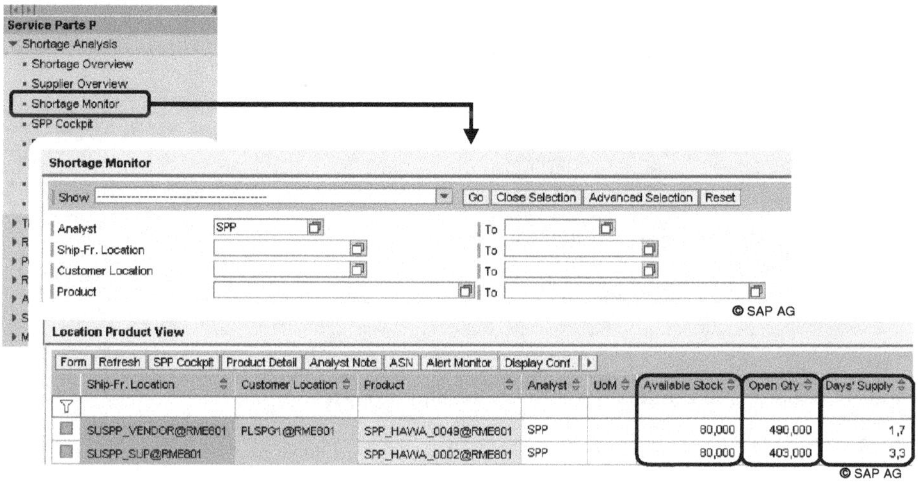

Fig. 14.4. Shortage Monitor

The shortage monitor shows at a first glance the available stock (80 pieces for the first product), the open quantity (490 pieces) and the days' supply (1.7 days). In the details of the location product additional information as the demand frequency, the backlog and others are displayed as shown in figure 14.5.

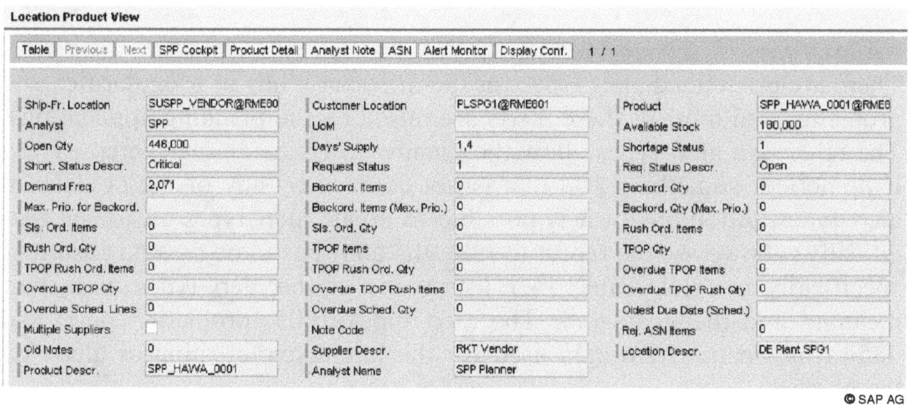

Fig. 14.5. Shortage Monitor – Location Product Details

It is possible to branch from the shortage monitor directly to other tools as e.g. the alert monitor, the SPP cockpit or the product detail.

The order in which the location products are displayed is defined with the customising path *APO → Supply Chain Planning → SPP → Monitoring → Shortage Analysis → Define Sorting in Location Product View* as shown in figure 14.6 – in this case descending according to the demand frequency and ascending according to the shortage status.

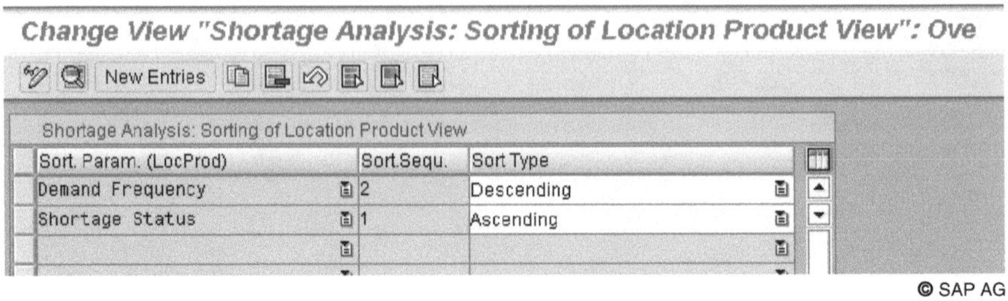

Fig. 14.6. Sorting of Location Products in the Shortage Monitor

14.3 Alert Monitor

The alert monitor notifies the planner about irregularities and problems in the supply chain. Some of the potential problems are connected with the procurement of the service parts. Since the alert monitor for service parts planning is part of SAP ICH™ the supplier can access the alert monitor as well and react and comment on the alerts that are connected with him.

• *Alert Types*
There are predefined alert types for the different kinds of irregularities and problems, and most of these alerts are raised by the planning applications. The other two alert types allow the planner to create an alert interactively if he notices something odd that is not covered by any of the predefined alert types. Additionally it is possible to create alert types customer specifically – however, the report to raise the alert has to be created customer specifically as well. Table 14.1 lists some of the alert types with their meaning and their category. The alert types 7805 (problem report) and 7856 (information) are only used for the interactive creation of alerts by the planner.

• *Alert Monitor*
The alert monitor is called from the navigation bar at the left as shown in figure 14.7. Here it is possible to select the alerts by planner (parameter 'analyst'), location, product, alert type and more. It is mandatory to select by alert type – in order to display all alert types '*' is allowed.

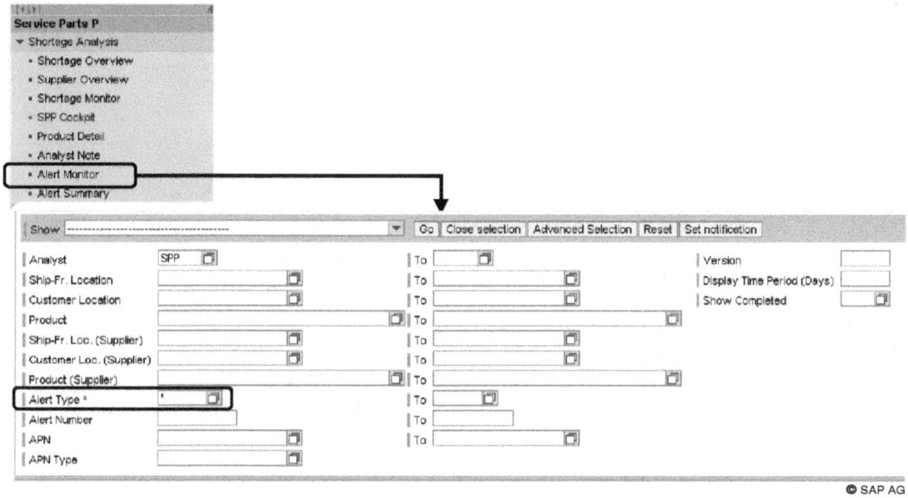

Fig. 14.7. Alert Selection

The result of the alert selection is displayed in the statistical view. Here all alerts are listed by alert type, and the number of alerts with their priority and their status (new, in process, completed, retained) are displayed as well, figure 14.8.

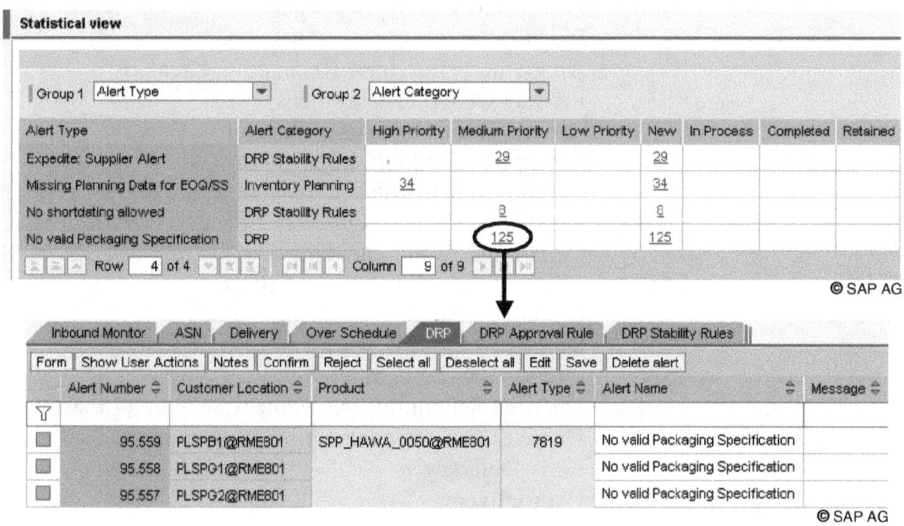

Fig. 14.8. Statistical View and Alert Type View

Table 14.1. Alert Types (Excerpt)

Alert Category	Alert Type	Alert Type Name
Forecasting	7815	Forecasting Phase-In
Inventory Planning	7842	Missing Planning Data for EOQ/SS
	7843	Safety Stock Has Too Large a Discrepancy
	7844	Missing Planning Data for Stocking
	7846	Missing Planning Data for De-Stocking
Surplus and Obs.	7875	No Surplus Quantity Determination for Location
Service	7876	Product is set to Obsolete
DRP	7816	Invalid or Missing Master Data (Location Product)
	7817	Invalid or Missing Master Data (Product/Shipment)
	7818	Inconsistency for Virtual Consolidation Location
	7819	No valid Packaging Specification
	7867	Inconsistency for Replenishment Indicator
	7820	Requirements Cannot Be Pulled
	7821	Supplier Shut Down and Supplier Split
	7822	Supersession: Firmed Schedules
DRP Approval	7824	Manual Review
	7827	New Product
	7828	DRP De-Expedite from Limited Freeze Horizon
	7829	Change in Limited Freeze Horizon
	7830	Discrepancy in Supply Figures
	7831	Pending Obsolescence Starts
	7833	Anonymous Purchase Requisition Created
	7834	Product Group Procurement
	7835	Ordering Reason Causes Manual Review
	7836	Maximum Schedule Line Value
	7837	Maximum Schedule Line Value Change
	7839	Outline Agreement Obsolete Bef. End of Freeze Hor.
	7840	Maximum Total Lead Time
External Order Approval (EOA)	7857	Value of Schedule Line too High
	7858	Quantity Change Over Limit Value
	7859	Value of Network Stock Over Limit Value
	7860	Excess days on hand
Over Schedule	7806	Overdue Scheduling Agreement Schedule Lines
	7812	Uncovered Conf. with Shipping Date in the Past
Delivery	7808	Early Delivery
	7809	Overdelivery
Supersession	7855	Stock Exhaustion Before Warning Date
	7870	Pending Obsolescence Date was changed
	7871	Inconsistent Supersession Master Data
	7878	Supersession Chain Not Released

The alerts that belong to the alert type are displayed by double click. Figure 14.7 shows the first three of the 125 alerts of the type 'no valid packaging specification'. Each alert has a number (here: 95557 to 95559), and in the first rows the location and the product are displayed. Additional details are displayed in the 'form'-view, figure 14.9.

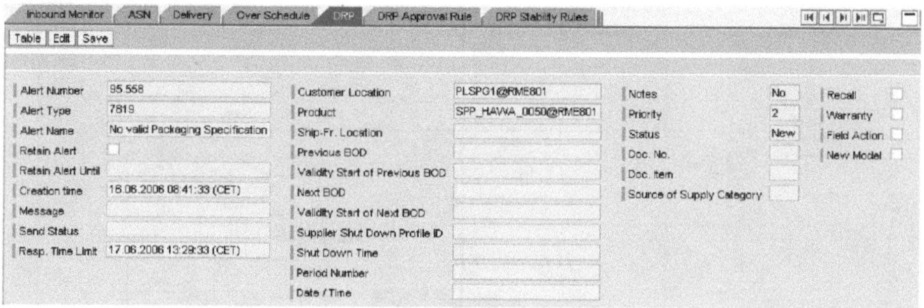

Fig. 14.9. Alert Details in the 'Form'-View

• *Status Sequence*

To each alert type a status sequence is assigned which defines the reactions to the alerts. When an alert is raised, the status of the alert is 'new' (SN). Other statuses are 'in process' (SP) and 'confirmed' (SC). The status sequence defines – depending on the current status of the alert – who (the planner respectively analyst or the supplier) is allowed to perform an activity (e.g. to edit, reject or confirm the alert) and what the resulting status is going to be. Figure 14.10 shows the definition of the status sequences with the customising path *ICH → Supplier Collaboration → Functions for SPP → Alert Monitor → Make General Settings for Alerts.*

Define Status Sequence

Status Sequence	BusPartner	User Role	Status ID	Activity	Next Status
1		Supplier	SN	Confirm	SC
2		Analyst	SN	Confirm	SC
3		Analyst	SP	Confirm	SC
3		Supplier	SN	Confirm	SP
3		Supplier	SN	Edit	SN
4		Analyst	SN	Confirm	SP
4		Supplier	SP	Confirm	SC
5		Analyst	SP	Confirm	SC
5		Supplier	SN	Confirm	SC
5		Supplier	SN	Reject	SP

Fig. 14.10. Status Sequences

The status sequence '2' describes a simple and common procedure where the planner confirms the new alert during the alert processing. In contrast to this simple procedure, the status sequence '5' describes a more elaborate procedure with interaction between the planner and the supplier, figure 14.11.

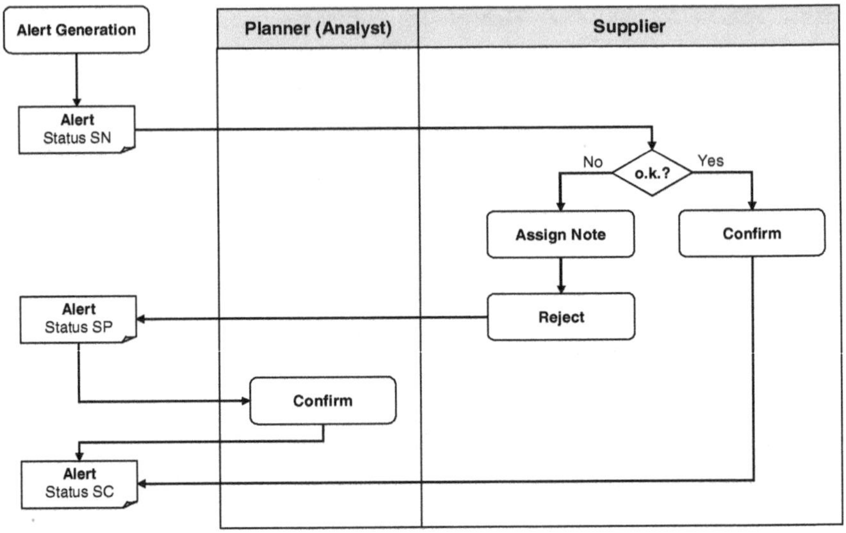

Fig. 14.11. Procedure for the Status Sequence '5'

The status sequence is assigned to the alert types with the same customising path.

• *Alert Type Customising*

The customising for the alert types is performed with the same customising path *ICH* → *Supplier Collaboration* → *Functions for SPP* → *Alert Monitor* → *Make General Settings for Alerts* as the definition of the status sequence. Besides the status sequence, each alert type has a validity period (in days) and a response time (in days) – after this time a response from the planner respectively the supplier is expected. Whether the alert is visible for the planner (analyst), the supplier or both is part of the alert type customising as well. Figure 14.12 shows an excerpt of this customising.

General Alert Type Settings

Alert Type	Validity Period ...	Status Sequence	Response Time...	SDPR-Relevant	Display	Create	Notification	Visible
7801	100	1	3,5	☑	☑	☑	☐	Supplier/Analyst
7802	200	2	3,5	☑	☑	☑	☐	Supplier/Analyst
7803	150	5	1,8	☑	☑	☑	☐	Supplier/Analyst
7804	100	5	2,6	☑	☑	☑	☐	Supplier/Analyst
7805	300	8	1,0	☑	☑	☑	☐	Supplier/Analyst

Fig. 14.12. Customising for Alerts Types

14.4 SPP Cockpit

The SPP cockpit allows the planner to gain a quick overview about some key measures of a service part – for all locations of the BOD. Among these key measures are

- available stock on hand
- stock in transit
- forecast

The forecast is the final forecast of the current period as displayed in the forecast planning book.

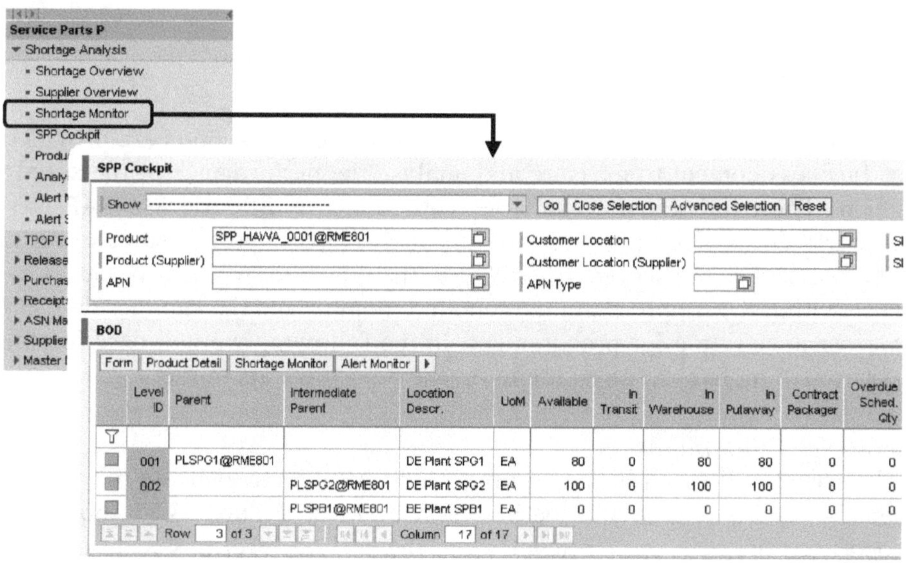

Fig. 14.13. SPP Cockpit

The forecast of the parent location is shown and not of the virtual child location. Figure 14.13 shows the SPP cockpit with all three location products of the BOD for the product SPP_HAWA_0001@RME801. It is possible to branch from the SPP cockpit to the shortage monitor, to the alert monitor, to the product detail and to a detailed view of the planning situation at a certain location (with the pushbutton 'forms'), figure 14.14.

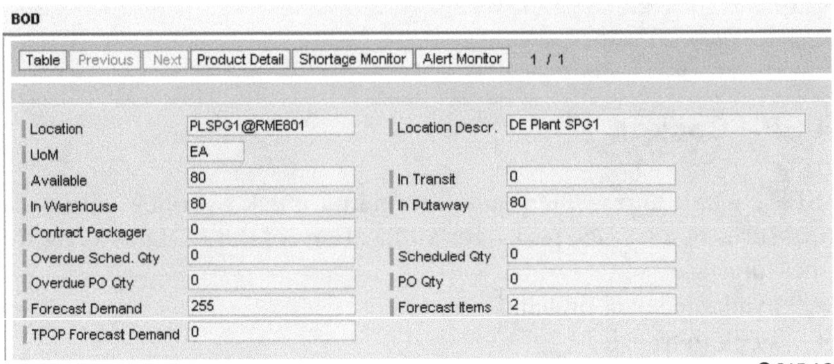

© SAP AG

Fig. 14.14. SPP-Cockpit – Detail for a Product Location

14.5 Reporting

Within the service parts management solution several reports are provided as business content to measure and analyse the performance of the supply chain. These reports are available with the SAP BI™ release SAP Netweaver™ 2004s. The report to measure the outbound performance towards the customer is the service fill monitor, the report to measure the performance within the supply chain the inbound monitor and the supplier delivery performance rating for procurement. In the following we will describe the service fill monitor as an example for the reporting capabilities.

• *Service Fill Monitor*
The service fill monitor is a report within SAP BI™ to evaluate the service level – both the alpha and the beta service level. Figure 14.15 shows the report for the beta service level – i.e. the service level based on the fulfilled quantities. The incredibly low service level in this example is due to the test data.

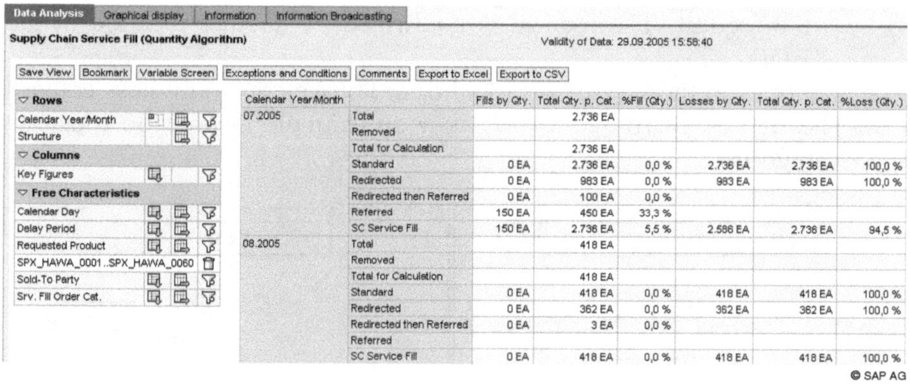

Calendar Year/Month		Fills by Qty.	Total Qty. p. Cat.	%Fill (Qty.)	Losses by Qty.	Total Qty. p. Cat.	%Loss (Qty.)
07.2005	Total		2.736 EA				
	Removed						
	Total for Calculation		2.736 EA				
	Standard	0 EA	2.736 EA	0,0 %	2.736 EA	2.736 EA	100,0 %
	Redirected	0 EA	983 EA	0,0 %	983 EA	983 EA	100,0 %
	Redirected then Referred	0 EA	100 EA	0,0 %			
	Referred	150 EA	450 EA	33,3 %			
	SC Service Fill	150 EA	2.736 EA	5,5 %	2.586 EA	2.736 EA	94,5 %
08.2005	Total		418 EA				
	Removed						
	Total for Calculation		418 EA				
	Standard	0 EA	418 EA	0,0 %	418 EA	418 EA	100,0 %
	Redirected	0 EA	362 EA	0,0 %	362 EA	362 EA	100,0 %
	Redirected then Referred	0 EA	3 EA	0,0 %			
	Referred						
	SC Service Fill	0 EA	418 EA	0,0 %	418 EA	418 EA	100,0 %

Fig. 14.15. Service Fill Monitor

The service fill monitor provides also additional information to analyse which location of the BOD causes the service loss. Since the use of rules-based ATP with location substitution is part of the service parts management solution and some locations are not stocked on purpose, this is not self-evident. The concept to differentiate between these cases is to review all the involved locations during the rules-based ATP check. The start location as determined by the first rule during the ATP check is the customer facing location (see chapter 13.3). If the replenishment indicator of the customer facing location allows stocking, this is also the first stockholding location. If the replenishment indicator is set to 'not stocked', the next location with a replenishment indicator for 'stocked' is the first stockholding location. The next location is defined by the location substitution procedure of the second rule of rules-based ATP. The first stockholding location is the location which is supposed to confirm and deliver the sales order. This is however not necessarily the case, and then the next location within the substitution procedure is checked. This location might or might not confirm the request. In order to distinguish between the different reasons for location substitution the following naming convention is used:

- standard: The customer facing location is the first stockholding location and confirms the request
- redirected: The customer facing location is set to 'not stocked' and the first stockholding location confirms the request
- referred: The customer facing location is set to 'stocked' but is not able to confirm the request. The request is confirmed by another location in the BOD
- redirected then referred: The customer facing location is set to 'not stocked' but the first stockholding location is not able to confirm

the request. The request is confirmed by another location in the BOD

The quantities in the service fill monitor are broken down to these categories. The figures 14.16 and 14.17 show an example in order to illustrate these categories.

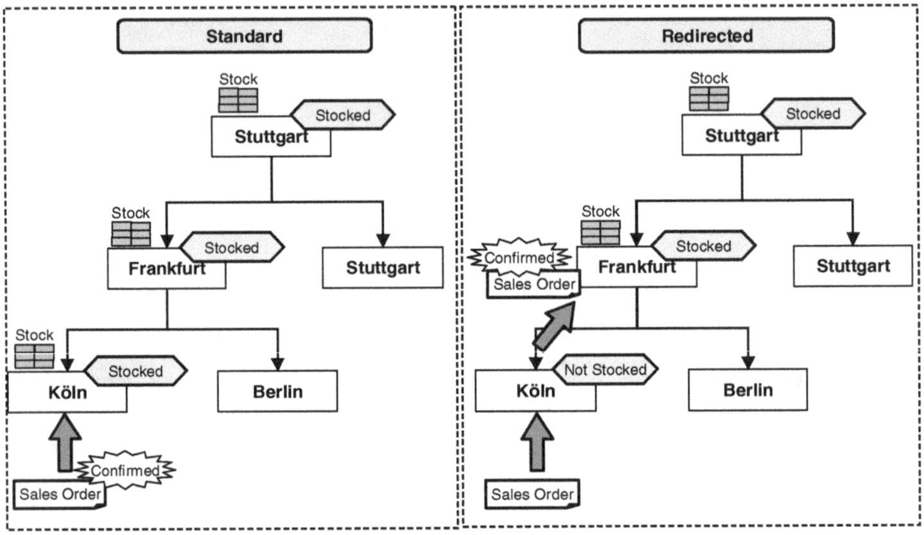

Fig. 14.16. Location Substitution: Standard and Redirected

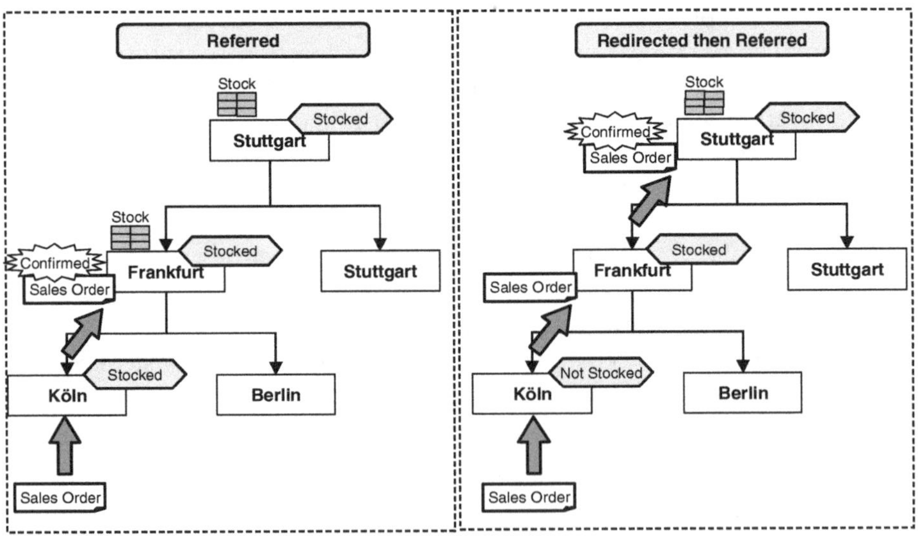

Fig. 14.17. Location Substitution: Referred and Redirected then Referred

The service fill monitor is primarily based on the sales order from mySAP CRM™ and the goods issue from SAP EWM™ via mySAP ERP™. The data is however first processed in SAP APO™: First the service fill decision is calculated and then the service loss analysis performed. The processed data is finally sent to SAP BI™. Figure 14.18 shows the data flow.

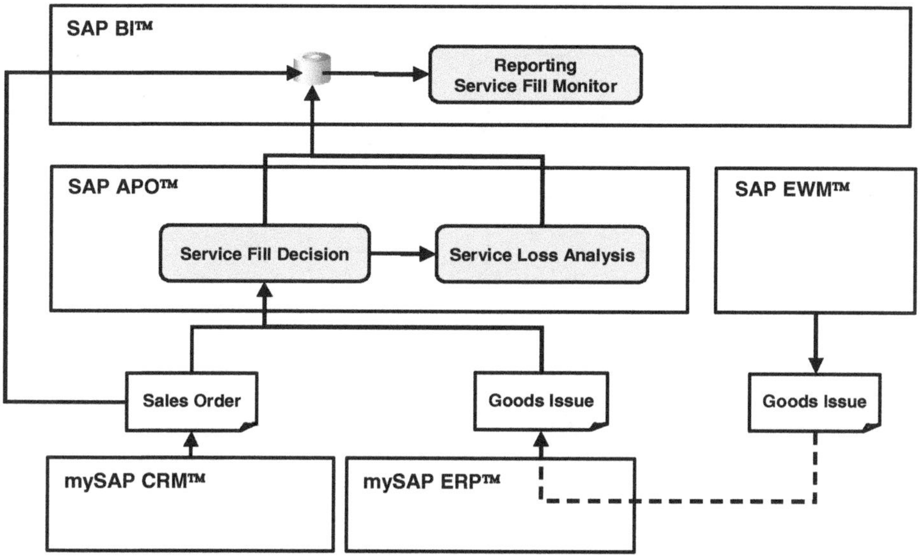

Fig. 14.18. Data Flow for the Service Fill Monitor

References

Literature

Arnold, D.; Isermann, H.; Kuhn, A; Tempelmeier, H.:
Handbuch Logistik.
Springer-Verlag, Berlin Heidelberg 2002

Dickersbach, J. Th.:
Supply Chain Management with APO.
Springer-Verlag, Berlin Heidelberg 2004

Muckstadt, J. A.:
Analysis and Algorithms for Service Parts Supply Chains.
Springer Science+Business Media Inc., New York 2005

Leitz, A.:
Supplier Collaboration mit dem mySAP SCM Inventory Collaboration Hub.
Galileo Press GmbH, Bonn 2005

SAP Online Help for SPP in SAP SCM 5.0
http://help.sap.com/saphelp_scm50/helpdata/en/a3/7ed240caeb752ae10000000a155106/frameset.htm

SCOR
Supply-Chain Operations Reference-model
SCOR Overview 7.0 1_06.pdf
http://www.supply-chain.org/site/scor7booklet2.jsp

OSS Notes

832393 Release Restrictions for SCM 5.0

902556 SPP pull deployment: ATP check of distributable quantity

913863 TDL: Composite SAP note for the transaction data layer

925171 DRP Approval: add new approval rule

929169 DRP Approval: add new approval rule (BAdI)

Abbreviations

ADC	Anticipated Demand Coverage
APO	Advanced Planner and Optimiser
ASN	Advanced Shipping Notification
ATD	Available-to-Deploy
ATP	Available-to-Promise
BAdI	Business Add-In
BAPI	Business Application Interface
BOD	Bill of Distribution
BOP	Backorder Processing
BI	Business Information Warehouse
CIF	Core Interface
CRM	Customer Relation Management
DP	Demand Planning
DRP	Distribution Requirements Planning
EDI	Electronic Data Interface
EDQA	Event Driven Quantity Assignment
EOQ	Economical Order Quantity
ERP	Enterprise Resource Planning
EWM	Extended Warehouse Management
FC	Forecast
FDO	Future Dated Order
FOES	First Order Exponential Smoothing
GUID	Global Unique Identifier
ICH	Inventory Collaboration Hub
IDN	Inbound Delivery Notification
JIT	Just In Time
KF	Key Figure

KPI	Key Performance Indicator
MAD	Mean Average Deviation
MRP	Material Requirements Planning
ODL	Order Due List
ODM	Order Data Manager
POD	Pending Obsolescence Date
POD	Periods of Demand
PSM	Planning Service Manager
qRFC	Queued Remote Function Call
RFC	Remote Function Call
RQDT	Retention Quantity Determination Table
RSG	Retention Strategy Group
SAD	Smoothed Average Deviation
SCM	Supply Chain Management
SED	Stock Exhaustion Date
SEWD	Stock Exhaustion Warning Date
SNP	Supply Network Planning
SOES	Second Order Exponential Smoothing
SPM	Service Parts Management
SPP	Service Parts Planning
SPPD	Successor Product Planning Date
SPRD	Successor Product Receipt Date
STO	Stock Transfer Order
TDL	Transaction Data Layer
TPOP	Third Party Order Processing
TSDM	Time Series Data Manager
TSL	Time Supply Limit
TSL	Target Service Level
UI	User Interface
VCL	Virtual Child Location
VLCO	Virtual Location for Consolidated Ordering
WSS	Warehouse Space Savings
XI	Exchange Infrastructure

Transactions

For the quick access of some functions this chapter provides a list of useful transactions for planning with characteristics. Most of these have been explained in the text.

Master Data

Description of the Transaction	Transaction in SAP APO™
BOD	/SAPAPO/BOD001
Assignment of Product to BOD	/SAPAPO/PROD2BOD_M
Display Assignment Product-BOD	/SAPAPO/PROD_DISP
Display Assignment BOD-Product	/SAPAPO/PROD2BODDISP
Regional Pattern	/SAPAPO/RGPAT01
Assignment of Product to RGP	/SAPAPO/PROD2RGP_M
Display Assignment Product-RGP	/SAPAPO/PROD2RGPDISP
Product	/SAPAPO/MAT1
Location	/SAPAPO/LOC3
Packaging Specification	/SCWM/PACKSPEC
Test Rounding	/SAPAPO/AC12
Planner	/SAPAPO/PLANNER
Planning Profile	/SAPAPO/PE_CFG
Execute Planning Service	/SAPAPO/PE_RUN
Planning Service Log	/SAPAPO/PE_LOG_DISP
Planning Service Log	SLG1
Trigger	/SAPAPO/TRIGGER
TDL Semantics	/SCMB/TDL_SEMANTIC
Time Series Type	/SCA/TSDMCFG
TDL Tools	/SCMB/TDL_TOOLS
Number Ranges for TDL	/SCMB/TDL_ORDERGUIDS
TDL Time Series Data	/SAPAPO/TDL_TS_TEST
TDL Order Data	/SAPAPO/TDL_ORD_TEST
TDL Inventory Data	/SAPAPO/TDL_INV_TEST
Simulation & Simulation Version	/SAPAPO/SPPSIM
Model and Version Maintenance	/SAPAPO/MVM
Snapshot	/SAPAPO/SNAPSHOT

Capture Demand

Description of the Transaction	Transaction in SAP APO™
Administrator Workbench	RSA1OLD
Administrator Workbench	RSA1
Info Object Master Data	RSDMD
Customising of Demand Categories	/SAPAPO/PDEMCUST
Fiscal Year Variant	OB29
Adjustment of Aggregated Demand	/SAPAPO/SPPDMDH
Adjustment of Order Items	/SAPAPO/SPPDMRD

Stocking Decision

Description of the Transaction	Transaction in SAP APO™
Maintenance of Decision Tables	/SAPAPO/SPPINVPDEC
Exclusion Tables	/SAPAPO/PINV_EX_MAIN

Forecasting

Description of the Transaction	Transaction in SAP APO™
Planning Book for Forecasting	/SAPAPO/SPPFCST
Semantics for Add. Key Figures	/SAPAPO/TDL_APO_SEM
Forecast Profile	/SAPAPO/SPPFCSTPRF
Historical Forecast	/SAPAPO/SPPFCSTTRACK
Forecast Approval	/SAPAPO/SPPFCSTAPPR
Product View	/SAPAPO/RRP3
Phase-Out Forecasting	/SAPAPO/SPPLONGFCST

EOQ and Safety Stock Planning

Description of the Transaction	Transaction in SAP APO™
Target Service Level Maintenance	/SAPAPO/PINV_TL_MAIN
Normal or Poisson Distribution	/SAPAPO/PINV_MS_MAIN
Planning Book for Inventory Plan..	/SAPAPO/SPPINVP
Deployment Indicator Determination	/SAPAPO/DEPL_IND_DEF

Surplus and Obsolescence Planning

Description of the Transaction	Transaction in SAP APO™
General Settings for Surplus	/SAPAPO/SORCUST
RQDT	/SAPAPO/SORRETQTYDET
Retention Strategy Group	/SAPAPO/SORRETGRP
RSG Selection Table	/SAPAPO/SORRETGRPSEL
Surplus Approval	/SAPAPO/SPPSOR

DRP and Procurement Approval

Description of the Transaction	Transaction in SAP APO™
DRP Matrix	/SAPAPO/SPPDRPM
Fixed Requirements	/SAPAPO/SPPFIXREQ
Transportation Lane	/SAPAPO/SCC_TL1
Procurement Relationships	/SAPAPO/PWBSRC1
Scheduling Simulation & Explanation	/SAPAPO/SPP_SCHD_EXP
Quota Arrangements	/SAPAPO/SCC_TQ1
Schedule Board	/SAPAPO/SPPDRPSB
Supplier Shutdown	/SAPAPO/SPP_SSD
Mass Approval	/SAPAPO/SPPDRPAPPR
Release Creation	/SAPAPO/PWBSCH1

Description of the Transaction	Transaction in SAP ICH™ and SAP XI™
Monitoring of XML Messages	SXMB_MONI

Description of the Transaction	Transaction in mySAP ERP™
Inbound Delivery	VL33N
Copy Inbound Delivery	VL60

Description of the Transaction	Transaction in SAP EWM™
Goods Receipt	/SCWM/PRDI
Post Stock from File (Test Only)	/SCWM/ISU

Deployment and Inventory Balancing

Description of the Transaction	Transaction in SAP APO™
Determination of the Deployment Indicator	/SAPAPO/DEPL_IND_DEF
EDQA Configuration	/SAPAPO/EDQA_PD
EDQA Event Linkage	/SAPAPO/EDQA_EC
EDQA Log	/SAPAPO/EDQA
TSL Parameters	/SAPAPO/TSLPAR
Service Profile for Deployment	/SAPAPO/DEPLSPRF
Priority Tiers	/SAPAPO/TIERDEF
Deployment Simulation	/SAPAPO/SPPDEPL
Inventory Balancing Area	/SAPAPO/RELHSHOW
Inv. Balancing Parameter Profile	/SAPAPO/RDPLPRF
Assign Inv. Bal. Par. Prof. to IBA	/SAPAPO/RDPLPRFA
WSS Storage Type Settings	/SAPAPO/RDPLWSTYPLOC
Warehouse Space Savings Profile	/SAPAPO/RDPLWSSPRF

Supersession

Description of the Transaction	Transaction in SAP APO™
General Settings for Supersession	/SAPAPO/SPRSCUST
Interchangeability Group	/INCMD/UI

Sales Order Fulfilment

Description of the Transaction	Transaction in mySAP CRM™
Sales Order	CRM_ORDER

Description of the Transaction	Transaction in mySAP ERP™
Display Unchecked Deliveries	VL06U
Check Unchecked Deliveries	VL10UC

Description of the Transaction	Transaction in SAP EWM
Outbound Delivery	/SCWM/PRDO
Confirm Warehouse Order	/SCWM/TO_CONF

Index

FSC
www.fsc.org
MIX
Papier | Fördert
gute Waldnutzung
FSC® C083411

Kolibri 360 GmbH
Ferdinand-Jühlke-Straße 7
99095 Erfurt, Deutschland
produktsicherheit@kolibri360.de